AFRICAN ETHNOGRAPHIC STUDIES
OF THE 20TH CENTURY

Volume 24

YAKÖ STUDIES

YAKÖ STUDIES

DARYLL FORDE

Routledge
Taylor & Francis Group

LONDON AND NEW YORK

First published in 1964 by Oxford University Press for the International African Institute.

This edition first published in 2018
by Routledge
2 Park Square, Milton Park, Abingdon, Oxon OX14 4RN

and by Routledge
711 Third Avenue, New York, NY 10017

Routledge is an imprint of the Taylor & Francis Group, an informa business

© 1964 International African Institute

British Library Cataloguing in Publication Data
A catalogue record for this book is available from the British Library

ISBN: 978-0-8153-8713-8 (Set)
ISBN: 978-0-429-48813-9 (Set) (ebk)
ISBN: 978-1-138-58624-6 (Volume 24) (hbk)
ISBN: 978-1-138-58637-6 (Volume 24) (pbk)
ISBN: 978-0-429-50467-9 (Volume 24) (ebk)

Publisher's Note
The publisher has gone to great lengths to ensure the quality of this reprint but points out that some imperfections in the original copies may be apparent.

Disclaimer
The publisher has made every effort to trace copyright holders and would welcome correspondence from those they have been unable to trace.

Okpebri, the Village Speaker of Umor (left) and Ina Abam, priest of the Kupatu fertility spirit, with their stool-carriers at the time of the Harvest Rites

YAKÖ STUDIES

DARYLL FORDE

Published for the
INTERNATIONAL AFRICAN INSTITUTE
by the
OXFORD UNIVERSITY PRESS
LONDON   NEW YORK   IBADAN
1964

Oxford University Press, Amen House, London E.C.4

GLASGOW NEW YORK TORONTO MELBOURNE WELLINGTON
BOMBAY CALCUTTA MADRAS KARACHI LAHORE DACCA
CAPE TOWN SALISBURY NAIROBI IBADAN ACCRA
KUALA LUMPUR HONG KONG

Printed in Great Britain by
Hazell Watson & Viney Ltd., Aylesbury

INTRODUCTION

I have, at the suggestion of several of my colleagues, brought together in this book a series of studies of the Yakö, of the middle Cross River region of Eastern Nigeria, that have been published in various journals over the past twenty-five years. I am aware that such a collection of studies written at different times and with reference to diverse aspects of Yakö culture and society is likely to lack the coherence and continuity of the longer monograph I had once hoped to write after a thorough reworking of my Yakö materials. But, since other obligations and preoccupations have prevented me from undertaking the further work in the field that I had hoped for, which would have made it possible to follow up many factual and theoretical questions that have subsequently arisen, it is perhaps more useful to present together as they were written these studies that are based on the field work undertaken in 1935 and 1939.

My sincere thanks are due both to the Council of the International African Institute for recommending and undertaking this publication, and to the Royal Anthropological Institute, the International African Institute, the American Anthropological Association, the Liverpool University Press, and Messrs. Faber and Faber for permission to reprint from articles and chapters originally published by them. I am also grateful to Miss Barbara Pym, Editorial Secretary of the Institute, for her very great help in collating and checking the text for this volume. As far as possible I have retained the original texts, but in order to avoid discrepancies in terminology and orthography and also to avoid the repetition of prefatory or explanatory material in the several papers, I have deleted redundant passages. I have also taken the opportunity, for the sake of greater clarity, to make a number of minor corrections in the text. Any significant supplementations or corrections have been indicated by footnotes. Terminology and the orthography for Yakö terms have been revised where necessary to make them uniform and to eliminate discrepancies that might give rise to confusion. The Africa orthography of the International African Institute (*A Practical Orthography of African Languages*, Memorandum I, 1930) has in general been followed in writing Yakö terms. But tones have not been indicated and no distinction has generally been made between open and close *e*, while *ö* has been retained for the obscure vowel (*ə*) as a matter of convenience in the name of the people, viz. Yakö. Velar 'n', as in English 'sing' has been written *ŋ*.

These studies cannot pretend to do full justice to the rich diversity of the culture of the Yakö or to the complexity and significance of their social institutions. Attention has been concentrated on a limited number of aspects and problems. An effort has been made to present as clearly and concisely as possible both the data and the analysis relevant to these but I am well aware of the limitations of my own experience and understanding of Yakö society. In two comparatively short periods of field study from July to December 1935 and June to October 1939 I was constrained to focus my attention rather closely on the aspect originally selected for study, the economy and its relation to the salient features of social organization. Thus the information and understanding of Yakö religion that I gained was largely obtained incidentally in the course of these inquiries or of outstanding events in the village of Umor. Here, however, I was fortunate in being able to follow closely the two main seasonal rituals of the village—the Harvest Rites in 1935, of which I have not yet published a detailed account, and the First Fruits Rites of 1939. Discussion of these with several of the leading officiants and other Yakö, at a time when the ceremonies and the various meanings attached to them were in the forefront of their minds, opened up in the most vivid manner a complex field of ritual action and belief of which I could pursue only some of the salient features. Among these the wide variation in the significance of spirit beings, which became apparent as one moved from public ceremonies to personal invocations at spirit shrines, is illustrated and discussed in the later chapters. The studies of religious belief and ritual action presented there have been supplemented by an analysis of Death and Succession among the Yakö published in *Essays on the Ritual of Social Relations*, edited by Max Gluckman (Manchester University Press, 1962).

Investigations of rights in land and other resources, including disputes to which they gave rise, and of issues concerning the scope of authority provoked by the growth of settlement and developing relations with the Nigerian Administration, afforded some insight into both traditional political processes and the innovations and the adjustments of outlook stemming from the establishment of a

Native Court for the area. An analysis of the several fields of social control and of their inter-relations is given in Chapters V and VI.

Among the Yakö I was concerned with a pattern of distribution of authority that did not correspond with either of the types of political systems that Fortes and Evans-Pritchard distinguished as a framework for the studies in *African Political Systems*. Distinct principles related to personally achieved status and territorial political association were seen to be major factors in the exercise of judicial and executive authority above the level of the discrete kin groups composing the larger society.

But I was not able to pursue the opportunities for close study of the recent history of the Yakö communities—a subject which would have thrown much light on the factors accounting for their remarkable growth and comparative stability from at least the later part of the nineteenth century, during a period in which there appears to have been a considerable widening of their external contacts and a remarkable assimilation and adaptation of new religious and other elements as well as an extensive restructuring of some of the village communities. The Yakö, it seemed, lived very much in the present. At least they had no institutionalized narratives of the past in relation to any of their major institutions. But several of my older friends in Umor, particularly *Okpebri*, the Speaker of the village, Arikpo Egede, the Court Member from and *de facto* head of Egbisum ward, and Ina Abam, the priest of the fertility shrine of the *Atewa* spirit, to whom I shall always be grateful for their sympathetic interest as well as a wealth of information and spontaneous commentary, showed in the many references they made to past events concerning particular groups, sites, and institutions, a very detailed and consistent knowledge of traditions concerning events and developments over the previous two or three generations.

I should also call attention to the very limited extent of my knowledge of rituals and other activities controlled by women. The references to these and the interpretations as far as they go are, I believe, correct but I made no close study of, for example, the *Ekao* cult of the women of a ward and did not investigate the significance of the institutionalized clowning of barren women (*kekoŋ*) on such occasions as the village Harvest Rites.

I hope, however, that those Yakö who may read these studies and others concerned to share some understanding of a disappearing phase in the culture and social life of a West African people, will excuse any errors of detailed fact and interpretation that they may find and will derive satisfaction from an attempt to record objectively and interpret faithfully, within the limits of an incomplete knowledge, the salient features of the way of life and social institutions of a remarkably vigorous and sympathetic people.

In the course of my first period of work I gained a fairly extensive command of Likö vocabulary, could generally understand informants' statements and take texts. But I did not really master the grammar and I could not follow rapid conversations among Yakö. For accounts of such discussions, and the checking of my own understanding of statements, I relied on several English-speaking Yakö informants and in particular on Ubi Okoi to whom I owe a great debt for his patient and thorough help as a teacher and interpreter. During the later part of my work he became a most conscientious field assistant, participating in many of my inquiries and obtaining both genealogical and quantitative information relating to households, kin groups, and farming activities. I was also greatly helped by Okoi Arikpo, a son of Arikpo Egede who is now Secretary to the Nigerian Universities Commission, but in 1935 was a senior pupil at Hope Waddell College. I was later happy to welcome him as a student of anthropology in London and have largely through his friendship been able to maintain my contacts with Umor.

It may be useful to call attention here to the relevance of some of the ethnographical and sociological aspects of these Yakö studies to anthropological interests at the time when they were first undertaken. There had then been scarcely any attempt to assemble the data for an analysis of the economy of a West African community as an organized system. There appeared to be little appreciation of the need for systematic study in which the inter-relations of ecological, demographic, and institutional factors were evaluated. Considerable information on separate aspects of techniques of production, customary land rights and, in unquantified terms, of control and distribution of supplies had been assembled for one people or another. But their inter-relations, and notably the extent to which features in one sphere depended on conditions in another, as, for example, among the Yakö the scale and character of kin group organization and its position in the wider social system in relation to the techniques of land use and the organization and protection of rights in land and other resources, had barely been carried beyond the separate recounting of customary methods and formal rules which did not reveal the connections between them. The attempt made in the study of land, labour, and exchange, and of the processes of growth, fission and fusion of the territorial groups by means of case studies, censuses, genealogies and mapping, made it possible, for example, to show the interconnections between both the assertion and the breaching and overriding of the doctrine of patrikin group solidarity and the features of cooperation required for the exploitation and protection of a manageable unit area by a body of patrilocally co-resident men. Analyses of the composition and genealogical history of samples of the co-resident groups showed, furthermore, how far a doctrine of recruitment and acquisition of rights by unilineal descent could be maintained and sustain sentiments of solidarity while allowing for *de facto* changes in composition and the allegiance of individuals and subgroups under the exigencies of demographic expansion, of particular shortages of land and house sites and inter-personal tensions. In other words, the principle of patrilineal kinship as the norm or ideal for residence and cooperation in productive activities and their protection, which may, as Yakö traditions assert, have initially been closely followed in an earlier phase when patriclans were small and discrete, has been retained under conditions of larger, denser and territorially more integrated populations; but individual adoptions, fissions of and accretions to kin groups have rendered the patrilineal descent largely fictive for the patriclan as a whole. I have further analysed this aspect of Yakö organization in an essay on 'Unilineal Descent, Fact or Fiction', in *Studies of Kinship and Marriage*, recently edited by I. Schapera and dedicated by the Royal Anthropological Institute to Mrs. B. Z. Seligman.

A study of first marriage among the Yakö, which analysed the obligations of and the relations between the kinsfolk of spouses and their age-mates, was relevant to the current discussion of the functions of 'bridewealth' (cf. Radcliffe Brown, *Man*, 1929, p. 96 and Evans Pritchard, *Man*, 1934, p. 174). It considered the influence of economic and other factors on changing marriage patterns among the Yakö and showed the importance of distinguishing the distinct elements in the complex of statuses involved. Published separately under the title, *Marriage and the Family among the Yakö*, it appeared initially as No. 5 in the London School of Economics series of *Monographs in Social Anthropology*, 1941, and has been reprinted by the International African Institute, 1951.

The original sources of the chapters in this book which are reprinted by kind permission of the editors and publishers concerned are as follows:

Chapter I   'Land and Labour in a Cross River Village in Southern Nigeria', *Geographical Journal*, vol. 90, 1937, pp. 24–51.

Chapter II   Chapter II of *Native Economies of Nigeria*, by Daryll Forde and Richenda Scott (ed. Margery Perham). London: Faber, 1946, pp. 49–64.

Chapter III   'Fission and Accretion in the Patrilineal Clans of a Semi-Bantu Community in Southern Nigeria', *Journal of the Royal Anthropological Institute*, vol. 68, 1938, pp. 311–88

Chapter IV   'Double Descent among the Yakö' *in African Systems of Kinship and Marriage*, ed. A. R. Radcliffe-Brown and Daryll Forde. London: Oxford University Press for International African Institute, 1950, pp. 285–332; together with passages from 'Kinship in Umor', *American Anthropologist*, vol. 41, 1939, pp. 523–53, as indicated in the text.

Chapter V   'Ward Organization among the Yakö', *Africa*, XX, 4, 1950, pp. 267–89.

Chapter VI   'Government in Umor', *Africa*, XII, 2, 1939, pp. 126–62 and 'The Governmental Roles of Associations among the Yakö' [Munro Lecture], *Africa*, XXXI, 4, 1961, pp. 309–23.

Chapter VII   'Spirits, Witches, and Sorcerers in the Supernatural Economy of the Yakö', *Journal of the Royal Anthropological Institute*, vol. 88, 1958, pp. 165–78.

Chapter VIII   'Integrative Aspects of the Yakö First Fruits Rituals', *Journal of the Royal Anthropological Institute*, vol. 79, 1949 (1951), pp. 1–10. [Presidential Address.]

Chapter IX   *The Context of Belief: a Consideration of Fetichism among the Yakö.* [The Frazer Lecture for 1958.] Liverpool University Press, 1958.

CONTENTS

INTRODUCTION   *page* v

   I LAND AND LABOUR   1

  II EXCHANGE AND CONSUMPTION   31

 III FISSION AND ACCRETION IN THE PATRICLAN   49

 IV DOUBLE DESCENT AND THE MATRILINEAL
      SYSTEM   85

  V WARD ORGANIZATION   135

 VI VILLAGE GOVERNMENT   165

 VII SPIRITS, WITCHES, AND SORCERERS   210

VIII FIRST FRUITS RITUALS   234

 IX THE CONTEXT OF BELIEF   254

    INDEX   284

ILLUSTRATIONS

PLATES

Okpebri, the Village Speaker of Umor   *frontispiece*

I *a*. A compound in Ndai   *facing page* 16

   b. Yam farm during the growing season, with a pile of early yams in the foreground   16

II *a*. Woman hoeing up yam hills   17
   b. Man digging yams   17

III *a*. Preparing the yam stack   32
   b. A full yam stack   32

IV *a*. Tapping a palm inflorescence for wine   33
   b. Men pounding palm fruit for oil   33

V *a*. Washing early yams   80
   b. Palm oil trading post, Ediba   80

VI*a*. House-building   81
   b. House interior   81

VII *a*. Head-loading harvest yams   96
   b. Hunter and palm-wine collector   96

VIII *a*. Making roof mats for house repair   97
   b. Wife carrying food to husband's feast   97

IX *a*. A patriclan area in Idjiman ward   112
   b. *Epundet* of Ibenda II   112

X *a*. Egbisum *kepun* house   113
   b. Egbisum *kepun* house interior   113

XI *a*. Pillar in Ukpakapi ward square, Umor (damaged by fire)   128
   b. Rite of Ward Leaders before the burial of one of their members   128

XII *a*. *Ebiabu* dance leaders   129
   b. Masked dancers of *Leko*   129

XIII   Leaders of *Eblɔmbe* dancing during a funeral rite   160

XIV *a.* Members of *Ŋkpe* carrying the 'Leopard Voice'   161
    b. *Leko* dancers with insignia   161

XV *a.* *Obot Lopon*, the Village Head of Umor, 1935   176
   b. *Ligwomi* initiate   176

XVI *a.* The *Elamalama* priest   177
    b. The leader of one of the younger age-sets with its
         decorated palm-wine jar   177

XVII *a.* *Obot Obuŋa*, Head of the Diviners   192
     b. *Ikpuŋkara* initiate   192

XVIII *a.* Scene during a ritual dance of *Ikpuŋkara*   193
      b. The Bench of the Native Court at a sitting in Umor   193

XIX *a.* *Opalapala*   208
    b. *Odjokobi*   208

XX *a.* Invocation by the Village Speaker before the
        altar of *Odjokobi*   209
   b. The *Ekui* dance before the *Yabot* on *Ledemboku*   209

XXI *a.* *Lite* dancers   240
    b. Diviners collecting leaves and roots   240

XXII *a.* Cooling the village   241
     b. The *Odere* dancers   241

XXIII *a.* *Yose* shrine house and cult objects   256
      b. *Kupatu* shrine interior   256

XXIV *a.* Invocation to *Yose Otabalusaŋa*, Ina Ibiaŋ   257
     b. One of the *Akota*, the foundation war stones   257

XXV *a.* *Kepun* funeral insignia   272
    b. *Edet*, Odjilebo in Idjiman   272

XXVI   The shrine of *Isɔ Obasi*, spirit of the diviners   273

MAPS

The Territory and Settlements of the Yakö and their Neighbours   2

Map of Umor   50

FIGURES

1. Sketch-map of Umor territory   5

2. Calendar of farm work   8

3. Diagram of plots belonging to a single household   10

4. A tract of farming land   12

5. Frequency distribution of yam hills   15

6. Dot diagram of area and yam harvest of 97 farms in Ndai   15

7. Diagram of fissions and recent migrations of lineages in the   60
   patriclans of Umor

8. House plans   91

9. Composition and affiliation of compounds   94

10. Diagram of matriclan links in Umor   104

11. Yakö terms for kin   118

TABLES

I. Sales of native produce   35

II. Basic annual household expenditure, Umor, 1939   45

III. Estimated annual cash income of household, Umor, 1939   46

IV. House sites of lineages of patrilineal kin groups of Ndai   54

V. Patriclans of Umor   57–8

VI. The lineages of Ndai   64–5

VII. Position in lineages of five living heads in Ndai   70

VIII. Living children in Ndai   80

IX. Distribution of the adult male members of four
    matrilineal kin-groups   101

X. Matriclans of Umor   105

I
LAND AND LABOUR[1]

M Y first expedition to the Cross River country in Southern Nigeria in 1935 was made possible by the generosity of the Leverhulme Research Fellowships Fund and by the courtesy of the Nigerian Government, to both of whom my sincere thanks are due. I arrived at Calabar towards the end of July and proceeded up the Cross River by paddle boat to Obubra. After a short reconnaissance of the country lying on either side of the Cross River in the Obubra and Abakaliki Divisions, I decided to work in the Yakö village of Umor. My main objective was the investigation of the economic life of a community of hoe cultivators in the West African forest zone, and I was concerned with the relations of this economy to both physical environment and social organization. For this purpose it would be necessary to select a group who would not only assent cheerfully to the sudden appearance of a European resident in their village but would also take kindly to detailed and persistent inquiries concerning that often difficult and dangerous topic—the land. I was also anxious to avoid in this instance a people whose economic life was deeply affected by an external market and whose agriculture and equipment had been extensively modified by the needs and opportunities of modern trade. These conditions were largely met in Umor, and to its people I owe a very great deal for their quick friendliness and their general freedom from suspicion. Although there were inevitable barriers of custom which made some lines of inquiry difficult, I was, so far as ease of human relations was concerned, particularly fortunate in my choice.

The Yakö of the Middle Cross River area of Obubra Division live in five compact villages a few miles apart, each of which was formerly autonomous in its political as well as its ritual organization. They have a common tradition that their forebears all came from the east together with the people of Okuni, a settlement some fifty miles away up the Cross River. They were not a river

[1] Reprinted from *Geographical Journal*, vol. 90, 1937.

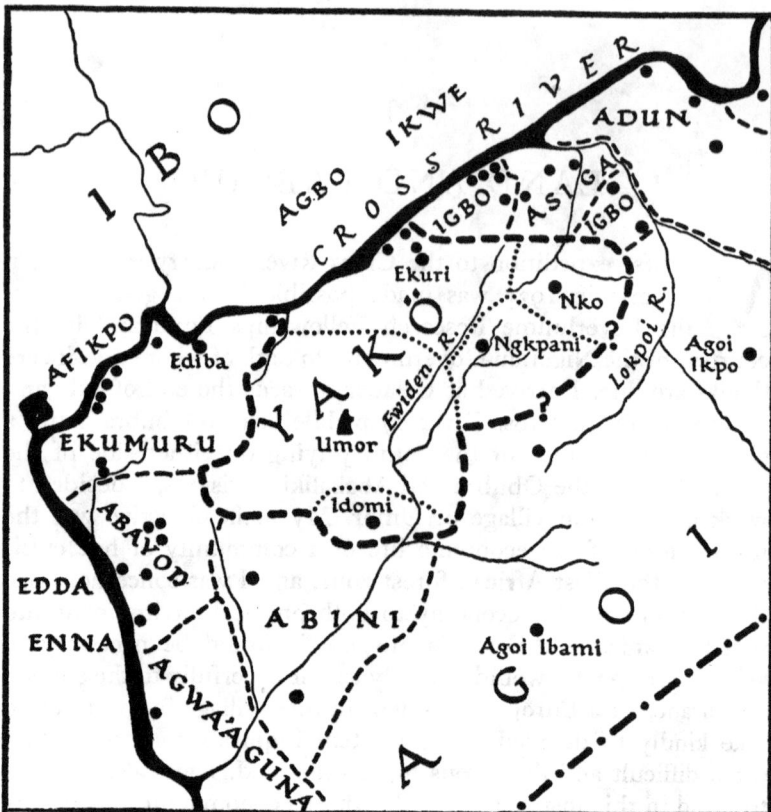

Map Labels

IBO

IKWE

AGBO

CROSS RIVER

ADUN

ASIGA

IGBO

IGBO

AFIKPO

Ekuri

Nko

Agoi
Ikpo

Ediba

YAKÖ

Ngkpani

Ewiden R.

Lokpoi R.

EKUMURU

Umor

?

?

Idomi

ABAYOD

A G O I

EDDA

ABINI

ENNA

AGWA'AGUNA

Agoi Ibami

Legend

● Nko   Settlements

━ ━ ━   Yakö tribal boundary

·············   Yakö village territories

- - - -   Boundaries of neighbouring tribes

━·━·━   Provincial boundary

Scale 0 ___ 5 ___ 10 Miles

SKETCH MAP OF THE TERRITORY AND SETTLEMENTS OF THE YAKÖ AND THEIR NEIGHBOURS

Inset map

Obubra

Cross R.

OGOJA PROV.

Afikpo

Itu

CALABAR PROVINCE

Calabar

Scale 0 ___ 50 Miles

S·E·NIGERIA

people and had moved overland in several parties and over some years. A distinction is made between those villages in which the original migrants settled—that is, Idomi, where a section of the main group which founded Umor remained, Umor itself, and the separately settled community of Ɖko—and the remaining villages of Ekuri and Ɖkpani which are held to have been founded a generation or two later by local migrations, following dissensions, from Umor. Two of the Yakö settlements, Umor and Ekuri which lie nearer the river, have grown considerably since the late nineteenth century during a period of increasing commerce and growing security. Umor had, by 1935, become exceptionally large for a single compact community, having a population of nearly 11,000. My 1935 estimates of population for the Yakö villages were: Umor, 10,900; Ekuri, 7,100; Ɖkpani, 4,400; Ɖko, 2,600; Idomi, 1,900. A very high degree of linguistic and cultural homogeneity has been maintained between the villages by a continual interchange of visitors and permanent migrants. But there is no centralized political organization and sporadic, short-lived fighting between villages, particularly between Umor and Ekuri, is said to have occurred in the past.[2]

Yakö settlement has been comparatively stable. In the larger and traditionally older villages of Umor and Ekuri the house sites of important ancestors four generations back are pointed out, and there are in places mounds several feet high said to have been formed by superposition of successive house floors. Of the smaller villages, Idomi and Ɖkpani are held to have been established by migrations from Umor, the latter after a bitter quarrel between two Umor wards. But despite a rapid increase of population over at least the past two generations and the growth of Ekuri and particularly Umor into very large and crowded settlements, there is a very strong tendency for men to remain with their own patrikin. When, as is increasingly common, dwelling areas in the village become fully occupied, the pressure is relieved by building hamlets (sing. *kowu*) on the nearest tract of farming land belonging to the group and within half a mile or less of the village. The occupants of these hamlets continue to participate as fully as they can in the life of the main village. With the increase in size of settlements the areas appropriated for cultivation and the collection of forest products have been extended, but the overall density of

[2] See Map I. Territory and Settlements of the Yakö.

population has not so far risen high enough to cause deleterious pressure on land. Even in the territory of Umor, where the density is highest, at about 230 per square mile, there are still some tracts of unfarmed land.

THE VILLAGE TERRITORY

Umor (lat. 5° 50′, long. 8° 10′ E.) is called Ugep by the riverside peoples and is so named on maps and for administrative purposes. The village itself lies 7 miles east of the Cross River and, although only 70 miles north of Calabar in a direct line, is about 120 miles away by river. It is a large compact settlement covering an area of nearly a quarter of a square mile and, like the other Yakö villages, is economically and territorially autonomous and has an independent native political organization. Approximately 11,000 people live in Umor, and the territory claimed by the village has an area of 47 square miles, so that the density of population in the village territory as a whole is approximately 230 per square mile.[3] There

[3] The basis for the estimate of population, which differs somewhat from the official estimate in the District records, may be explained here. A 'Nominal Roll' of the adult male population of the village had been taken by the District Officer in connection with tax assessment only a few months before my arrival at Umor. In this roll absentees not expected to return permanently were noted. In the course of my work I made a detailed census of the households of a kin group comprising 112 adult men. Unknown names and double entries of individuals under different names in the Roll of this kin group were largely matched by records in my census of men omitted from the Roll, but a small discrepancy remained. As the household census was a prolonged inquiry which was several times rechecked, I have assumed that a discrepancy of this order would be likely to apply to the male population as a whole and have applied the ratio of the discrepancy (112:115) to the Nominal Rolls as a whole (less absentees) in estimating the number of adult males in the village. From my census data on the kin group investigated I obtained a ratio of adult females to adult males and also of minors to adults of both sexes. These are 176 adult females per 100 adult males and 123 minors per 100 adults of both sexes. The results may be tabulated as follows:

Number of adult males in Rolls of 1935 (less absentees)   1,801
Number of adult males recorded for Ndai kin group in Rolls (less absentees) 115

Household census of Ndai Kin Group

Adult Males	112	
Adult females	198	310
Minors		382
Total		692

Estimated population of Umor 1935

Adult males	1,754
Adult females	3,101
Minors	5,982
Total	10,837

are at least 4 or 5 square miles of continuous unfarmed forest on the eastern borders and a square mile of uncultivated swamp land in the north-west, but the remainder of the 40 square miles of territory is penetrated by a web of farming paths, which give access to periodically cultivated tracts of land on either side as well as affording routes to neighbouring villages (see Fig. 1). Farmed land

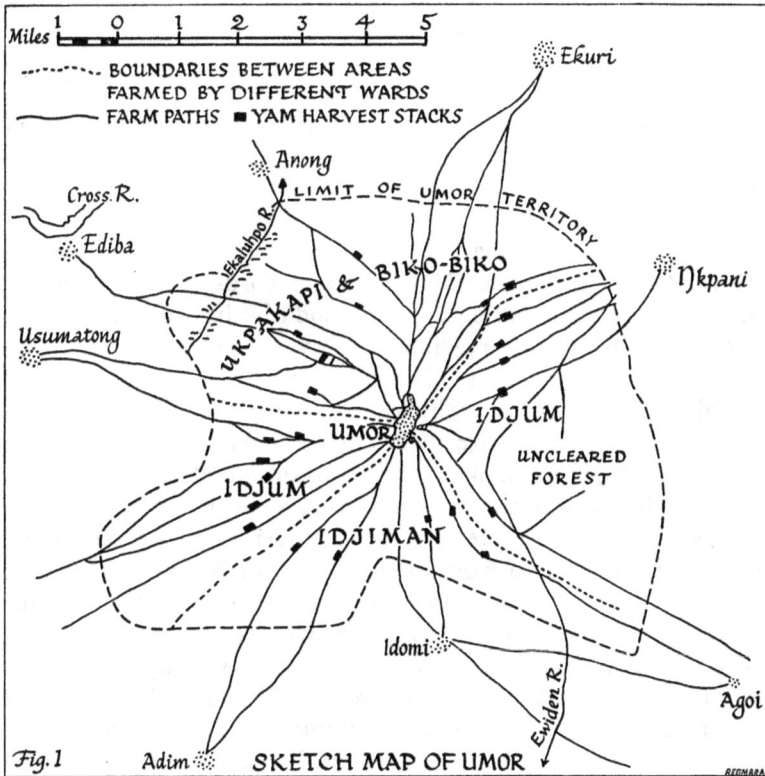

Fig. 1   SKETCH MAP OF UMOR

appears rarely to extend to a distance of more than a quarter of a mile from these main paths while it is often restricted to a fringe only 200 yards on either side, so that there are at present numerous islands of uncultivated land between the more widely spaced farming paths. Thus, in accordance with my estimates, the aggregate area of land cleared for cultivation amounts to only 18 square miles, and of this, as will be seen later, a total of only 3 or 4 square miles is actually cultivated in a single year.

The village territory lies athwart a low undulating ridge of Cretaceous sandstone which never rises more than 200 or 300 feet above the level of the Cross River. It is crossed by a multitude of streams which drain broad open valleys aligned roughly parallel with the Cross River, and immediately east of the village a steep cliff face, descended by a precipitous path, overlooks a wide low-lying basin which is drained circuitously by the large Ewiden stream to the Cross River.

Climatic Conditions

The country lies in the northern part of the forest belt of Southern Nigeria, in which there is a clear distinction between wet and dry seasons. From early in April to the end of October there are heavy rains every few days, followed by a dry season of four months during the climax of which, in December and January, the rainfall is negligible. No climatic records are available for Umor itself, but rainfall data for a period of thirty-one years down to 1935 are available for Afikpo, a Government station approximately 20 miles to the east. The Afikpo records give a mean annual rainfall of 80·12 inches, of which 71·65 inches fall during the seven rainy months and only 8·47 inches in the remaining months of the year. The rainfall normally rises to a maximum of about 15 inches in September, and in the period 1931–5, for which more complete data were available, there were on the average twenty-one rainy days in this month. In November the rainfall falls away abruptly, although there were at Umor in 1935, several heavy falls accompanying the violent tornados that are characteristic at this season. December is a month of real drought, while in January and February only occasional light showers occur. Although this régime is normal there is an occasional break in the rains in the middle of the wet season. This was very marked at Afikpo in 1932, when only 1·67 inches fell in July, and it is a feature of the climate well known to the natives, who believe it to be very harmful to the yam crop.

Short-period data (9.0 a.m. and 3.0 p.m. shade readings for 1931–5) for Afikpo show a small annual range of temperature which rises to a 9.0 a.m. monthly mean of 79°F. in March at the end of the dry season with increasing insolation. There is a slight fall in April and May with moderate rains and a marked fall from June to August after the onset of the heavier rains. The mean daily range rises from little over 10°F. in the wet season to nearly 20°F.

in the dry season (March 1931–5: 19·1°F.). The relative humidity is high throughout the year in the early morning, and at Afikpo the monthly mean at 9.0 a.m. is rarely below 85 per cent. in any month, but 3.0 p.m. readings fall to around 60 per cent. in the dry season.

This part of the Cross River region thus lies in the zone of heavy equatorial monsoon rainfall, but the length of the dry season and the period of two months of virtual drought in December and January are likely to affect the composition of the vegetation and the cycle of agricultural activities. The geological and soil conditions over the greater part of the territory of Umor are such as to intensify the effects of the marked dry season, for the Cretaceous sandstone is highly permeable and the soil weathered from it has very low water-holding qualities.

The natural vegetation is dense tropical forest which appears to be transitional from the evergreen forest to the mixed deciduous forest. This is indicated by botanical data from the general region collected by the Nigerian Forestry Department and by the composition of the dense forest tracts round Umor itself.

The Cycle of Cultivation

The people of Umor are yam growers; practically every household is a farming unit and the sequence of agricultural tasks and rewards dominates the economic life of the village. The sharp seasonality of rainfall and the moderate natural fertility of the soil are clearly reflected in the agricultural cycle. There is only a single planting at the beginning of the rains each year, and since there is no effective fertilizing, farmland is usually rested for four years after a single harvest has been obtained. Yams, the large tubers of *Discorea* spp., which are the staple food of the people, constitute by far the largest and most important crop. As all other cultivation is subordinated to the requirements of the yam harvest, the calendar of farm work can best be considered in connection with yam cultivation (Fig. 2).

Early in January, after the second moon cycle of the dry season, clearing of the farm lands for the coming season begins. As these tracts have not been cultivated for four years they have grown up into a dense bush of saplings and undergrowth about 20 feet high. This is cut down by parties of men, whose formation will be described later, and yam hills, mounds hoed up to an initial height of

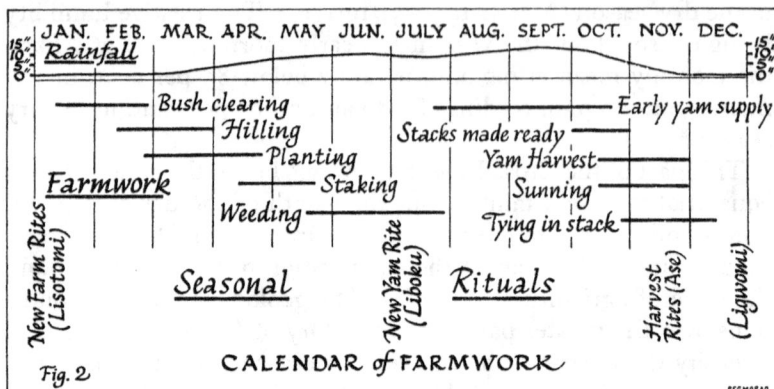

Fig. 2   CALENDAR of FARMWORK

about 2 feet 6 inches and set close together, are made by women
or foreign workers as the clearing progresses (Plate II).

Planting, undertaken jointly by men and women, follows as
soon as the first plot or section of hills has been prepared in each
farm and it continues as clearing and hilling progresses until the
end of April. A number of subsidiary crops such as coco yams
(*Colocasia* and/or *Xanthifolia*), maize, okra, pumpkins, and less
commonly beans and cassava (*Manihot*), are planted after the yams
on the slopes of the yam hills. Small patches of ground nuts are
also planted, and round the margins of the farm pepper bushes
are transplanted from the previous farming site. The preparation
and erection of the stakes and strings for the yam vines rest with
the men, but all the subsequent tending of the farm, including the
heavy task of a double weeding which continues throughout
June, is done by the women (Plate I*b*).

In July the first crop of an early variety of yam (known as
lidjofi), which is generally planted in every fifth row of yam hills, is
available, but these may not be dug or eaten until after the performance of the First Fruits (*Liboku*) rites which are regarded as
essential to the success of the main harvest. Early yams are said to
be ready for eating from the middle of June as a rule, but before
Liboku they can only be dug and brought into the village surreptitiously. From July onwards the women in their daily visits to the
farms dig the early yams, as they are needed to feed the household
until the main harvest begins in the last weeks of October.

This harvest is stored in great yam stacks, open air barns built
on all the farm paths 2 or 3 miles from the village. The stacks are

made ready for the harvest by the men in October, while the yams which the men and women have dug together are carried by the women to the streams for washing and then to the stacks. Here they are laid out to dry in the sun for a week or two before the men tie them in the stack. When the yam stacks have been filled the cycle is complete and there is a short lull in farm work until the clearing for the next year begins (Plates III and VII).

Farm crops are not the sole vegetable products obtained through the year. Supplies of bananas, plantains, kola nuts, native pears (*Pachylobis edulis*), pawpaws, and coconuts are obtained from groves of planted trees laid out along the farming paths, round the yam stacks, and in the village. The tending of these trees is entirely in the hands of the men, about half of whom are also daily engaged in exploiting the outstanding wild food plant of the forest—the oil palm, from which oil, kernel nuts and sap-wine are obtained.

PROBLEMS AND FIELD METHODS

The rhythm of agricultural activities just outlined will be recognized as characteristic of many parts of the forest belt of the Guinea coast, and my object here is not a detailed discussion of the technique of cultivation but a preliminary analysis of the organization of labour, and the consideration of that organization in relation to the resources of the territory and the production and distribution of the food supply and other wealth. In the course of my field work I made a census of the agricultural and other economic activities of about one hundred households, obtaining data on the composition of the household, the lands farmed, the crops grown, the division of labour, and the size of the harvest.

The effective study of the economic activities of primitive peoples demands more systematic and objective data than have hitherto been commonly obtained. Discussion of the efficiency of native methods and the limitations of physical conditions on the one hand, and of the relation between economic activities and social institutions on the other, cannot be securely based on general impressions or even on more detailed knowledge of a few individual cases, when such matters as division and intensity of labour, volumes of production, and accumulation and distribution of food supplies and materials are involved. But very real difficulties face the ethnographer here. He works alone in an area for which there has been no land survey, with maps, if any, that are only most

approximate and small scale, among people whose numbers have
been only most roughly estimated, if at all, and whose measures
of time, value, and area, are difficult to assess in objective terms.
The people may be extremely suspicious of minute and systematic inquiries into their numbers, customary land rights, wealth,
and property, and may refuse or falsify information. Data approaching the scope and accuracy of those obtainable for a western
country could only be secured with the aid of a considerable party
of surveyors and investigators; and such a procedure might well
defeat its own ends by arousing suspicion and hostility, which would
frustrate any investigation of other related problems in which every-
thing depended on the good will and confidence of informants.

Neverthelss it is often possible with resourceful use of the local
standards of value and knowledge, and with approximate, even if
unorthodox, methods of survey to achieve reasonably accurate
estimates in the economic and demographic field. I therefore
devoted some considerable time to attempts to work out and employ
methods for assessing quantitatively the economic conditions and
activities in Umor, which would be feasible with the co-operation
of the people themselves and would yield in a relatively short
period results adequate for ethnographic and statistical analysis.

FARM AREAS

The farm lands in Umor are held by adult men individually and
a man of middle age will have established and recognized rights to
half a dozen sets of plots (Fig. 3). Only one-fifth of the aggregate
area is however cultivated in any one year while the rest remains in
bush. One of my earliest tasks in Umor was that of finding a

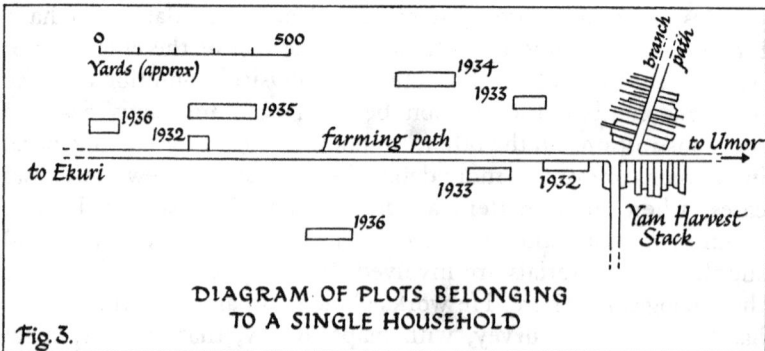

DIAGRAM OF PLOTS BELONGING
TO A SINGLE HOUSEHOLD

Fig. 3.

method of estimating with reasonable accuracy the size of these farm plots. Owing to the reluctance of their occupiers, the time required, and the difficulties of movement and sighting among the yam vines, it was impossible to make an instrumental survey of a sufficient number of farms to obtain adequate data on area and productivity. But the nature of the cultivation and the laying out of the farms in Umor permitted safe generalization as to the mean area and variation of farm areas. The process of clearing, hoeing, and planting farm lands proceeds piecemeal on each plot as the collective labour of a group of kinsmen becomes available to each individual in turn. A party of a dozen or so men clears a small stretch of bush day by day for each of their number in turn. These sections are hoed and planted by the women as they are cleared. The boundary between sections is marked and every man knows how many sections he has planted and the relative size of each. Further, the yam hills are made very methodically row by row across each section, forming an approximate rectangle (Fig. 4), and since the number of yam hills on two sides in each section could be readily counted, an estimate of the number of hills could be quickly reached. The mean area of the individual farms of 97 adult able-bodied men of one patrilineal kin group (the Ndai *kepun*) obtained in this way was approximately 1½ acres (1·40), the equivalent of 2,440 yam hills. Thus a representative Umor household of a man, two wives, and three or four children is likely to have about 7 or 8 acres of farming land at its disposal, of which 1½ acres are cultivated each year. The estimated aggregate area of farm land in Umor (a minimum of 18 square miles, of which 3·6 are actually under cultivation in a given year) is obtained by the application of these results to the total adult male population. The Ndai kin group consisted of five sub-groups or lineages of closer kinsmen in which the number of farm holders ranged from 16 to 27. The means for the farms of these component lineages lie fairly close to the general mean, and some knowledge of conditions in other kin groups also indicated that a fair sample had been obtained. But the areas of individual Ndai farms cultivated in 1935 ranged widely from 0·25 to 8 acres. Although only five of the 97 were 4 acres or more and only ten were less than 0·5 acres in area, there was a large group, about 40 per cent. of the total and not confined to the farms of young recently married men, which lay well below the average (between 0·5 and 1 acre in area).

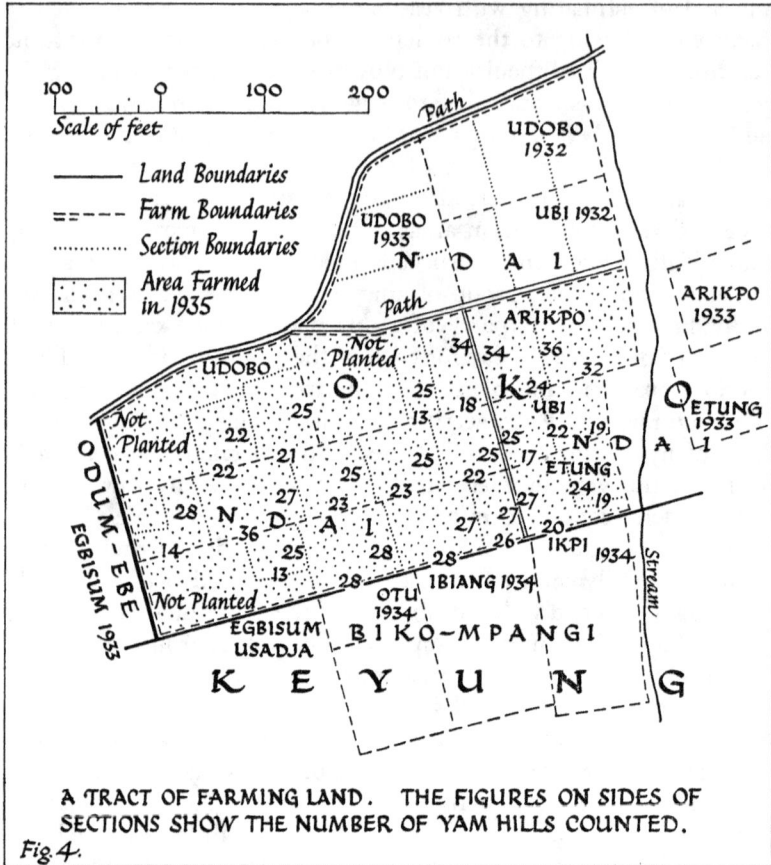

A TRACT OF FARMING LAND. THE FIGURES ON SIDES OF
SECTIONS SHOW THE NUMBER OF YAM HILLS COUNTED.
Fig. 4.

The frequency distribution of farm areas is shown by the graph
of yam hills in Fig. 5, in which the very high proportion of farms
in the lower classes is clear. This distribution, although it confirms
a general impression that very small and very large farms were
rare, is much more precise and striking than could otherwise have
been obtained. The size of the farms of a few individuals, which
appreciably raise the mean for the group, was very surprising.
There were five farms of 4 acres or more and they were in some
cases disproportionate to the size of the household. The larger
farms were, as in the case of the exceptional 8-acre farms, those
which provided most of the surplus sold outside the village and
contributed to the considerable Cross River trade in yams. The

adult strength of a household farming unit will obviously set limits to the area which can be cultivated, but the area of farms was found to bear no simple relation to the size of the household, whether considered as a farming unit of adults or a consuming unit including minors. Many other factors, such as interest in trading and hunting, seed yams available for planting, the capacity of the man and women, and the services of kinsmen, all affect the farm area of individual households. The people themselves are well aware of differences in farming capacity among both men and women. A youth is often told to choose as his wife a girl whose mother goes early to farm, while some of the elders often remarked that so-and-so did not care enough about seeing his yam stack grow bigger.

It is very significant, in view of the large stores of food that chiefs and leaders of social groups are said to accumulate among many peoples, that none of the very large farms in this kin group belonged to kin group leaders and priests or to heads of associations, who might be expected to have a special claim on the services of a wider circle of kinsmen or supporters. Indeed the priest-head of the Ndai group had a farm of only 1·2 acres, less than the average for the group as a whole, while that of his assistant was little above the average. It was clear from other instances that there is little tendency in Umor for men of prestige and authority to accumulate a large surplus of yams or other food supplies and marketable products, either by making large farms or by receiving gifts of these from others. The acquisition of currency, cloth, etc., by other means is a different matter which is discussed later, see pp. 45–8

THE SIZE OF HARVEST

At the end of the farming season I undertook a census of the yam harvest of the ninety-seven farms whose area I had estimated.[4] This was based on a native practice which lent itself to numerical estimation. At harvest-time the yams are stored in the stacks by tying them to raffia midribs or long stakes, each 10 or 12 feet high, set close together on the solid timber frame. The harvested yams, when they have been sunned, are graded according to size for greater ease in handling and are tied in neat, close-packed, vertical rows to the poles, so that they form a solid wall of yams 8 to 10 feet

[4] Data were actually obtained for 104 farm harvests, including those of six households for whose farms a count of yam hills could not be obtained.

high. Every person refers to his yam harvest by stating the number of upright sticks which he has tied with yams. Such an estimate may be rather misleading because the actual size of the harvest will vary according to the height of the sticks and the bulk of the yams. In addition to the large yam tubers a number of small yams, sometimes attached to the neck of the main growth, are formed, and these small yams, often little larger than a big potato, are used extensively for planting in the ensuing year. At the harvest of 1935 I found that the greater part of the larger yams were between 9 inches and 12 inches long and that very few exceeded 18 inches in length, while the small yamlets ranged from 2 to 6 inches in length. A closer estimate of the bulk of the harvest was made possible by counting the number of sticks in each of three sizes (under 6 inches, 6 to 12 inches, and over 12 inches), and by obtaining at each harvest stack a mean value for the number of yams on the sticks in each size group.[5] In terms of units of medium-sized yams the mean production for the 97 farms investigated was 2,545. The individual harvests ranged from a single exceptionally low value of 235 to a maximum of 11,410 units of medium-sized yams, and the frequency distribution of the yam harvest is given in Fig. 5 (Plate III).

It will be observed that, while the harvest variation is of the same general character as that for farm area, an even larger percentage of farms falls in the lower class intervals, which suggests that a considerable number of farms of more than average size do not yield a correspondingly large harvest. This is to be expected, since yield will be considerably affected by care in cultivation, and the household data indicate that there are a considerable number of farms of more than average size with relatively low labour power as measured by the number of adult members. In such farms there would tend to be some falling off in efficiency of cultivation. This cannot, however, be directly concluded from the graph and must be determined from a consideration of all the data concerning the households.

As the size of farms and the bulk of the harvest have been

---

[5] In the task of counting and recording the yam sticks, as well as in the earlier work of counting the yam hills along the sides of the farm sections, I was able to secure the untiring and very thorough help of an Umor man, Ubi Okoi. He was a member of the kin group which was the subject of my census and had returned to the village some years ago after a considerable period at a mission school. Speaking English and having an aptitude for figures, his help was invaluable when so short a time was at my disposal.

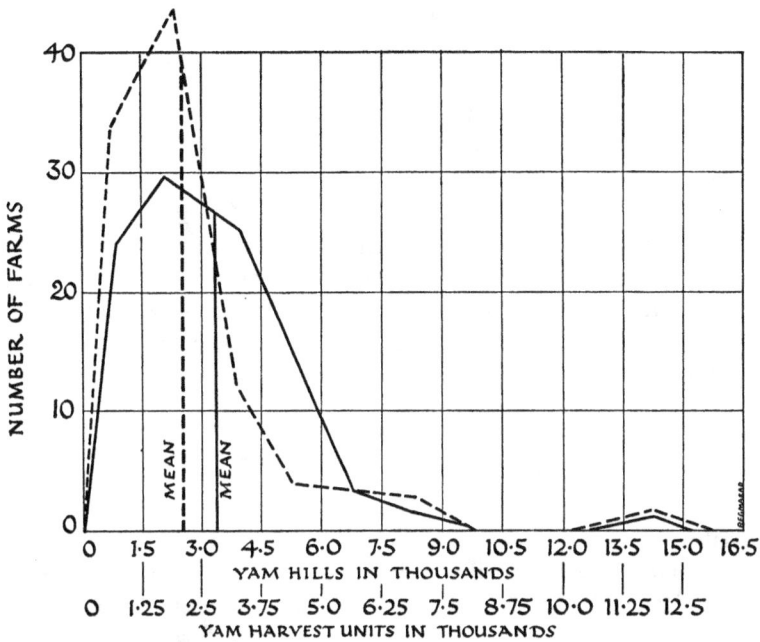

FIG. 5. *Frequency distribution of yam hills* (- - - -), *and yam harvest* (———)

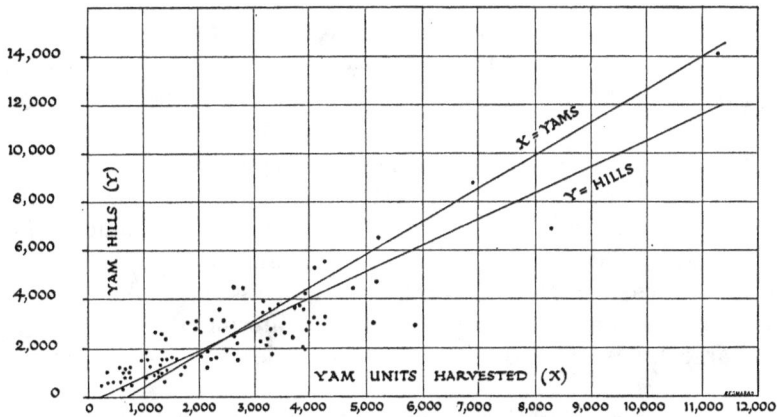

Fig. 6. DOT DIAGRAM OF AREA AND YAM HARVEST OF 97 FARMS IN NDAI

Means	OBTAINED BY DEVIATION	CALCULATED	STANDARD DEVIATIONS	*Coefficient of correlation*
YAM HILLS	2,418	2,440	2,061	0.89 ± .02
YAM UNITS HARVESTED	2,603	2,645	1,752	

estimated independently, reliability of the estimates can be tested by investigating their correlation. Despite differences in fertility and in efficiency of cultivation, a high correlation between size of farm and bulk of harvest is to be expected for the series as a whole, and is shown by the data plotted in Fig. 6,[6] where the distribution of the dots indicates the degree of correlation. This has been calculated from the diagram as 0.89 ± 0.02 and is graphically indicated both by the narrow elliptical clustering of the dots and by the small angular distance between the regression lines for yam hills and harvest units respectively. The probable loss of efficiency in the cultivation of many larger farms is also suggested in this diagram by the downward sag of the dense dot cluster in the class intervals above the mean for yam hills.

KINSHIP BASIS OF FARMLAND RIGHTS

The farm and harvest data discussed above relate to one of the patrilineal kin groups in Umor through which men acquire rights to farmlands. Each patrilineal kin group or *kepun* (plural, *yepun*), which has collective rights to a delimited dwelling area in the village, has also rights to a number of tracts of farming land. The number and strength of the *yepun* in Umor cannot be stated definitely, for there are several quasi-*yepun* which lack one or more characteristic features, but from the point of view of farming rights there are about 30 kin groups ranging in size from 30 to nearly 200 adult men and their households. At the same time the *yepun* fall into larger territorial groups concerning which there is no principle of internal kinship. These larger groupings are wards (*yekpatu*) of the village, and it is on a ward basis that the village territory is primarily divided, since the patrilineal kin groups of the different wards as a rule share a number of common farming paths. Fig. 1 shows the way in which the farming paths, and consequently the sectors of land reached by them, are distributed among the four wards. The people of the four wards thus farm lands lying in great blocks round the village; but the lands of the kin groups within a ward are as a rule considerably intermingled.

Large tracts of land, each a square mile or more in extent,

---

[6] I am indebted to Mr. G. H. Daniel for the construction of this diagram and for the statistical analysis based on it, and also for much help with the tedious preliminary calculations involved in assembling and checking the farm and harvest data.

I *a*. A compound in Ndai

I *b*. Yam farm during the growing season, with a pile of early yams in the foreground

II *a*. Woman hoeing up yam hills

II *b*. Man digging yams

lying along the farm roads are known by names usually referring to some natural feature, and their boundaries are known to all farming on these roads (see Fig. 4). But these named lands appear to be largely functionless with regard to property rights and are no longer the basis on which land is shared among the *yepun*. The control of land by the men of a particular kin group is subject to slow but continual change by processes of piecemeal accumulation or abandonment. For each farm road used by a *kepun* there is a 'farm path elder' (*oponotam eta*), who is expected to know the established rights of all individuals of his *kepun* on that road, to mediate in any disputes between those individuals, and to act as spokesman in disputes with other *yepun*. In general the majority of the men of a single lineage within a *kepun* farm on the same path —often in a cluster of contiguous plots in each year—and the path elder is often a leading member of the lineage which provides the majority of the *kepun* members farming from that path. He is thus a close kinsman of the majority of the kin group concerned.

The kinship basis of farmland tenure does not, however, completely circumscribe the farming rights of the individual. In the first place individuals or small groups of relatives are able, if welcomed, to migrate from their own *kepun* area in the village and go to live in the dwelling area of another *kepun*, and may, without formal adoption, be given farming sites in the lands of that *kepun*. A man may also obtain temporary rights to make a farm in the land of another kin group. This is fairly often done where the man's own *kepun* is short of lands on the particular road he has elected to farm. He visits a path elder of another *kepun* (generally on the same path) which has a surplus and asks to be shown a tract which he may clear. A large gourd of palm wine must accompany such requests, when he visits the path elder in his house towards sundown. No other payment or gift is made for this right, but it can only be obtained by this formal recognition of the owning *kepun's* right and an appeal to its generosity. This is a very characteristic Yakö attitude. Few economic opportunities are bought and sold, but there is great emphasis on correct form of procedure, and on open recognition of favour.

If serious pressure develops on the farming land, new and permenent farming paths are opened. These are as a rule only shallow loops from the main paths. Considerable labour is involved in opening up such paths and in keeping them clear of vegetation.

Every year, as will be seen, large parties are formed to clear the farming paths at the opening of the new season, and despite the daily passage to and fro of people going to their farms a second clearing is often needed towards the end of the rainy season. Most of the old-established paths have been used so long that the daily passage of human feet has worn a gully in the soft sandstone 5 or 6 feet below the level of the surrounding ground which may become a torrent after heavy rains.

A man first takes up farmland when he marries: that is, when he first brings a wife to live with him in an independent household. Before this he has helped his father, and his prospective father-in-law. The provision of an elaborately coiled bundle of yam tying strings and a season's work in the farm is an important obligation of a youth to his prospective father-in-law. In his first year of farming the youth usually receives a part of his father's farmland. If the father needs to replace part of the ceded land he, not the son, goes to the path elder of his *kepun* to ask for and establish his claim to an unoccupied area.

In the first year the young man will probably farm only one or two sections of about one-quarter of an acre in total area. For the next two or three years he may continue to receive part of his father's farm plots as these are successively cleared for cultivation, while his father will as before recoup himself elsewhere if necessary; but after three or four years of farming he will endeavour to increase the area of his farm, both because there will by now, with average harvests, be a larger surplus of yams for planting in the coming year, and because he may already be taking a second wife. For his first year's farm the young man usually obtains his seed yams for planting from his parents, half a dozen sticks from his father and two or three from his mother. If his parents are poor or dead he will seek gifts from other close kinsmen. His wife will receive two or three sticks from her father and one or two from her mother, and she will get from her mother her supply of the early yams which belong entirely to women.

These two sources of planting yams—the man's and the wife's—are recognized as distinct, and the harvests they yield remain so throughout, for it is an important principle of Yakö farming that the husband and wife each have their own yams. Yams although they are the staple food play no part in marriage payments and both parties to the new household thus bring their own farming capital.

It is necessary to emphasize here that, while the division of farm tasks is applicable to the farm as a whole, the yams of the man and his wives are planted and dug separately and are tied on distinct groups of sticks in the harvest stack. The husbands and wives have distinctive marks, which they incise on the base of their yams as they are dug at harvest time, and the yam harvest of both is used to maintain the family according to well-established rules. The husband's yams are usually completely dug, washed, and sunned first. He then proceeds to dig some yams for each of his wives every day that he is in the farm. During the period of digging, sunning, and tying, which lasts about two moons, food yams are taken from the husband's or the wives' supplies according to whichever is being handled at the time. When the yams are being tied each wife also takes the equivalent of one stick, say thirty medium-sized yams, equally from her own and her husband's heaps. These are tied separately and are for food in the period immediately after the harvest, that is, from about the end of December, and when they are exhausted, the wife is expected to use two sticks of her own yams for household food, before asking for a stick of yams from her husband. These four sticks of yams (120 or so medium-sized yams) are considered to be sufficient for the wife, her children, and her share of the food provided for her husband for two moons (late December to late February). By this time bush-clearing for the new farm is well advanced, and before a wife asks her husband for another stick of his yams, she should have begun to make yam hills on the first section of the new farm. When this fifth stick is exhausted at the beginning of March, yam planting should have begun and the woman can then use the tips of the planting yams for food as well as the good parts of any decaying yams she may find on the sticks.

Hill making and planting generally occupy nearly two moons and after that, from late in April until the new yams may be dug in the latter part of July, the household must depend on a surplus of unplanted yams left in the stack. The area planted may therefore be limited by the minimum food requirements for these three moons, and inefficient cultivators find it hard to increase their farm areas on account of their very limited surplus after planting each year. In 1935 Ubi Okoi of Ndai, who had a farm of 2 acres with two wives, two young children, and one dependent relative (a youth who helped him in farm work and was fed by his senior wife), had tied 100 sticks of yams of his own at the previous harvest. His two wives had 40 and 16 sticks of harvest yams, a total of 156 sticks. Eighteen of these were used for food in January and February, 125 were used for planting and eating in March and April, and after planting he was left with eight sticks himself and his wives had three and two sticks for food until late July. Ubi gave four sticks to one wife, two to the other, and had two for feeding visitors during the three months before new yams were available.

While I heard nothing of serious famines in the past among the Yakö and most households are able to keep an adequate, if not lavish, supply of yams for food in the period after planting, only a small minority regularly have a considerable surplus beyond this. For these there is a ready market both in the village, among those who need more yams for planting, and also in the riverside villages of the lower Cross River and at Calabar itself. It should be noted that a man can sell only his own yams, and a wife's surplus is similarly her own.

The early yams, which provide food for three months from mid-July are almost always the property of the women. A woman receives a small supply at marriage from her mother and she is entitled to plant them in every fifth row of hills in each section of the farm, including those sections that are otherwise planted with her husband's yams. From July to November about a fifth of the year's crop is thus removed from the farm. Although these early yams are normally the property of the women they are used to feed the entire household during this later part of the farming season.

GROUP LABOUR IN FARM CLEARING

It is now necessary to review the farm cycle again and consider the special arrangement made for different phases of farm work. Both before the planting and the harvest each year the farm roads and the narrow paths leading to the lands have to be cleared. This is effected by obligatory co-operative labour. The path elders of the different kin groups farming on a road ask the ward heads to announce the day, and parties set out before daybreak working outwards from the village, cutting back the bush on the main road. These consist of all the able-bodied age-sets of the ward (see Chapter V, Ward Organization, pp. 143–6). When this has been done, smaller groups of men who propose to farm adjacent plots in different areas clear the branch paths giving access to their lands.

Fines may be imposed on able-bodied men who refuse to co-operate and one or two days is generally enough to complete the work.

The clearing of bush from the new farmlands is men's work, and it is also the occasion of co-operative labour. Farms are nearly always cleared and planted by stages in approximately rectangular sections, which vary according to the labour available from 200 or 300 up to 3,000 square yards, although exceptionally large sections made only by older men with numerous sons and helpers may extend to over 5,000 square yards. A party of a dozen men or more can clear a moderate section in a morning. Working parties are formed by the group labour of parties constituted within the *yepun*. Each man wanting a party to work on his farm goes to the *kepun* head bearing a calabash of palm wine and expresses his desire. This is generally done at an informal meeting in the compound of the *kepun* head or in the *kepun* assembly house at the opening the farming season. All *kepun* members have an obligation to help for one day and they later go to the house of the applicant to make final arrangements. These *kepun* parties usually work only in the morning and on market, i.e. non-farming, days, and the man whose farm is being cleared provides a mid-day meal of baked yams in the farm. The Yakö have a six-day week of which the second and fifth days are market and ceremonial days and the others farming days. It is a general rule that services in public and co-operative work and other group activities should not be demanded on farming days, and most rituals, whether of the *yepun*, clubs or other groups, are also generally confined to non-farming days.

The number of individuals taking part in the bush-clearing groups, in the farms of one Ndai lineage alone, ranged from 5 to 50, but the number usually lay between 12 and 30. A man who intends to make a farm of some three acres or more will need the services of four or more of these parties, but an attempt at fair rotation is made by the *kepun* head and the path elders. Claimants can be called on to give their own services or those of their older sons to those who have helped them on an equal number of occasions. At farm-clearing time there may be lively disputes as to priority in receiving parties and reciprocity of services. In practice strict reciprocity is not expected or obtained, and as a rule it only becomes a point in debate when disputes arise on some other head.

Kepun bush parties are usually enjoyed for their own sake, and since a minority of farms greatly exceed the average area there are always a few men who will need more help than can be required of them in turn. But if they offer a meal and a generous supply of palm wine later, they will not as a rule lack helpers from among their kinsmen who have few yams. If a man requires more help than he can readily get from *kepun* parties, or if a man is at odds with his fellow *kepun* members concerning his rights and obligations either in the actual clearing or in connection with some quite different matter, and therefore refuses to take part in the *kepun* clearing parties, he has recourse to reciprocal parties of friends. These friends are as a rule farming a group of adjacent plots but are not necessarily members of the same kin group. Such a party generally numbers only about half a dozen men and successively clears sections of each member's farm, until the work is completed. Several instances occurred in Ndai of individuals who took little or no part in the *kepun* parties and relied on these parties of friends.

The clearing parties merely hack down the saplings and bush, and grub up the larger roots; the occupier often has to spend several farming days on a section of average size, digging out the mass of smaller roots and laying the land quite bare. Ten to fifteen days later he burns the dried vegetation which has been piled up in a number of heaps. Here again the services of a few helpers are needed, and men farming adjacent plots commonly help each other in starting and controlling the fires. Charred wood is cleared off and often carried back to the village, and the making of yam hills proceeds immediately after the ashes have been scattered over the section.

The hoeing of yam hills is traditionally women's work and in ordinary circumstances no Yakö men undertake it. But for nearly a generation now parties of 'strangers' visit Umor at this time and share in this work as paid labourers. These foreign labourers are Ezza Ibo living west of the Cross River, among whom a considerably greater share of the farm labour is done by men. Parties of young men arrive at Umor in January and may stay for two months or more. They are hired by individuals, usually in parties of from five to thirty, and may work on one farm for from two to ten days. In 1935 they were being given their food, shelter, and 2d. per day.

Minor Crops

After the yam planting—carried out jointly by the man and his wives in the intervals of clearing and hilling, and usually without help from outside—the farm work devolves almost entirely on the women. They plant between and on the sides of the yam hills the minor crops of maize, coco-yams, okra, pumpkins, and beans which are left entirely to their care. These minor crops afford welcome variety in a diet consisting so largely of yams. A capable wife is expected to be able to offer her husband dishes in which corn, okra, and other minor crops are used, and small supplies of most of these crops are stored—often in the house—after the harvest. On the other hand the people are aware that hills overloaded with minor plantings are likely to yield poorly in yams and fairly strict limits are set to this interculture.

From May to September the women work their way through the farm removing the weeds that rapidly spring up. The whole farm should be weeded twice and a third weeding is needed if a late ripening variety of bean, gathered a month or more after the yam harvest, is grown. Ground-nuts, which are also valued as a relish, gourds whose fruit cases are used to make a variety of receptacles, and cassava, which is generally regarded as a foreign and insipid yam substitute, are, however, planted by men. Ground-nuts often occupy a separate corner or the end of the last section of the yam

Number and Percentage of Ndai Farms Growing Minor Crops

	Ikpi Omengka	Itewa	Lineages Etang Enamuzo	Obeten Ogometu	Ubana Mkpiyen	Ndai Total	% of Total
Total no. of farms	20	20	16	25	22	103	100
*Coco-yams	18	19	16	24	21	96	93·2
*Corn	19	20	16	25	22	102	99·0
*Pumpkins	19	18	13	24	22	96	93·2
†Gourds	18	4	5	18	14	59	57·3
†Cassava	3	5	10	3	4	25	24·3
†Ground-nuts	18	19	11	25	22	95	92·2
*Okra	19	20	14	25	22	100	97·2
*Sword beans	16	11	12	22	20	81	78·7
*Curly beans	—	1	2	—	1	4	3·9
*Flat beans	—	—	2	—	—	2	1·9
*Sugar cane	5	10	12	4	6	37	35·9
*Peppers	19	19	15	18	22	93	90·3

*Grown by women.   †Grown by men.

farm and are planted in long wide ridges after the fashion of Hausa ground-nut cultivation in Northern Nigeria.

Although the amounts grown are small most of these minor crops are raised on the majority of farms, and the above table of data from the Ndai farms shows that only cassava, sugar cane, the later ripening curly bean (*okpoma*) and the flat bean (*kekpoma-babali*), said to have been recently introduced, are absent from the majority of farms.

Harvest Labour

The labour involved at harvest in the digging, carrying, washing, and stacking of yams may be indicated by the actual numbers of yams tied in the stacks. In Ndai in 1935 the totals (for yams of all sizes) ranged from 350 in the case of a young man farming for the first time to 11,400, the harvest of an exceptionally large household from a farm of 8 acres. The mean was nearly 4,000 per household and the average number of yams handled was over 2,500 per acre of farm land.

OIL PALMS

While the farm plots are by far the most productive areas of the village territory and demand the greatest expenditure of labour, they are not the only economically productive areas. In addition to a wide variety of materials for food and crafts, collected on a small scale from the bush, the products of the wild oil palm are obtained regularly in large quantities throughout the year. About half the able-bodied men of Umor are daily engaged in obtaining palm wine and palm fruits, while the fronds are also collected in large quantities for house roofing. The oil palm grows abundantly throughout the territory and is left standing when land is cleared for farming. Rights to oil palms are acquired through patrilineal kin groups, each of which collectively claims the oil palms in tracts of territory reached from the farming paths. These tracts are not limited to the lands that are periodically farmed by the kin group but may extend into uncultivated areas, and there may apparently be considerable discrepancies between farming and oil palm rights. In detail the groups of palms actually exploited are constantly changing according to the yield and the convenience of their situation. Each man desires palms that are fairly easily accessible on his journeys to and from his farm, but side tracks have often to be kept open in the dense bush to reach them. Usually groups of two or three men co-operate to make a path into a promising and convenient area, settling their claims to particular palms by agreement.

A distinction is, however, recognized between palms tapped for wine and those from which fruit is collected. Palm wine—the fermented sap obtained by piercing the flower stalk and attaching a collecting calabash—has to be collected twice daily and considerable labour is involved in each tapping of an inflorescence which yields for only a month or so. To obtain about a gallon of palm wine some six to ten trees have to be climbed twice a day. Trees that are being tapped, have been prepared for tapping, or are being rested for three moons or so after tapping, are claimed by those who have worked on them and should not be interfered with by others. The owner generally places some leaves in a cut in the trunk near the ground to indicate that it is reserved to himself. An individual can, however, cut palm fruits anywhere in his *kepun* palm land so long as he does not interfere with the tapped palms of others. In practice most individuals collect fruits in a tract round their current tapping area, and since there is a surplus of fruits there are few disputes. Surreptitious cutting of accessible palm fruits by men from other *yepun* is said, however, to be more frequent. Among 103 men of the Ndai kin group, 50 were tapping palms for wine and 48 were collecting fruit. In nearly all cases part of the product was sold in the village (Plate IV).

Trade in Palm Oil and Kernels

The preparation of palm oil is a household matter shared between men and wives. It is done at convenient intervals when a sufficient supply of fruits has been collected. Although the extraction of the oil is, apart from the pulping of the fruits, carried out by the wives, the oil, save for household requirements belongs to the men alone. The wives receive as their share the nuts which they and the children crack to extract the kernels for sale.[7]

The relatively small quantities of oil and kernels produced in

[7] The kernels are in aggregate more valuable in trade than the oil, but they are shared among a greater number of women, since many men have two or more wives. In connection with the production of palm oil and kernels, which has increased enormously during the last generation and is by far the most important source of money income, there have grown up customs of division of labour and product as precise as those associated with farming.

the individual households are bought by one or other of the twenty or so men in the village who devote themselves to trading. Using kerosene tins with graduated dipsticks to measure the amount of oil, the traders endeavour to adjust their payments to the prices they are likely to receive at Ediba on the Cross River or in Calabar. In Umor oil trading is regarded as a specialized and somewhat risky business, and very few oil traders have practically given up farming to devote all their time to the trade. When traders think that the price offered at Ediba is too low they may have their oil carried by canoe to Calabar, where they can offer it to a number of competing firms (Plate V).

Since nearly half the men of Umor are producing palm oil, which is their only important source of money, the fluctuations in wholesale prices, which have been very great in recent years, have had a considerable effect on the purchasing power of trade goods and on the tax-paying ability of the people. Ediba prices for a kerosene tin of oil ranged from 1/1d. to 3/3d. in the twelve months from November 1934, and the highest price was of course far below that of the boom period. It is difficult to estimate the amount of palm oil exported from Umor, but nearly 200 tons of oil reach the Cross River from this region and Umor is likely to produce some 60 to 70 tons a year, which at 1935 prices would have a value of only £400 to £500.

Trade in palm kernels is a more widespread venture and a considerable number of the younger men engage in it. They often get their wives and older children to go about the village offering to purchase kernels by the cupful. When a man has got together one or two bags[8] he takes them to the river for sale. About 1,000 tons of kernels reach the Cross River from the Yakö villages every year, and of this the likely share of Umor, 400 to 500 tons, was worth about £2,500. There are, however, more women selling kernels than men selling oil in Umor and probably two or three times as many kernel traders.

There are approximately 1,500 households in Umor, so that their mean money income from the palm oil production of the village is probably slightly more than two pounds. This income is however very unequally distributed in the village.[9]

---

[8] Jute salt bags which are the current native unit of measurement. In 1935 a bag of kernels was worth about 3/6d. at Ediba.
[9] For further estimates of the volume and value of this traffic see p.33 below.

The other forms of external trade are concerned both with an entirely native product—smoked bush meat—and with European trade goods, particularly cloth and cutlery. It should be noted that as the one involves long journeys into the forest of Agoi to the east where game is abundant, and the other frequent visits to Calabar and Port Harcourt for European goods, this trading is more specialized and time consuming than that in palm products. Although oil traders occasionally buy cloth in Calabar for sale on their return to Umor this combination is not common, and the cloth and cutlery traders are for the most part young men who enjoy frequent visits to the coast and often return with an assortment of personal luxuries ranging from scented soap to cricket blazers.

HUNTING

A considerable number of Umor men hunt in the forest tracts and farm bush in the village territory. Game is taken in a variety of spring traps set along the paths and round the farms and is also shot with Dane guns—the long-barrelled flint locks that are widely used in Southern Nigeria. While a number of duiker and other forest buck and small game (of which the more common are lemurs, genets, civets, porcupine and the pangolin or scaly ant-eater) are obtained, this source of meat is very small in relation to the total population. Smoked bush meat brought in from Agoi is always available in the market, but the effective demand is apparently low, for only small quantities are usually displayed and it is only on the occasion of feasts of kin groups and associations that it is seen in large quantities. Organized hunting appears to have been more active a generation ago. There is still, however, an association of hunters in each ward which resorts periodically to a hunting camp in the bush and plays a part in ceremonials; see pp. 155-7.

LIVESTOCK

Livestock do not contribute very substantially to the food supply. The Southern Nigerian dwarf cattle are found in Umor but there were only 32 head of cattle in the possession of 103 men of Ndai in 1935, which suggests that the entire village stock is little more than 500, and some of this is sold every year to Ibo who visit Umor to obtain cattle for their title feasts. Goats are more than twice as numerous and are a common food at feasts, the excellence of which is judged by the amount of meat provided. There are practically no sheep, although neighbouring villages have them, and the pigs which foul some of the other Yakö settlements are not numerous in Umor. In fact the chickens and occasional ducks are the only livestock that are at all common: there were on the average nearly two per household in Ndai kin group. There is little doubt therefore that the Yakö diet is poor in animal proteins, for meat is normally available only in minute quantities as a relish, and the local fish supply is negligible. Imported stockfish is however brought for sale to the village market.

The economic activities of 112 adult men of Ndai can now be conveniently summarized as follows:

FARMING, TRADING, HUNTING, AND LIVESTOCK IN NDAI

Lineage	Number of men	Farming	Old or Idle	Trading entirely	Trading auxiliary	Hunting	Cattle	Goats	Pigs	Chickens
Ikpi										
Omeŋka	21	20	0	1	3	5	5	10	7	14
Obeten										
Ogometu	28	26	2	0	4	7	4	9	0	19
Ubana										
Mkbiyen	26	23	3	0	3	1	0	12	1	18
Etuŋ										
Enamuzo	16	16	0	0	1	2	4	2	0	9
Itewa	21	20	1	(no data)		1	3	6	3	9
Totals	112	105	6	1 (in 91)	11 (in 91)	16	16	39	11	69

TRADING IN NDAI

Adult men	Total Traders	Exclusive	Auxiliary	Oil	Kernels	Cloth	Bush meat
91	12	1	11	2	5	1	4

LAND RIGHTS OF MATRILINEAL GROUPS

The land rights and labour services so far considered all take their rise from the collective claims and activities of the patrilineal kin groups—the *yepun*—and of their larger aggregations—the wards. But the patrilineal principle is not all-pervading among the Yakö. There is also a matrilineal organization of great importance in the village government and responsible for rituals of greater prestige than those performed at the *yepun* shrines. Furthermore, while individual claims to economic resources are usually established within the patrilineal kin group, the greater part of accumulated wealth and movable property is inherited by matrilineal kinsmen. This practice controls among other things the disposal of the yam harvests of men and women when they die and may involve matrilineal relatives in obligations to supply labour in a farm to complete the cycle of cultivation of a deceased kinsmen. The structure and significance of the groups of matrilineal kin groups thus formed are discussed below; see pp. 96–112.

The economic rights of matrilineal kin groups may also, in certain circumstances, override those of the patrilineal groups, for the former lay certain claims to tracts of land which are at the same time cultivated and exploited by the *yepun*. At the funeral rites of an elder the dead man's matrilineal kinsmen can enter their tract and take wine from any or all of the tapped oil palms, despite the fact that these palms have been prepared by men who are not their kinsmen and who at all other times have exclusive rights to the palms, which they could defend in the village court. In these same tracts the valuable raffia palm may be planted in swampy ground by members of the matrilineal group, and these cannot be claimed either by the patrilineal kin group farming there or by patrilineal descendants of the planter. More recently the matrilineal groups have established a claim to the village share of the royalty fees which now have to be paid for felling within their lands certain valuable timber trees scheduled by the Forestry Department. As the patrilineal and matrilineal land rights coexist, over the same territory and the boundary lines of the divisions do not coincide, there is an intricate dual mosaic of established rights to the resources of the village territory.

Although no farming rights or duties normally derive from the matrilineal kin organization, that system is nevertheless closely associated with the general prosperity of agriculture. Three village rituals each year—the First Planting rites, the First Fruits or New Yam feast (*Liboku* rites), and the Harvest rites—are all performed by the priests at the spirits of the matrilineal kin groups, and it is the response of these which is sought for the prosperity of cultivation.

CONCLUSION

Although the basic economic activities in Umor operate within a framework of established rights of kin groups, these are not simple or comprehensive in character. Rights to farm land are acquired through membership in the patrilineal *kepun*, but the area of the farm and the co-operation of the kinsmen are subject to but slight group control, and the farm once planted is regarded as household property into which a fellow *kepun* member will not lightly enter lest his motives be misconstrued. There are great contrasts in farming prosperity among the individual members of a kin group, which are reflected in the ability of individuals to pay for membership in the village associations. Similarly the establishment of rights to bush products within the *kepun* lands is left to the initiative of individuals or small groups. At the same time specific but more restricted claims are made to the resources of the territory by kin groups of an entirely different order.

The *kepun* organization of farming activities involves some obligation of mutual assistance in path and bush clearing but little or none in other farming activities. In times of misfortune, indeed, it is to the matrilineal kin as often as to the *kepun* that the distressed individual or household turns. A man who through sickness or absence cannot attend to his farm is likely to ask a younger matrilineal kinsman for help in caring for his farm. The rights of matrilineal kin to inherit the greater part of a man's movable property are but a partial explanation of this attitude. The sentiment of matrilineal kinship, perhaps because it is not subject, owing to territorial dispersion, to the day to day rivalries and differences within the *kepun*, is surprisingly strong. Within the *kepun* there is marked individualism, and except on ceremonial occasions few effective demands can be made on the individual for the benefit of *kepun* fellows outside his lineage.

There is not at present in Umor any severe competition for land or forest products, for the village has adequate territory. The continuance of the great increase in population that can be inferred from village expansion in the last two generations may eventually result in land hunger if other sources of wealth are not developed, but assuming no basic change in the present economy, the population could probably increase by another 50 per cent. before severe strains would show. The need in Umor, however, as so generally in Southern Nigeria, is not a further increase in density of population but modifications in economy which will improve the quality and variety of the food supply of the West African; a need from which arise the most important social and scientific problems of the country.

II

EXCHANGE AND CONSUMPTION[1]

PRODUCTION FOR EXCHANGE

PROBABLY every household in Umor produces some surplus which is disposed of by sale. But the variations in the amounts are as great as the means of disposing of them are various and some analysis is necessary before an attempt can be made to assess the importance of exchange production within the households or to estimate the amounts of cash income that are secured.

Foodstuffs

In the village market women engage in a petty trade in food-stuffs, but it is very difficult to estimate the amounts of produce involved, nor is there any hard and fast line between cash sales and barter.[2] About half the women of the village dispose of small surpluses in this way as they become available.

The traffic in yams, the staple food, appears to be small in relation to the total harvest. Investigation of a sample group of households in 1935 revealed not merely a high degree of self-subsistence in yams, but also that surpluses are normally small and largely disposed of by gifts and sales among kinsfolk. Only 15 per cent. of men produced a surplus sufficiently large to be offered for sale to an outside trader for export from the village, while less than half the men and a quarter of the women sold any yams in quantity. Excluding yams disposed of in petty barter, the aggregate surplus probably amounted to less than 3 per cent. of the main harvest and of this less than half left the village. On the other hand, on account of their value, a man with a considerable yam surplus, such as 500, could, at a typical village price of 7s. per hundred, derive there-from a comparatively large item of cash income.

The numbers of livestock kept are in general so small that no

---

[1] Reprinted from *Native Economies of Nigeria*, 1946, pp. 49–64.
[2] At any given period recognized exchange values exist between several of the main items of farm and bush produce. Yams, either singly or five at a time, and bowls of palm-oil kernels function as a local currency for the purchase of other goods in small quantities.

substantial addition to income either by direct consumption or through sales is derived from this source. A small number of more prosperous men secure considerable, if sporadic, returns from the sale of dwarf cattle most of which are not butchered in the village but bought and taken away by Ibo traders. With good fortune a man who owns a cow may hope to sell a calf every year or two for a pound and obtain from £3 to £6 for the cow when he comes to sell it. Livestock is quite markedly concentrated in a minority of more prosperous households. In fact the keeping of livestock is in general an indication of means secured from some other source rather than an important source of income itself.

Forest Produce

Most constructional materials such as raffia poles and thatching leaves are produced by the men of each household as needed, but there is a considerable demand for dried lianes and other fibres for use as roping in house-building and yam-tying. This is in part met by supplies provided by the younger men, who will collect for sale up to a dozen or so bundles at about 6d. each in the course of the year.

But by far the most important, and as has already been indicated, the most remunerative element of surplus production is that based on the exploitation of the wild oil-palms. Palm-wine is produced for local consumption, edible palm-oil is made from fresh fruit for local use and, most important of all, palm-oil and palm-kernels are produced for export. Nearly all the more active men tap palm-trees for wine and a very large proportion of them sell part of their supplies to others in the village. A fairly active palm-wine producer can probably make 10s. or so in the course of the year by sales of his surplus wine at the local price which varies from ½d. to 1½d. a calabash of about half a gallon; while those concentrating on palm-wine collection, who are, however, few, can earn more than £1 in this way.

The returns from palm-oil and kernel production are, however, more considerable and are by far the largest single source of cash income. These involve, as has been indicated, the joint activity of both man and wife among whom the produce is shared. Without exceptional concentration on this production, the household of a man with one wife will produce from 10 to 20 tins, of approximately 4 gallons or 36 lb. each, of semi-hard oil in a year, while in a few

III *a*. Preparing the yam stack

III *b*. A full yam stack

IV *a*. Tapping a palm
inflorescence for wine

IV *b*. Men pounding
palm fruit for oil

households in which the services of younger men and several women are available for its preparation over 50 tins are produced.

No adequate data on the labour costs of palm-oil production were obtained in Umor, but a number of estimates for the production of semi-hard oil under similar conditions elsewhere in the eastern and western provinces[3] suggest that for one 36 lb. tin of oil about 25–30 bunches or 300 lb. of fruit are required. The cutting and transport of the fruit demand from ½ to 1½ days' labour according to their accessibility, removing fruits from the stems would take a further day, while the process of extraction would require another 1 to 2 days, apart from half a day's labour for securing wood and water needed in the cooking process. Thus, the total labour cost per tin would be from 3 to 5 days, of which, among the Yakö, from 2 to 3 would be contributed by the women. About ¼ cwt. of kernels can be secured from the nuts by a further 2 days' labour by the women.

At 1939 village prices of 2s. 6d. approximately per 36 lb. tin of oil and 1s. for ¼ cwt. of kernels, the cash return would have been from 7d. to 8½d. per labour day. At the depression prices of 1s. or less per tin of oil, the return on a day's labour would have been 3d. or less.[4]

At the local prices current in recent years, which have ranged from 5s. to less than 1s. per tin, a man's income from the sale of palm-oil may be estimated as ranging from 75s. to 12s., according to the ruling price, in the case of ordinary producing households, while the larger producers have received cash returns of over £13 to only 36s. in similar circumstances. While prices as low as 1s. per tin are locally regarded as very inadequate and probably have the effect of diverting some effort to other more remunerative activity where it can be found, even the highest prices during the period between 1935 and 1939 were compared unfavourably with the 'twenties when 10s. or more was obtained for one 4-gallon tin.

The output of kernels is normally greater than that of oil since almost every women endeavours to produce kernels for sale whether or not her husband produces oil. If he does not, the wife will

[3] Summarized by Mr. A. F. B. Bridges in his unpublished *Report on Oil Palm Survey: Ibo, Ibibio and Cross River Areas*, 1939. It should be noted that the process for making soft and edible oil from fresh fruits involves twice or three times as much labour.

[4] Casual unskilled wage labour, such as porterage or grass cutting for Europeans in this area, was paid 6d. per day. Among themselves the Yakö would pay 3d. to 4d. per day for such labour.

demand that he should cut palm-fruit for her for this purpose, for, apart from petty trading in foodstuffs, women have fewer alternative opportunities for securing cash incomes than men. While some were in 1935 producing and selling kernels at the rate of £1 or more in a year, very many were not obtaining more than a few shillings.[5]

Total Household Sales

An inquiry into returns from production for exchange among the 81 men of one kin group showed that three in four produced and sold a surplus of any of the leading exchange products[6] but none of them produced surpluses of all.[7] The quantities and values for each category of produce are summarized in the accompanying table.[8]

The value of the produce exported from the village was approximately 60 per cent. of the total value of sales.[9] Since the number of men deriving considerable cash income from other activities remunerated outside the village, i.e., a few itinerant traders, road labourers, etc., is very small, the bulk of the cash-payments for locally purchased native produce must be ultimately derived from the sale of produce leaving the village. In other words, sales of produce outside the village are the only substantial source of new funds. If the group studied be taken to be a representative sample of the village as a whole, the average cash income per household

[5] Unfortunately no adequate data could be obtained on the actual outputs of a sufficiently representative group of households to permit a direct estimate of village production. It could, however, be estimated that about 1,500 tons of kernels were sold in the local Cross River markets to the 'factory' of a European firm and to native wholesalers in 1935. If a third of this be attributed to Umor, the value of the village kernel output would, at an average price of £4 10s. per ton for that year, have been £2,250 or an average of £1 10s. per household, or 15s. per adult female. In any case there are great variations from household to household in palm-kernel outputs.

[6] Data were obtained separately for yams, palm-oil, palm-wine, and native rope, which are the only produce regularly sold in any quantity by men.

[7] The data do not unfortunately cover a whole year. It is, however, possible on the known seasonality of production to estimate the totals for a full year, while the number of sellers would not show an increase.

[8] It will be observed that the return from the sale of yams is not much smaller than that of palm-oil but, whereas almost the entire output of marketed palm-oil is exported, a great part of the yams are sold in the village for local use. Yam prices were, moreover, considerably higher and oil prices lower at the time of this census in 1941 than they were in 1935, when data for the estimates of output and values referred to earlier were made.

[9] On the assumption that half the yams marketed and all the palm-wine and native rope are purchased locally, c. £25 worth of the sales, or about 40 per cent. out of a total of c. £60 are to local buyers for local use.

TABLE I[10]

SALES OF NATIVE PRODUCE BY THE 81 MEN OF A SAMPLE KIN GROUP, EGBISUM KEPUN, UMOR, OBUBRA DIVISION, EASTERN PALM BELT, 1941

I. Records for Jan.– Aug. Inclusive

	No of Sellers	Total Sales Amount	Total Sales Value (£ s. d.)	Average Sale Amount	Average Sale Value (s. d.)	Largest Amount	Largest Value (£ s. d.)	Smallest Amount	Smallest Value (s. d.)	Correction for Full Year
Yams . .	25	4,940	22 14 0	198	18 2	720	3 0 0	50	5 0	$\times\frac{1}{1}$
Palm-Oil .	37	411 tins	20 14 0	11 tins	11 2	50 tins	2 10 0	4 tins	4 0	$\times\frac{9}{8}$
Palm-Wine .	31	2,297 bottles	9 11 0	74 bottles	6 2	180 bottles	0 15 0	12 bottles	1 0	$\times\frac{10}{8}$
Native Rope .	7	38 bunches	8 19 0	5½ bunches	2 9	10 bunches	0 5 0	2 bunches	1 0	$\times 1\frac{2}{8}$
All Sellers .	59		£53 15 0							

II. Estimate for Full Year

	No of Sellers	Total Sales Amount	Total Sales Value (£ s. d.)	Average Sale Amount	Average Sale Value (s. d.)	Largest Amount	Largest Value (£ s. d.)	Smallest Amount	Smallest Value (s. d.)
Yams* . .	25	4,940	22 14 0	198	18 2	720	3 0 0	50	5 0
Palm-Oil† .	37	462 tins	23 2 0	12½ tins	12 6	56 tins	2 16 3	5 tins	5 0
Palm-Wine .	31	2,871 bottles	11 18 9	93 bottles	7 9	225 bottles	0 18 9	15 bottles	1 3
Native Rope .	7	57 bunches	1 8 6	8 bunches	4 0	15 bunches	0 7 6	3 bunches	1 6
All Sellers .	59		£59 3 3						

* No. of men selling both Yams and Palm-Oil: 7

† No. of men selling both Palm-Wine and Palm-Oil: 21

[10] I am indebted to Okoi Arikpo, of Umor, for the data on which this table is based. They were obtained in 1941 during a period of leave from his duties as an instructor at Yaba Higher College.

from sales of men's produce, omitting petty traffic and occasional and exceptional items such as stock, would be approximately 15s., while the sum received from external sales averages only about 9s. per household. These estimates omit one important source of household income from produce, namely, that received by wives from their sales of palm-kernels. If a value be assigned to these on the basis of the independent data referred to earlier concerning typical palm-kernel outputs, a sum of about £62 should be added as the contribution of palm-kernels produced by the 123 wives at an average of 10s. each. This would give an average per household of about 25s. for total sales and of about 19s. for sales of exported produce. Actual household sales would, however, range from a few shillings to over £5.

TRADING

Trading in Umor falls into three fairly distinct categories which are to a large extent in different hands. They are: first, the purchase for resale of palm-oil and kernels with which is often combined trading in exported and imported food supplies; second, the retailing of European goods; and third, the local traffic in native food supplies and manufactures which is mostly in the hands of women.

Palm Products

There are no large-scale palm-oil wholesalers in Umor. The bulk handling of oil is concentrated in the Cross River village of Ediba seven miles away, where the 'factory' of a European firm and native wholesalers buy up oil which is brought in from the villages of the surrounding area. The oil traders in Umor confine themselves to buying for resale oil produced from time to time by individual households, offering a cash-payment for each lot according to the price they expect to receive at the riverside.[11]

Oil trading is regarded as a specialized and risky business, in which only those who can afford to lose money will engage on any scale. There appeared to be at most a dozen men in the whole village who regularly traded in palm-oil. One man who did devote

[11] If the price actually offered at Ediba either by the 'factory' or by native wholesalers proves unsatisfactory, a trader may hire a space in a canoe to have his oil carried to Calabar, where he can offer it to a number of competing firms, or leave it on deposit at Ediba in the hope of a rise in price. Oil is quite often held up either in the village or at the river for several months before it is sold.

nearly all his time to it and purchased most of the food for his household, accumulated from 10 to 40 tins of oil every two or three weeks when he was buying. He considered a net profit of 3d. per tin satisfactory and 6d. very good. An annual turnover of 300 tins at a 'satisfactory' profit of 3d. would yield £3 15s.[12] (Plate V).

Palm-kernels are bought up from the women by petty kernel traders by the bowlful. When one or more hundredweight sacks have been filled, these are carried to the river for sale to the factory or to native wholesalers, or for further transport to Calabar and other down-river markets. A few shillings is all that is needed to set up as a kernel trader, and this venture is popular among the younger men. The trader's gross profit per bag may be quite considerable as compared with that from oil, but the turnover is usually smaller. In 1939 when the kernel prices were low, the trader had a margin of 1s. to 1s. 2d. on a cwt. bag, selling for 4s. at Ediba, although the actual profits were said not to increase greatly with higher prices.

A very active kernel buyer will fill up to 10 bags in three months or about 40 bags in a year, which, at a steady price, would yield a gross profit of about £2. On the other hand, a fall of a shilling or more per sack, which has not been at all unusual in recent years, would wipe out most of the profit. Many kernel buyers claim that they have lost more than they have made in recent years. The majority of the young men engaged in this trade marketed only a few bags in the course of a year and typical individual profits have amounted to less than 10s. The village kernel traders do not confine their activities to their own community. The more enterprising visit the surrounding villages on their market days. On the other hand a number of buyers from the riverside villages are also to be found in the Umor market.

Analysis of data for one year[13] concerning trading journeys with palm and farm produce undertaken by the men of one ward showed that out of the total adult male population of 390 only 31 men were engaged in these forms of external trade. Of these 21 traded mainly in oil, 15 in kernels and 18 in farm produce; while 12 of them purchased supplies for further trading on their return.

[12] The local oil traders obviously could not be handling more than a small fraction of the oil produced in the village, and the greater part of the output is carried by the producers themselves to Ediba, when they have accumulated a tin or two for sale.

[13] From October 1938 to September 1939.

If this be taken as representative of the village as a whole, it implies that about 8 per cent. of the 1,750 men in the village, or about 140 in all, were engaged in one or other of these lines of trade. Moreover a great deal of this trade is on a very small scale and in the hands of youths who have not yet taken up farms of their own. While all the recorded traders were below middle age, fully half of them were under 25 years of age.[14]

Trade Goods

The trade in European goods varies even more in scale. On the one hand, there are a few well-established specialist traders who do not farm, have several assistants and cover a wide circuit of village markets. At the other extreme are a considerable number of young men who, with a loan of a few shillings, travel to Calabar or Port Harcourt to buy a few lengths of cloth which they attempt to sell at a profit on their return. Most traders have their favourite 'lines', but there is a good deal of overlapping. The majority sell cloth and combine this with other goods as opportunity offers. The outstanding trade goods brought to the village are: cloth and clothing in considerable variety;[15] salt;[16] stockfish; yellow soap; hardware, especially enamel bowls and matchets; matches; lump sugar, consumed by the women and children as a sweetmeat; gunpowder; patent medicines and miscellaneous personal articles such as beads, combs, mirrors, and pomades.

With the development of lorry road-services in the country west of the Cross River, Onitsha and Port Harcourt have largely superseded Calabar as the markets from which cloth traders get their supplies, but kernel and oil traders taking supplies to Calabar frequently buy trade goods there for resale in Umor. In all cases these are mostly bought at their ordinary retail prices in the European or Syrian stores.

The largest trader in Umor in 1939 was visiting one of these

[14] Of the 21 men trading oil, only one was operating on a really considerable scale, marketing 100 tins, and only 4 others marketed 20 tins or more in the year. Only 2 of those trading in kernels were operating on any considerable scale and half were marketing less than 10 bags per head in the course of the year. Although it was a common practice on trading journeys with oil-palm products to market farm crops at the same time, this trade too was very petty.

[15] This includes 'Manchester' prints and Yoruba (native) dyed cloth, khaki drill (which is made up by native tailors into shirts), cotton and artificial silk vests.

[16] The imported bagged salt is 'cooked' by the trader into cylinders about 6 inches in diameter, which is then sold in slices of about 1 inch thick.

centres every three months to purchase cloth and other goods to
the value of £15 to £20 on each occasion. He considered a gross
profit of 25 per cent. to 50 per cent. on cloth to be reasonable,
since each journey cost 10s. to 15s. and he had to maintain two
assistants, who traded some of his goods in outlying markets.
His gross annual profits were between £20 and £30, against
which expenses from £5 to £10 for journeys and payments in
kind to his assistants had to be set.[17]

There appeared to be only two other traders in cloth and miscellaneous goods in the village who had abandoned farming to
operate on this scale and only 8 others who, while maintaining
adequate subsistence farms, devoted much of their own time and
energy to trading in cloth, visiting a distant factory about every
three months to purchase about £10 worth of supplies. On a turnover of £40 of goods in a year, such men might be expected to
obtain gross profits of £10 or more, of which £2 to £3 would be
expended on travelling and assistance.[18] Finally, there were about
a hundred younger men trading sporadically in cloth and miscellaneous goods, sometimes in combination with kernel buying.
They made few journeys to distant markets for supplies, and
might buy their goods from as close at hand as Ediba. Their turnover and profits were considerably smaller and are likely to range
from a few shillings to not more than £2 in the course of a year.[19]

The total net profits of cloth and miscellaneous trading by
villagers in the course of the year could therefore be roughly estimated at £200. While, however, the local traders visit other villages,
traders from other districts also visit Umor, so that the activities
described above do not directly indicate the level of local consumption of cloth, hardware and miscellaneous goods. There will be
over thirty men offering these for sale in the bi-weekly village
market, of these two-thirds will be local men and the remainder
strangers, mostly Ibo from the far side of the Cross River. If we

[17] He claimed that his trading capital, which in 1931 had been of the order of
£60, had by 1939 been reduced to little more than £20 and attributed this to
losses due to the undoubted shrinking of trade during the prolonged period of
low palm product prices. But he had in the meantime built a mudblock cement-
faced house with an iron roof on which more than £50 was spent.

[18] Detailed costing of an actual journey for supplies from Onitsha showed an
expenditure of 10s. 4d.

[19] Soap, matches, sugar, and other minor household articles are another largely
separate trading line which is engaged in by petty traders, nearly all of whom are
local men, although a few stranger women also participate. From 10 to 20 stalls
of such goods are to be found in the market.

assume that the local traders dispose of two-thirds of their goods in the village and that they share equally with strangers in the total trade, the annual village purchases of these goods will be about £1,000 to £1,500, or from 14s. to £1 per household.

Imported dried cod, known as stockfish, is a separate trading speciality, although dealing in it is sometimes combined with kernel buying. It is purchased by the bag at Calabar for £2 10s. and sold in small pieces at 1d. to 6d. a time according to size, at a gross profit of 15s. to 16s. on a bag. About a dozen local men regularly sell stockfish in the market, but no detailed information as to their turnover and profits were obtained.

Native Food Supplies and Manufactures

There is practically no large-scale trade in native food supplies. Traffic is mainly confined to the sale of small surpluses from household farms and to petty purchases of imported specialities. Reference has already been made to the occasional petty sales by women of their own farm surpluses, to the small-scale external trading in farm produce by men who are primarily engaged in other trading activities and to the occasional larger-scale of yams by surplus producers to local consumers or visiting traders.

Extremely few Umor women engage in trading outside the village, although about 5 per cent. make occasional visits to neighbouring villages to obtain supplies, mostly of fish and peppers, for resale in the Umor market. Trading in food supplies imported into the village is largely in the hands of 'foreign' women who come in considerable numbers to this the largest village market for some twenty miles around, bringing dried local fish, coco-yams, cooked food such as bean cakes, and miscellaneous vegetable produce. A number of these 'foreign' women reside in the village for several months at a time, making frequent journeys abroad for supplies. The records of household sales and purchases of food supplies strongly suggest that the village as a whole was a net importer of native food supplies other than yams, but that the quantities and values involved were small.

Smoked bush meat prepared by the Agoi peoples, whose small villages are scattered through the high forest to the east of Yakö territory, is marketed both by Umor and a few Agoi men, who engaged in a two-way trade taking gunpowder, cloth, and other trade goods to these villages in exchange for bush meat, creeper-rope, palm-kernels, and cam-wood. There are usually three or four men selling this bush meat at every market, and it is also sold in the compounds by traders who often make journeys to fulfil special orders for a club, kin group, or other feast. Apart from such occasional large purchases, it can be roughly estimated that the equivalent of only some half-dozen duiker carcases would be sold in a week—a negligible amount in relation to the population of the whole village.

The Yakö rely largely on 'foreign' traders for their supplies of native manufactures. Those purchased in the largest amounts are baskets, pots, hoe blades, tobacco, and prepared chalk used for ceremonial and cosmetic purposes. Although a considerable quantity of these products is purchased by villagers who have gone to outlying markets for other purposes, there are, except in the case of native tobacco, few if any resident traders in native manufactures who keep stocks of these goods.

LEVELS OF CONSUMPTION AND MONEY INCOME

While there is no recollection or tradition of serious famines among the Yakö and the majority of households are able to provide an adequate, if not lavish, supply of yams for food in the period after planting, only a minority regularly have a considerable surplus. Wives are expected to grow adequate household supplies of the secondary crops which they plant between and on the sides of the yam hills. On the other hand, it is well known that hills overloaded with minor plantings are likely to yield poorly in yams, and men set fairly strict limits to this interculture, especially where a wife is securing a surplus for her own trading activities.

In view of the smallness of the external trade in yams, the consumption of this staple may be taken a little below the total available output. The average household harvest in the sample discussed earlier was equivalent to approximately 2,500 medium-sized yams of 3 to 4 lb. weight, but the modal value for farm harvests was approximately 1,900.[20] It is reasonable, therefore, to assume that a small household of one man and wife with two or three children will in ordinary circumstances have a harvest equivalent to about 2,000 medium-sized yams. Of this about one-quarter must be deducted for replanting and losses in the stack, while a further

[20] The total *number* of yams is much higher as it includes a large proportion of small yams only a pound or so in weight.

hundred will probably be used in barter, minor gifts and hospitality, leaving some 1,400 for household use. This implies a mean daily consumption of about 1·3 medium yams per adult unit, or 4 or 5 lb. weight of unprepared yam.[21] The value of this yam consumption at a middle price of 7s. per hundred yams would be £4 18s. per annum.

Actual household consumption varies considerably, however, through the year. Even well-provided households with large harvests do not reserve sufficient yams to maintain consumption at earlier levels during the period between planting in April and the first digging of early yams in July. Consumption may, according to the resources of the household, fall to a half of what it has been during the rest of the year or even lower. At this period coco-yams are substituted as far as possible, but many households have only one substantial daily meal during these two months. The yam consumption following the harvest and during the digging of new yams is correspondingly higher than is suggested by the average daily estimates given above.

It would, however, be incorrect to assume that there are no substantial variations from household to household in yam consumption. Although there is probably no gross insufficiency of supply of this staple food, there are at opposite ends of the scale households which, through inefficiency, sickness, or other misfortune, secure much less than they need by local standards, and others in which the fufu[22] bowl is always heaped full.

The supply of coco-yams, which are eaten in quantity only during the growing season for yams, is met by both home production and by import from other villages. A normal consumption for a small household would be from 300 to 400, worth 4 or 5 shillings. The ordinary household is largely self-sufficient in okra, beans which are dried and stored for use through most of the year, as well as in plantains, pawpaws, peppers, maize, ground-nuts, native 'pears', and other vegetable produce including edible palm-

---

[21] Two children have been counted as one adult in this estimate. The consumption indicated accords closely with independent estimates of the amounts consumed by households. Thus, a prosperous trader with a household of this size reported his annual yam consumption as 1,000 purchased and about 500 produced by his wife on her brother's farm. His standard of living did not deviate noticeably from general food habits save that his supplementary purchases of coco-yams during the period of yam shortage and his consumption of rarer foods, e.g. meat and stockfish, was probably higher.

[22] The general southern term for mashed yam which is the main element of the evening meal.

oil. The annual consumption of these crops by a small household appears to be worth about £1 at the prices ruling in the local market. A daily calabash of palm-wine would have a further annual value of £1 10s. Thus, the total value of typical vegetable food consumption in a small household would be about £7 12s. per annum.

The most important further item of food supply is animal protein. Most households will consume the equivalent of one or two goats and two or three chickens in a year, though they may actually be provided outside the household diet and be eaten mainly by the men. Small quantities of smoked bush meat, stock-fish and dried fish are purchased by many of the households at the main market every sixth day. But the quantities are extremely small, amounting in many cases to one or two ounces at a time, to be used in flavouring the stew in which the mashed yam is dipped. Thus, in the ordinary small household meat constitutes a relish and represents an expenditure of at most 10s. or so in a year. The total value of the annual consumption of food at local prices is therefore not likely to exceed £8 2s. per year for a small household, or about £2 5s. per adult unit.

Dietetically, despite its overweighting of carbohydrate and deficiency in animal protein, the food supply has redeeming features. The regular consumption of palm-oil in stews and of the oily native 'pear' (*Pachylobis edulis*), eaten in large quantities when in season, ensures a reasonably high intake of vegetable fats, while palm-oil, palm-wine and the considerable quantities of green stuff eaten both raw and cooked provide, as has been seen, 'protective elements' in sufficient quantities.

The most valuable of the further items of household consumption are clothing and hardware, most of which are imported trade goods. Although the outlay in any one year varies considerably, scrutiny of a number of household budgets indicated that the annual expenditure on clothing of men who are heads of small households varies from 5s. to 10s., representing one or two lengths of cloth. Some of this was for gifts to wives, but the latter also made smaller purchases themselves, and the typical total outlay, for a small variation, more especially since there is a tendency when funds are available to buy surplus cloths for putting by. The actual expenditure on clothing over one year by men alone in a sample of 81 households ranged from nothing to £8.

Some additions and replacements to domestic and working

equipment are made every year in most households. In the sample referred to above, the norm for a small household appeared to be 3 to 4 shillings on machets or knives, but a shilling or less on pots and enamelware. Here again, however, the variation in outlay was considerable, ranging from 25s. to nothing.

Expenditure on cosmetics and ornaments, both native and imported, may be very considerable in a prosperous household, since purchase of expensive bead necklaces worn by both men and women on ceremonial occasions is a recognized way of displaying wealth. While therefore a typical outlay on soap, perfume, chalk, cam-wood, etc., is only a shilling or so and most households buy few if any personal ornaments, a prosperous household will spend several shillings on cosmetics and from 10s. to £1 on ornaments.[23]

Every household is involved in a system of gift exchange of food, clothing and ornaments made on a variety of ceremonial occasions, but it can be assumed for the present purposes that the exchanges cancel each other out and the consumption involved is included in the norms described above.

Yakö houses are, with minor repairs, durable for 8 to 12 years, but the roofing must be replaced, sometimes piecemeal, at least every two years. The total cost of building the small house used by the man and the larger house of the wife and children can be estimated fairly closely. Only the skilled construction of the dried mud partitions, beds and ledges are usually paid for in cash, the other work being provided by the members of the household and by friends and relatives who are rewarded with food. The value, at local prices, of all the housing construction required by one small household is about 28s., of which £1 represents durable construction, good for 10 years, and 8s. items that must be replaced every two years. Thus the average annual value of work and supplies for housing will be approximately 6s., of which only about 2s. takes the form of payments in cash or kind[24] (Plate VI).

[23] Occasional purchases of the very expensive cornelian necklaces costing £10 or so are not included here as items of current consumption. They are more appropriately regarded as a form of saving.

[24] The approximate values of component items for a woman's house of ordinary size are:

	s.	d.
Framework: materials and construction . . .	3	4
Walling: prepared mud and construction . .	1	8
Skilled plastering (cash-payment) . . .	3	6
Roof matting (materials, making and erection) .	5	4
	13	10

TABLE II

BASIC ANNUAL HOUSEHOLD EXPENDITURE, UMOR, 1939

Composition of household: 1 man, 1 wife, 2 children.

	Value at Local Prices	
	Home-produced	Purchased
Food Supply:	£ s. d.	£ s. d.
Farm Products—Yams . .	4 18 0	
Coco-Yams	4 0[25]	
Other .	1 0 0	
Palm-Wine[26] . . .	1 10 0	
	£7 12 0	
Meat		10 0
Clothing		12 6
Cutlery and Utensils . . .		4 0
Tobacco[27]		5 0
Cosmetics and Ornaments .		2 0
Housing	4 0	2 0
	£7 16 0	£1 15 6

i.e., a total consumption of £9 11 6

The foregoing survey of basic consumption suggests that a small household needs funds for an annual cash outlay of about £1 15s. 6d. per annum. But money is also needed to meet other demands outside the direct household consumption. The most rigid of these is the annual government capitation tax of 5s. payable by each able-bodied man; but cash for a variety of other purposes is needed. These include payments for admission to clubs, contributions to marriage payments,[28] fees for the minority of children attending the small mission school, payments of court

[25] A large number of households buy part or all of their coco-yams.

[26] About half the households purchase palm-wine, but most younger men provide their own and sell a surplus.

[27] Tobacco is not universally smoked or taken as snuff, and is not purchased by poorer men.

[28] These may include arrears on the head's own payment or contributions to the payments of kinsmen. There is not space to analyse the economic situation here, but it can be roughly estimated that the equivalent of an annual accumulation of 5s. is needed to meet such demands. The standard level of marriage payments has declined in Umor from £5 5s. to half that amount during the last decade of falling palm produce prices. See Forde, C. D., *Marriage and the Family among the Yakö*, 1941.

charges, fines and consideration money to the native court, ward heads and others, all of which would require an average annual expenditure of about 10s. on the part of the household head, and a further 2s. by his wife. Thus, the money income needed to meet the basic cash outlay of a small Umor household can be estimated as being from £2 10s. to £3 a year, although in any one year the need may be considerably above or below that sum.

While there are wide variations in the extent to which savings are made when a cash surplus is available, most household heads and married women do hold over savings in coin from year to year, and it is also possible to obtain interest-free loans from matrilineal kinsmen to meet demands which exceed one's own resources.[29] In addition to cash savings, every household has assets, household equipment and personal property, some of which can be realized at need. It is difficult to estimate the value of such equipment but sample inventories indicate that for a small household it is likely to be worth £2 or more, while for an exceptionally prosperous one it will exceed £10.

TABLE III

ESTIMATED ANNUAL CASH INCOME OF HOUSEHOLD,
UMOR, 1939

Man:		s.	d.
Sales of palm-oil, 12 tins at 1s. 2d.		14	0
,, palm-wine .		8	0
,, harvest yams, 100 at 7s.		7	0
,, rope, etc.		4	0
		£1 13	0
Wife:			
Sales of palm-kernels		15	0
,, early yams .		4	0
,, other vegetable produce		2	0
,, mats .		2	0
		£1 3	0
Total for man and wife		£2 16	0

[29] Inquiry among 81 households revealed that 55 of the heads held cash savings which ranged in value from as high as £30 in a few instances, such as ward head and large-scale trader, to 5s. at the other end of the scale. The average, excluding the two very large items, was in the neighbourhood of £1 10s. The total of savings far exceeded the aggregate debts. These were recorded for a total of 13 men, mostly of long standing, and ranged from £3 to 5s.

It will be useful to compare the estimate of annual cash outlay needed by a small household with the cash income attainable by that household with reasonable industry, at the prices of recent years.

Estimates for all the items here are moderate and very approximate. The output in all cases could, without great effort, have been exceeded, but on the other hand the majority of households do not in fact produce substantial surpluses of all these goods.[30] One or other is generally omitted. The level of cash incomes has during the past decade, fallen below the level of the norms of cash expenditure established when palm produce prices were high. Curtailment of expenditure does not appear, in fact, to have kept pace with the fall in current cash incomes the difference being met by depletions of savings and the receipt of loans from more fortunate kinsmen. The average level of household expenditure, low as it is, has probably not adjusted itself fully to current levels of money income, but is still influenced by standards established in the 'twenties.[31]

The levels of output and consumption in Umor have been presented above for a small household unit of one man, one wife and two young children. It should, however, be emphasised that the more energetic and prosperous men have in the recent past had two or three wives.[32] At the same time a considerable number of the petty traders are young men who have not yet taken up farms of their own and contribute to their parents' household outputs both from their trading receipts and by help in farm work at busy times. There are, therefore, a considerable number of households containing from three to six adults and these are generally the most active in the community. From the sale of palm products and considerable surpluses of yams, they appear to secure a cash income more than proportionately greater than the norm for a small household as estimated above. On the other hand, there are 'poor relations', generally members of small households who, through disability or misfortune, have outputs well below the general level. In many such cases both the men and women offer their labour at times of planting and harvesting in return for payments in yams which enable them to make up the deficiences

[30] See p. 45, Table II above.
[31] Marriage payments, for example, remained so high that several years were required to complete the transaction.
[32] For the social and historical contexts of Yakö polygyny see Forde, *op. cit.*

in their own farm outputs. Some such men also attach themselves to prominent kin group or ward leaders, or to traders, serving as messengers and supporters in return for occasional gifts of food and clothing.

The economic condition of the households of Umor ranges from that of a prominent man who may be head of his ward, and a leader in one or more clubs, with several wives and male dependants and whose income from various sources, including consideration money in connection with court cases, may exceed £10 a year, with savings of between £20 to £40, to impoverished household heads who feed very poorly, and can barely afford to buy a single cloth and a few utensils in the course of a whole year.

III

FISSION AND ACCRETION
IN THE PATRICLAN[1]

THE Yakö recognize and distinguish clearly between patrilineally and matrilineally derived rights to property and status. Although the greater part of accumulated wealth in rod-currency, livestock, and harvested crops passes at death to matrilineal kinsmen, patrilineal succession is paramount in the territorial organization. Rights to farm-land, house-sites and benefit from co-operative labour are established within and by the general consent of the group to which the individual belongs normally in virtue of his patrilineal descent. The structure of these patriclans and the social processes by which they are maintained and modified will be analysed in this chapter.

THE KEPUN

The most obvious of the larger social groups in Umor are the *yepun* (sing. *kepun*). They are manifest in the plan of the village, while the economic and ceremonial activities organized within them are the most frequent and prominent in the daily life. Each *kepun* has a dwelling area (*lekuma*; pl. *yikuma*) in which the great majority of its men and their wives and children reside and pass most of their time. Each *kepun* has a name which is used to refer both to the people and to the dwelling area.[2] The boundary between the dwelling areas of two *yepun* is often marked by a narrow gap, a pathway or a shallow ditch, and the adjacent houses of the two groups are built back to back on either side of the boundary, emphasizing by their very orientation the separateness of the two groups. But the blank walls, ditches and alleys, the posts and boundary trees do not always effectively immobolize the *yepun*,

---

[1] Reprinted from *J.R.A.I.*, 68, 1938, pp. 311–38.
[2] These are not, however, personal names and have no apparent reference to ancestors, actual or mythical. Some refer to natural features, suggesting that conditions connected with the site led to the naming. Loseni, for instance, is the name of a tree. But several names are common to *yepun* in different wards, and their significance will be discussed elsewhere.

Map of Umor

and accusations of encroachment are fairly common, since houses are frequently demolished and rebuilt on adjacent sites.

This residential unity of the *kepun* within the village obviously strengthens its social coherence. Born and growing up in one dwelling area, playing from childhood with others who will later be his neighbours in the village and his companions in farm work and palm tending, a man comes to regard his *kepun* group as a community within the larger village. Inside the dwelling area there is a large open-sided meeting house built of massive timbers, in which the *kepun* gong is kept. Here, rather than in their own houses, men spend their leisure hours and often bring some task they have in hand. In the *kepun* meeting house (*lepema*), as well as in his own courtyard, the death of a man is ceremonially recognized when his name is drummed on the *kepun* gong (see Plate X*b*). The *kepun* house is not formally barred to women, but they never assemble there and rarely loiter as they pass; they have no concern with it. Near the meeting house is the shrine of the *kepun* spirit (*epundet*; pl. *yepundet*), a low mound of small boulders surmounted by some chalk-stained pots, usually set in the shade of a tree. The *epundet*, and the recurrent rites performed there, symbolize for everyone from childhood the corporate group. Every few weeks a daughter is brought for the pregnancy rite at the *epundet*, and occasionally there is a more solemn expiation ritual for an offence that would otherwise injure the prosperity and fertility of the group (see Plates IX and X).

But the *kepun* is not merely a territorial group the coherence of which is maintained by contiguity alone. It is in native theory, and to a large degree in fact, a group of kinsmen. The *kepun* membership of every person is normally established at birth, for a child born in the village is automatically recognized as a member of its father's *kepun* and continues to be so regarded unless special circumstances result in a *de facto* transfer of membership later in life. Although individuals may be adopted into the group either as children or even when adult, the majority of the members of a *kepun* at any one time belong to it in virtue of patrilineal descent.

Not only does residence alone fail to establish *kepun* membership, but *kepun* membership may be maintained despite non-residence throughout several generations. The fundamental importance of patrilineal affiliation, and the degree to which actual residence may be irrelevant, are very fully demonstrated in the situation of Obeten Okoi, a man of the Ikpi Omeŋka lineage of Ndai *kepun*.[3] Obeten's household lives in the dwelling area, not of Ndai, but of Egbisum *kepun*. He himself was born there and has lived there all his life, and his father too, had been brought up in Egbisum. The father had gone as a boy, on the death of his mother, to live in the household of an adult half-brother, a son of his mother by a previous marriage with an Egbisum man, and on reaching manhood he had been given a house site in his half-brother's compound in Egbisum. He obtained his farm plots in Ndai lands, however, and did not, as he might otherwise have done, seek to be regarded as an adopted member of Egbisum *kepun*. In fact he succeeded his own father as head of his lineage of Ndai, although he continued to reside elsewhere. His children grew up in Egbisum, but all the sons except Obeten returned to Ndai to live when they were adult. Obeten has also farmed in Ndai land, and his affiliation to Ndai has in no sense been impaired by his residence in Egbisum. He participates in the *kepun* funeral feasts of Ndai, but has no such right in Egbisum. Moreover his senior living wife is a woman of Letekem *kepun*, whom no Egbisum man could marry, for Letekem and Egbisum constitute a single exogamous unit.

This unusually prolonged residence in the territory of an alien *kepun* is likely to be continued for another generation, since Obeten's eldest son Udumo, who was about to marry at the end of 1935, shared his father's house, and his wife's house was to be built in Obeten's compound. But the woman he was marrying was from Egbisum, a girl of the *kepun* in which he will live. Such a marriage would, as will be seen, be impossible if Obeten and his son were regarded as members of the Egbisum group.

For women there is no continuous residential association with a single part of the village. By the rule of *kepun* exogamy a woman at marriage leaves the house, compound, and *kepun* in which she was born. Save for returned widows, the *kepun* as a residential group does not normally include the adult married daughters who nevertheless belong to the *kepun* as a kin group. On the other hand, in the residential group there are many adult women, the wives of the men, who are not members of the *kepun* kin. Apart from anomalies of the kind cited above, every wife in a *kepun*

---

[3] No. 12 in Table VI, B.1.

area has come from elsewhere and here female *kepun* kin are scattered, according to their marriages, all over the village.

The corporate sense of the basically patrilineal *kepun* extends to the outlying forest and farm lands, since the *kepun* organization provides the framework and security within which each family head establishes his claim to the farm lands from which his food supply is obtained. A farm road elder (*oponotam eta*) adjusts the claims of individuals in each tract of land occupied by men of the *kepun*, while the weight of group opinion defends individual claims to forest products.

A *kepun* of Umor may therefore be summarily and provisionally described as an exogamous patrilineal and territorial group, with rights to a delimited dwelling area in the village and to farm in the village territory, possessing a shrine and an assembly house for group rites and social intercourse.

To the Yakö of Umor a *kepun* is characterized by all these attributes. But all social structures are plastic and liable to departures from the recognized norm, consequent on growth, decay, and the impact of other social institutions. Umor is no simple aggregation of perfectly formed *yepun*. Increase of numbers, the development of friction within groups, the concomitant recognition of matrilineal ties, opportunities for house-building on new sites and for farming in new directions have all operated to complicate the, formal plan.

LINEAGES

While the *kepun* is a corporate group of men and their children, united by common residence, co-operative farming activities, exclusive rituals, and a theory of common descent, it is itself frequently composite, the relations of the individual to his *kepun* fellows being often effected through a sub-group within the *kepun*. These sub-groups, intermediate in size between the household and the *kepun*, and consisting of persons who claim to trace actual patrilineal relationship or are recognized as belonging to the group in consequence of specific adoptions, are known as *yeponama* (sing. *eponama*) and can conveniently be called 'lineages'.[4] The more

---

[4] In the sense first suggested by Gifford for small unilineal kin groups tracing common descent but lacking the formal attributes and functions of clans. The native etymology of the term *eponama* is *epo* (begotten) *nama* (urethra). Whether correct or not it expresses the sense of the principle of patrilineal descent as the basis of lineage membership.

completely filiated character of the lineages is reflected in their names, which, unlike the *yepun* names, are those of ancestors whose existence can usually be confirmed by genealogical analysis (see Table V). But, while the household is an active economic unit and the *kepun* has concrete symbols of unity, the lineage has little formal organization; coherence depends on the sentiments of closer kinship within this segment of the larger *kepun*, and their expression when specific questions of patrilineal succession and inheritance arise. The conditions of neighbourly residence, of contiguous farming, and of co-operation in funeral rites, which affect the *kepun* as a whole, operate even more intensively within a lineage.

A *kepun* dwelling area consists of a number of clusters of houses, each grouped round a small open space, or along either side of a broad path. An analysis of the residence arrangements of the men of a *kepun* shows that men of a single lineage tend to

TABLE IV

House Sites of Lineages of Ndai

Lineages	Number of Ndai men in compounds of Ndai area									Number in Lek-paŋkem area*	Number in new outlying settlement	Number in other dwelling areas or absent	Total number
	A	B	C	D	E	F	G	H	I				
1			7		3	2				3	1	5	21
2	10		1					3				2	16
3			8	1	5	7	5	1				1	28
4			2		13	2		4					21
5	5		7		5		1	3	3		1	1	26
	10	5	18	8	26	11	6	8	6	3	2	9	112
No. of lineages represented	1	1	4	2	4	3	2	3	2	1		2	

* Adjacent to Ndai area and occupied by other patrilineal kin of Ndai men.

live together, often occupying a single compound group.[5] Of the
nine compound groups in Ndai, four are almost exclusively
occupied by men of one lineage, and the majority of the men of
three of the five lineages living in the *kepun* area are found in
single compounds. For details of this distribution see Table IV.
That this follows from a tendency for sons to build their houses
in the same compound as their fathers is seen from the fact that,
despite the considerable growth of population in recent times and
a consequent movement to outlying areas, 19 of the 32 adult men
of Ndai whose fathers are alive occupy the same compounds as
their fathers (Plate I).

The provision of food supplies at funeral rites is a special concern of the dead man's lineage, and succession to membership in
cult associations falls to a lineage-fellow before it is offered to, or
expected by, other members of the *kepun*. Moreover the most
important offices in the *kepun*, that of *kepun* priest and his assistant,
are usually regarded as properly filled by members of certain
lineages only. The choice of the *kepun* priest and of his assistant
in the larger *yepun* is almost always restricted to one or two
lineages; when more than one lineage is concerned, these provide
the priest in rotation.

Variations in *Kepun* Structure

The *yepun* of Umor, which, as Table V[6] shows, generally range in
size from 50 to 150 grown men, are relatively small groups in a
village of over 1,800 adult men. The dwelling areas are grouped in
four districts or wards of the village, known as *yekpatu* (sing.
kekpatu).[7] The significance of the wards will be considered more
fully elsewhere, and it is necessary here only to emphasize, first,
that the grouping together of certain *kepun* dwelling areas within
a single ward does not imply any genealogical affiliation of these
yepun in fact or in native theory,[8] and, second, that organization
and social activities based on the ward do not control or conflict

---

[5] See below, p. 94 for a diagram of the compound.
[6] The figures after each *kepun* or quasi-*kepun* refer to the number of adult
males recorded as present in the dwelling area in a government roll made early
in 1935. As will be seen later, these figures do not afford an exact indication of
the number of adult males who are actually members of the *yepun* concerned,
but they suffice as a general indication of their strength.
[7] See map, p. 50.
[8] Several *yepun* have admittedly been established by fission from others
situated in different wards, e.g. Lekpaŋkem in Biko-Biko from Loseni in Idjum.

with the organization and social life of the *kepun*. The occupants
of a ward do not consider themselves a kin group, and there is no
native authority in the ward with rights to limit or direct the customary activities of the priests and elders of the component *yepun*.

The dwellings of Umor do not, however, lie entirely within the
wards proper. When approaching the village from most directions,
outlying groups of houses are met with a few hundred yards before
entering the main settlement. These suburban house clusters,
known as *kowu*, are all said to have been established in recent times,
that is, within the lifetime of the older men, and they are undoubtedly a consequence of the recent growth of the population. Most
of the *kowu* are severally occupied by men of a single *kepun* and lie
fairly close to the *lekɔma* of that *kepun*. While none of the present
kowu claims the status of an independent *kepun*, there are indications that some of the quasi-*yepun* now within the main village,
such as Lekpaŋkem in Biko-Biko, and indeed the whole ward of
Biko-Biko, began as outlying settlements.

The data summarized in Table V and on the map reveal the
fact that the actual *yepun* of Umor in some instances diverge
considerably from the ideal structure indicated at the outset. If the
groups are defined in terms of the named dwelling areas alone, we
find twenty-six in all. But it is apparent on investigation that there
are sometimes two shrines (each with its own priest) within a
single area, and that there are often two assembly houses in these
areas; such, for example, are the conditions in Ibenda (in Biko-
Biko) and in Akugum (in Idjum). There are in fact five named
dwelling areas with dual *kepun* shrines. In each there are two sets
of lineages with independent rituals forming separate exogamous
groups, for there is no bar to marriage between members of the
two groups. Some of these groups unite in farm activities and
recognize a single leader for each of the paths to their farm tracts,
others do not. One of these double *yepun*, Kikoŋkula, has but
a single priest, although there are two shrines. I did not have an
opportunity to investigate closely the situation there, but the
independent shrine appears to belong to a single lineage, the priest
of the larger of the two segments performing the rites at both
shrines.

On the other hand there are named dwelling areas the occupants
of which have their own elders, farm road leaders and assembly
house, but lack an exclusive shrine. The members of a group of

TABLE V

Patriclans of Umor

This table shows linked groups, sites of *yepun* shrines, the number of component lineages, and the number of adult males in dwelling areas.

Yepun with a single shrine are bracketed on the left, those with combined dwelling areas on the right. *Yepun* with their shrines in their dwelling area are italicized. (K) = *yepun*, a considerable number of whose male members live in outlying settlements (*kowu*).

	Lineages	Adult Males in Dwelling Area[9]
Idjiman Ward		
1. { *Lebokem* (K)	2 (+ 1 in 6)	52
2. { Lekpaŋkem I	1	
		89[11]
3. { Lekpaŋkem II	1	
4. { *Ugom I* (K)[10]	1 } (+ 1 in 22)	70
5. *Ugom II*	1 }	
6. *Letaŋkem* (K)	1	27
7. *Lebulibulikom* (K)	1	62
8. *Aboni* (K)[11]	1	
9. *Kebuŋ*	1	35
10. *Otalosi* (K)	1	49
11. (Utoŋ, migrants from 18 and foreign)	3	58
Ukpakapi Ward		
12. { *Lekpaŋkem* (K)	2 (+ 1 in 25)	56
13. { Ndai	5	115
14. { *Egbisum*	3	83
15. { Letekem	3	66
16. *Usadja* (K)	3	77
Idjum Ward		
17. *Anedja–*	1 }	
18. { *–Lekpaŋkem*	6 } (+ 1 in 11)	132
19. { Lewaŋkem	2	51

[9] From Nominal Rolls (unadjusted).

[10] This group has its own shrine (Elamalama) but this lies in the dwelling area of Otalosi Kepun.

[11] Aboni resident males included with Lekpaŋkem.

TABLE V—*continued*

20.	*Loseni*	3 (+ 3 in 31, 25, 21)	27
21.	*Akugum I* (K)	2 }	
22.	*Akugum II*	? }	192
23.	*Kikoŋkula I*	? }	
24.	*Kikoŋkula II*	1 }	132
25.	(Unebu, migrants from 12, 20, 26)		99

BIKO-BIKO WARD

26.	*Emeŋko*	3 (+ 1 in 25)	50
27.	*Lebokem*	3	61
28.	*Mpangi*	3 (+ 1 in 20)	73
29.	*Ibenda I*	1 }	
30.	*Ibenda II*	2 }	96
31.	(Lekpaŋkem (K), migrants from 20)	1	49

this type resort to a shrine elsewhere for the performance of *kepun* rituals, and men of such groups may actually act as the priests of those shrines. In Idjum ward, for example, the head of Lewaŋkem is the priest of the Lekpaŋkem shrine. In all such cases the two named groups form a single exogamous unit and frequently co-operate in farming organization. There are eight shrineless *yepun* in Umor. In most cases they lie within the ward in which their shrines are found and are often adjacent to the *yepun* containing them, but two of them, Lekpaŋkem (Biko-Biko) and Utoŋ (Idjiman), are linked with *yepun* in other wards.

In native thought and practice the exogamous patrilineal group includes all persons who supplicate a single shrine (*epundet*), so that there are in Umor on the one hand nominally distinct *yepun*, like Lekpaŋkem and Ndai in Ukpakapi, which constitute a single ritually united exogamous group, and on the other hand nominally unitary *yepun* (like Akugum in Idjum or Ibenda in Biko-Biko) which in fact consists of two exogamous groups each with its independent *kepun* ritual. The position may be summarized thus:

Yepun names	26
Exogamous groups each with its own shrine	22
Named groups with separate dwelling areas but lacking an exclusive shrine	8

Exogamous groups with named sub-groups occupying distinct
    dwelling areas   6

Groups with a single name and dwelling area, consisting of two or
    more exogamous units with separate shrines .   .   .   5

Exogamous groups, many members of which (all or part of one or
    more lineages) live in the dwelling area of another group .   7

As a result of these anomalies only six of the group have the full complement of single and exclusive name, shrine and dwelling, area (see Table V and Fig. 7). These conditions suggest themselves as effects of fission and accretion whereby the structure and composition of many of the patrilineal kin groups has been modified. Such processes cannot be observed in action from day to day, and the stability of the groups themselves implies their relatively infrequent expression, but evidence of their operation and some clues to the conditions in which they develop are to be seen even over a short period of time.

Since, as will be seen, Umor is, and has been for two or three generations at least, a rapidly growing community, it is likely that processes of fission will have been more active than those of fusion, but both fission and recombination are apparent in two anomalous groups in which lineages of admittedly distinct filiation are assembled. Two of the three lineages of Utoŋ of Idjiman ward are said to have come from other Yakö villages (Nko and Idomi), and are regarded today as having combined with the single native lineage, since they now recognize and resort to the traditional shrine of that lineage. Furthermore the shrine itself lies in another dwelling area, that of Anedja-Lekpaŋkem in Idjum, from which the Utoŋ lineage itself migrated. The three lineages of Unebu in Idjum ward are similarly recognized as having come severally from Loseni in Idjum, Emeŋko in Biko-Biko and Lekpaŋkem in Ukpakapi. Here fusion has not progressed so far. Two of them resort to the shrines of their parent *yepun*, while a step recently taken by the Ubi Otomise lineage of Lekpaŋkem (Ukpakapi) origin demonstrates a stage in the process of actual *kepun* fission. About ten years ago this group in Unebu, after a dispute over the provision of materials in connection with a *kepun* rite at the Lekpaŋkem-Ndai shrine, determined to create their own shrine in Unebu. The story of the prolonged debate that this involved reveals clearly the strength of the sentiment of *kepun* continuity, but the outcome demonstrated the possibility of fission.[12]

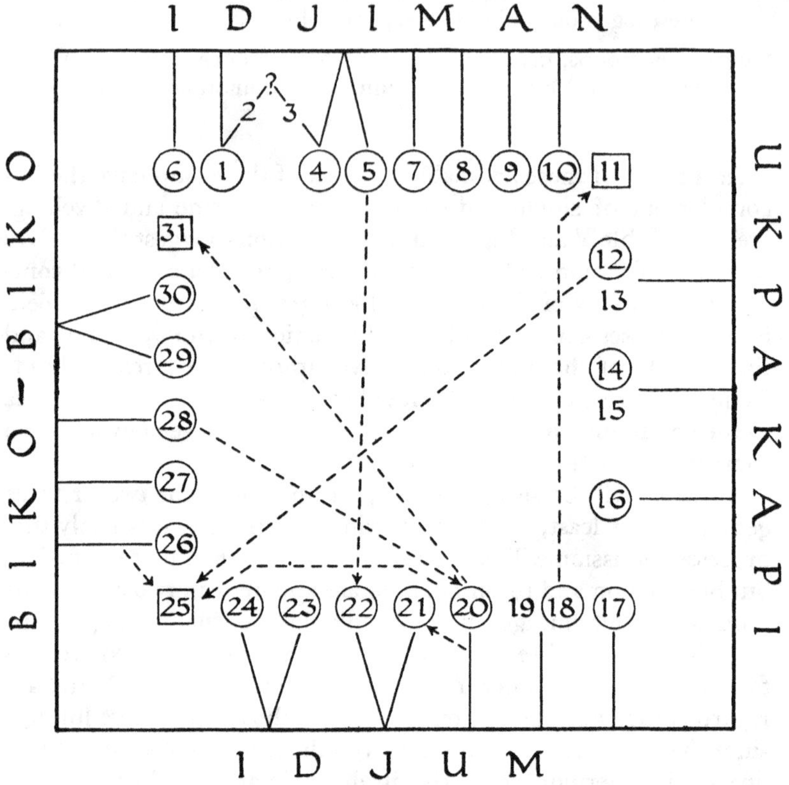

FIG. 7.—DIAGRAM OF FISSIONS AND RECENT MIGRATIONS OF LINEAGES IN THE PATRICLANS OF UMOR.

Groups are numbered as in Table V; those with shrines in their dwelling areas are encircled. Migrations of lineages to other group areas are indicated by broken lines with arrows.

[12] The elders of the Unebu group were allowed to take a few boulders and a pot from the Lekpaŋkem shrine. To these they added boulders collected and carried in from the bush, and new pots of the required kind, which they obtained from the Ibo village of Afikpo on the far side of the Cross River. With these they created their own shrine. The members of the Unebu group now recognize no bar to marriage with Lekpaŋkem folk and also urge that the *epundet* they have established should be recognized and used by all the men of Unebu. The older Lekpaŋkem men with whom I talked about this affair considered the action a bad one. It was punished, they said, by the death a few years later of all the men who took a direct part in it, but at the same time they regarded the detachment of the migrants as permanent.

The creation of a new *epundet* with a material nucleus of pots and boulders obtained from an earlier foundation is a recognized, if rare, procedure, and several *kepun* shrines are said to have been established in this way within the lifetime of older men. The manner in which another such shrine was established discloses a further element in the native theory of filiation. A lineage of Akugum in Idjum determined to separate from its fellows after a dispute. It sought and obtained the nucleus of boulders and pot, not from the shrine it had formerly used, but from the shrine of Ugom I *kepun*, known as Elamalama, which is uniquely eminent in the village. The importance of Elamalama and its priest is connected with the belief that it was the first *epundet* to be established at the foundation of the village. Having quarrelled deeply with their *kepun* fellows, the disaffected lineage of Akugum went back to the foundation shrine to secure the materials and supernatural force necessary for their own. The shrine of Ugom II[13] is said to have been similarly established some twenty years ago, although in this instance the Elamalama *epundet* was itself the former shrine of the separating group. All the *kepun* shrines of Umor are believed to derive ultimately from Elamalama, but it is generally agreed that six of the others were established at a time which is not within the memory of any living person.[14]

It has also been seen that there are *yepun* with distinct names, dwelling areas and assembly houses which also have only a single shrine. It will be useful here to consider as an example the situation in the double *kepun* which I came to know most intimately, namely that of Lekpaŋkem-Ndai in Ukpakapi. Numerically Ndai, with over a hundred adult males, is one of the larger groups. It has its own elders and meeting house, but it is at the same time linked with Lekpaŋkem, with which it shares a shrine and priest. The genealogical data for Lekpaŋkem and Ndai illustrate both community of descent and the process of fission in the formation of distinct lineages. Logically, of course, the naming of lineages from real or putative ancestors may be taken to imply the branching of collateral lines in the *kepun* as a whole. The genealogical

[13] The name is written thus because the group, like several others of recent formation, has no distinct name of *kepun* type. Members of such groups do, however, distinguish themselves by using the name of the priest, i.e. by calling themselves 'the *kepun* of So-and-So', or by using lineage names; e.g. Ibenda I and II are distinguished as 'Ibenda Iwara Kekbiyen' and 'Ibenda Iwara Edo'.

[14] These are Lekpaŋkem and Egbisum in Ukpakapi, Akugum I and Lekpaŋkem in Idjum, and Lebokem in Idjiman.

tables of Lekpaŋkem and Ndai confirm this, and there are two lineages now separated and belonging to different groups, which trace the descent of their truly filiated members from a single ancestor of five or six generations back (see Table VI, A). The historicity of this ascription may be doubted in the absence of records, but it implies the recognition of fission by the people themselves.

Ndai is largely independent of Lekpaŋkem in farming activities and building sites, although there is no demarcated boundary between the Ndai and Lekpaŋkem houses which interdigitate in an unsurveyable fashion. But the possession of a common shrine and pregnancy ritual maintains both the exogamy and the patrilineal continuity of the Lekpaŋkem-Ndai group as a whole. Although the shrine is adjacent to the Lekpaŋkem meeting house, the priest is selected from one of two Ndai lineages (Etuŋ Enamuzo or Obeten Ogometu). It may be said that Ndai lacks only an independent shrine, and since, as has been seen, new shrines may be created, it can easily be imagined that a serious dispute between considerable numbers on each side, over such a matter as rights to house sites or farm lands, might result in a declaration of independence and the creation of a separate shrine. It is, however, pointless to attempt to decide whether Ndai and Lekpaŋkem are one or two *yepun*. In some social activities they are independent, whereas in one which profoundly affects marriage they constitute a unit. The internal relations of four other sets of paired *yepun* are substantially similar to those of Lekpaŋkem and Ndai, and here again any summary statement of their character must be largely a matter of convenience, or of relevance to the topic under consideration.

The effects of fission and amalgamation are thus clearly apparent in the patrilineal kin structure of Umor. The wide range of social activities that should in principle be grouped within a coherent *kepun* unit are in practice by no means always so tidily arranged. The customs of exogamy, of economic and ritual co-operation, and the underlying sentiment of kinship maintain a general stability, but all can be terminated by internal strain and then reforged in a new grouping under conditions of territorial proximity.

SIZE AND COMPOSITION OF *Kepun* AND LINEAGE

The estimation of the numerical strength of the groups will of course depend on the criteria adopted to define them, and some of the difficulties involved in such definition have already been indicated. If Lekpaŋkem-Ndai be considered as a single *kepun*, and men who reside in other dwelling areas, but retain their affiliation, are included, it comprised 183 adult males in the latter part of 1935.[15] The separate totals for Ndai and Lekpaŋkem were 112 and 71 respectively. The estimates of the strength of other *yepun* which are given in Table V, on the basis of the Nominal Roll prepared for taxation purposes early in 1935, indicate that Lekpaŋkem-Ndai is an unusually large group.[16] My data are not complete enough to permit of a definite statement of the mean size, and the variation in size, of the *yepun*, but it is clear from the table that where the group greatly exceeds 100 adult men some form of sub-division is nearly always found.

There are seven lineages in Lekpaŋkem-Ndai, of which five form the Ndai group, and the mean of the number of adult men in these is 22. Since a few of the men born in these lineages have been fully adopted into other *yepun*, in circumstances to be considered later, and since there are a few adult males who have not founded families of their own, the characteristic number of households in a lineage may be put at about 20.[17] The number of lineages in other *yepun* (indicated in Table V) suggests that 15 to 30 households is a fair estimate of the range in size of the patrilineal sub-groups or lineages in Umor, and this is the group within which mutual aid in farm work and patrilineal rights and obligations of inheritance are primarily effective.

Four of the lineages of Ndai are connected with an alleged immigrant to Umor, who came from the neighbouring Yakö village of Ekuri. Two of them (Obeten Ogometu and Etuŋ Enamuzo) have a nucleus of members who are lineal descendants

[15] This figure is taken from my own census, and excludes young men who had not yet made farms or built houses of their own.

[16] These totals include any non-members resident in the dwelling areas, and exclude non-resident members. The discrepancy is, however, likely to be small, and may be the present purpose be considered insignificant. More important is the fact that the Roll disregards the sub-divisions of dual *yepun* and quasi-*yepun*. There are *yepun* even larger than Lekpaŋkem-Ndai in Idjum ward, but they are dual, with separate shrines. The number of adult men in the majority of the *yepun* units with a single shrine for which estimates could be made lay between 50 and 100, of which typical examples are Usadja, with 77 men, and Lebuli, with 62. But others are much smaller, as for instance Kebuŋ, with only 35.

[17] The number of living adult men born into the two Lekpaŋkem lineages is considerably higher (40 and 32), but since a number of them have in fact migrated to other dwelling areas, the effective size of these groups is not significantly higher.

TABLE VI

THE LINEAGES OF NDAI.

Numbers refer to living adult male members of lineages. Lineage heads are underlined and numbered in order of succession. Present assistants to heads are indicated by three dots.

/ =division between half-brothers   =adoption of an adult

x =deceased men   =adoption of a minor

A =living men adopted into other groups   =purchase of a foreign child (*ofoli*)

A.—*Ancestors of Lekpaŋkem-Ndai Kepun Showing Relations of Lineages*

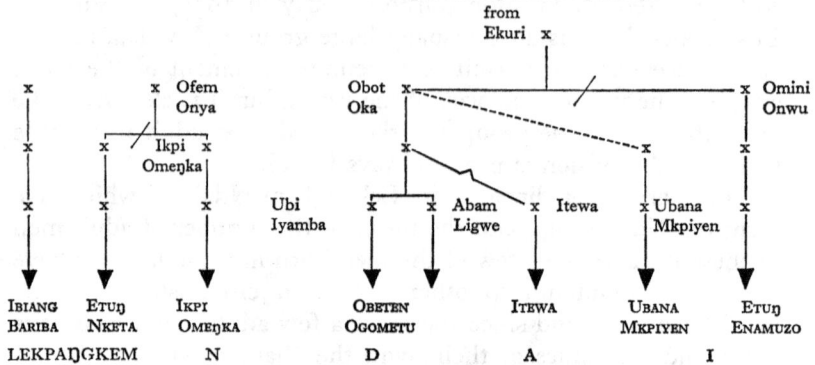

B. 1.—*Lineage of Ikpi Omeŋka*

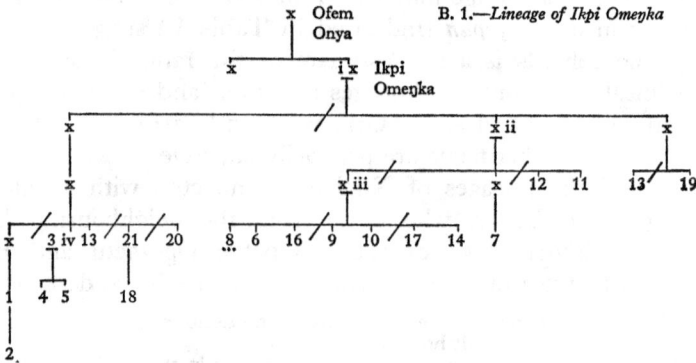

B. 2.—*Lineage of Etuŋ Enamuzo*

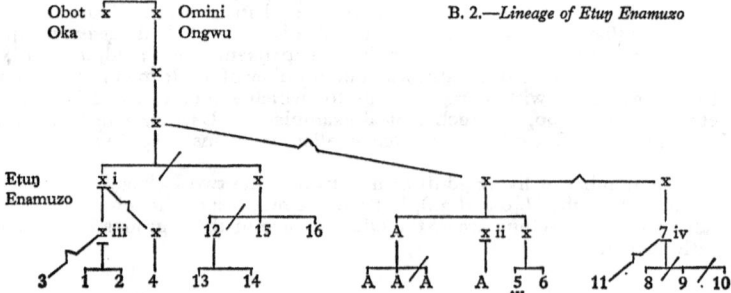

TABLE VI (*continued*)

B. 3.—*Lineage of Obeten Ogometu*

B.4.—*Lineage of Itewa*

B.5.—*Lineage of Ubana Mkpiyen*

of two sons of this man, Obot Oka and Omini Oŋwu. The remaining two are mainly composed of the descendants of men
adopted by the former into the *kepun*. No precise or generally
accepted account of a true filiation between the two Lekpaŋkem
lineages could be given. The relationships of the Ndai lineages
and their connection with those of Lekpaŋkem (shown in Table V)
reveal clearly, first, that the part played by strict genealogical
descent has been only that of providing a nucleus to which individuals of other origins and their descendants have adhered, and,
second, that the line of separation between the linked groups of
Ndai and Lekpaŋkem is one which does not correspond with any
formal recognition of degree of relationship, but is fortuitous from
the point of view of genealogical descent. Events unconnected
with genealogical succession, which have occurred in the course of
the growth of the Lekpaŋkem-Ndai group, are likely to have been
responsible for the present alignment.

We are now in a position to consider the actual composition of
the lineages. The 21 men born into Ikpi Omeŋka are all descended
from three sons of the eponymous ancestor, and range over four
generations (Table VI, B.1.). Three of them (Nos. 18, 19, 21)
have, however, gone to live in the area of the anomalous Unebu
group, in Idjum ward, on the far side of the village. The other
four Ndai lineages all trace their origin to a single immigrant, but
the genealogical data afford many examples of individual adhesions.
Of the 16 living adult men of Etuŋ Enamuzo only 7 are lineal
descendants, while there are four groups of descendants of
separate adoptions. Similarly in Itewa only 5 of the 21 present
adult members are lineal descendants, while the rest are members
in virtue of four adoptions at various times.[18] In the large group
of 26 men of Ubana Mkpiyen only two living men are lineal
descendants of the eponymous ancestor and five adoptions have
occurred.

---

[18] In one of the compound groups mainly occupied by the households of
Itewa men lived three men of the Lekpaŋkem lineage Ibiaŋ Bariba, whose
relations were closer with the Itewa group than with the men of their own lineage. Their descent from Ibiaŋ Ebun in the Ibiaŋ Bariba lineage was well known,
but they farmed plots which had been transferred to them by Itewa men and regarded themselves as virtually adopted into the Itewa lineage. On the other hand,
a fourth descendant of Ibiaŋ Ebun remained with the Ibiaŋ Bariba group. He,
it was said, did not farm land obtained from Itewa men and could have nothing
to do with them. I was told that it was because the other three men had asked for
and received some vacated land first cleared by Itewa men that they were now

The Obeten Ogometu group, in which adoption has been responsible for present membership to a lesser extent (five adoptions are recorded, which account for only nine of the living members) presents an instance of the opposite tendency towards fission. While accretion tends to occur through the incorporation of individuals, fission follows more often from the separation of relatively large groups, and an early stage of the process appears to exist in this lineage. While most people in Ndai regarded Obeten Ogometu as a single lineage, some, including one section of its own members, habitually referred to two lineages: those of Ubi Iyamba and of Abam Ligwe, the two sibling grandsons of Obot Oka. Indeed, my inquiries concerning the structure and composition of the Ndai group were for a time confused by this discrepancy in nomenclature. The junior, Abam Ligwe, group in Obeten Ogometu accounts for 12 of the 28 living members of the lineage. Some of these men told me that they constituted a separate lineage and, while their number falls below the usual lower limit of lineage size, there is no doubt that the Abam Ligwe men are tending to consider themselves as a separate group with Abam Usani (No. 23) as their head.

This situation throws light on the problem of the stability and durability of lineages. Here, where the senior and junior branches are tending to drift apart, the men of middle age (from 30 to 35 years[19]) belong to the fourth generation of descendants of those who are regarded as the ancestors of the incipient sub-groups. The disposition towards fission is associated with, and is likely to be in part a consequence of, the abnormal size of this group. In conditions of increasing population the lineages are likely to exist as stable and integrated groups for only four or five generations. The lineage is thus a small group of kinsmen with their adopted adherents, the internal coherence of which lasts so long as the group remains small and intimate.

associated with the Itewa lineage and that if they continued to occupy Itewa land they would become Itewa men. There can be little doubt that if this close association is maintained their children will be regarded as members of that lineage on the ground of the adoption of their parents, though no formal declaration of transfer had been made either by the men themselves or by their Itewa hosts. Adoptive transfer may thus take place even between lineages within a single exogamous group.

[19] The approximate ages of adult males have been determined by collating the successive formations of age sets in each ward with datable events in the Cross River district during the past fifty years.

HEADSHIP OF *Kepun* AND LINEAGE

The performance of *kepun* rituals and the arbitration of more serious internal disputes are responsibilities of the *kepun* head, who is known as the *Obot Kepun*. Although he relies considerably on the opinions and support of the older men of the *kepun*, the *Obot Kepun* is regarded with very considerable respect and deference.

He has no insignia or paraphernalia of office other than the pots and chalk which are used in rituals at the *kepun* shrine. He receives a gift from the participants in these rites, and at the time of the annual New Yam rites all adult males in the *kepun* are expected to make him a gift of a yam and a calabash of palm wine. The men of his *kepun* can be called upon to give him assistance in clearing land for his farm, but he makes no personal claim to the lands cultivated by the *kepun* members as a whole, nor does he interfere with any arrangements for the occupation of such lands unless a dispute arises.

He investigates and arbitrates between the men of his *kepun* when any farming dispute cannot be settled by the elders, or if any individual refuses to submit to the judgement of a farm elder or the lineage heads. In general, such cases are referred to the *Obot Kepun* by the elder and lineage head, and not by an aggrieved individual, in the first place. Other serious disputes between two persons of his *kepun*, and any case of injury or damage by a fellow-member of the *kepun*, are usually brought to him, and he calls the *kepun* elders to join in the hearing. In addition to ordering restitution or reparation, *kepun* heads have imposed and successfully collected small fines (amounting to 2s. or 2s. 6d. at the most today) from the individuals judged to be guilty in this type of case. Such fines are kept by the Obot and the elders.

The present head and priest of the Lekpaŋkem-Ndai group is Oka Agbo, of the Etuŋ Enamuzo lineage of Ndai (No. 7 in Table VI, B.2). This lineage traces its ancestry to the younger son of the migrant from Ekuri, but Oka Agbo himself is not a genealogical descendant. His connection with that ancestor is, indeed, through two successive adoptions. Like other *kepun* heads, Oka Agbo has an assistant, and Omini Oka (No. 5) of the Obeten Ogometu lineage, who holds this position, is thereby designated as his successor. This is in accordance with the rule in the Lekpaŋkem-Ndai group that the priestship should be occupied alternatively by the heads of these two lineages. The fact that such a succession holds good in practice is a tangible expression of the general feeling that these two lineages, the nuclei of which are traced to two brothers, are the core of the Ndai group. Why neither of the lineages composing the Lekpaŋkem group, which is often said to be the older, today claims a right to succession to the priestship never became clear. Certainly no historical or mythological justification was brought forward, or felt to be necessary, to explain the situation.

Within each lineage there is usually an accepted leader who, without any formal authority or ritual functions, is nevertheless turned to, in the Yakö manner, to advise his fellows and act as their spokesman. The genealogical positions of the leaders of the several Ndai lineages throw further light on the Yakö attitude to succession within groups of nominal kinsmen. Save where the priestship of the *kepun* shrine falls to a particular lineage, there is no installation, formal recognition or specific ritual function in connection with this headship, but the lineage head, referred to as *uwo womon* (our father) is expected to show concern and accept responsibility for the solidarity of the lineage.[20] It is recognized as fitting that the head should take the initiative in composing any internal disputes, and he is expected to speak on behalf of any individual or group in the lineage accused of an offence or suffering from a grievance. Both men and women make him small gifts when they seek his services.

Although the people themselves, when speaking in general terms, emphasize seniority in patrilineal descent, succession to the leadership of a lineage is not in fact necessarily determined according to any strict rule of descent. A leader usually chooses, from among his male relatives a few years junior to himself, an acceptable lieutenant who acts as a messenger and general supporter. This man, if he gets on well with his fellows in the lineage and shows the qualities of moderation that are so much appreciated, is gradually recognized as the deputy of the head, whom he later succeeds without discussion or formal appointment. As with the

---

[20] Ibiaŋ Iyam, the head of Ikpi Omeŋka lineage (No. 3), would not admit, for instance, that the three men living in Unebu, among whom was one of his own brothers, would become permanently affiliated there, and was most anxious that I should include information as to their households and farms in my census of the Ndai *kepun*, although they were farming on land used by the *yepun* of Idjum.

headship of the *kepun*, the undisputed succession of this lieutenant or assistant of the lineage head is regarded as normal.

The successive holders of the headships in the Ndai lineages are shown in Table VI. The fact that the living head is in no case removed by more than three successions from the eponymous ancestor supports the other evidence indicating that the lineage, as a self-conscious group, is of very limited duration. In only two lineages (Table VI, B.2 and 3) has the succession passed directly from a father to his son and then to his grandson. There is, however, a tendency for the headship to revert to a descendant in the line of a former head. In the Itewa and Etuŋ Enamuzo lineages there is also a suggestion that alternate succession may occur when the lineage has two branches. The position in their lineages of the five living heads in Ndai is summarized in Table VII.[21]

TABLE VII

Lineage	Approx. Age	Oldest living man	Senior descendant*	Descendant in senior branch	Descendant of an adoptee	Younger of two living brothers
I.O.	60	v		v		
E.E.	68	v			v	
O.O.	63				v	v
It.	57		v	v		
U.M.	76	v			v	

* Of his generation by primogeniture.

[21] In the Ikpi Omeŋka lineage, Okoi Ikpi, who was head fifteen or twenty years ago, chose his eldest son as his helper. This son succeeded as head, but took as helper, not his own son, but a kinsman called Ibiaŋ Iyam, who was little younger than himself, and who is head of the lineage today. Ibiaŋ Iyam was recognized as head of Ikpi Omeŋka lineage, it was said, because he was the oldest living son in the senior line of descent in the lineage. But Oka Agbo (No. 7), the head of the Etuŋ Enamuzo lineage of Ndai, who is thereby also the priest of the Lekpaŋkem-Ndai *epundet*, is not a lineal descendant of a senior line. He is the son of an adopted man whose foster-parent had also been adopted into the lineage (see Table VI, B.4), and is senior to his fellows only in years. The leader of the Obeten Ogometu group, Omini Oka (No. 5), is similarly not a lineal descendant of Ubi Iyamba, the older of the two brothers from which the lineage descends, and there are no less than three men actually senior to him in years who are true descendants of Ubi Iyamba. Indeed, Omini has a living half-brother senior to himself. The leader of the Ubana Mkpiyen lineage (No. 11) is the oldest living man in the group, but he too is the son of an adherent who came from outside the lineage. In the Itewa lineage alone do we find a leader, Obeten Ibomi (No. 2), who is both genealogically and in years the senior living descendant of the ancestor.

Although the number of cases studied is too few to permit secure generalization, these instances of leadership in the Ndai lineages indicate that while absolute age, and seniority to others and in descent, are regarded as qualifications, none are indispensable, and all may be overridden. The head of a lineage should not merely be eligible by descent and seniority; he should be notable and prosperous, impressive and conciliatory. When these qualifications are not combined in one person, the acceptance of a man as the actual successor usually depends on the dominance of his supporters within the lineage. Reference to the actual ages and kinship positions of the heads shows that they are all relatively senior in years. This situation accords with Yakö views expressed at various times on rights of succession, from which it was apparent that several possibly conflicting principles are entertained. In the case of lineages from which the *kepun* priest, i.e. the leader of the whole *kepun*, is selected, a critical situation might be expected if disputes arose over succession, since indispensable ritual functions are involved in this office. But, as has been seen, every priest-head has a recognized and active assistant —'the pourer of palm wine' in *epundet* rituals—to whom the priestship passes automatically, and his prior recognition as assistant in fact depends on his being already either the established head of another lineage, or the designated and accepted successor to the priest in the headship of the lineage of which both are members.

ADOPTION

All fellow-members of the *kepun* are addressed according to seniority by terms also used for one's own father (*uwo*) or brother (=father's child, *wenuwo*), and the sense of patrilineal kinship within the *kepun* is also expressed in many rights of succession. But, as indicated above, there are many men whose status within their *yepun* derives not from unbroken patrilineal descent, but from adoptions. The more recent adoptions are well known to everyone in the group and, while ordinarily ignored, may form the basis of an excuse, of a gibe in a personal quarrel, or of a counter-claim when a right is in dispute.

The circumstances and motives involved in these adoptions, which may be effected in childhood, youth, or occasionally late in life, are very varied. They may bring into the group men from other *yepun* within Umor itself, men from other Yakö villages, and also strangers from other language groups. Adoption is not marked by any rite whereby a man's status is formally and abruptly changed and an earlier kin allegiance annulled in favour of his new status. It may often be impossible for an observer, or, indeed, for the people themselves, to assert at a particular moment whether or not a man has become a member of a new kin group by adoption. A boy coming to live with his mother's brother, as often happens on the death or divorce of the mother, may form many ties as a young man within the *kepun* of the man who has thus become a foster-father, and he may be offered farm land on his mother's brother's land when he first marries. Acceptance, which would normally imply an intention to associate himself permanently with the *kepun* group of his foster-parent, will depend on particular circumstances. Much will depend on whether the youth's actual father is still living and is sympathetic to him, whether he has brothers or half-brothers with whom he is intimate in the *kepun* of his birth, on the one hand, or whether, on the other hand, he desires to join a society or an age group in the ward of his foster-father's *kepun* rather than in his own. But the crucial issue here is often the provision of funds for marriage payments. If the funds for his marriage payment[22] are provided by his foster-parent, the youth will be expected henceforth to behave as a member of his *kepun*. He will certainly receive farm lands from its farm path elders, and be entitled to live permanently in its dwelling area, and he will also be required to make contributions at funerary and other rites of the *kepun*.

If, however, the youth goes back to his father's *kepun* after having begun to farm on the lands of his foster-kin, the foster-kin will be likely to remind him that he is but a guest and cannot lay any permanent claim to plots, although the farm path elder may, for a time, find a place for him from year to year. Again, the provision of funds for the marriage payment by his father or brothers puts the youth under an obligation to return to his patrilineal kinsmen, among whom he can seek a house site and farming lands. He may return as an orphan, lacking the aid of a father in his first years of farming, but he will have brothers or other close kin within his lineage to whom he can go for support and gifts.

---

[22] The matrilineal kin usually share in the provision of money and materials for the marriage payment. This need not be discussed here, except to point out that a mother's brother who becomes foster-father assumes the patrilineal as well as the matrilineal duties.

Adopted children or wards (*yawunen*; sing. *owunen*) do quite frequently remain permanently with their foster-fathers, who are usually related to the mothers. They are often pressed to stay by these foster-kin who desire to increase the number of their descendants. The foster-father then undertakes the marriage negotiations for his adopted son, and sponsors him in all claims to status in the new kin group. Love affairs or marriage with people of that *kepun* will be forbidden as incestuous to the ward's children, but those children will, on the other hand, be free to mate in the kin group in which their father was born. Disputes actually arise on this point. Parents may attempt to prevent the youthful son of a man adopted out of the husband's *kepun* from approaching their daughter's, i.e. girls of the boy's father's *kepun*, but instances were found of men who had in this way married women of their father's *kepun*.[23]

The decision to adhere permanently to the kin group of a foster-father does not, however, entitle the man himself to seek a wife in his father's *kepun*. Many of the associations and obligations connected with his kinship status during infancy still cling to him.

It may happen that a man will leave the *kepun* of his birth in adult life. When a man succeeds to a matrilineal priesthood he often desires, or is compelled to live in the *lekɔma* where the shrine is situated. Leaders of some cult associations may also migrate for similar reasons. Achieving prominence in everyday matters among the men of the *kepun* in which he now resides, and perhaps accepting an offer of farmland, he may in some circumstances identify himself almost completely with their *kepun*. A man who changes his *kepun* affiliation in this way in adult life cannot, of course, abolish the ties and reciprocal obligations of his earlier life. He may neglect his obligations and expect little from his former *kepun* kin, but the link still exists, for he will have brothers or father's brother's sons to whom he should make gifts in case of need. Apart from his personal feelings, it would be scandalous for him to ignore the obsequies of his close patrilineal relatives, so that he will have added to, rather than transferred, his kinship obligations by his migration.

As already noted, the majority of adopted boys are the matri-

---

[23] Eta Utere, whose father Obono Utere (born in the Etun Enamuzo lineage) left Ndai as a child to become the ward of his mother's brother, has married a Ndai woman, Oden, the sister of Ina Usani (No. 19) of Ikpi Omenka lineage. See Table VI for the genealogical positions of these men.

lineal kin of their foster-fathers, and usually their nephews. Such
is the case with the two living Etuŋ Enamuzo men who were
adopted in childhood, Nkasi Arikpo (No. 11) and Eno Edjedje
(No. 3). Nkasi is a son of his foster-father's older sister, who was
married to an Ekuri man and went to live with him there. Nkasi
came to live with Oka as a small boy, and has remained permanently in Ndai. In consequence of this, Nkasi is a close kinsman
and an heir of Oka, in virtue not only of their matrilineal, but of,
their adopted 'patrilineal' relationship as well. He can, in fact
claim a part in the succession to Oka's status and wealth both in
the *kepun* and in the matrilineal line by which most of the wealth
in movable goods is inherited among the Yakö.

Eno Edjedje is also by birth a sister's son of his foster-father. He
came from Loseni *kepun* in Idjum, where his mother had married.
A further instance of sister's son adoption occurred in an earlier
generation, for the father of Omini Ibiaŋ (No. 4) was a maternal
nephew of Etuŋ Enamuzo, the eponymous ancestor of the lineage.

On the other hand the adoption of sisters' sons has removed
male descendants from this lineage. A group of five men so adopted, who by patrilineal descent should be members of the Etuŋ
Enamuzo group, are actually members of the Lewaŋkem *kepun* in
Idjum (see Table VI, B.2). The senior of these, Obuŋo Utere, the
oldest son of Ewa Akpa—himself an adoptee—was given into the
care of Ewa's wife's brother, one Obasi Mgbai, when he was a
small boy. Neither Oboŋo's three sons, who are now grown men,
nor their children now have any formal relations with or obligations to the Etuŋ Enamuzo lineage or the *kepun* of Lekpaŋkem-
Ndai; the eldest of the sons, Eta Utere, has, as described above,
married a woman of Ndai. Oboŋ Utere himself is today the head
of the lineage into which he has been adopted, and also assistant
to the priest of the Lewaŋkem *epundet*; he is, in fact, the accepted
successor to the present *kepun* priest-head. His history thus fully
illustrates the status of an adopted child as a potential successor
to *kepun* rights.

A further adoption followed Oboŋo Utere's transference. His
younger brother, Obeten, had remained and grown up as a
member of his father's household. He married, but died young,
and on his death Oboŋo took charge of his only son, Onen. Onen
is now married and he, too, ranks with Oboŋo's begotten sons as
a member of Lewaŋkem *kepun*. His adoption by his father's brother

has, however, involved transference to another *kepun* only because Obono had himself been adopted by a matrilineal kinsman. But for this the adoption would have been of the intra-*kepun* type which is a usual arrangement on the death of a father during a son's youth.

The adoption of a sister's son springs from conditions and motives which derive from the recognition of matrilineal kinship, and as such it demands further analysis in that context. For the present it may be viewed as one of the common processes whereby the theoretical patrilineal unity of the lineage and *kepun* is affected both by the introduction of non-kin and by the loss of true kin. At the root of the practice lies the Yakö rule that, with minor exceptions, movable property is inherited by matrilineal and not by patrilineal kin, and that sisters' sons have prior claims to such property.

The cases of adoption so far considered involve transfer from one *kepun* group to another within the village, but the adoption of persons from other settlements does not involve such transfer. While matrilineal kinship is held to extend beyond the limits of the village, and to embrace in a somewhat tenuous fashion even persons in other linguistic groups, no *kepun* rights or obligations in Umor exist initially for those coming from outside. Such individuals may have come originally at the invitation of some *kepun* elders because of their skill in a craft such as wood carving,[24] but the majority have come as the kinsmen of foreign women who have been brought to the village as wives.

A widowed or divorced woman from another village, whether it be in Yakö or in one of the neighbouring territories such as Ekumuru and Adim, may, with the consent of her new husband, bring with her a youthful son who by the time he is adult will be accepted as a member of his step-father's *kepun*. Similarly an

[24] Specialist craftsmen from remote areas occasionally come to Umor. The majority of these are either smiths, or people working at new crafts such as sawyers, carpenters, and shirt makers. They are few in number, and, although they may come from distant places in Onitsha, the Cameroons and elsewhere, they strike no roots in Umor. They usually return at intervals to their native villages; they bring wives from among their own people; and though they live as the guests of Umor men they do not seek incorporation in the *kepun* group with which they live. They can maintain this independence because they do not farm and are thus largely concerned in the everyday affairs of a *kepun*. Again, partly because they do not need to farm, they rarely spend the whole of their lives in the same village, but are free to pass on after a few years to another place and finally return to their homes. Their social remoteness reflects their economic independence, and they are the guests, not the wards, of their sponsors.

adult brother or kinsman of the foreign wife, who seeks an opportunity to leave his own village, may also come. Arriving as a guest, he may stay indefinitely, help his brother-in-law in the farm lands for a season or two, and eventually be taken by the brother-in-law to the *kepun* head and farm path elders to beg for a plot of his own. The great majority of the adopted foreigners recorded in the genealogical tables whose history could be obtained were found to be the relatives of foreign wives.

A second class of extra-village adoption arises from the recognition of matrilineal kinship. It consists essentially in the adoption in childhood of a boy or, less often, of a girl from among the foster-parent's matrilineal kin in another village. This form of adoption also commonly results from extra-village marriages. The sons and daughters of an Umor woman who has married into another village will normally become members of that community. But, as has been seen, a man often seeks to adopt a sister's son, more particularly if he is without sons of his own, while, on the other hand, such a child may be offered to his care in consequence of some dislocation in the sister's household. When the sister has married a man of another village, such an adoption involves the transfer of the child from one community to another. In addition to actual sisters' sons, more remote and putative matrilineal kinship may be the occasion for such extra-village adoption. The majority of the children in Ndai households who were found to have been adopted from other villages were the matrilineal kin of a man or, more rarely, of a wife. The affiliation of such a child to a kin group in the community of its birth is not formally abrogated, but the earlier affiliation will never be implemented if the child continues to live in Umor. The child remains a member of the matrilineal group of whichever foster-parent was its real or putative relative, and at the same time becomes a *de facto* patrilineal kinsman of the foster-father as an adopted son or daughter.

But a considerable number of children with no original affiliation in Umor, and completely alien in origin, have also been adopted into Umor households and so into the *yepun*. These children, known as *yafoli* (sing. *ofoli*),[25] have been brought to the village by

---

[25] Dr. Meek has kindly pointed out to me that this term is related to the term for 'slave' found in various forms among the Ibo, Ibibio and other peoples of S.E. Nigeria.

strangers and have been handed over in return for payments, usually made in money. It is not admitted that children are still obtained in this way today, for the practice is subject to severe penalties under the Ordinances relating to slave-dealing, but the genealogical data indicate that the kin groups investigated have been considerably augmented by the descendants of *yafoli* (see Table VI, B). There may be more instances of the introduction of foreign boys than the genealogical data reveal, for the condemnation and punishment of the sale and purchase of children have probably led to the concealment of such past actions, and to the misrepresentation of *yafoli* as *yawunen*, or actual begotten children. On the other hand, after I had gained the sympathy and interest of the Ndai men, the recorded instances of purchased boys were readily admitted to be correct, as were also a large number of cases of purchased girls who had become the wives of men in Ndai. There was uncertainty, however, as to whether some of the more remote adoptions in some lineages were of kinsmen's children or of *yafoli*.

While I had neither the time nor the opportunity to investigate child-trading closely, the situation in Umor during the past two generations became fairly clear. To purchase an *ofoli* was a meritorious display of wealth, and was one of the achievements necessary for a man who claimed to be a man of substance (*osu*, pl., *yasu*), and partook in the reciprocal funerary feasts of the rich. *Yafoli* have been acquired far more frequently by men than by women, but childless wives often urged their husbands to obtain a child in this way. Both boys and girls were obtained, but girls more frequently than boys. The adoption of girls, as was expressly stated by the people themselves, reflected the desire to increase the numbers and prestige of the matrilineal kin. It was also valued as giving a woman a companion and helper in her farm work.

The status and significance of a girl *ofoli* becomes that of a daughter. For a short period she may make possible an increase in the size and productivity of her parents' farm, and later a marriage payment is received by her foster-father and his close kin. After that she is likely to have little significance for the *kepun* unless serious matrimonial disputes arise, but a girl *ofoli* ranks as a member of the matrilineal, as well as the patrilineal, group of her purchaser, and her children are matrilineal heirs. Her household after marriage, therefore, continues to be of close concern to her foster-father. The boy *ofoli* likewise ranks as a matrilineal heir, but he also grows up as a virtual member of the *kepun* of his purchaser.

Arriving as young children, the *yafoli* are said to have soon lost any visible sign of their foreign origin. But although a boy *ofoli* could inherit status from his foster-father, as if he were a begotten son, the term itself might be used against him in abuse in moments of anger both by *kepun* members and by other villagers. Only a few old people, who admittedly themselves arrived in Umor as *yafoli*, were known or pointed out to me, but the descendants of *yafoli* are numerous and their status is not today inferior to that of native-born men, either in the *kepun* or in the other social groups of the village. Obeten Okoi (No. 12 in Ikpi Omeŋka), whose mother was an *ofoli*, is a member of the Ikpuŋkara association and a *kepun* elder in Ndai.

The adoption of foreign children by purchase probably developed considerably in Umor with the early growth of the palm-oil trade, which enabled a considerable number of men to amass a source of transferable wealth in rod currency or coin. I obtained various statements as to the size of the payments made for children; sums of from £10 to £50 were named, but it is in any case clear that the amounts were substantial. These children were rarely offered by their own parents, and those selling did not pretend to parentage.[26] In the period of stability and increasing wealth which has extended over the past four or five decades there have probably been fewer orphans than would-be foster-parents in Umor, and the adoption of *yafoli* has certainly contributed to the growth in the population which is indicated by the expansion of the village site.

The adoption of children in Umor is sought in order to satisfy economic, social, and mystical needs which might otherwise be

---

[26] I was almost always told that they were brought by Aro Chuku men, and that Umor buyers often went down to the river to meet them. This may, however, merely reflect the notoriety of the Aro Chuku cult and of the traffic associated with it. Certainly the children came from the west and could be obtained in the river villages, or at such markets as Abomege and Uberu in the eastern Ibo country. It is generally said in Umor that many of these children had been deliberately stolen, while others were obtained in exchange for payments from impoverished families crowded on the poor soil of parts of the southern Ibo country; but I had no opportunity to inquire into the source and mode of their acquisition. Police investigations of recent cases pointed to frequent theft, and to the fact that the children might change hands many times before they found a permanent home.

inadequately fulfilled. The economic and social needs are closely linked. While a large household is an obvious responsibility to its head, its size and activities enhance both his prestige and his importance. Direct responsibility for feeding and maintaining children ceases within a few years after puberty, while care for their interests and the arrangements for farm plots, house sites, and marriage payments for his sons afford the father an opportunity to express his interest and ability in conducting *kepun* affairs. An adopted youth can often be a direct economic asset. A man will farm and build, collect palm products and engage in petty trading for at least fourteen years before any son of his own is old enough to act as a regular and effective male helper. A young married man, therefore, often welcomes an opportunity to adopt a boy ten or twelve years of age. When Obeten Okoi went to Agoi, on hearing of the death of a matrilineal kinswoman who had left an orphan child, his brother Ubi asked him to endeavour to bring the boy back to be his *owunen* 'if he looked good'. Obeten satisfied the boy's patrilineal kin and brought him back to Umor. Ubi, whose own children are all under ten, now has a virtual son of fourteen, who helps in many of his farming and household tasks.

Although there are overt social and economic benefits to be derived from adoption, the strong and widespread desire to enlarge the household and increase the number of descendants must also be recognized. Pleasure at the birth of a child and the welcome of an opportunity for adoption do not result from a nice calculation of ultimate economic benefits, but arise largely from the satisfaction of a general attitude which permeates the society, an attitude the prevalence of which is not invalidated by the fact that it may be submerged in a particular situation by other emotional or practical objectives or difficulties. Men, for example, quite often make little effort to retain their children by divorced wives in their own households, merely saying that the former wife and her new husband or the children in question are 'hard to speak to', or that he has no woman to give them to. While the boy children of divorced parents who have stayed with the mother are usually expected to return to help their father soon after puberty, some fathers appear to make little effort to secure this return, although the need for farmland and a house site does often lead a son to turn to his father and his patrilineal kin at the time of marriage. The giving of help with marriage payments need not of itself lead an absent son to resume his life in the kin group, however, for youths should and do frequently receive contributions towards their marriage payments from both their patrilineal and matrilineal kin, and the latter sometimes make the greater contribution.

THE COMPOSITION OF HOUSEHOLDS

The vicissitudes of polygynous marriage, death, divorce, and adoption give a somewhat heterogeneous character to many of the households within the *yepun,* and while the patrilineal group is one of the nodes of social and economic relationships, conditions of residence may profoundly affect the sentiments and activities of individuals.

The circumstances that affect the stability of marriages require more extended discussion than can be given here, but it is important to consider the effect of the death or divorce of parents on the custody of children. The question is best approached through a study of the present composition of the households of a *kepun.* The data from Ndai, for 109 husbands and their 187 wives, are summarized in Table VIII.

TABLE VIII
LIVING CHILDREN IN NDAI
In households

Sex	Of present wives	Of departed wives	Of wives by earlier husbands	Adopted kin of man or wife	Total	Away	All living minor children of husbands
M	123	9	16	39	187	22	154
F	137	0	41	17	195	21	158
	260	9	57	56	382	43	312

Of the 382 children in Ndai 113 (about 30 per cent.) were not children born to the men in whose households they were living. On the other hand 43 (about 14 per cent.) of the children born to living Ndai men were not resident in their fathers' households. The introduced children were equally divided between (i) the adopted kin of men (or, more rarely, of their wives), of whom the majority were boys, and (ii) the children of wives by earlier husbands, most of whom were girls.

V *a*. Washing early yams

V *b*. Palm oil trading post, Ediba

VI *a*. House-building

VI *b*. House interior

While only 24 of the boys and 19 of the girls born to Ndai men are living away from their fathers' households, 55 boys and 58 girls who are not children of Ndai men are living in their households. On balance, the Ndai group as a whole appears to receive a net gain of 72 children by means of these transfers of children from the households of their parents, a position which must be matched by a corresponding net loss elsewhere. But apart from the possibility that there are concealed *yafoli* among them, the situation cannot be viewed in terms of the gains and losses of kin groups as units, for some of the transfers are internal to the group, i.e. from one man's household to that of a *kepun* kinsmen. Moreover, the fostering of children is a matter which is normally decided between individuals, according to their needs and opportunities on particular occasions, and is often effected on the basis of matrilineal kinship. Further, it cannot be assumed that all these children, and particularly the boys, will when adult be affiliated with the *yepun* of their present foster-parents.

The great majority (72 per cent.) of the absent children of Ndai fathers are living with their divorced mothers or with the kinsfolk of their divorced or deceased mothers. While this accounts for all the girls a few of the boys (4 of the 24) are with their fathers' kinsfolk.

Of the children that have been brought into Ndai households from outside, half are the children of Ndai men's wives by earlier husbands, and over 70 per cent. of these are girls. The other 56 introduced children are the sons and daughters of kinsfolk of the Ndai men or their wives. Among these there is a very marked predominance of boys among the children coming from the men's kinsfolk (33 out of 37), and of girls among those coming from wives' kinsfolk (13 out of 19), and there is at the same time a significantly greater number coming from the men's kinsfolk than from the kinsfolk of their wives.

This distribution results from general conformity with the definite and accepted practices whereby the immediate needs and the ultimate status of children are both safeguarded. Very young children nearly always accompany their mother when a marriage is dissolved, and if their mother dies they are as often given to the care of relatives of the father or of his deceased wife as to other wives. With older children the customary attitude differs with regard to boys and girls. A man is held to have more concern in the disposition of boys. Although he may in a particular case agree that a son should go with the mother, this does not imply his consent to adoption by the mother's kin, and he is upheld by the *kepun* head and by the village head if he refuses to let the child accompany her. Girls, however, almost always accompany the mother, and the matrilineal kin of the mother in such circumstances normally accept complete responsibility for her marriage, receiving the marriage payment and meeting any claims for later repayment if they arise. In the 109 households analysed, there are only nine children of deceased or divorced wives living with their fathers, and all of them are boys, while there are 43 children living away with the absent mothers or their kin, or with relatives of the father. Thus the retention of children during early infancy in the household of the father after the departure or death of the mother appears to be comparatively rare, and in this sample took place in only one case in six.

The father or his patrilineal relatives will, however, usually maintain contact with an absent son during his childhood, and encourage his return at manhood to the *kepun* of his birth. If the son is with a step-father he does nearly always return. It is only when the child is entrusted to his mother's brother, for which the father's explicit consent would be required, that he is likely to associate himself permanently with the *kepun* of his foster-father. Such a transfer has the effect of increasing the number of descendants of the latter's lineage and *kepun*, and since both a large household and large and influential groups of kinsmen, patrilineal as well as matrilineal, are consciously sought in Umor, the adoption of matrilineal kin into the patrilineal group in this way is welcomed at any convenient opportunity.

The balance between these sentiments and customary rules, and the circumstances of the close matrilineal and patrilineal kinsmen who may be concerned, will obviously affect each individual case in which the disruption of a family may involve the separation of a child from one of its parents. It should be realized also that, while there is great variety in the character of the transfers, none of them need affect the social and future economic status of the adopted child in any irrevocable way. A particular adoption may favour *de facto* transfer at manhood from the *kepun* of birth, but it is rare that any undertaking is given or demanded either by the true father, the foster-parents, or the child.

CONCLUSION

If any social structure is to be maintained over a series of generations, customary rules must be generally accepted by the component individuals and groups for the transmission of rights from one generation to the next. In the majority of small communities mere propinquity and common existence in a territorial group are regarded as less significant and binding than the social cohesion and continuity which arise from the biological events of parenthood, an attitude which is still dominant despite the elaboration of territorial organization, in many spheres of social and economic organization in the Western world.

But the duality of parenthood confronts every society with the need for the selection and emphasis, in however unformulated a fashion, of particular practices, since the recognition of ties of kinship must be restricted if corporate groups are to be maintained. Only on the basis of a unilineal reckoning can definite and stable relations persist in a self-perpetuating kin group. The widespread occurrence of unilineal kin groups and their fundamental importance as matrices in primitive social organization have long been recognized. Their prominence has, however, led to schematic formulations, in which they have been claimed to operate in too all-inclusive and automatic a manner.

While instances may be found of the extreme dominance of one unilineal reckoning of kinship and succession, pervading all spheres of social life, the opposed patrilineal and matrilineal principles may also operate simultaneously over distinct fields within a single society. Participation in some group activities may depend on patrilineal descent, while participation in others follows from recognition of matrilineal kinship. Succession to status and the inheritance of property rights may be divided into spheres subject to the two opposed principles. A fairly even weighting of the two may be rare, and such a situation may not often endure for a long period, but it has existed for at least several generations among many eastern Nigerian people,[27] of whom the Yakö of Umor afford an instance.

Such a situation undoubtedly tends to produce a conflict of interests and loyalties, and the analysis of the patrilineal groups of Umor presented here reveals the manner in which the principle of matri-

[27] For other brief illustrations of this phenomenon in different groups see Meek, C. K., *The Northern Tribes of Nigeria* (Oxford, 1925), i, p. 493, ii. p. 555.

lineal inheritance of property has stimulated the adoption of sisters' sons and their admission to the mother's brothers' patrilineal group.

Quite apart, however, from the pressure of the co-existent matrilineal principle, membership of the nominally patrilineal group may be established by a legal fiction for outside persons, children and adults, villagers and strangers, who are acceptable to the particular group. With a rising population and the adherence of individuals from beyond the community, fission of the patrilineal groups and the accretion of non-kin have been very considerable. But the breaking of filiation, on the one hand, and the affiliation of aliens, on the other, do not destroy the patrilineal character of the groups; for the living members of a group, though they may not include all the patrilineal kin of the putative ancestor, and may include individuals known not to be actual kin, nevertheless accept patrilineal succession as a basic principle for the future continuity of the group.

The structure and composition of the patrilineal kin groups of Umor illustrate in an extreme form processes in the history of clan organizations which have probably been more frequently operative than is generally recognized. The adaptation of a pattern of unilineal succession to vicissitudes both in particular households and in the larger community must be effected in all such societies, and is likely to result in discrepancies between theory and practice of the kind which this analysis reveals.

IV

DOUBLE DESCENT AND THE MATRILINEAL SYSTEM[1]

INTRODUCTION

THE relations arising from parenthood extend in all societies to form a wider system of kinship whereby, both for individuals and groups, rights of inheritance and succession, and ties of mutual obligation, are established on accepted principles of descent. But parenthood is dual, and if recognition were symmetrically accorded through both parents at each generation, kinship ties would proliferate indefinitely in ever widening aggregates. Moreover, the sex differences among both parents and siblings are a pervasive factor in differentiating cultural activity and attendant social status. In the process of establishing coherent and continuing social relations between kin, endless variety is possible in the stress and limitations set on the recognition of particular ties. The sex distinction may in some contexts be so dominant that women are grouped and succeed through their mothers, while men are grouped and succeed through their fathers.[2] But in the maintenance of groups of wide social relevance the sex difference between individuals is normally subordinated to the principle of affiliation of both sons and daughters through one of the parents to give rise to mutually exclusive kin groups of both sexes.[3]

Among many peoples one line of descent, either that through fathers or that through mothers, is stressed and a single system of

[1] The greater part of the essay on Double Descent among the Yakö, in *African Systems of Kinship and Marriage*, 1950, is reprinted here. But the more detailed passages concerning the patrilineal system have been omitted. Some case material from the earlier paper on Kinship in Umor, in *Amer. Anthropolo·gist*, vol. 41, 1939, has been added as indicated by footnotes.

[2] This tendency which gives rise to distinct descent groups among, for example, the Gê tribes of the Matto Grosso in South America, is exemplified over limited fields of inheritance in Africa.

[3] For a discussion of the range of conditions under which this tendency finds expression in the formation of a stable system of mutually exclusive unilineal kin groups, see my paper, 'The Anthropological Approach in Social Science', in *The Advancement of Science*, London, 1947.

unilineal groups is formed. But the ascription of status within groups based on one unilineal reckoning does not exclude the concurrent establishment of rights and obligations, if only between close relatives, with kinsmen in other lines of descent. The unilineal tendency itself contains the alternatives of patrilineal and matrilineal reckoning and these are not, as was once assumed, mutually exclusive. Both may be operative as principles of affiliation and group organization in distinct social fields, so that rights of succession and inheritance fall into distinct categories.

Systems of double descent or double unilineal kin-group organization have long been encountered in Africa, but they have often been misunderstood and few of them have been closely studied.[4] The Yakö are of importance in this connection, for their kinship systems afford an instance of full and simultaneous development of both patrilineal and matrilineal groups.[5] Until the present generation, among whom many features are, as will be seen, being modified under the impact of Western institutions, matrilineal descent has been as outstanding in its sphere as patrilineal, and both are corporately organized.

HOUSEHOLD AND FAMILY

The elementary family is the nucleus of the Yakö household, but the majority of the older men have more than one wife. In polygynous households every wife has a right to occupy a separate house provided by her husband and has personal property in food-supplies and domestic equipment (see Fig. 8, Woman's House). She rears her own children and in both productive and recreational activities is in principle free from the interference of any other wife. Although co-wives normally occupy adjacent houses there are, from the point of view of daily food-supply, as many households as there are able-bodied women. The single household head has equal rights and obligations in each. Food should be prepared for the husband by each wife in turn, but the length and regularity of the periods appears to be very variable. But in farming, a man with his several wives normally constitutes

[4] On the Herero system, which still awaits full analysis, see I. Schapera, *Notes on some Herero Genealogies*, University of Cape Town, 1945.

[5] Other neighbouring peoples who have a similar dual system of kin grouping are the Ekumuru, Abayoṇ, Agwa'aguna, Enna, Abini, Agoi, and Asiga. The Agwa'aguna and Yakö share a common tradition of overland migration from the north-east. Among them both 'friendship' and social distance are expressed in taboos on fighting and intermarriage and in joking relations.

a single farming unit, although each wife has her specific interests, rights, and duties which do not extend over the entire farm plot, and one wife does not control the farm labour of the others. The close proximity of the houses of plural wives and their common concern with the affairs of one husband involve personal relations between the wives, but these are informal in character. They depend on individual temperament and vary according to the particular circumstances. Attitudes are not determined in advance either by rules of domestic co-operation or by the relative status of wives. The first married or the senior existing wife has no formal superiority or prerogative. Yakö say that each wife has an equal claim on the time, attention, and energy of the husband. Similarly each wife has an equal obligation to participate in household duties, including especially farm work and preparing food for the husband, and is responsible for the well-being of her own children. In practice, owing to differences in the aptitudes and inclinations of wives and in the sentiments of the husband towards them, there may be considerable differences among them, both in their participation in domestic activities and in their prestige in the compound. But such differences are not subject to the control of the senior wife. On the farm it is the husband who tells each wife what he wishes her to do. Mutual helpfulness between wives in farming and domestic activities is by no means absent, but at the same time it is quite common to find an age-mate of one wife helping her in some task at home or on the farm while the other wife is working independently. The relations between wives of one man may range from real companionship to a minimum of contact punctuated with outbursts of hostility. The failure of a wife to live amicably with another in the compound is a recognized ground for dismissing the aggressor.

The yams of a man and those of his wife or wives are planted and harvested separately. They are tied on distinct groups of uprights in the husband's harvest stack and the separate harvests of each are used in turn to provide household supplies according to well-established rules. The lesser crops are the wives' responsibility. Each owns and controls her own harvests, but she is at the same time under obligation to provide her husband and children with adequate supplies during the year. A wife who, for any reason, is unable to carry out all the farm work that falls to her lot should find and recompense helpers from among her age-mates or her kin.

If she lacks sufficient yams to supply her share for the needs of her husband and children she is expected to work on other people's farms at busy times, and especially at planting and harvesting, when she will be given yams for each day's work which will help to remedy her own deficit. But a husband with a large harvest of yams will himself give a wife extra yams in recognition of her farming services to him if her own crop is short.

On the other hand, fruit-trees and oil-palms are not held by women. They are planted or tended individually by men, and rights to them are transmitted to male heirs. A husband is expected to provide his wife with supplies of palm-nuts for the preparation of kernels which she sells, and failure to do so is a very common source of friction between them. This he commonly does in the course of his collection of palm-fruit for the preparation of palm-oil, the marketable surplus of which belongs to him. There is a division of labour between men and women in the successive processes, the wife normally receiving the nuts for cracking and disposal of the kernels as part of her share in the product and her reward for assisting in the production of the oil.[6]

There is no limitation, apart from inclination and the resources he commands, on the number of wives that a man may have at any one time, and demographic conditions at least in the recent past, have been favourable to a high incidence of polygyny.[7] Plural marriage is an undoubted advantage in maintaining a large farm every year, for weeding the farm, cultivating secondary crops and carrying the yam harvest, and also in the preparation of oil-palm products for sale. Men frequently explain their later marriages by saying that increase in their yam harvests or the death of one wife made it necessary for them to seek another without delay. But plural marriage is also valued as a means of rearing a larger number of children and so of increasing the strength of a man's patrilineage and of his own prestige within it. On the other hand, the increasing adoption of trading pursuits by younger men who, in consequence, can clear only small farms, is rendering polygyny difficult or expensive for them. Such men also tend to be less

[6] Wives retain for their personal use any oil left over after filling the 4-gallon tins used as units in oil trading. Any surplus less than half a tinfull the wife claims for domestic use and for disposal in small occasional gifts to kin, affines, and neighbours with whom she is on good terms.

[7] See my *Marriage and the Family among the Yakö in South-Eastern Nigeria*, Monographs on Social Anthropology, No. 5, London, 1941; new edition, 1951.

strongly concerned in the traditionally high value placed on numerous offspring. Moreover, there is little emphasis on the number of wives as a direct expression of an individual's status or prestige. The priest leaders of the clans, both patrilineal and matrilineal, for example, are not distinguished by a markedly higher degree of polygyny than the adult male population in general.

A man takes further wives according to his needs and opportunities throughout his earlier life, but as old age approaches he does not marry again. Elderly widowers, although they maintain their own farms, often do not remarry late in life, but are dependent on the aid of daughters or sons' wives for farm work. There is thus no tendency among the Yakö for old men as a class to secure a disproportionate number of women as wives at the expense of younger men.

Young men usually marry girls of their own age in the first instance. On the other hand, in later marriages men often take women who differ widely from them in age, and the general tendency is to marry younger women. There is a particular inducement to take a second wife very shortly after the first if the latter has borne a child, for a child is normally suckled for two years during which intercourse between the parents is forbidden. In such a situation the second wife is often a previously unmarried girl.

The sex ratios at birth and at marriageable age appear to be normal among the Yakö.[8] It is therefore likely that the general practice of polygynous marriage has been made possibly only through the purchase of foreign children, mainly from Ibo country, west of the Cross River, who are known as *yafoli*, and are adopted into the household and kin groups of the purchaser, and the great majority of whom have been girls. There has recently been increasing governmental check on this trafficking in children, but it has for a considerable period made available a surplus of girls especially for marriages to older men as later wives.

Divorce as well as polygyny is frequent among the Yakö and both produce a situation in which a man's children fairly often consist of several groups which are half-siblings to one another. All will be members of the father's patrilineage, but their matrilineal affiliations and considerable rights and obligations associated with them will be divergent. A man is not usually concerned, for example, in his paternal half-sister's marriage; her children are not among his

[8] See Forde, D. and Charles, E., 'Notes on some population data from a Southern Nigerian village'. *Sociological Review*, xxx, 2, 1938.

heirs. But a full sister and a maternal half-sister are equally among his closest matrilineal kin.

The household of an older man will often include not only his wives but also divorced or widowed kinswomen, among whom mother, sisters, daughters, and sisters' daughters are the most frequently encountered. A woman widowed late in life usually joins one of her sons in whose farm she will plant her crops. A younger woman who has been widowed or divorced may temporarily rejoin her parents or go to her mother's brother or to an older brother. Such women are given houses of their own, but, unless they are infirm, they provide their own food-supplies and assist the head of the household. Their rights and obligations are in many respects similar to those of the wives, and any young children with them will be treated like foster-children. Elderly widowers are also to be found as dependants in the households of sons or other patrikin. There are, too, in many Yakö households young children of previous marriages related to only one of the spouses.

The majority of household heads provide themselves with a separate man's house, usually a smaller and simpler dwelling than a woman's, in which they keep their personal belongings, meet their friends, and often sleep. Young men before and after marriage frequently share the house of a father, elder brother, or other male relative living in the same compound. (See Fig. 8, Man's House, and Fig. 9.)

Yakö feel that physiological paternity constitutes a right to social fatherhood which, where they conflict, may be asserted against the rights derived through marriage. Although, as will be seen, social fatherhood may be later attenuated if not extinguished following adoption by a foster-father and his lineage, a man's physiological paternity of his wife's child is generally axiomatic, for there is not usually any knowledge or assumption to the contrary. But rights to social fatherhood based on physiological paternity outside marriage can in another context be successfully asserted over those derived from marriage to the mother. In other words, an adulterer can in some situations successfully claim the social fatherhood of his child. It is said that claims which would give rise to such a conflict are not frequently made, but they are held to be justified where a woman has left her husband and has a liaison with another man, before any divorce has been arranged

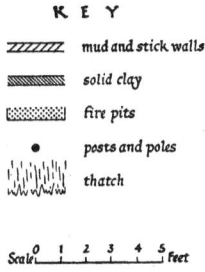

KEY

▨	mud and stick walls
▨	solid clay
░	fire pits
•	posts and poles
⁙	thatch

Scale: 0 1 2 3 4 5 feet

WOMAN'S HOUSE

rack

rack cupboard

opening ---to--- Lekpekpeli (store room)

lebelibō

A

B

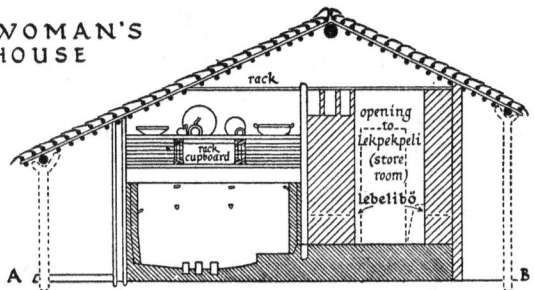

Section A-B, with distance, facing C, superimposed in broken lines

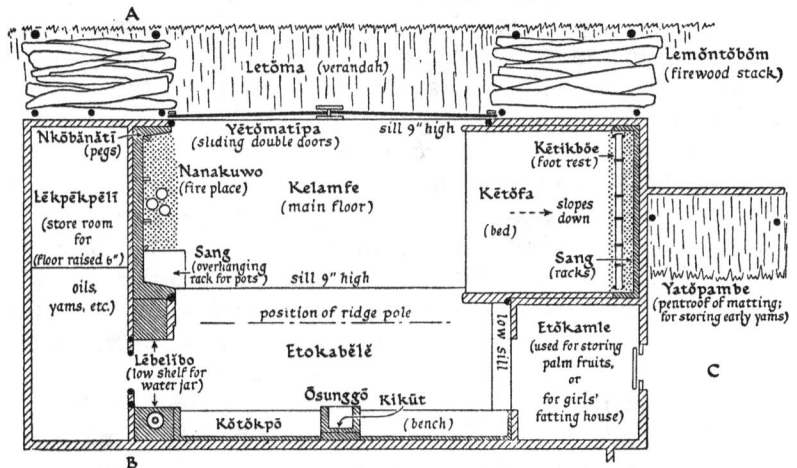

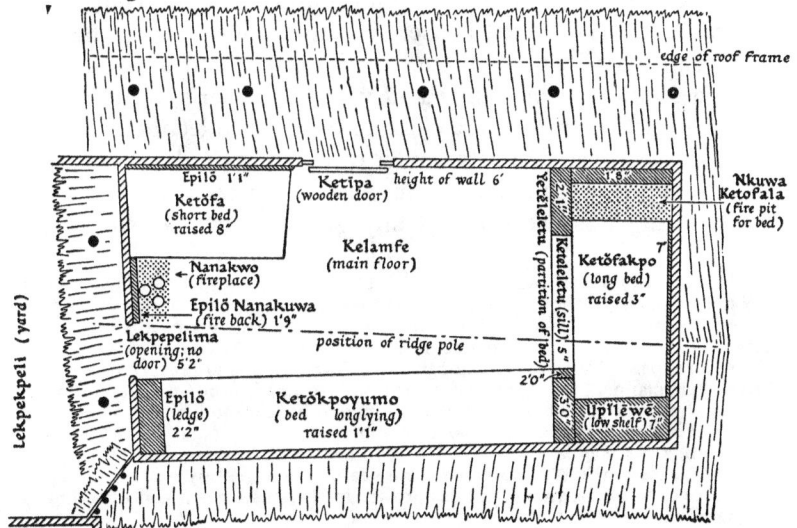

A

Letōma (verandah)

Lemōntōbōm (firewood stack)

Nkōbānātī (pegs)

Yētōmatīpa (sliding double doors) sill 9" high

Kētikbōe (foot rest)

Nanakuwo (fire place)

Kelamfe (main floor)

Kētōfa (bed)

slopes down

Lēkpēkpēlī (store room for (Floor raised 6") oils, yams, etc.)

Sang (overhanging rack for pots)

sill 9" high

Sang (racks)

Yatōpambe (pentroof of matting; for storing early yams)

position of ridge pole

sill 10"

Etōkamle (used for storing palm fruits, or for girls' fatting house)

Lēbelībo (low shelf for water jar)

Etokabēlē

C

Ōsunggō Kikūt (bench)

Kōtōkpō

B

edge of roof frame

Epilō 1'1"

Ketīpa (wooden door)

height of wall 6'

Yeteleleu (partition of bed)

Nkuwa Ketōfala (fire pit for bed)

Kētōfa (short bed) raised 8"

Kelamfe (main floor)

1'8"

Kētōfakpo (long bed) raised 3"

Nanakwo (fireplace)

Keteleleu (sill) 5"

7'

Lekpekpeli (yard)

Epilō Nanakuwa (fire back) 1'9"

Lekpepelima (opening; no door) 5'2"

position of ridge pole

2'0"

Epilō (ledge) 2'2"

Ketōkpoyumo (bed longlying) raised 1'1"

3'0"

Upilēwē (low shelf) 7"

MAN'S HOUSE

FIG. 8

by repayment of marriage money. The rights of the husband and his patrikin are then confined to compensation for the adultery and a return of the marriage money, but do not include fatherhood of the child or its membership of his patriclan. And this has been held to be so even when the woman eventually returns to her husband.[9]

PATRILINEAGE AND CLAN

Yakö dwellings are usually built round small four-sided compounds (*akəmsuŋa*, sing. *lekəmsuŋa*) on to which face from five to ten separate women's and men's houses. A compound usually contains the houses of several household heads, but the latter, as will be seen, are nearly always close patrilineal kin and despite the crowding of houses in the parts of the villages that have been long occupied, an effort is made to extend the compound and maintain the unity of the related households if they increase in number. Thus a Yakö child brought up in the house of its mother is one of a considerable group of children of various ages. Most of them will be linked in patrilineal kinship both among themselves and to the men in the compound, although, as will appear later, foster-parentage, and the fact that young children usually accompany their mother if she leaves her husband's compound on divorce, introduce some who are connected by other ties. More important at this stage is the fact that a child grows up in the company of age-mates from different households and, as it grows up, takes an increasing part in the activities of the compound as a whole. A boy goes out with his father and with his father's brothers from an early age, when they are clearing bush or collecting palm products. Unless relations between his own parents and others happen to be strained, he is made to run messages or take food out to the farm during busy seasons for any grown-up of the compound.

---

[9] In one case, which came for decision to the village head in Umor, a woman left her husband, went to live under the protection of a matrikinsman, and had a liaison with one of the latter's neighbouring patrikin, giving birth to a son. Her husband, wanting her to return, had not brought a charge of adultery or claimed return of the marriage money and a year later she did return to him. The lover then claimed the child before the village head, who, with some of the council, held that the child belonged to him and his clan to which it should later return. The lover was told he should compensate the husband for the adultery, but more stress was laid on their living in peace, and no compensation was in fact made. Nevertheless at about twelve years of age the boy was brought back by the lover to his patriclan and has grown up there as his son and a member of his patrilineage.

Later he becomes a regular helper in work on his father's farm and in the co-operative working parties of kinsmen and others in which his father joins. A girl accompanies her mother to the farm or looks after younger children in the compound when the older women have to be away farming or at the market. When a young man reaches eighteen or nineteen years and payments have been made for his first marriage, he is given his first farm plot and help in building a house by his father and other patrilineal kin in the compound (see Fig. 9).

But the compound in which a man is born and grows up is, as been has shown, only one segment of a larger settlement group of patrilineal relatives and their wives. And it is this larger group, normally a cluster of several adjacent compounds, which collectively maintains rights to a section of the village site and to tracts of farmland in the surrounding country. In one house area examined in Umor, 19 out of a total of 32 men, whose fathers were still living, lived in the same compound or house cluster as their fathers. Of the 9 adjacent compounds in this dwelling-area, 4 were almost exclusively occupied by men who were close patrilineal relatives. Each of these sets of close patrikin neighbours, together with a few individuals living elsewhere, constitutes a self-conscious group, an *eponama* (pl. *yeponama*), a corporate patrilineage whose members trace descent through birth or adoption from a common ancestor three to five generations back, from whom they name themselves as a corporate group, e.g. *Eponama Etuŋ Enamuzo.* The patrilineage rather than the single compound is the most important corporate group beyond the household of which a Yakö is conscious. Its members claim and distribute among themselves succession to rights in house sites, farm plots, oil-palm clusters, and planted trees that are not made use of by actual sons. A senior man of standing, referred to as *uwo womon* (our father), arbitrates in disputes among them and is their leader in affairs with other groups. And they may also speak of themselves and be referred to as his people, e.g. *Yanen bi Ikpi Esua.*

But, as we have seen, the patrilineages are aggregated into patriclans which are also territorially compact. Each has a recognized and even demarcated dwelling-area in which live the great majority of its men with their wives and children. Each has a name which is used to refer both to the members and to the dwelling-area. These names do not refer to ancestors, actual or

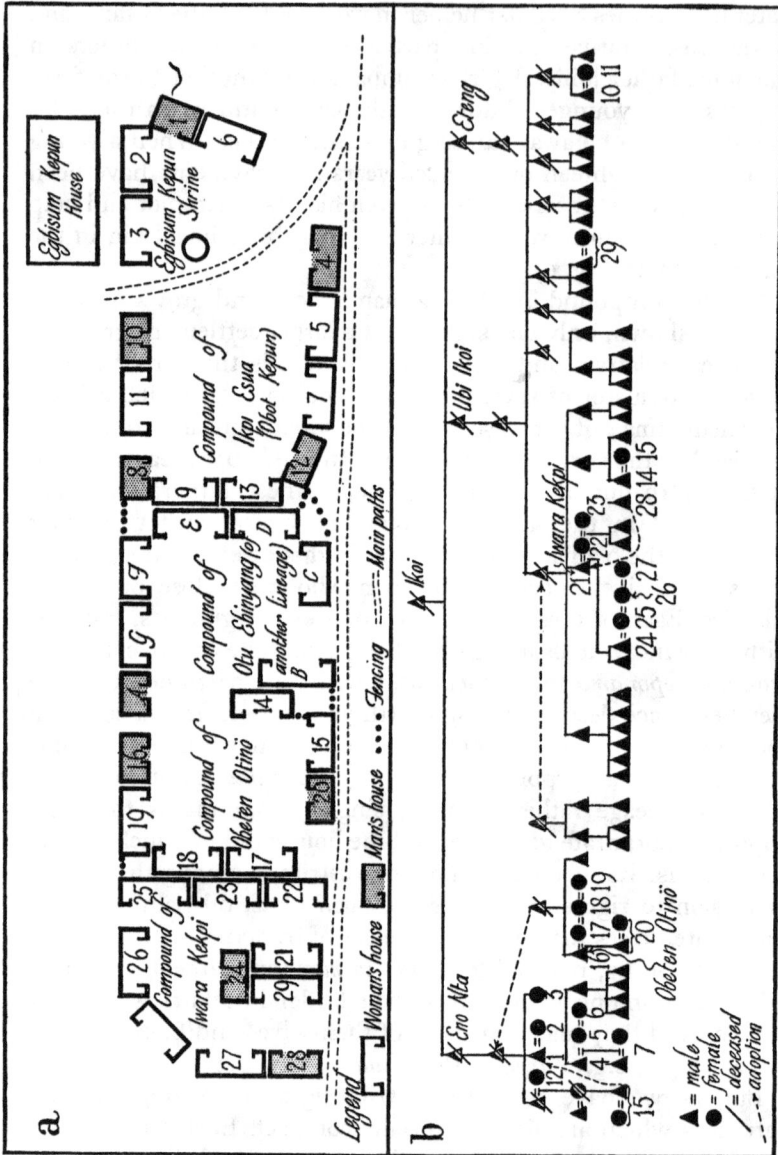

(a) Diagram af four adjacent compounds in Egbisum Kepun, Umor.
(b) Lineage of Ikpi Esua (*Obot Kepun*) to show affiliations of occupants.

Numbers refer to houses in the diagram of compounds. All living adult males of the lineages are shown. Those without numbers live elsewhere.

Fig. 9.—Composition and Affiliation of Compounds

mythical. Some refer to natural and other features suggesting that conditions connected with the site led to the naming, though several *yepun* in different wards have the same name.[10]

The coherence of the *kepun* is not conceived in terms of contiguity alone, however. The *kepun* membership of every person is normally established at birth, for a child born in the village is automatically recognized as a member of its father's *kepun*, and continues to be so regarded unless special circumstances result in a *de facto* transfer of membership later in life. Although, as has been seen, individuals may be adopted into the group either as children or even when adult, the majority of the members of a *kepun* at any one time belong to it in virtue of patrilineal affiliation.[11]

On the other hand, the *kepun* is not usually a single lineage of wider span than the *eponama*, in the sense that all members are held to be descended from a single ancestor to whom genealogical connection is traced or even ascribed. Yakö may and do say of their *kepun* fellows, 'We are all brothers', and imply common descent in this way, but in other contexts, particularly in disputes over dwelling-sites or prior claims to the use of tracts of farmland, the separateness of the lineages and their alleged distinct origins are emphasized.

The patriclans are, nevertheless, strictly exogamous and the rule is enforced with no great difficulty, since post-marital residence is patrilocal. At marriage a woman leaves the compound and *kepun* of her birth to join her husband, usually elsewhere in the same village. Thus, apart from returned widowed or divorced daughters, the women living in a patriclan area are wives and not members of the *kepun* kin. The women who are *kepun* kin are scattered, according to their marriages, all over the village and to a lesser extent in other villages.

In Yakö thought and practice patriclanship and exogamy apply to all persons who supplicate at a single shrine (*epundet*), so that there are in Umor, as has been shown, on the one hand, nominally distinct residential groups, which constitute a single ritually united exogamous entity, and, on the other hand, single residential groups which in fact consist of two exogamous units each with its independent ritual.

---

[10] Many *kepun* names incorporate the Yakö term for dwelling-area, e.g. *letekǝm*, place of smithing; *lekpaŋkǝm*, place of *kekpan* (= grouping). Others, however, e.g. *ibenda*, *unebu*, etc., omit this combination.

[11] See Chapter III.

MATRIKIN AND MATRICLAN

The patrilineal *kepun* is not, however, the only group of kin within which an Okö has rights and obligations. It has already been seen that ties of matrilineal kinship underlie many of the adoptions of men into *yepun*. These ties not only involve rights and duties between persons closely related in this way; they are also the foundation of matriclans, known as *yajima* (sing. *lejima*), complementary to the patriclans just described. Apart from full siblings, the persons composing the patrikin and the matrikin of each individual are normally distinct, and it is of importance for the understanding of the social relations that are established through matrilineal kinship to bear in mind that, among close relatives, only full brothers and sisters will of necessity belong to both groups. Since residence is patrilocal, the members of a matriclan must be dispersed among the patriclan territories of a village while a minority will be living in other villages (Table IX).

The rights and obligations which derive from matrilineal kinship do not formally conflict with those derived patrilineally. Over the greater part of the fields of economic activity, ritual observance, and succession to property, a clear distinction between their spheres of application has, until very recently, been maintained. Matrilineal kinship should take precedence over patrilineal in the inheritance of transferable wealth, especially livestock and currency, in the receipt of payments made to a woman's kin at her marriage, in the corresponding responsibility for the return of payments received for women who later unjustifiably leave their husbands, in responsibility for debts incurred by an individual, and also in obligations and rights in respect of recompense for bodily injuries. On the other hand, patrilineal rights and obligations, as has been seen, largely relate to the use of land and houses and to the provision of co-operative labour, especially in the annual farm-clearings at the beginning of the agricultural season. Yakö say that 'a man eats in his *kepun* and inherits in his *lejima*'.

In the present generation, however, matrilineal ties are being undermined, especially in the villages of Ekuri and, to a lesser degree, Umor, by successful claims of sons to their father's personal possessions and by the retention of marriage payments by fathers. Administrative confirmation of decisions in this sense in the Native Authority courts has strengthened this tendency.

VII *a*. Head-loading harvest yams

VII *b*. Hunter and palm-wine collector

VIII *a*. Making roof mats for house repair

VIII *b*. Wife carrying food to husband's feast

But in the thirties the majority of the Yakö still adhered to earlier custom, and, although some are now determined to flout them, no one denies that matrilineal rights exist.

Close matrilineal relatives will be in touch with all important events and circumstances in each other's households and will give mutual support within the framework of the accepted kinship obligations. Although in the larger villages many members of one's matriclan may be encountered only occasionally, all are made vividly aware of their fellowship two or three times a year in rituals which are the visible symbols of the unity and social reality of the matrilineal groups.

The matriclans are similar in numerical strength to the patriclans. The largest do not much exceed 100 adult males and some are much smaller. The prefix *ya*, signifying 'the people of . . .', is incorporated in the names of the matrilineal kin groups which are quite distinct in form from those of the patrilineal groups.[12] Some are held to have been independent groups at an indefinitely remote period. Such clans have priesthoods. Others are ritually attached to one or other of these groups and are in some cases held to be offshoots of the clan from which the priest of the spirit (*yose*, pl. *ase*) they recognize is chosen. Other secondary groups are held to have transferred their ritual dependence to another shrine when they separated from a parent group. Fig. 10 and Table X summarize the position in the village of Umor, where it will be seen that although 23 distinct matriclans are recognized, there are only 10 cult groups. Twelve of the former, although they are independent with respect to other rights, depend for their supernatural benefits and for the ritual validation of decisions by their elders on rites carried out by the priests of other clans. All but four of the priests officiate for more than one matriclan and these four are said to be priests of groups which were themselves dependent on others before they established shrines and priesthoods of their own.[13]

The actuality of the fission in the matrilineal kin groups implied by this situation and alleged by the people themselves was con-

[12] Thus *yabaye* refers to one matriclan as a corporate entity as well as to a plurality of members. An individual member is an *obaye*. But the name of a *kepun* such as Egbisum is distinct from the term for members, who would be referred to individually as Ogbisum and collectively as Yagbisum.

[13] The documentation of these processes which follows is taken from my earlier paper 'Kinship in Umor'. *Amer. Anthropologist*, xli, 4, Oct.–Dec. 1939, pp. 531–6.

firmed for two of them by the assertion that appointments of the first priests of the *ase* concerned were said by the older men to have been made within their lifetimes. It was also said that in several instances of alleged fission in the past the subdivision had transferred its allegiance to a *yose* other than that which it recognized before the division.[14]

The process of *lejima* fission could be observed in an early stage in one instance. The Yakpambot people have for some time regarded themselves as linked with the Yabot II people in recognizing the *yose* Obolene. About ten years ago the elders of the Yakpambot *lejima* living in Idjiman ward declared their intention of making their offerings to Oseŋawekoŋkoŋ, *yose* of the Yakumiko and Yabuŋ *yajima*, which is situated in Idjiman. I was not able to investigate closely the circumstances of this declaration which was said to have arisen out of a dispute over rights to *lejima* raphia palms and I did not learn the views of the 'Idjiman Yakpambot' elders, but the transfer has been effective. It will be noted that in this instance only part of the *lejima* transferred its allegiance to a new spirit and that this group was at the time territorially limited. But, as has already been pointed out, the *yajima* are inevitably non-territorial groups, since a woman who alone can transmit *lejima* membership to the next generation cannot rear her children in the dwelling-area in which she was born.[15] This matrilineal subgroup which began as a small local division is already losing its territorial character and the fact that it arose in Idjiman ward over some particular dispute will soon have lost all significance.

Concerning other of the 'secondary' *yajima*, such as Yakunkunebot (not distinguished from Yabot I in the table) there was no native theory of transfer of cult allegiance in the past. Such *yajima* were regarded as having taken a distinct group name while re-

[14] The *lejima* of Yakpölö, for instance, is regarded both by its own elders and by people in general as having formed in the past a part of Yabot I *lejima*. After its separation from the main Yabot I kin group, its members sought the performance of rituals not at the Yabot spirit Odjokobi but at that of the Yaboletete *lejima*, Esukpa. A similar transfer was said to have been made by the Yanali people. Quarrels were the alleged occasions of these transfers of allegiance from one *yose* to another, but I had no opportunity of inquiring closely whether there was any confirmatory evidence of this.

[15] It therefore follows that the matrilineal descendants of the Yakpambot people living in Idjiman ward at any one time would within a few generations be scattered right through the village. This is already beginning to happen. Children of girls who were associated with the Oseŋawekoŋkoŋ spirit, whatever the ward in which they are born, are regarded as members of the *lejima* of their mother and are being brought to Oseŋawekoŋkoŋ spirit at the public rituals.

maining ritually a part of the cult-holding groups from which they were derived. Yakunkunebot people have, for example, in the native view 'grown out from Yabot people. Odjokobi is *yose* for Yakunkunebot just as for Yabot people, but Yakunkunebot never make a *yose* priest. Only Yabot people know how to be priests to Odjokobi.'

While each matrilineal kin group has, as a rule, its own name, there are two anomalies. One of these, the Yakpambot group originating in Idjiman, has already been considered; the other is more difficult and was at one stage very baffling when I was endeavouring in the field to grasp the alignment of these kin groups. A brief review of the stages of my own understanding of the position may help to make the situation clear.

It was early apparent that a matrilineal kin group with the title *Yabot* existed in Umor. This term *Yabot* has the general connotation 'the Leaders'. It is also used as a collective title for the priests of the *ase* and certain others who, as a group, constitute a corporation of village priests ordering and conducting the great seasonal rites and who also maintain by supernatural sanctions—and formerly by invoking the action of men's associations—law and order in the community as a whole.[16]

It soon became apparent, however, that two *ase*, Odjokobi and Obolene, each with its own *ina*, were claimed by the Yabot people. These two *ase* were said to 'stand in front of all other *ase* in Umor', while of Odjokobi it was claimed 'He is for all Umor. Yabot have him but he exists for the whole village.' The *ina* of Odjokobi, the manner of whose selection and appointment from among the Yabot people is generally similar to that for other *ase* priests, has nevertheless a special position and title which clearly gives him rank as a village priest-chief. He is known as *Obot Lopon* (Leader of the Village), is head of the corporation of priests also known as *Yabot*, and goes to live on appointment in a special site, Lebokem, which is not within the territory of any of the wards or *yepun*.

But some of the Yabot people asserted that their *yose* was Odjokobi, others that it was Obolene, and others that all the *ase* could be invoked on their behalf. It later became apparent, when I had obtained genealogical data and came to know the priests and some of the Yabot elders, that there were in fact two matrilineal kin groups both of which used the title Yabot. This was confirmed

[16] See Chapter VI below.

by later inquiries on inheritance and succession. Neither disputed the use of the title by the other, although one was frequently said to be a branch of the other. One claimed the premier spirit, the Odjokobi *yose*, and their elders nominated its priest who became in virtue of this appointment the Village Head. The other, while its elders would often claim equality of status with the Yabot people of Odjokobi, declared their direct association with the Obolene spirit. The Yabot people do in fact, when a distinction between the people of Obolene and those of Odjokobi arises, use distinct but obviously improvised terms for the groups, calling the one *Lejima-z-Obot-Ikpi* (i.e. the *lejima* of Obot Ikpi, who is the present priest of Odjokobi and 'Leader of the Village') and *Lejima-z-Ina-Uket* (i.e. the *lejima* of Ina Uket, who is the present priest of Obolene). These two Yabot *yajima* are distinguished as Yabot I and II in Table IX.[17]

The beliefs and attitudes of the people of Umor on the formation of the *yajima* and their mutual relations may be summarized as follows:

The *yajima* are of varying antiquity and size but all have their own elders and are independent groups within which property and status are transmitted according to matrilineal filiation.

Some are said to have existed when the Yakö first settled at Umor and are believed to have constituted independent kin groups at an indefinitely remote period. Each of these has its own super-natural spirit of which one, the *yose* Odjokobi, is also a source of fertility and prosperity for the village as a whole. These are (i) Yabot I with the *yose* Odjokobi; (ii) Yaboletete with the *yose* Esukpa; (iii) Yapuni with the *yose* Otabelusaŋa; (iv) Yakaŋkaŋ with the *yose* Atewa.

There are two further *yajima*, which as a combined ritual unit are also believed to be of independent and remote origin. These are Yakumiko and Yabuŋ, with the *yose* Oseŋwekoŋkoŋ. They are believed to have been formed by the fission of a single matrilineal

---

[17] The Yosenibot *lejima* is also of interest in his connection. Its title includes the two terms Yabot and Yoseni. It is believed to have come into existence by fission from the Yabot group, and the term Yoseni is the plural of Loseni which is used as the name of the *kepun* in whose *likuma* the *yose* must permanently remain. It was asserted that the *lejima* owed its name to the site of the *yose*, and it appeared likely that it had begun as a breakaway of Yabot people living in Loseni *kepun* after the manner of the recent separation of the Yakpambot people in Idjiman ward. The name Yoseni, and the belief that it is associated with the present site of the *yose*, is in any case another instance of the effects of territorial conditions on the essentially non-territorial matrilineal kin groups.

TABLE IX
Distribution of the Adult Male Members of Four Matrilineal Kin Groups (Yajima) Among the Wards and Patrilineal Kin Groups (Yepun) in Umor

Yepun in wards	Matrilineal Kin groups (Yajima)				
	Yakoibot	Yabot I	Yabot II*	Yabaye	Yakun-kunebot
UKPAKAPI	28	45	8	37	45
Egbisum	3	9	1	12	9
Letekem	4	3	—	4	11
Ndai	9	13	5	17	14
Lekpaŋkem	4	6	—	3	3
Usadja	8	14	2	1	8
BIKO-BIKO	25	23	3	27	18
Mpaŋi	3	5	1	3	3
Emeŋko	9	3	—	4	2
Ibenda I	1	4	—	4	—
Ibenda II	5	6	1	4	—
Lekpaŋkem	4	2	1	7	4
Lebokem	3	3	—	5	9
IDJUM	17	21	12	14	26
Loseni	—	1	—	3	3
Unebu	1	4	2	1	3
Kikoŋkula	10	3	6	2	6
Anedja-Lekpaŋkem	3	12	1	3	11
Akugum	3	1	3	5	3
					89
IDJIMAN	15	5	10	14	no data
Aboni	2	—	1	1	
Kebuŋ	2	—	4	1	
Letaŋkem	—	—	—	2	
Lekpaŋkem	1	—	3	3	
Otalosi	—	—	—	2	
Lebuli	10	1	—	—	
Lebokem	—	—	—	1	
Utoŋ	—	4	1	4	
Ugom	—	—	1	—	
Total	85	94	33	92	

* Part only (one lineage).

kin group, but they have both retained the right, exercised in alternation, to provide a priest for the *yose*.

There are four *yajima* (Yabot II, Yakoibot, Yosenibot, Yaŋyo and Yabaye) which, although they have severally their own *ase* and select their own priests, are believed to have come into existence by separation from other older matrilineal kin groups.

There are also ten secondary groups which are severally derived from present groups which alone select the priest of the *ase* they recognize. Such are the Yakunkunebot people who recognize the Odjokobi spirit of the Yabot I *lejima* and the Yabuna, Yakamafe, and Yatebö people, who all recognize the *yose* of Yaboletete.

Finally there are 'secondary' groups which transferred their relations to another *yose* when they separated from the parent group. Such are Yakpölö and Yanali people, who now recognize Esukpa whose priest is chosen from the Yaboletete *lejima*.

This statement of the relative positions of the matrilineal kin groups of Umor reveals, as does an analysis of the patrilineal groups discussed earlier, a characteristic of Umor society which was continually obtruding itself, namely the weakness of any tendency among the people themselves, whether leaders or elders of social groups or not, to formulate a comprehensive ranking of groups. The use of the term 'secondary' in the preceding paragraphs must not be taken to imply that the matrilineal kin groups themselves, as distinct from certain *ase*, are regarded as having any definite ranking in status.

Composition of a *Lejima*

In order to appreciate the character of the individual matrilineal kin groups it is necessary at this point to consider in more detail the composition of one such group, and the present membership of the small Yabot II[18] *lejima* will be analysed in order to exemplify the outstanding features.

Only 33 grown men of Yabot II actually living in Umor were known to me and they were scattered through the village (see Table IX). Twelve lived in Idjum ward, 10 in Idjiman, 8 in Ukpa-kapi and 3 in Biko-Biko. Of the 7 accepted elders (*yajimonotam*) 3 lived in Idjum, 3 in Idjiman and 1 in Ukpakapi. Thirty-five women with 24 boys and 25 girl children were also members of

[18] By this term I distinguish the second of the unnamed sections of the Yabot people which provides the priest of the Obolene *yose*.

the group. The somewhat feeble coherence of the matrilineal groups in every day life was suggested at the outset by the considerable difficulty I experienced in obtaining a complete enumeration of the members. I am not indeed certain that the material obtained, though it was sought from men in all the wards, is as complete as that which I readily obtained for much larger patrilineal kin groups.

The *yose* priest of Yabot II, Ina Uket, had moved into the compound containing the Obolene shrine (in the dwelling area of Loseni *kepun* in Idjum) at the time of his election some ten years before. Nearly all the living members were said to be descendants of a single ancestress, Ma Ete, four generations senior to the majority of the younger adult members (i.e., their great-great-grandmother). Whether the numerous alleged descendants of the generations next below were all children of an actual Ma Ete may be doubted. More significant was the assertion that one of them was a man, Akpam Emori, a former priest to the *yose*, who increased the strength of the *lejima* by purchasing no less than 4 foreign girl children (*yafoli*) of whom there are 9 male and 4 female adult descendants today.

A further group in the *lejima* consisting today of 3 adult men and 7 married women traces its ancestry to a man from the neighbouring village of Idomi, who was a matrilineal kinsman of Akpam Emori married to a foreign woman and came to live with Akpam at Umor. On account presumably of his anomalous status and his alien wife his children were accepted as members of *his* own and Akpam's *lejima*. In their own view therefore 12 of the adult men and 11 of the married women of Yabot II are descended from adopted ancestors. There are also others who were descended from foreign children adopted in later generations. Indeed of the 31 men only 14 and of the 35 women only 8 could claim a true and continuous *matrilineal* descent within the *lejima*. True matrilineal descent is valued, however, and the fact that he had an adopted ancestor may be used in trying to prevent an older man who is unpopular from being recognized as an elder. There is also strong sentiment that a truly lineal descendant should be preferred when selecting a successor to the priesthood. This was expressed on several occasions and Ina Uket, the priest of Obolene, the *yose* of this group, is in fact a lineal descendant. But his predecessor Ina Onun was not, for Onun's mother, Leman Okoi, was said to have been a foreign child adopted by Okama Ubi, a sister of Akpam Emori.

In every matriclan there is a group of elders known as *yajimanotam*—old men and women of the *lejima*—from 6 to a dozen of the more senior and active members and leaders in component lineages who, although they have no ritual functions and no ceremonial duties and maintain their numbers by informal co-option from time to time, do in fact exert considerable influence

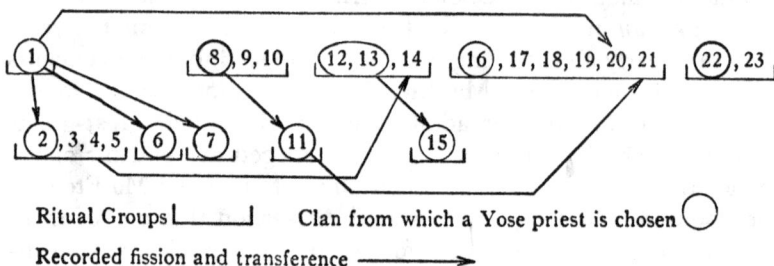

Ritual Groups └────┘　　Clan from which a Yose priest is chosen ◯

Recorded fission and transference ──────▶

FIG. 10—DIAGRAM OF MATRICLAN LINKS IN UMOR

both on the members and on village affairs that concern the group. Recompense for offence by one member of the matriclan towards another can be enforced by requesting the priest of the *yose* to declare the offender excommunicated. By appeal to the village council they are able, as will be seen, to protect the interests of particular members of the group in the payments and responsibilities involved in the marriages of their matrilineal kin. On the death of a matriclan priest they nominate his successor.

Within each village one of the matriclan spirits is held to be superior in power and in ritual status. Its cult is maintained, not only for the benefit of members of the matriclan of its priest and of any others secondarily attached to it, but also on behalf of the village as a whole. Its shrine has precedence in all village rituals and the priest, as ritual head of the local community, is known as *Obot Lopon* (Leader of the Village). But this does not confer any formal authority or superior status on the members or elders of the matriclan itself. Indeed, the matriclan organization, like the patrilineal groups already discussed, exhibits a characteristic absence of systematic ranking of groups.

While all members of a matriclan within a village are not only ritually associated but regard one another as kin, they are not an

TABLE X
Matriclans (Yajima) of Umor

Lejima	Yose		Lejima	Yose
1. YABOT I	Odjokobi*	12.	⎰YAKUMIKO	Osengawe-
2. ⎰Yabot II	Obolene*	13.	⎱YABUɖ	koŋkoŋ*
(from Yabot I)		14.	Yakpambot of	(Obot Lo-
3. Yakpambot	—		Idjiman	kona)
4. Yawambot	—	15.	Yaŋyə (from	Obete Edet
5. Yadjemi	—		Yakumiko-	
6. Yakoibot	Kupatu*		Yabuŋ)	
(from Yabot I)		16.	⎰YABOLETETE	Esukpa
7. Yosenibot	Okarefoŋ*	17.	Yabuna	—
(from Yabot I)		18.	Yakamafe	—
8. ⎰YAKAɖ-	Atewa*	19.	Yatebə	—
KAɖ		20.	Yakpələ (from	—
9. Yatioma	—		Yabot I)	
10. Yayale	—	21.	Yanali (from	—
11. Yabaye (from	Atalikumi		Yabaye)	
Yakaŋkaŋ)		22.	⎰YAPUNI	Otabelusaŋa
		23.	⎱Yadjokpoli	—

Capitals indicate matriclans providing *ase* priests and not known to have separated from another group.

Italics indicate matriclans said to have separated from others as indicated to create their own *ase*.

Ase which may not be moved from the site of their alleged foundation indicated by *.

Nine matriclans have an exclusive right to elect priests; 2 have rights in alternation; 12 provide no priests; 1 is in process of fission; 8 (7 and a section of an 8th) have transferred their allegiance and 5 of these have created new *ase*. Part of Yabot I is claiming to be a separate *lejima* known as *Yakuŋkunebot*.

---

undifferentiated group. The exercise and transmission of rights operate within smaller units of close relatives known as *yajimafat* (sing. *lejimafat*). These matrilineages are comparable in size and span to the patrilineages and it is within these smaller groups that most rights and obligations between matrilineal kin are exercised and transmitted. The collective term for matrilineal kin—*yatamban*—usually refers to the matrilineage, although it may apply also to the clan.

It is only within the matrilineage that exogamy is now strictly enforced. Formerly marriage within the matriclan was strongly disapproved. Old people still hold that such a marriage is likely to be sterile and to weaken the beneficient power of the *yose*. But during the thirties, starting first in Ekuri, both practice and attitude were changing in connection with the conflict over inheritance rights between sisters' sons and sons. There has been a general tendency in recent years for sons to lay successful claim to at least a share in the movable goods left by their father which, by former custom, passed entirely to matrilineal heirs. Marriage with a girl of another lineage in one's own matriclan has come to be encouraged as a device whereby this conflict can be resolved, the son of such a marriage being regarded as the matrilineal heir of his father. Such sons are successfully claiming sole inheritance of their father's movable goods as members of his matriclan and virtual members of his matrilineage, while young men are being encouraged by elders of their own matrilineage to make their first marriage with a girl of another lineage in the matriclan, so that they will be able to transmit their wealth to their eldest sons.

Unlike the patriclan system, which does not extend beyond the village, the matriclans in one village are held to correspond with clans in others. There are no common rituals, but there is a considerable parallelism in names of clans and clan spirits, and even a vague belief in ultimate common descent. People coming from another village, including not only individuals bent on trade or visiting a close kinsman who has migrated but also parties of young girls who commonly make stays of several weeks in the rainy season, can expect hospitality from members of the corresponding matriclan. Women marrying into another village are, together with their children, automatically accepted as members of the appropriate matriclan there. Formerly sons of such women lost no rights as matrilineal heirs of their mother's brothers in her village of origin.[19]

MATRILINEAL RIGHTS AND OBLIGATIONS

It has been seen that rights to dwelling-sites, farming land, and the more important forest resources are obtained by virtue of membership of a patrilineal group; but that when attention is transferred from rights in economic resources to the transmission of accumulated wealth, matrilineal kinship comes into prominence.

---

[16] Marriage with women of other villages appears to have been largely confined to Umor.

The funeral and the disposal of a dead person's property are supervised by a close matrikinsman, a mother's brother or a sister's son, who in the case of a man is chief heir. All currency, whether it be in brass rods or modern coinage, and all livestock, should by custom pass to matrilineal relatives, who also receive the greater share of the implements, weapons, household goods, and any stores of food. The movable property of women, which is usually less considerable, passes mainly to their daughters, but sons should expect very little from their parents. A man may obtain a gun or cutlass that was his father's; the rest will be claimed by his father's brother or sisters' sons.

With these rights of inheritance are associated corresponding obligations, and, in particular, responsibility for debts of matrikinsmen, a readiness to make reasonable loans at need, and the duty of providing a part, although a minor share, of the currency and goods transferred by a sister's son at marriage. If an outside creditor is unable to obtain satisfaction for a debt he will often seize a goat or cow belonging to a close matrilineal kinsman of the debtor, who can obtain no recompense through either the Village Council or, in more recent times, the Native Authority court, if the existence of an unduly prolonged debt is satisfactorily established. Considerable payments are involved in membership of men's associations among the Yakö and debts are often contracted in this connection both with individuals and the clubs themselves. If the debtor is dilatory, his matrilineal kinsmen are summoned and requested to make arrangements for settlement. If they refuse or fail to carry out their agreement, the Village Council would formerly have approved the seizure of their livestock by one of the associations. Nowadays most disputes over considerable debts are taken to the Native Authority court established by the Nigerian Government, but the responsibility of an offender's matrilineal kin to contribute if necessary has been recognized there. The court likewise summons the matrilineal kinsmen of a bankrupt debtor and orders them to undertake a settlement. Finally, if a man at his death leaves outstanding debts, his matrilineal kinsmen succeed to the obligations.

When a man dies, his household usually continues to function as a productive unit with the aid of brothers and sons until the yam harvest of the farm is gathered in. The dead man's crop, which will be considerably larger than those of his wives, is at the disposal of his matrilineal kin. But the chief claimant, who may be a full brother, and thus also a patrikinsman, undertakes obligations to young children of the dead man if they remain in the *kepun*, a considerable part may in fact be used for the benefit of these children. The widows will remarry or join either their grown sons or their own parents, and unless they are still caring for young children of their dead husband, when they will be given a portion, they have no right to any share of their dead husband's yams. The rest of the surplus is taken by brothers and adult sisters' sons for planting in their farms or for sale. But the dead man's children will themselves go later to his brothers' or sisters' sons, as to a 'father', for a supply of yams to make their first farms.

The position of women as wives and as owners of property in their husbands' farms is similarly the concern of their matrilineal kin. When a wife dies, both her rights and duties in her husband's farm pass for the rest of the farming-season to one or more matrikinswomen. If she dies after a harvest, her yams in the houshold yam store are claimed by her matrilineal kin and are usually taken by a sister or a grown daughter. If, on the other hand, a woman dies during the growing-season, the husband asks to be given the services of one or more of her 'sisters' to care for the farm and carry in the harvest. When the crop is dug, the yams of the deceased wife are carried away by the women who have taken her place, for distribution among themselves and other matrilineal kin.

Apart from the recent open challenging by sons of the inheritance rights of matrikin referred to earlier (p. 96), some evasion by men and their sons is said to be of long standing. Hoards of brass rods and later of Nigerian currency have not infrequently been hidden by secretly burying them in farmland. Apart from the ease of concealment, the profound suspicion of magical malpractice which is aroused by trespass on another's farmland and the magical safeguards against it render such a cache in farmland fairly secure. A man may confide in one or more of his sons the whereabouts of such a hoard while withholding knowledge of it from his matrikin so that the former may quietly take possession after his death.

Matrilineal kinship confers no settled right to economic resources which are exploited within the patriclan, that is, to farm plots as distinct from specific harvests, to oil-palm groves or to planted fruit trees. But the categories are not entirely clear cut, since matrikin should supply one another when there is special and occasional need. A man should never refuse a reasonable request from a sister's son or other matrikinsman for some of the produce of his planted trees and will seek approval from the head of his patrilineage for him to collect palm products on their land. Moreover, a considerable number of the valuable clumps of raphia palms, largely confined to swampy ground not used for farming, which provide much valued building material for houses and yam stacks, are in fact the property of matrilineages. It is recognized that a man who plants a new clump may share it during his lifetime with his sister's sons and leave it to one or more of them at his death. The right of control then passes matrilineally, although conversely owners' sons in each generation are then allowed access to the clump for their own needs. This practice runs counter to the general principle of patrilineal succession to farm and forest resources and appears to be related to the very uneven distribution of the scarce raphia-bearing swamps among the lands of the patriclans.[20] Finally, each matriclan claims the right to collect palm-wine over a tract of village territory for use in the funeral rites of matriclan elders, at the installation of their priests, and in certain other rituals. This temporarily overrides the rights of those who have prepared the trees in their patriclan lands, and enables a matriclan to act corporately in assembling a large supply of palm-wine.[21]

Membership in most of the men's associations among the Yakö is obtained by succession to a deceased member. This may be

[20] Some of the raphia clumps, like those on the Obuli farm road on the south-west side of the village, which are very large and belong to Yabot II people, are owned by the *lejima* as a corporate group. The elders of the group call on their fellows to help clear the surrounding bush to promote the growth of the clump and also control the cutting of the palms by members of the *lejima*. Other smaller raphia clumps are transmitted individually from single men or a group of close relatives to their younger brothers and sisters' sons. As it is, men in Ukpakapi ward, for example, often have to seek out *lejima* elders in Idjiman ward to obtain permission to cut raphia stems on the far side of the village.

[21] The *yajima* have also in recent years successfully established new claims over natural resources in the village territory. Since the introduction of Government control of forest trees, a royalty has to be paid for felling any of the valuable forest trees. Part of this royalty is repaid to the village and in Umor the priests and elders of the *yajima* have successfully claimed any payments that are received for trees felled in their wine-collecting and raphia-planting tracts. This is probably due to the fact that the payment is received in the first place by the village head. As he and the other *ase* priests are dominant on the native village council, in which the patrilineal clan organization as such is unrepresented, claims by the priests themselves and the other leaders of the *yajima* would not unnaturally have found favour.

either patrilineal or matrilineal, since a man's right, which is also an obligation, to join an association may be inherited from either a matrilineal or a patrilineal kinsman and this right should pass on by the same rule as that whereby the deceased succeeded. The close kin, both matrilineal and patrilineal, are expected to contribute to the fees required, but the more substantial payment is made by the group providing the successor, and in their case the obligation extends beyond the close relatives and concerns all the older members of the lineage and other notables of the clan.[22]

Homicide within a village also initiates a series of customary claims for compensation which are the concern of the kinsfolk of those directly involved. Formally no distinction is made between deliberate and accidental homicide, and while it is not admitted that the killing of one villager by the deliberate violence of another is a danger to be guarded against, anger is little tempered by evidence, however obvious, that the injury was accidental. If a man is killed, the reactions and claims of the two sets of his kinsfolk, patrilineal and matrilineal, are clearly distinct. In both groups anger is aroused, but the immediate crisis and the danger of retaliation is much greater among the patrikin. When the body is brought into the compound, there is a likelihood that the close patrilineal relatives will urge the men of the patriclan to attack the offender and his patrikin. Fights arising in this way have fairly frequently occurred. Indeed it is customary for the offender to seek shelter in the compound of the Village Head, and stay there while the Village Speaker is sent to the assembly house of the dead man's patriclan bearing the village elephant-tusk trumpet and drum which, by supernatural sanction, impose restraint and an obligation on the bereaved patriclan to keep the peace. The offender, or one of his close patrikin, has also on occasion been seized as a hostage by the *kepun* of the dead man and held until payment was made to them for his release.

Nevertheless, if one of their number, man or woman, is killed the patrilineal kin have no customary right to compensation, material or ritual, from the patriclan of the offender. This concerns only the matriclans of the deceased and the person held responsible. A matriclan which suffers loss by the violent death of a grown member at the hands of an outsider has a recognized right

---

[22] There is a lien on part of the deceased member's wealth for this purpose as described below, see p. 184.

to compensation which is ritually safeguarded. It is also required that the offender and, where an adult man has been killed by another, one of the former's matrilineal kinswomen be transferred to the dead man's *lejima* in a ceremony at its *yose* shrine.[23] A little more than a year before I first came to Umor, Ina Udomo, an Idjum man of Yaŋyo *lejima*, had been killed while hunting in the bush near the Egoiti path on the Umor border by a fellow-hunter and companion, Okpata Ikoŋ, of the Yabuŋ *lejima*. Ina Udomo was brought in mortally wounded, accusing Okpata of deliberate murder. Okpata asserted that he saw something moving in the bush which he took to be a buck; he fired his Dane gun and found only on running up that he had wounded Udomo. Two other men of the party supported his claim that the affair was an accident, but serious trouble between the *yepun* of the two men was only averted by the intervention of the Village Head. Okpata was later taken to the District Headquarters where, according to the village account, he was eventually exonerated by the District Officer. On his return, however, he was summoned to the compound of the Village Head at the request of the *lejima* of the dead man. There, he and the elders of Yabuŋ, his own *lejima*, were reminded by the *Yabot* of their obligation to the Yaŋyo *lejima*. They were required to make an immediate payment of £3 and this was shared between the *Yabot* and the elders of Yaŋyo. They were also told to pay £30 to the Yaŋyo *lejima* within a reasonable period of time. At the same time Okpata himself and a matrilineal kinswoman of child-bearing age were ordered to be transferred to the Yaŋyo *lejima*. One of Okpata's closest matrilineal kinswomen, the daughter of his sister, a young girl not yet married, was selected for this and a few days later they came to Obete Edet, the *yose* of Yaŋyo, with the materials for an offering. The *Yabot* assembled at the shrine and the transfer was effected by a declaration by the priest that the people of Yabuŋ gave these persons to Obete Edet. Okpata's membership of Yaŋyo *lejima* need continue only until the money debt has been settled, but that of his sister's daughter is permanent, and her children will be members of Yaŋyo *lejima*, although they may at the same time claim rights of inheritance from Okpata and their other matrilineal kin by birth. Down to the time when I was given this account of the past events no further money payment

[23] The account of an instance which follows is taken from my earlier paper, 'Kinship in Umor', *Amer. Anthropologist*, vol. 41, 1939, pp. 544–5.

had been made by Okpata and his kinsmen to the elders of Yaŋyo, and I was told that several seasons might elapse before they would settle the debt. It was also clear that although a particular sum was named there would be bargaining from time to time, when instalments were handed over, as to the total amount for which the elders of Yaŋyo would agree to the return of Okpata to the *lejima* of his birth—a return which would be performed at the Oseŋ-wekoŋkoŋ *yose* of Yabuŋ. In the recent past a money payment to enable the injured *lejima* to purchase an *ofoli*—a foreign child of the appropriate sex who was adopted by the dead man's relatives and became a member of the *lejima*—was usually accepted instead of one or both of the members of the offending *lejima*. Transfers could also be cancelled later by providing acceptable *yafoli* to re-place the man and woman.

There is a keen sense of loss over those who have been trans-ferred, but they must attend and contribute conspicuously at the funeral rites of members of their new matriclan and must avoid ostentatious participation in rituals of their former matriclan. The transfer of a woman, which is always permanent, results, if she bears children, in the numerical increase of the matriclan she has entered and also in the transfer, by inheritance, of property from the people of the offending *lejima*. It was fairly clear that restora-tion of the strength of the injured *lejima* was the most vital aspect of these transfers and they reflected a sentiment, more con-sciously developed in the matrilineal than in the patrilineal groups, which is being continually enhanced by the fertility rituals at the *ase* shrines.

This practice of compensating the matrilineal kinsfolk alone is not intelligible from a material point of view. Any children that a man who is killed might later have begotten would have been no concern of his matrilineal kin and, since his existing property should pass to them in the ordinary way, any loss to the matriclan is confined to wealth he might subsequently have accumulated. The patriclan, on the other hand, suffers the loss of a breadwinner and a progenitor by the death of a grown man, yet it can legally claim no compensation from the offender's patriclan either in services or supplies of food for the household, nor are any males transferred to membership of the bereaved *kepun*. The strong sentiments concerning fertility and peace within the *lejima*, as described later, appear to be responsible for the maintenance of

IX. *a*. A patriclan area in Idjiman ward

IX *b*. The *epundet* of Ibenda II. *Kepun* shrines are only regarded with reverence or awe on ritual occasions. On the right is the entrance to a closed compound of lineage kinsmen including the priest of the *epundet*

X *a*. Egbisum *kepun* house

X *b*. Egbisum *kepun* house interior. The upright stones surrounded by boulders are not the *kepun* shrine which is outside the house. Known as *Etaŋ* Egbisum, they are believed to have supernatural power and can be approached by any members of the *kepun*, but they are the special concern of one lineage whose head performs the rite. An ancestor of the lineage is believed to have established the cult. Similar subsidiary cults exist in many other *yepun*. The children are seated on one of the log benches and on the far side is the large slit gong beaten at funerary and other *kepun* rites

these practices, but there is nevertheless a lack of symmetry. The matrikin are given the emotional satisfaction of restitution but the patrikin are not, while in economic terms the matrilineal kin are over-compensated and the patrilineal kin remain without recompense. It is held that these obligations to the matrilineal kin of victims of homicide are not affected by close patrilineal kinship between the parties. The murder or killing of a half-brother, a son, or other *kepun* kinsman would involve restitution to the bereaved matrilineal kin in the ordinary way. On the other hand, no claim for compensation could arise from a killing that involved two men of the same matrilineal group.

Rights to inheritance of property, to aid in the accumulation of their marriage payments, and sometimes to succession in associations inevitably strengthen the ties between youths and their senior matrilineal relatives, and there is usually an intimate relation between a man and his sister's son—the classic relationship which cuts across parental ties in societies stressing matrilineal descent. And among the Yakö this relationship is often converted when opportunity arises into foster-fatherhood, with subsequent adoption of sisters' sons into the patriclan of the mother's brother.

RITUAL AND POLITICAL AUTHORITY OF MATRICLAN PRIESTS

Every matriclan is associated with a fertility spirit—*yose* (pl. *ase*). This is embodied in a miscellaneous set of cult objects, including decorated skulls, figurines, helices, and penannular rings of brass and copper and various pots, which are kept on an altar in a miniature house in the compound of the priest and arranged on an adjacent open-air altar at public rituals. The successive invocation of the fertility spirits at these shrines constitutes the central act of the village rituals at various stages in the farming year, and the *ase*, not the *yepundet*, spirits of the patriclans, are in native belief the spirits primarily active in maintaining the well-being of the village. Every girl is brought by a close matrilineal kinsman, usually an older brother or a mother's brother, to the shrine of the fertility spirit of her matriclan during her first pregnancy. Gifts and materials for an offering are brought on an appointed day when a rite is performed to safeguard her and her unborn child, a future member of the group. A corresponding ritual, in which the woman is accompanied by her father, is performed at her patriclan shrine, but is regarded as less powerful. The priests of the *ase*, each known as the *ina* (pl. *bi'ina*) of the spirit in question, e.g. *Ina Atalikumi*, have, in consequence of this greater ritual power, a prestige and authority superior to those of the priests of the patrilineal kin groups. This power of the *ase*, to which their priests alone have direct access, is the ritual sanction of authority in the wider field of social control in the village as a whole, which over-rides authority within the several patriclans. The *ase* priests are the nucleus and strength of a sacerdotal council in each village which has the power to invoke the destructive or beneficient actions of the spirits themselves, and thus commands the strongest supernatural sanctions in the village. (Plates XIX, XXIIIa and XXIVa)

Each is chosen from a certain matriclan and proposed by its elders but acts on behalf of every clan dependent on the spirit concerned. Although a close matrilineal relative of a former priest is considered most appropriate, succession is not rigidly prescribed. Choice usually falls not on one of the elders but on a man in early middle life and, although he is selected by the clan elders, he must be approved, and then instructed in his ritual duties, by the group of *ase* priests as a whole.

A priest should reflect in his own physical well-being, in the serenity of his temperament, and in his peaceable behaviour the beneficient power of the spirit, and he will usually ask the priest of another spirit to deputize for him if he is ailing or has suffered distress at the time of a ritual. If two or more priests of a single *yose* die in succession after only a few years of office, a notion of restoring life-maintaining power by infusing new blood into the priesthood comes into play. It is believed that a weakness revealed by the chain of misfortune can be overcome by selecting as a successor a son of a man of the matriclan, an *okpan*, that is, by breaking the rule of succession within a group of matrilineal kin. This may also occasionally be done apart from previous mis-fortunes, if a man, well fitted by physique and temperament on whom the clan elders and the *ase* priests are agreed, cannot be found within the group. A priest appointed in this way is ritually adopted into the *lejima* at his installation.

Although each priest carries out private rituals at his shrine for all persons of the matriclans concerned, the seasonal rites are conducted jointly by all the priests and for the village as a whole. In each village one of them is, as has been said, recognized as the

Leader of the Village (*Obot Lopon*), in virtue of his control of the cult of the premier spirit which is regarded as the fertility spirit of the village and the most powerful supernatural force within it. Selected from a single matrilineal kin group, he is as pre-eminent among the priests as is that spirit among the others and he is recognized as the religious head of the village.

This corporation of priests, known collectively as the Leaders (*Yabot*),[24] does not consist solely of the *Bi'ina* but the other members such as *Okpebri* (the village Speaker and prayer-leader in collective rituals) all belong to it in virtue of their appointment to ritual offices at the instance of the other priests. Its functions are not, however, restricted to ritual performances and the securing of supernatural benefits. It also guides village affairs, reaffirms customary law, and attempts to settle major disputes. In Umor the priest of *Odjokobi* is *Obot Lopon* and head of this council. His compound, known as *Lebokem*, is situated on one side of the village assembly square (*Keblapoŋa*), near the centre of the village and not in the territory of any patriclan or ward. In his compound at the *Odjokobi* shrine all the public rituals of the village are initiated and reach their climax and in it, too, the council assembles to discuss village affairs and to hear disputes that are brought before them.

The *Yabot* thus form a close-knit corporation whose members are linked to the rest of the village through the matriclan system. They are not representative of the patrilineal groups or of any territorial section. They are responsible for announcing the times at which many seasonal activities should begin, and for refusal to comply with their regulation of such activities they impose fines. They have authority both in civil disputes, where they serve as a court of appeal, and in public offences, for which they can impose fines and order expiation.[25] Disputes between persons and groups which cannot be settled by the arbitration of the elders of the kin

---

[24] The term *Obot* (pl. *Yabot*) can best be translated as Leader or Head, but its connotation varies with its context. Used alone in the plural it is usually understood to refer to the indigenous sacerdotal council of the village; the *kepun* heads are distinguished as *Yabot Yepun*. The same term is also, however, the title of two matrilineal groups from one of which the *Obot Lopon* is selected (see Table X, p. 105).

[25] The establishment first of a Warrant Chief's Court and more recently of Native Authority Councils and Courts in the Yakö area have reduced the judicial and executive authority of the *Yabot*, but civil disputes, especially those between kin groups, are brought to them and they still intervene against ritual offences. These governmental roles are more fully discussed in Chapter VI.

groups concerned, or by the ward heads in the larger villages, are taken to them by one or other of the contestants. They would also intervene on their own initiative to deal with public offences both secular and religious.[26] The *Yabot* command powerful sanctions to enforce their decisions. But only the supernatural sanctions lie in their own hands. They can refuse an offender and his close matrikin all access to the shrine of his matriclan spirit. More drastic is a ceremonial declaration of the offence to the *yose* and a request that the beneficence of the spirit be withdrawn from the offender and if need be from his *lejima*. By coming in procession and placing their staffs before the entrance to his compound or his house, they can forbid a person's entering or leaving the dwelling until the fine imposed for an offence has been paid. If their decisions are flouted one of the men's associations is authorized by them to despoil the offender and his close kin.

YAKPAN

It will be appreciated that, with the tracing of distinct lines of descent and the formation of groups of kin through father and son on the one hand and through mother and daughter on the other, every person will, through parents and children, have kin to whose lineal groups he or she will not themselves belong. Such will be the matrilineal kin of one's father and those of a man's children and the patrilineal kin of one's mother and those of a woman's children. The children's kin of the other group will, of course, be those with whom affinal ties were established for the parent at marriage, but the relation is felt as distinct from, or at least as a special reinforcement of, affinal ties as such. Because they are kin groups of one's own closest kin, mutual consideration and helpfulness second only to that expected between patrikin and matrikin is felt to be meet. A man can, for example, seek assistance from them or from the elders of their clans if he is in need of additional land to farm or of raphia supplies for house-building. More specifically both men and women are under obligation to visit and bring gifts at the funerals of members of these patri- and

[26] Their power of action in the public interest may be exemplified as follows: it is the duty of the Speaker acting on behalf of the *Yabot* to quell serious disorders arising from civil disputes and summon the offenders before them. Anyone alleged to have caused a fire in the village would be tried by the *Yabot* and if guilty pay them a fine of a cow and 10 brass rods. For abortion, as a grave ritual offence believed to impair fertility in the community as a whole through action of the *ase* spirits, they impose a fine of a cow which is sacrificed and eaten in a rite of expiation at the shrine of the offender's matriclan.

matriclans, occasions when many of them are assembled and sympathy and support can be expressed at a time of loss and grief. For this relation, as will be seen, the Yakö employ the specific and reciprocal term *okpan* (pl. *yakpan*). It is, it should be emphasized, not a relation within and between groups, but between a person and groups of kin to which he or she is individually linked by the cross-ties arising from patrilineal and matrilineal kinship.

THE TERMINOLOGY OF KINSHIP

The kinship terminology of the Yakö clearly expresses the dichotomy between matrilineal and patrilineal affiliation as well as the unity of the kin group so formed. But, save on formal (ritual or periodical) occasions and when there is emotional stress, kinsfolk below the grandparental generations are usually addressed by their personal names. The terms discussed here are therefore most frequently used for reference (see Fig. 11).

The terms used for parents (*uwo* = (my) father; *muka* = (my) mother)[27] may also be employed in a classificatory sense when referring to collateral kin of their generation, if they are of the same sex as well as the same lineage as the parent, i.e. to male patrikin and to female matrikin of this generation. Thus father and father's brother and father's father's brother's son are all referred to and may be addressed as *uwo*, but a mother's brother will not. Similarly, mother's sister and mother's mother's daughter will be called *muka*, but father's sister will not. These terms can also be extended to all men immediately senior in generation in one's patriclan and to all women senior in generation in one's matriclan.

Step-parents are not kin. Another wife of one's father is referred to as such, *yanen wuwo*, and a stepfather is known as *uwo keplaku* (father in daylight), a term which conveys the element of quasi-paternal authority and responsibility he may have as head of the domestic group.

A mother's brother, as are all men immediately senior in generation in one's matriclan, is *wenyaka wamuka* (child of mother of mother). A father's sister, like all women immediately senior in

[27] The terms for parents are as follows:

my, our father,	*uwo*,	—mother,	*muka*
thy, your father,	*awo*	,,	*aka*
his, their father,	*yate*,	,,	*yaka*
my, our fathers,	*buwo*,	—mothers,	*bamuka*
thy, your fathers	*bawo*,	,,	*ba'aka*
his, their fathers	*bəyate*,	,,	*bəyaka*

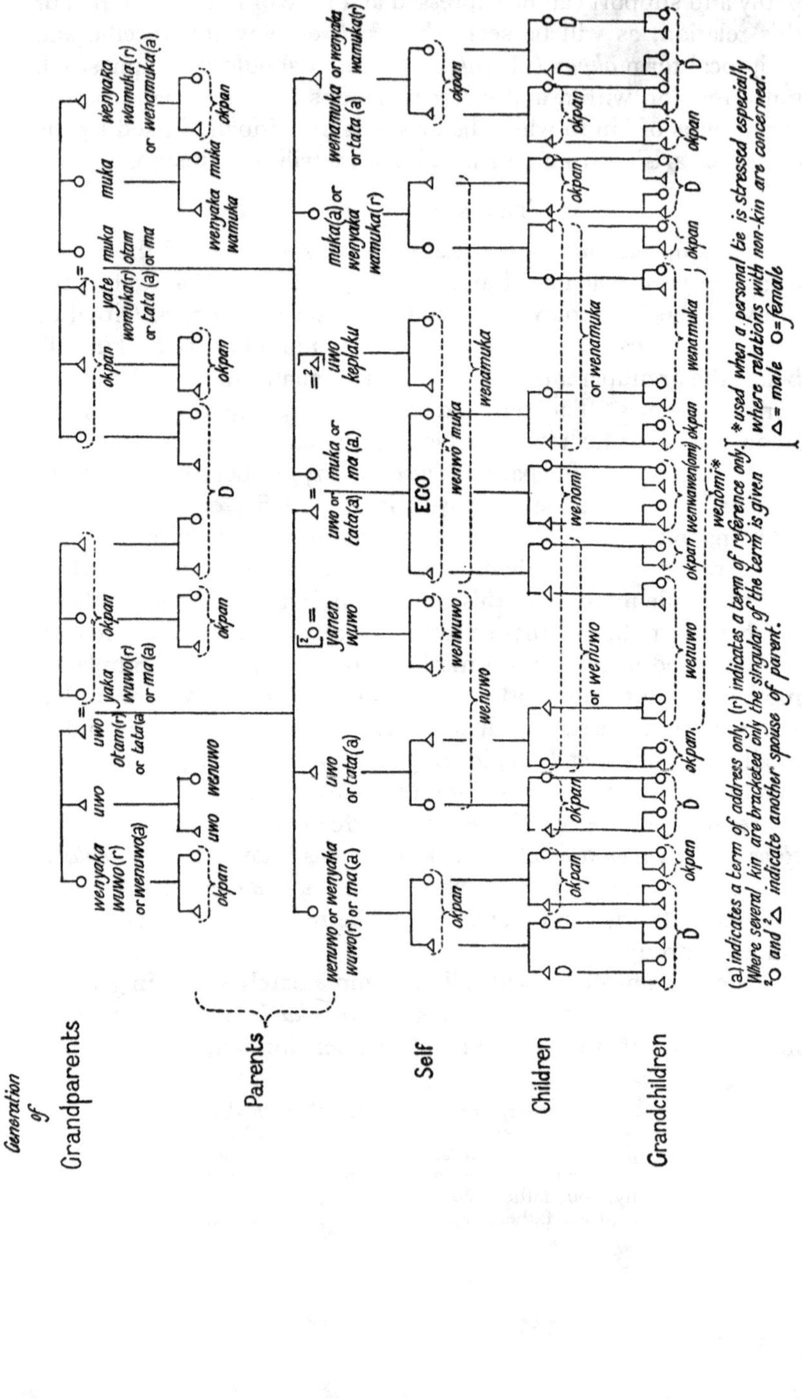

FIG. 11.—YAKÖ TERMS FOR KIN

generation in one's patriclan, is *wenyaka wuwo* (child of mother of father).

Among siblings the maternal link has precedence whereby full and maternal half-siblings are designated *wenwəmuka* (child of my mother, pl. *benbəmuka*), while only paternal half-siblings are called *wenwuwo* (child of my father, pl. *benbəwuwo*).

Patrikin and matrikin junior in generation are, however, merged and may be referred to individually and collectively by the term *wenomi* (pl. *benomi*) which is more specifically used for one's own child.

The paternal grandfather is called *uwo otam* (old father) and the maternal grandmother *muka otam* (old mother) The paternal grandmother may also be called *muka otam* if the grandchild has been much with her, but she is more usually addressed and is always referred to as father's mother (*yaka wuwo*), while the maternal grandfather, of whom a child usually sees little, is never referred to as 'old father', but always descriptively as mother's father (*yate womuka*). These terms are not, however, applied to other kin of the grandparents' generation. Those who are male patrikin and female matrikin are merged with the father's and mother's generation as *buwo* and *bamuka* respectively; female patrikin and male patrikin are addressed and referred to by terms which stress lineage membership but ignore generation level, while only descriptive terms, or in some cases a reciprocal term (see below), are applied to those belonging to neither of one's own lineages. Here, again, the patrilineal and matrilineal ties are emphasized throughout.

One's own grandchild is called *wenwawen* (*omi*)—child of (my) child—without distinction between children of sons and those of daughters, although they will be members of different patri- and matriclans. But this term is not extended to collaterals of this generation; the latter as kin junior in generation may, as indicated above, be merged with the generation of one's children as *wenomi*. But they may also be referred to according to affiliation by the merging terms for patrikin, for matrikin, or for the members of one's father's matri- or mother's patrikin (see below).

More inclusive classificatory terms which further ignore generation differences are more usually employed in referring to unilineal kin outside the elementary family. They are *wenuwo* (pl. *benuwo*), which refers to all members of the patriclan, and *wenamuka* (pl.

benamuka), which correspondingly refers to all matrikin. These terms are not, however, applied individually to one's own father, paternal grandfather, or grandchild, or to one's own siblings, children, mother, or maternal grandmother, save when included in a wider group of unilineal kin. They combine the roots for child and father, and child and mother respectively, but are, it should be noted, distinct from those used specifically for siblings—*wenwə-muka* and *wenwuwo*—given earlier.

A single reciprocal term (*okpan*, pl. *yakpan*) is used to express the kinship ties between a person and the father's matrikin, the mother's patrikin, the matrikin of a man's children, and the patrikin of a woman's children, i.e. the members of the unilineal groups to which one's parents or children belong but to which one does not belong oneself. Thus, if ego's father is a member of the Yanyə matriclan, ego is an *okpan* of Yanyə, and they are *yakpan* to him. If his mother was born in Anedja patriclan, he is also an *okpan* of Anedja and they are *yakpan* to him.

The patrikin, matrikin, and the two sets of *yakpan* comprise all the persons who are grouped together under broad classificatory terms. There is no single word for kin as such and remote cognates who fall outside these classes can be and are designated when occasion arises only by compound descriptive terms which state the genealogical links (D in Fig. 11). They are, like other persons, addressed by their proper names. The terms applying to wide classes of kin are not customarily used in address, since, as mentioned above, both patrilineal and matrilineal kin other than own parents and grandparents are addressed by personal names usually prefixed, in the case of those senior in generation, by the terms *tata* (for men) and *ma* (for women). These last terms like *wen* (child) are expressive of generation difference rather than of descent itself and may be used in addressing all elders.

In addition to the terms for parents, children, siblings, grandparents, and the classificatory terms for the various groups of unilineal kin to which a person is related, descriptive terms are also employed to designate the kinship links between persons by combining the roots for child (*wen*), the father (*yate*), or the mother (*yaka*). To these may be added where required an indication of the mode of descent: borne by (a female)—*womani*—or begotten by (a male)—*wəmponi*—together with the sex of a person: male—*wodo'-odəm*, or female—*wodəyanen*, compounded from the terms *odəm* (male) and *yanen* (female) plus kin. In these fuller descriptive terms, precedence is again given to matrilineal descent in that the maternal link is used where, as among full siblings, there is both a matrilineal and a patrilineal relation. We have seen that children of one mother, whether full or half-siblings, are all *wenwəmuka* to one another, while only paternal half-brothers and sisters are *wenwuwo*. Similarly, where a relationship between patrilineal kin is to be more precisely indicated by the use of a descriptive term, the link is traced back to the mother, not to the father of the siblings from whom they are respectively descended. Thus a father's sister is designated *wenyaka wuwo wodoyanen* (child of mother of father: female). Grandchildren can be distinguished as *wenwa-wenwəmponi* (child of child I begot) by a grandfather and *wenwa-wenwomani* (child of child I bore) by a grandmother. They too may be differentiated in sex as *wodo'odəm* (male) and *wodəyanen* (female).[28]

MARRIAGE AND AFFINAL RELATIONS

It will already be appreciated that marriage, with the establishment of a new household and family, is the concern of several distinct sets of relatives, of the matrikin and patrikin of the husband and those of the wife. In addition to the direct affinal relations of each spouse with kin of his or her partner, certain of these relatives also undertake obligations to one another. But the roles of the matrilineal kin of the husband and those of the wife are not symmetrical. The domiciliary factor, with patrilineal succession to house sites and land, is dominant on the husband's side and his patrikin are most concerned in the marriage. His children will be members of his patriclan but not of his matriclan. On the woman's side, however, the dominant aspects both of fertility and of the responsibility accepted in receiving marriage payments are felt to be preponderantly a concern of the matrilineal kin. Her children will be members of her matriclan, they will be the matrilineal successors and heirs of her brothers—her own mother's sons. The links of the children with her patriclan will, like their links with their father's matriclan, be limited to occasional acts of kindness and the ceremonial expression of friendship and sympathy due from them as *yakpan*.

---

[28] A full list of terms and the contexts of their uses have been given in 'Kinship in Umor', *Amer. Anth.* vol. 41, 1939, Appendix I, pp. 550–3. Affinal terms are discussed later; see p. 129.

During betrothal and the marriage ceremonies, indeed until she actually takes up residence in her husband's dwelling-area, which is generally subsequent to the birth of her first child, a wife has little contact with and no formal obligations to her husband's patrikin. Later, when resident with the patriclan of her husband and children, she is likely to be a close neighbour of her father- and brothers-in-law with whom she will in favourable circumstances be on easy terms, being treated as a daughter and sister. Apart from her mother-in-law, she has much less to do with her husband's matrikin, although these will be *yakpanen* (*yakpan* people) of her children.

For a man, on the other hand, the affinal relation of major significance is that with one or more of his wife's senior male matrikin. During the betrothal he is as a suitor dependent on the goodwill of his future wife's parents. But once the marriage payments have been accepted and, more particularly, when his wife has come to live with him, it is her mother's brother, or one of her own elder brothers acting in his place, who, as her closest senior matrikinsman, takes responsibility should serious disputes arise and the marriage be threatened or actually dissolved.[29]

During the period of betrothal (*keplɔ kesi*) before the first marriage of a girl, which may last from one to two years, the suitor is obliged to perform specific services for his prospective bride and her parents and to make them gifts. He will be asked to help and to bring his age-mates to assist in any considerable tasks that the father-in-law undertakes, such as the lifting and tying of yams at harvest, building and repairing houses. And it was formerly customary not only to bring the future father-in-law a daily calabash of palm-wine but also to carry water for the mother-in-law, a task which otherwise is woman's work. During the annual new yam rites, at the time when parents give special food and ornaments to their children, a suitor should make gifts not only to his betrothed but also to her parents.

In the ceremonials and exchanges of marriage itself there are no direct relations between the kinsfolk of the bride and those of the groom. Indeed, a most remarkable feature of Yakö marriage ceremonial is the emphasis on the relations of the chief participants each to their own friends or age-set mates, who need not be

---

[29] For an account and fuller analysis of betrothal and marriage see my *Marriage and the Family among the Yakö in South-Eastern Nigeria.*

and often are not kin, and the lack of emphasis on their relations to either kinship groups or particular circles of kinsfolk as such.

Apart from later rituals at her matriclan and patriclan shrines, when the bride is pregnant, the clans of the bride and the groom have no corporate relation to the marriage ceremonies. The patriclans of the bride and groom have an interest in maintaining the exogamic rule which would be sustained by the intervention of their Heads if an infraction was threatened, but they otherwise take no corporate action concerning the marriage. Nor does the matrilineage of the bride, although it has, as will be seen, an interest in the maintenance of the marriage once established, participate in its ceremonial recognition. It is only after the last wedding feasts which the bride's parents severally give to their own personal friends, particularly their age-mates, that her father should go, or send a message to, his wife's brother as the closest senior male among the matrilineal relatives of the bride, informing him that the wedding feasts have been concluded, that the marriage payment has been made, and that he is ready to hand over the customary portion to him.

In considering the provision of the marriage payment (*libeman,* marriage money), which formerly consisted mainly of brass rods, but is now, apart from a few token rods, handed over in Nigerian currency, a distinction must be made between the first marriage of a youth and the later marriages of older men. For the latter the responsibility for payment is usually entirely the husband's, although he may often borrow from matrikin. But for his first marriage, while labour services are made by the youth himself, his father normally takes the main responsibility, although his mother's brothers and often more distant kin on both sides will make contributions varying according to the individual circumstances. If the mother's brother is the foster-father of the groom he replaces the father as the main contributor. The marriage payment should properly be handed over by age-mates, i.e. age-set friends, of the groom to the father or foster-father of the bride when she returns to the village after the clitoridectomy rite which should form part of the marriage ceremonies. Frequently only a portion of the payment is transferred on this occasion and the balance is later handed over informally in a number of instalments. By the wife's father and mother's brother the marriage money is regarded as provided by the husband. It is he, not his father or any other kinsman, who claims its return and the fact that it is the groom himself who offers it is emphasized in the transfer.

Transfers involved in marriage payments are not directly reciprocal between the households or kinsmen involved. A father receives for his daughter much less than he gives for his son. A mother's brother receiving for a bride does not give correspondingly for her brothers. There is no doubt that it is the transfer of the *libeman* which gives the husband legal rights to his wife's services and to the social fatherhood of the children born to her during the marriage. The retention of a portion of the marriage money by the father, like its initial transfer by the groom to him, is not regarded by the Yakö as an indemnity for any economic value of a daughter. It is to be explained by the fact of paternal authority in the household. A father has the established right to control the domicile of his unmarried children. No daughter may go or be removed from his household and parental authority without his consent. The acceptance of the marriage money and the retention of a portion of it mark the curtailment of the father's parental authority and signify his consent to his daughter's departure from his household. His share of the marriage payment is a consideration for that consent.

But the husband is securing at marriage not merely the curtailment of paternal authority over the bride. He is also placing the bride under a positive obligation to perform certain services. Should she fail, compensation cannot be secured from the bride herself and the obligation to return the marriage money to the husband devolves not on the father but on those who in Yakö law have responsibility for ensuring the fulfilment or compensation of all personal obligations, namely, the matrilineal kin. It is on account of this potential obligation that a matrilineal kinsman is considered entitled to receive from the father the greater part of the payment. It should be observed that the obligation to return what was received relates to the whole of the marriage money, including the portion retained by the father. That the kinsman who undertakes it and in consequence receives the greater part of the marriage money should be the mother's brother is consonant with the Yakö principle of matrilineal transmission. As the closest matrilineal kinsman senior in generation to the wife, compensation would be claimed from him if she should fail in her marital obligations, while her matrilineal brothers are successors both to this obligation and to the property of the mother's brother.[30]

Thus the Yakö marriage payment is variously related to the several interests involved. It expresses the value of a wife to her husband and confirms his intention to maintain a stable union. It rewards the bride's father for the renunciation of his parental authority while establishing his consent and that of the matrilineal kin to the assertion of marital rights by the husband. It reinforces the responsibility of matrilineal kin for ensuring that the wife shall fulfil her marital obligations by giving the closest senior matrilineal kinsman of the bride a pecuniary obligation with regard to her good conduct.[31]

The relations of a widow to her deceased husband's kin depend on whether she has grown sons. There is neither leviratic marriage nor widow inheritance and a widow, if she is young, is free to remarry where she and her own kin wish. Only if she is widowed while suckling a child has she a right to remain for any length of time in her late husband's compound and to be given farming facilities by one of his patrikin. She may or may not prefer to join her parents or other relatives, but in any case she cannot remarry until she is ready to wean the child; she is therefore dependent on either the late husband's or her own relatives for farming facilities and food-supplies. On the other hand, a widow has no claim to the

[30] The customary obligation of the bride's father to hand over the greater part of the marriage payment to her mother's brother or other close matrilineal relative has, as already mentioned, been increasingly disregarded in recent years, and in a third of the cases in a sample studied it was all retained by the father or someone acting in his place. This was particularly common where the father was a rich man (osu, pl. yasu), and was not a matter of cupidity but rather an assertion of paternal authority and also of wealth and independence. For a mother's brother can rely on his matrilineal kinsmen to assist him in providing the means of returning a marriage payment, but a father cannot, since the marriage is not the concern of the father's matrilineal kin; nor do his daughter's children belong to his patrilineage. Thus a father who retains the marriage payment faces the possibility of having to refund a large part of it, perhaps many years later, entirely from his own resources: a risk a poor man would be more reluctant to assume.

[31] The role of mother's brother in relation to a girl's marriage and other juridical and ritual obligations should properly be assumed by the senior among the brothers (including maternal half-brothers) of the mother, and where there is no true brother the senior matrikinsman in the senior collateral line should act. But, while this is fairly strictly adhered to in ritual contexts, in situations requiring personal initiative and responsibility the rights and duties may be assumed by a younger brother or other matrikinsman who, through personality or possessions, has greater prestige. Thus marriage payments are not infrequently nowadays handed over by the mother's eldest brother to a wealthier junior who is more ready to accept the contingent responsibility for repayment.

livestock and personal possessions of her late husband, although she may, at the distribution of his goods during the funeral rites, be given a cloth, and a few other small objects by the matrilineal relative of her husband who is the chief heir. A young widow usually remarries within a year or two. She leaves her late husband's compound after the harvest following his death and joins the household of either her parents or a senior matrikinsman. On the other hand, an older widow who has adult sons living in the patriclan area, and usually in the same compound as her late husband, will often remain there and join the household and farming unit of one of her sons, who is, of course, her close matrilineal kinsman.

It is rare for a man to take the initiative in divorcing a wife, but if he determines to do so he informs her parents and the matrikinsman who received the marriage money that she must go. As a last resort he will refuse to admit her to his farm in the coming year. But, unless the woman's conduct has been outrageous, the husband forgoes all claim to a return of the marriage payments and the woman is free to marry elsewhere. Divorces arise far more frequently from the voluntary departure of the wife from her husband's compound, and the husband then becomes entitled to a return of his marriage payment. If she goes to live with another man, her new mate becomes liable, not only for the payment of damages to the husband on account of the adultery, but also for refunding to her matrilineal kinsman the amount of the marriage payment which the latter is required to restore to the husband. When, and only when, this payment has been made, is the divorce accepted and the adulterer recognized as a second husband. In recent years, however, deserted husbands, finding it difficult to obtain payment from the wives' matrikin, have been successfully making claims before the *Yabot* and the Native Authority courts for direct recompense by the men with whom their wives have gone to live. If several children have been born, the husband is considered entitled to a return of only a portion of the original marriage payment, usually little more than half. A wife is rarely prevented on divorce from taking young children with her, but she is not always allowed to take older boys and the husband often insists that young sons shall return to him when they reach puberty.

Some aspects of the relations between spouses have been indicated earlier. It is also important to emphasize in connection with their several relations with affines, that outside the wife's house, and to a lesser extent the farm, a man and wife are rarely found together as companions. Not only are men and wives separated in their memberships of productive groups such as age-set path-clearing parties and farm-working parties, as well as of ritual groups including cult associations, but they also tend to remain apart in both ceremonial and recreational activities. The feasts at a Yakö wedding are given by the bride's father to his friends and by her mother to hers. They are not joint feasts given by the parents to common friends of both sexes. A similar alinement is found in Yakö funerary ritual. There is co-operation between men and wives in ceremonial activities, but they do not constitute a couple in relation to others. This separation extends to minor economic activities, even to those of a strictly household character. Thus it is very unusual to see a man and wife walking together on a bush path to their farm. Wives go alone or in parties of neighbouring women; husbands likewise go independently or with their friends. On the farm itself each is usually engaged in separate tasks, sometimes with the aid of friends of the same sex. In the preparation of oil-palm products husbands and wives each carry out separate customary operations; a husband will get one or more kinsmen, age-mates or youths of his patriclan, but not his wife, to help him pound fruits in the great log mortar. He, on the other hand, does not take part in boiling the fruit or skimming the oil, while cracking nuts to extract kernels is a woman's task and the kernels are the wife's reward for her share in the work.

Old couples, on the other hand, often do much of their work in common and some depend greatly on each other for companionship; they are, for example, found sitting together at funeral and marriage feasts where the sexes are otherwise segregated. By this time the man usually has only one surviving wife and she needs assistance in all stages of the farm work. The age-mates with whom he might otherwise spend his lesiure will be few, while his wife after the menopause will not be excluded from groups of men or male secular activities.

A wife can place no legal restriction on the sexual activities of her husband, but he is entitled to claim monetary compensation from a man with whom she has committed adultery, to divorce her, and receive back the marriage money.

Wives in a polygynous household are not formally graded in

status according to seniority in marriage or age and there is similarly no fixed opinion concerning the relative desirability of becoming a first or a later wife. It is probable that the majority of
young girls prefer to wed youths who are marrying for the first
time, but this appears to be associated rather with the pleasures of
courtship and the claim at that time on the exclusive attention of
the bridegroom than with any conventional or personal attitude to
post-marital status. A man's later wives may, since they are often
divorcees or widows, be junior only in order of marriage and not in
age-set or years. To be a man's first wife by no means implies therefore that a woman will always be the senior in age or the most
experienced woman in the compound, nor does it confer any authority over the other wives. The relations among co-wives range
widely from companionable equality to hostility or considerable
domination, but these depend on differences not of formal status
but of personality and prestige.

The pattern of personal relations between affinal relatives does
not appear to be specific among the Yakö. Towards their parents-
in-law both man and wife behave in general as they would to senior
kinsfolk, and the considerable variations in the degree of intimacy
and sympathy between affines appears to depend on the tempera-
mental qualities of the persons involved. Sexual relations with an
affinal relative are regarded as highly improper, but most informants said that there was no specific penalty for it because it would
not occur, and I did not in fact encounter any instance in marital
histories, court records, or discussions of sexual irregularities.

During the period of betrothal and in the early months of
marriage a man may become an intimate of his wife's parents'
household. He may talk freely to and before his mother-in-law,
who will give him food and ask him for gifts. There is neither
avoidance nor any exceptional intimacy. A man may, if there is
need and relations are good, continue to give his father-in-law
occasional help in farm-clearing, house-building, and other work
after he has taken his wife to live with him in the area of his own
kepun. But apart from funeral gifts and annual New Yam gifts, a
husband has few personal relations with his parents-in-law after
his wife has come to live with him. Although his wife will frequently go there, he rarely visits his father-in-law's compound and
then only on a definite errand. If a wife misbehaves or deserts her
husband, it is only when the father is known to have a preponder-

XI *a*. Pillar in Ukpakapi
ward square, Umor
(damaged by fire)

XI *b*. Rite of Ward Leaders before the burial of one of their members

XII *a*. *Ebiabu* dance leaders

XII *b*. Masked dancers of *Leko*

ant influence and especially if he has retained the marriage payment, that he, rather than a mother's brother, is approached.

A wife has normally more frequent contact with her parents-in-
law than a husband has. The wife–father-in-law relation often
becomes one of considerable affection. A man may frequently be
seen gossiping in his daughter-in-law's house. A young wife may
also be asked by her mother-in-law to help in a farm or compound
task and will generally be ready to do so, but such help is an
expression of regard not an obligatory service. But a wife's relations with her parents-in-law may range from the warm friendliness of quasi-parentage to open hostility in which a wife will speak
vituperatively to and about her mother-in-law. A man is usually
benevolent towards his son's wife, but Yakö regard the relation
between a wife and her mother-in-law who is also her close neighbour as a difficult one, and if the two are not mutually sympathetic,
a man will take care to keep his farming and household activities
strictly separate from those of his father. On the other hand,
although her own mother can freely visit a wife to assist in household emergencies and should always be present at a birth, the
mother-in-law is also expected to advise and assist in the care of
her son's children, who are among her closest *yakpanen*, and it is
in this situation that friction often develops.

There are no specific terms for affinal relatives who are referred
to by descriptive terms; thus a man's father-in-law is *yatewəyanenomi* (father of my wife), a sister's husband is *odəmwawenwamuka*
(husband of the child of my mother). Parents-in-law are addressed
as *Tata* . . . or *Ma* . . ., and a mother-in-law may even be called
muka (my mother) where relations are cordial, while a man often
speaks of a favoured son-in-law as *wenomi* (my child). The wife's
brother who is the matrilineal guardian of a man's children is not
verbally distinguished from other members of the wife's matriclan,
who are known as *wenyaka wəyanenomi* (mother's child of my
wife). The wife's mother's brother who is trustee for the marriage
payment may, however, where the wife's father is dead, be
referred to as wife's father (*yatewəyanenomi*). His status in relation
to the marriage is ceremonially emphasized by token presents of a
yam and palm-wine made to him at the time when gifts are made
to children and between betrothed couples during the annual
New Yam rites.

CONCLUSION: THE DUAL SENTIMENTS OF KINSHIP

This account of the patterns of those personal and group relations among the Yakö which are conceived in terms of kinship ties will have made clear the manner and extent to which the individual is led through childhood and adult life to accept very distinct obligations according to the nature of the bonds of kinship and affinity. The ideas of right and wrong concerning attitudes and actions towards various groups and classes of kin, which are inculcated in each generation, constitute established norms by which individual conduct is judged. But these in turn rest on more general sentiments which are not maintained by kinship behaviour itself, or by exhortations to right conduct. These sentiments, the nature and conditions of which the anthropologist slowly and vaguely perceives amid the welter of heterogeneous events, emerge clearly only from an analysis of the forms in which they find expression in various contexts over the whole range of social life. They may find emphatic and verbal expression in rituals and social crises, but they can only be fully defined and assessed in relation to the culture as a whole. These underlying attitudes have sustained the kinship system of the Yakö and maintained its general structure by providing its axiomatic foundations in thought and feeling. It is only possible to indicate them in outline here and to make some prediction as to the outcome of present trends.

The striking problem presented by the Yakö system lies in the strength of matrilineal bonds despite the virtual absence of continuous association and frequent co-operation among matrilineal kin and in the presence of such close association and co-operation among patrilineal kin. Men who are patrikin live together, jointly control and utilize tracts of land for farming, collecting, and dwellings. A growing son works for several years on his father's farm plots and collects materials for him and the household. Brothers and patrilineal cousins help each other in farm tasks and have first claim to the use of lands formerly held by their fathers and grandfathers. In manhood brothers will often share a man's house in the same compound. Brothers may and do quarrel. There are jealousies and disputes among them and between sections of patrilineages and clans over rights of succession. But these are disputes, within a framework of habitual co-operation and collective rights, among those who should, and have many inducements to, live and work together.

When, however, we turn to the matrilineal relations, we find no such foundation in the routine of daily life, in the organization of essential production for livelihood, in ties of neighbourhood. The rights and obligations of matrilineal kinship are validated on a different plane. Practical assistance to matrilineal kin, the rights of a matrilineal kinsman such as a mother's brother, and above all the authority of a priest of a matrilineal clan, are linked not with the technical and economic advantages of co-operation and organization in practical affairs nor with inevitable and frequent daily contact and need for adjustment. They are associated, as becomes plain in common speech and in rituals, with mystical ideas concerning the perpetuation and tranquillity of the Yakö world. Central among these are the mysteries of fertility, health, and peace. The fertility and well-being of crops and beasts as well as man, peace between persons and in the community at large, are deeply felt to be associated with and passed on through women. It is by a wife that offspring are produced; it is from one's mother that one's life comes. The children of one mother are bound to mutual support and conciliation. The children of one's mother's sisters are part of one's own lifestream and this extends backward and forward through mothers and daughters. Thus the matrilineage is held together by mystical bonds of common fertility and within it anger and violence are gravely sinful. These sentiments are expressed and reinforced in the cult of the matriclan spirits, whose priests are ritually given the qualities of women—by the rite of chipping and blackening the teeth which is normally the mark of adult status, of wifehood and motherhood, for women. They are also the source of concepts of specific obligation which cut across the patrilineal ties and ordain mutual helpfulness and protection among matrikin despite their segregation in scattered and often opposed patriclans.

Matrilineal bonds can, as we have seen, provide a means of compensating and even replacing patrilineal ties which fail to meet particular needs and difficulties. A young man can be adopted into his mother's brother's lineage and clan. His mother's brother and other matrikin will assist him when resources within his own patriclan are lacking. Further, the organization of ultimate authority in the village in terms of the religious sanctions deriving from the matriclan spirits curbs the rivalry and potential conflict of the patriclans or the wards in which they are grouped. All this is not, however, thought out by the Yakö as a reason for, or justification of, a dual reckoning of descent. For them paternity and maternity contain inherently the different qualities from which flow the rights, obligations, and benefits, both practical and spiritual, which have been outlined.

The same sentiments are, as has been seen, operative with less intense expression at a further remove. One owes and expects consideration and helpfulness in relation to those kinsfolk of one's parents and one's children to whom one is thus linked, even though one does not belong to their patri- or matri-lines of descent. The matrikin of the father and those of a man's son are, for example, extensions of his own self. Their mourning is therefore one's own mourning, and where need arises they should help and be helped. For the Yakö they stand in the special position of *yakpanen*.

These sentiments underlying kinship are, however, being variously affected by the impact of Western trade and administration. The growth of trade in palm-oil and kernels and in imported goods has resulted in the emergence of trading as a specialist occupation. The more adventurous young men can obtain cash incomes for a period before their farming responsibilities become heavy. They are often dependent on an older man, but he may be a substantial trader who is not a kinsman, and where a young man works with or for an older kinsman, a father or a paternal or maternal uncle or an elder brother, the ties and obligations are personal. Individual aptitudes, training, and experience for these new activities are coming to the fore. The solidarity of siblings and of the patrilineage, and the ties between a man and his mother's brother have been weakened by this growing financial independence and differentiation among young men.

At the same time wealth in movable goods, which formerly passed matrilineally, has come to loom larger in Yakö economy. The prestige associated with a large yam farm maintaining a large compound household has shrunk in comparison with that of stocks of cloth, new-style furnishings, and above all accumulations of currency. And status in the organization of the farming economy, as a road elder, as a leader in patrilineage and patriclan affairs concerning both internal and external arrangements for the allocation of farming land, has accordingly declined relatively to the possession and display of wealth in imported goods and to holdings of currency with which services and favours can be bought and children sent to school. Sons and other patrikin are challenging with increasing success the rights of sisters' sons to succeed to such wealth. The matrilineal bonds are being sapped from within in the economic sphere of inheritance.

The superposition of the colonial administration on the indigenous political system has, largely unwittingly, weakened matrilineal ties at the opposite end of the social system. The 'warrant chiefs' recognized in the first phase, although they were often at the outset unofficial nominees of the village council in which succession was matrilineal or subject to the matriclan priests, came, in the exercise of their new duties and powers as agents of Government, to act as independent and alternative sources of internal political power. Although the Yakö seem originally to have thought and acted as if the two spheres, that of internal control of their own affairs and that of adjustment to the requirements and instructions of Government, were independent, the latter has progressively encroached. The Native Court and later the Native Authority were not only 'official' but possessed of physical sanctions backed by Government, while the ultimate physical sanctions which the indigenous village council could formerly invoke became subject to challenge or prohibition in the Native Court.

The prestige and powers of the village councils did not, of course, suddenly collapse, for the pressure of westernization and external administrative action has grown but gradually. The sacerdotal council is still significant, but its power has been subjected to frequent piecemeal erosion. There is rather the general sense that in the last resort on any major issue an innovation has a good chance of being upheld by the administration and any customary declaration of the council of being overruled. Custom is an ageing king, and with the weakening of their real power the matrilineal basis of the old village councils is itself losing its binding force.

Christian ideas and injunctions are beginning to undermine the influence of the rituals of the matriclan priests. Again not rapidly or dramatically, for although mission chapels and elementary classes conducted by visiting African pastors have been established in the larger villages, the numbers of seriously professing Christians in the thirties were still few and by no means all who sent their children to the school to learn to read and write showed interest in either the ethics or the dogmatic teaching of the missions. But there are those who hold the rituals to be savage customs and declare that they should be stopped or boycotted. Moreover Western attitudes in the sphere of morals by no means come only directly from the mission church or school for, though visits of Europeans to the Yakö villages are few and usually brief, African residents, including Yakö, who have gone afield, who know and can expatiate impressively on European ways, are a growing force.

Gradually, therefore, but cumulatively in the spheres of economics, politics, and religion the bonds of matrilineal kinship and the role of the matrikin groups are being reduced. The dogmatic principle that children of one mother and the children, notably the sons, of a man's sisters, have a special bond and are entitled to specific rights not shared by sons is being challenged, not only directly and indirectly by the European bias towards patriliny, but also by the economic and political processes of westernization.

Patrilineal ties might appear not to be affected in this way and even to be reinforced, but reinforcement is effective only within a narrow span. The tie between father and son may often be strengthened, but solidarity with collateral patrikin is weakening in the fields of new wealth and political power. Patriclan and patrilineage remain miniature corporations within the wider village community, since residence and the production of food and cash crops are organized in the old way and there is no serious shortage of land. And politically collective action is encouraged, for the patriclans now have their representatives in the Native Authority Council and Court, but the expression of patriclan solidarity is being cast in a more territorial idiom. As occasion prompts men move their dwellings from one place to another far more easily than they did. Locality as such and individual aptitudes are playing a greater part than a generation ago, and the stress on kinship as the ground for duties and rights outside the family is weaker and more uncertain.

V

WARD ORGANIZATION*

UMOR was, in 1935, exceptionally large for a single compact
community, having a population of nearly 11,000. Ekuri
had over two-thirds of this, Ŋkpani and Ŋko were smaller,
but only Idomi remained at less than 2,000. All the Yakö villages
except Idomi are divided territorially into wards (*yekpatu*, sing.
kekpatu) with populations of from 1,500 up to more than 3,500
in one case.[1]

A ward consists of the adjacent dwelling-areas (*yikəma*, sing.
lekəma) of about half a dozen patriclans (*yepun*, sing. *kepun*).
Some of the patriclans in a ward may have traditions of ultimate
common descent, but this is exceptional and in no sense a sanction
for membership of the same ward. There is no ancestor cult
among the Yakö and there is no stress on remote origin or its
genealogical expression. Indeed, on division, one of the segments
of a patriclan has usually sought a dwelling site and also farming
lands in another ward.[2] Marriage is virilocal and rights to house
sites and farmland are held and transmitted patrilineally by
men, so that the men of a patriclan grow up together and establish
their households in close proximity. Thus, although a Yakö village
appears as a continuous spread of compounds, separated only by
narrow alley-ways, each ward has its assembly place, or square,
for meetings, rites, and festivals, on which most of the alley-ways

---

* Reprinted from *Africa*, XX, 4, 1950, pp. 267–89.
[1] The estimated population of the four wards in the village of Umor in 1935
(based on a total count of adult males and a sample household composition of
two patriclans) was as follows (figures rounded to nearest 100 and 10):

Idjiman Ward	(11 patriclans, total	2,700	adult men	470
Idjum Ward	9 ,,	,,	3,800	,,	620
Ukpakapi Ward	5 ,,	,,	2,400	,,	390
Biko-Biko Ward	6 ,,	,,	2,000	,,	320
Total			10,900		1,760

The number of adult males in the component patriclans ranged from 50 to
180 with the majority having somewhat less than 100. The villages of Ekuri and
Ŋkpani consist each of three wards with a similar range of population.
[2] See Chapter III, p. 61.

converge. As will be seen, much of the secular life outside the patrilineage and clan is organized within the ward, and the layout of compounds, alley-ways, and meeting-place has been adapted to this end. Near the centre of the ward square there is a massive pillar (*əbagbə*) carved from an iroko trunk and surrounded by boulders.[3] At its foot protective rites are carried out seasonally and at times of crisis and all dancers performing in the square pour a libation of palm-wine into the ceremonial pot which is placed there. Along one side of the ward square another forest tree of smaller girth but 20–30 feet long is laid on the ground and covered with a long thatched shelter to provide a bench for the Ward Leaders and others on ceremonial occasions (Plate XI).

From the ward square one or two paths lead more or less directly to the village centre and to the adjacent sites for village rituals and assemblies. Here is the large compound of the Village Head (*Obot Lopon*) whose office, as the ritually premier member of a council of village priests, is primarily sacerdotal. The ritual duties of these priests and their moral authority centre on the cult of a series of fertility spirits each of which is accessible to one or more dispersed matriclans (*yajima*, sing. *lejima*). For, as described more fully elsewhere,[4] every Yakö is, by a principle of double descent, affiliated through the mother to a matrilineal group of real and putative kin simultaneously with the patrilineal affiliation to a *kepun*. The members of a matriclan, men as well as women, are dispersed through the village but each has its recognized Leaders (*yajimonotam*, sing. *ojimanotam*), and from some of them—those accepted as ritually senior in a cluster of matriclans—is selected the priest who intercedes with the spirit whose cult they observe. The Village Head is the priest of the premier matriclan spirit and the custodian of its shrine, which, through the priest, is made accessible to all in the village who are free from grave impiety or wrongdoing.

Outside the patriclan, status in the village is established for the ordinary man in the first instance within the framework of his ward, not in the village as a whole. Every few years, in the early

---

[3] In Umor these pillars were destroyed or badly damaged in a great fire in the twenties and have not been restored. The carvings, which are similar on all the pillars, represent a woman with a child across her knees and a number of crocodiles (*efem*) and iguanas (*krite*). Prayers are offered at the pillars to the creator sky god (*obasi*) by a diviner in each ward (see Plate XIa).

[4] See Chapter IV.

dry season after the harvest (December–January), boys of the ward who have reached 6 or 7 years of age since the previous occasion are initiated into the male community of the ward in a ritual known as *Ligwomi*. In Umor, where there are four wards, *Ligwomi* is normally performed on successive years by each ward in rotation so that it recurs every four years in each ward. Until he is initiated a boy is not regarded as a male; he is not distinguished socially from a girl-child and his parents should see that he keeps the same taboos as women and in particular that he is not given meat from feasts of men's organizations (Plate XV*b*).

In the morning of the *kokə*[5] (non-farming) day appointed for *Ligwomi*, the young boys of the ward are brought by their fathers or by other patrikinsmen to the assembly house of the patriclan of the *Ogbolia* (Ward Head) where the Leaders of the ward (*Yakambən*), 20 to 30 in number, have assembled, and two of them, the *Yawuna* (Singers), have donned masks and costumes to represent the Spirits of the ward (*Yakowa*), one male and one female. The Leaders are seated in a semicircle close behind the crouched figures of the *Yakowa*, with the *Ogbolia* and his deputy, *Ogometu*, in the centre. The boys with their sponsors assemble at the other end of the assembly house and are brought up one at a time to stand before the masked figures. Each boy carries the customary gift of a brass rod which his father takes from him and hands to the *Ogbolia* over the heads of the crouched *Yakowa*. He also places on the ground the customary offering of food, a small pot of palm-wine and a slice of cooked yam garnished with cooked leaves.

Ogbolia then tells the boy to place his right hand on the male *Okowa*, pointing to it. As he does so, a falsetto voice comes from the mask crying out '*Kakapana* (Don't touch)' which makes him shrink back, but his father urges him to do so and when he has overcome his fear, the *Ogbolia* leans forward and makes a transverse mark with white chalk paste on the back of his hand (a symbol of peace and well-being), saying as he does so:

---

[5] The Yakö have a six-day week, including one main non-farming day or market and a second non-farming day four days later. These days, especially the former, are selected for ceremonial as well as market activities, and are the basis on which forward reckonings and intervals in ritual sequences are calculated. The Yakö terminology is: *aiyo kokə* (before *kokə*), *kokə*, *kokəbləka* (after *kokə*), *aiyo oponyobi* (before *oponyobi*), *oponyobi*, *oponyobibləko* (after *oponyobi*).

Wo toli fai o fai   *To ya etom*
Body should be cool, cool   Let (him) live long

        Okpomo
    Let (him) be well spoken of

Obe banen   *Opon ben yaso*
Marry women   Beget children many.

This procedure is then repeated with the second (female) masked figure on the left. The boy is then told to pass in front of the Leaders, first to the right and then to the left of the *Yakowa*, holding out his hands with up-turned palms towards the Leaders, who one after another blow out breath on the palms, saying:

Tufa to fai ofai

Let (things) be cool, cool (for you), i.e. May you be peaceful and prosperous.

When all the boys have been presented and blessed in this way, the Elders remain behind to consume the wine and food which has been offered before dispersing.

    In the afternoon, the Leaders reassemble outside the village at a small clearing surrounded by high bush known as *Kegomitan* (*Ligwomi-Ketam*: *Ligwomi* meeting-place); it is approached by a single path, and in it there is an open ring of low stone boulders serving as seats. The *Yakowa* masks are donned again by the *Yawuna* and the *Yakambɔn* dance round them in a circle, singing and shaking their basketry rattles, while a few remain outside the ring whirling bull-roarers. The sound of this dancing is the signal for the initiates to be brought out from the village by their sponsors and they wait in a crowd at the entrace until they are summoned one by one into the clearing and made to dance within the circle of Leaders who switch them with freshly cut withies as they dance round. As each boy leaves the circle he is taken by one of the Leaders, smeared with soot in patches on face and back, told to sit at the edge of the clearing, and given miniature rattles of the same pattern as those of the Leaders. Older boys who have already been initiated and men of the ward have also come out and assembled round the edge of the clearing bringing rattles.[6]

    [6] The *Ligwomi* rattles (*ntesaŋ*, sing. *etsesaŋ*), are shaped like a large handbag, with a rectangular wooden base and sides and handle of basketry. During the public ceremonies of *Ligwomi*, i.e. the later processions and dances in the ward squares, all initiated men are free to use them, but at other times they may be

At the end of the dance all present form a procession headed by the Leaders with *Ogbolia* and *Ogometu* in the front brandishing bifid swords. The new initiates bring up the rear and, if very young, are carried on their fathers' shoulders. The *Yakowa* weave in and out of the procession as its proceeds first to its own ward square where the *Yakambən* dance again in a circle round them. The procession re-forms and proceeds to each of the other ward squares in the village where the dance is repeated and the Leaders of that ward bring out palm-wine for the visiting Leaders. Finally, there is another dance by the Leaders in their own ward square, during which *Ogbolia* slaughters a he-goat which is taken away to his patriclan assembly house to be cooked in readiness for the Leaders who assemble there later to eat it.

SPECIAL MOURNING *Ligwomi* AT THE DEATH OF AN *Ogbolia*

When *Ogbolia*, the head of the Ward Leaders, dies, a special *Ligwomi* is held at the next season of initiation, additional, if necessary to the four-year cycle. Any young boys who are available are initiated and one, who must be a close patrilineal relation of the dead *Ogbolia*, is selected to 'carry the Leopard' (*oto ekpe*) of the deceased *Ogbolia*, in a dance procession to all the wards of the village, which takes place the third *kokə* (non-farming) day following the initiation; the boy is carried on his father's back at the rear of the procession, holding the *Ligwomi* rattle of the dead *Ogbolia*, which has a live chick tied to its handle and is draped in raffia leaves.

The dancing at the bush site is omitted on this occasion, but, as a sign of mourning, a dozen or so boys up to 15 years of age are selected from among those initiated in earlier years to serve, together with the new initiate who will 'carry the Leopard', as mourners of the *Ogbolia* during this protracted *Ligwomi*. The boys or their parents must offer a rod and a calabash of wine to the Ward Leaders when offering themselves as members of this group. Their bodies are then blackened all over with soot and they are referred to as *Yabələmbəben* (sing. *Obolobowen*), Black Children. They have to sleep and spend much of their day in the patriclan assembly shed of the newly appointed *Ogbolia* where there food

carried and used in dances only by the Leaders (*Yakambən*), as, for example, at the funerary rites of a Leader. The rattles of the Leaders are, like the paraphernalia of the *Yakowa*, stored in the *Ogbolia's* patriclan assembly house. Others keep them in their houses and bring them out for *Ligwomi* celebrations.

is brought to them and they are catechized from time to time on the standards of good conduct of ward members. Such questioning is allowed only to youths and to men who have themselves in their time been *Yabalambaben*, led by one or two of the Ward Leaders. Whipping is the penalty for a stupid or defiant answer. During the day they are otherwise free to move about the ward where they have to collect firewood, a piece at a time, from among the piles under the verandahs of women's houses to supply the fire they must build and maintain in the assembly house. They have also to go in the later afternoons to the path leading from the ward area to the bush to collect palm-wine from all men returning to the village after tapping their palms. This provides a supply of wine which the Ward Leaders drink when they assemble in the evenings. While wandering through the village they are also free to take for themselves small supplies of foods, such as ground-nuts, melon-seeds, and okra, that are drying on the roofs of the houses at this season.

On the third *koka* day (18 days) after the initiation, the Ward Leaders assemble again for a procession with the *Yakowa* and dance in their own and other ward squares. On the following *koka* (six days later) the Leaders again dance in their own ward square, and visit those of other wards (but without the masked figures), before ending the mourning period by assembling the *Yabalambaben* to wash the soot from their bodies.

Kɛkpan—Ward Rite after Farm Clearing

The Ward Head, *Ogbolia*, and certain of the Leaders (a dozen or so in all) also carry out an annual rite when land has been cleared for the new farm plots of the men of the ward patriclans. Participation in this rite is restricted to the ward officers among the *Yakamban* —*Ogbolia, Ogometu, Edjukwa* (the ward crier), *Okaladji* (the cook who prepares their feasts)—together with certain others who have inherited the role from their fathers or other patrilineal predecessors. It is thus largely a prerogative of certain patriclans or, more precisely, lineages within the ward. A new member of this group is named by his patrikin during the funerary rites of his predecessor and is required to provide meat and palm-wine for feasts and payment both on admission to this ritual group and at later *kɛkpan* rites. In the thirties each member was expected, in the years following admission, to provide a total of four goats, a cow, and small amounts of bush-meat at successive feasts, together with considerable supplies of palm-wine, as well as the skin of a bush-cow the significance of which was obscure.[7] In this he would be assisted by his patrikin who shared in the prestige of his participation in the annual *kɛkpan* rite in the ward.

The Ward Head announces the *kokə* day on which he will carry out *kɛkpan*. The word '*kɛkpan*' in ordinary speech refers to clearing charred branches and rooting up stumps on a new farm plot after the bush has been burnt; and on the preceding day *Ogbolia* and his lieutenant (*Ogometu*) each bring in a bundle of charred wood—wood which is not normally carried back to the village but is burnt on the farm. The next morning the Ward Leaders assemble in *Ogbolia's* patriclan assembly house where a fire is made with the charred wood. The two masked figures of the ward spirits (*Yakowa*) appear and crouch behind it throughout the rite. On the fire *Ogbolia* roasts a yam and heats a sauce of oil, peppers, salt, and roasted mango-seeds. He provides palm-wine purchased with funds derived from fees and fines. He shares out the yam and the Leaders sit drinking until the fire has burned down but without other ceremony or invocation. The Ward Head finally puts out the fire, scatters the ashes and places any remaining charred wood in the *Legwomikpa* (*Ligwomi* Bag)—a large cigar-shaped basket of palm-fronds, which is said to contain an accumulation of charred wood from *kɛkpan* fires and the spirit object (*edet*) of *Ligwomi*. This basket, together with the Leaders' rattles and the two *Ligwomi* masks, is kept wrapped up in matting in the roof beams of the *Ogbolia's* patriclan assembly house.

MOURNING RITE AT THE DEATH OF A WARD LEADER

The Leaders of a ward also assemble in his compound whenever one of their number dies. They dance there with their *Ligwomi* rattles and, just before he is buried in the grave that has been dug in his house floor, they clear the house of other mourners and dance round the body addressing him in song (see Plate XI*b*).[8]

This final dance with its song is believed to ensure the reincar-

---

[7] The livestock provided by Leaders and by members of the *kɛkpan* group during and following their admission are handed over to the *Ogbolia* who keeps them as a stock to be drawn on for appropriate feasts.

[8] Earlier, the Leaders also dance in the compound and perhaps elsewhere in the ward. They alone may do so with *Ligwomi* rattles, and such restricted dances of the Leaders are known as *Kekambən*.

nation of the spirit of the deceased in a future male child of the ward.

SELECTON OF WARD HEAD AND LEADERS

Ligwomi and the other ward rituals are thus in the hands of a permanent group or organization of Ward Leaders, known as the *Yakambən* (sing. *Okambən*) headed by *Ogbolia*, the Ward Head, and his deputy *Ogometu*, who instruct the ward crier (*Edjukwa*) and the two *Yawuna* who impersonate the two ward spirits (*Yakowa*) in masked dances. Membership of the *Yakambən* is automatically open to all men in the ward who are priest-leaders of either patri- or matriclans, and also to other acceptable men of distinction who, like the priests, can provide, with the help of their kinsfolk, if need be, the substantial admission fees valued at 200 to 300 or more brass rods (£5–£7) which are used for the feasts and distributed among those already members. My records of a sample of 111 men in the Ukpakapi ward of Umor taken in 1935 indicate that approximately 35 per cent. of men were accepted as members of the *Yakambən*. Their age distribution, as obtained from age-set memberships, confirmed the impression that membership was by no means confined to the old men. The largest set of members (36 per cent.) were in the age group 40–9, but there were as many members from each of the age groups 30–9 and 25–30 (21 per cent.) as in the oldest group of men over 50 (also 21 per cent.).[9] Yakö themselves recognized that the admission of younger men had increased in recent years, an increase which they attributed to greater ease during the palm-oil boom in obtaining funds for the admission fees. It is to be noted that membership in the hereditary *kɛkpan* group was much smaller, at only 4 per cent. of the adult male strength, and all the members in the sample were 40 years old or more.

There is also at any time an informal group of younger men in the ward who are aspirants to admission as Ward Leaders. These make gifts to, and perform services for, the *Yakambən* especially at the time of a *Ligwomi* rite, and are given some share in the feasts. They are said to be 'putting their seat right' (*kenoma keyone*), a reference to the restriction to *Yakambən* of a seat on the great forest log in the ward shed on ceremonial occasions and at public meetings.

[9] This was agreed to be a considerably larger proportion than a generation previously, when, it was said, there were only about 30 members. For methods of calculation see note 15 on p. 145.

Succession to the office of *Ogbolia* is not a matter of kinship.[10] The *Yakambən* choose a new *Ogbolia* as occasion arises and they usually select one of the younger and more active members of their group. For capacity for the exercise of secular authority and conciliation are important in an *Ogbolia* since, as will be seen, he is, as head of the *Yakambən*, not merely a ceremonial leader, but a continuing authority in the affairs of the ward. He should be in the prime of life and command the esteem and respect of his fellows. On appointment an *Ogbolia* nominates, subject to the approval of the *Yakambən*, his deputy *Ogometu*, who would expect to succeed him if his death were untimely, but would not do so when an old man.

The Authority of the Ward Head and Leaders

The rituals of *Ligwomi*, of age-set recognition, of *kɛkpan* and those at the death of a Leader, all serve to develop and sustain sentiments of ward solidarity and the acceptance of the authority of the *Yakambən* in the public affairs of the half-dozen or more patriclans in a ward. For the *Yakambən* are not purely ritual leaders, nor do they rely only on ritual sanctions in case of conflict between patriclans in the ward. The *Ogbolia*, advised by the *Yakambən*, is expected to intervene to compose any serious disputes between members of different patriclans, to maintain friendly relations with other wards, and to represent their own in matters of trespass on lands or other property involving other wards. Corporate rights to land are not stressed in the wards. Among the Yakö these are phrased in terms of persons, lineages, patriclans and, beyond that, of the village. On the other hand the tracts of farmland and bush claimed by the patriclans of a ward form, for the most part, a compact segment of the village territory, so that interclan disputes within a ward tend to be taken up by the Ward Head and Leaders in the first place before there is resort to the Village Council or to the leading men's associations of the village which investigate and give judgement in such disputes.[11]

It is to be noted that, while in the larger Yakö villages *Ogbolia* and the *Yakambən* are ritual and executive authorities within the wards, in Idomi, where there are no ward divisions, the same or-

[10] See, however, Chapter VI, p. 170, concerning inter-clan competition and claims to this office.
[11] See Chapter VI, p. 178.

ganization and titles operate on a village-wide basis, as do the other organizations discussed later. No historical data are available to determine whether Idomi originated from a ward segment of a larger community, but there the *Yakambən* co-exist with the Priests' Council as village authorities.

AGE-SET FORMATION

Men's age sets (*nko*, sing. *eko*) are formed within each ward and in Umor the formal establishment of a new age-set from young men about to marry should in principle follow the four-yearly *Ligwomi* ritual. A new set is then called into existence by the Ward Head to whom it declares its chosen leader and his deputy. The large decorated wine-jar of the new age-set is prepared by them and set out in the ward square for the first time. The other sets bring out their jars and, when the new set has collected palm-wine to fill them all and offerings of food, before the drinking begins, the Ward Head, surrounded by the elders, sprinkles chalk on the new set's jar while blessing it and exhorting the members to good conduct. Although four years is regarded as the proper interval between the formation of two sets and, in the past, appears to have been generally observed, in recent years, with increasing population, the interval between calling for the leaders of one set and the next has tended to diminish[12] (Plate XVI).

At any one time there are about sixteen sets in existence in each ward and among them are distributed men ranging in age from 17 or 18 to over 70 years, but the numerical strength of the sets diminishes sharply after middle age with increasing seniority. In the wards of Umor in recent years an age-set of men has been of the order of thirty or more strong at the time of formation.[13] The age-sets in each ward are alternately labelled *okprike* and *agbiagban*,[14] and each set is further identified by the name of its senior leader,

[12] In Umor three-year intervals appear to have occurred recently in Ukpakapi ward, while one interval of only two years was recorded for the larger ward of Idjum. At the same time the ceremonial recognition of an age set has sometimes been postponed for several years on account of failure by the new set to accumulate in good time the food supplies necessary for the feast. Thus the Ukpakapi set, whose leaders were called for by the Ward Head and recognized in 1936, did not give their establishment feast until 1938.

[13] Thus in the Ukpakapi ward of Umor, with an adult male population of 387 in 1935, there were sixteen sets in existence, of which the youngest were 40 to 50 strong, while the oldest contained less than 10 each.

[14] Terms derived from the names of two villages of the Agwa'aguna people situated on the opposite bank of the Cross River.

being known as the *okprike* or *agbiagban* of so-and-so. The sets of the different wards, although they are formed independently and there is no co-ordination of establishment ceremonies, are in practice equated. Thus a man of one ward in a village can name the sets which correspond with his own, and are regarded as equivalent in age, in the other wards. In the same way, although it is less frequently needed, a man in one village can determine the age-set of any ward in another village which is held to correspond in seniority with his own. Should he migrate when adult he will be accepted as a member of such a set in the ward of his new residence.[15]

The principle of age-grouping operates long before the formal recognition of a set and a man's age-set membership has, in fact, been already established in childhood. Gradually during their childhood the boys of a ward sort themselves out into a series of groups of increasing seniority and as the members of each group reach the age of marriage it is formally established as an age-set. If, however, a potential set is too large or too few in number in the opinion of the Ward Leaders, it can be split or joined to its next junior group at this time.

Age-groups are similarly formed among the girls of a ward during childhood and the separate groups are distinguished in the ward dancing parties which take place especially during and after the New Yam festival. But women's age-sets similarly formed by combinations of the smaller groups, although they choose leaders and, like those of the men, act corporately in performing tasks such as path weeding at the request of the Ward Head, are not formally established in a public ceremony like those of the men.

---

[15] This age-set system affords a means of determining the approximate chronological age of any person. The assumption of a four-year interval between all but the most recent sets corresponds very well with the age obtained independently for particular men by means of dated events at their births and first marriages. Thus if the sets extant in a ward in 1939 be numbered in order of juniority, an Ukpakapi man of age-set V, the approximate age of whose members was estimated to be 62–5 in 1939, could be independently estimated, from the occurrence of his first marriage in the year of a British military expedition through the Cross River country, to be 61 years old. In the same way, a man of age set XVI (the age of whose members was estimated at 22–5 in 1939) could be shown to be 26 years of age, since the year in which he went away to school was 1925 and that was also the year of the second time that his father who farmed a six-year cycle of plots had again cleared a farm on the particular land (Ebe) where he was farming when his son was born. The man was thus 12 years old in 1925 and 26 years in 1939. Similar independent age estimates have confirmed the estimates of the age ranges of other sets. Owing to more frequent reductions of intervals between age-set formations in the large Idjum ward of Umor two groups of two sets are equated with two single sets in the other three wards.

An age-set of men continues to be divided within itself into a number of groups of closer friends or companions known as *liboma* (sing. *koboma* = finger). These groups of age-mates are conceived as sub-groups of the larger set and an analogy with lineages of a clan is made: 'We have *liboma* in *eko* just as we have *yepōnama* in *kepun*.' But the age-mate groups are not strictly mutually exclusive and comprehensive sub-divisions of an age-set. A man may, although it is exceptional, belong to more than one *koboma* at the same time, so that the memberships of the various groups overlap to some extent. Furthermore, even the ward boundaries of the age-set system can be overstepped by accepting in an age-mate group a man of an equivalent age set in another ward.[16] An age-set is concerned in any marriage or death of one of its members or of a member's close relative, and the part of the relevant age-sets in the conduct of rites and feasts whereby marital status is established is considerable.[17] But the entire age-set does not usually function as a corporate group on these occasions; the age-mates of the members concerned are the main participants to whom may be added less intimate age-set fellows who have other ties with him.

The age-sets do have, however, as corporate groups definite obligations to the ward, of which the most prominent is that of guarding the houses against fire during the dry season, when most people are away from the village by day clearing land and hoeing the ground for new farms. A spark is then sufficient to set a palm-frond thatch ablaze and the slightest breeze will carry the fire from house to house and set the whole village on fire in a short time.[18] For this guard all men's age-sets are expected to serve a day at a time in rotation, but the older sets, if they are very weak in numbers, join together to form a single group. A party of women from

[16] Thus a man of a lineage of Kikuŋkula *kepun* in Idjum ward at Umor had as *koboma*-fellows seven men of his own patriclan, five other men of his ward, each from a different patriclan, and three men of two different patriclans in another ward. The *koboma* of a man of Ukpakapi ward included three men of his own patriclan, two of another patriclan in Ukpakapi, one of another ward, and one or two others whose clan and ward affiliations were not recorded.

[17] This is described in my *Marriage and the Family among the Yakö*.

[18] A large part of the village of Umor was almost entirely burnt out in this way in 1919 and there have been other less disastrous fires in recent times. There is a strict rule that all house fires must be stamped out before leaving the compound, and breach of this regulation is punishable by fine; but the ward endeavours to protect itself further by maintaining a guard which is also protection against thieving from houses which are deserted for most of the day.

the corresponding set is sometimes required to stay in the ward as well, ostensibly to cook for the men. Two or three times a year men's age-sets are called out to cut back the growth of vegetation choking the main paths leading through the farmlands of the ward. This is done when farm clearing is about to start in January, again after the New Yam festival in June, and always just before the main harvest in November. Save in January, when a senior set should remain in the ward on fire-guard, all the age-sets are called out for this work. They begin at dawn and break off before midday, after having worked their way along the paths in squads, each working as a unit, towards the boundary of the village territory. The maintenance of the main springs from which the domestic water-supply of the ward is obtained is also regularly assigned to the age-sets. The clearing of springs is usually undertaken during the growing season in June or July by one or more of the junior sets under the direction of a few older men. In addition to these regular duties one or more of the sets can be called upon to undertake a particular task in the ward, such as cutting a new bush path or, more occasionally, joining with sets from other wards to do some work required for the village as a whole, such as the rebuilding or repairing of the house of the Village Head. The calling out of the age-sets is one of the duties of the ward crier, *Edjukwa*, who also summons other persons or assemblies at the instance of the Ward Head. When any work has been decided on *Edjukwa* walks through the ward beating his drum and calling out the name of the group concerned and the time and nature of the work.

In general an age-set takes care of its own backsliders and exacts a penalty in food or palm-wine from any one who fails to do his share without good excuse; but a person or set which refused customary duties without good reason would be punished with a fine by the Ward Head or, nowadays, be brought by him before the Native Court.

Ebiabu: A MEN'S ORGANIZATION WITH POLICE FUNCTIONS

Apart from their authority over the age-sets of the ward, the *Ogbolia* and the *Yakambən* formerly had at their disposal for the constraint of recalcitrants an organization of the majority of the able-bodied men of the ward known as *Ebiabu* (dog ghost, from *ebi* = dog, *abu* = ghost). Membership in *Ebiabu* is not obligatory but most men who can muster the fee seek admittance soon after marriage; it is open to all who are not *yafoli* (purchased children of alien origin). About 85 per cent. of adult men claimed membership in the thirties.[19]

Ebiabu is regarded by the Yakö as both a recreational club and an organization of the able-bodied and energetic men of a ward for the maintenance of public order. The *Ebiabu* in each ward has its own costumes, insignia, and songs[20] which may not be used or sung by non-members. It dances to celebrate successes of its own members and on many ritual occasions. At the same time it accepts the obligation to act at the instance of *Ogbolia* and the *Yakambɔn* in supervising arrangements for public amenities such as the positions and use of refuse dumps and latrines and the maintenance of farm paths and springs. Public work on such tasks is the duty of the age-sets to which it is assigned by the Ward Head on any occasion. *Ebiabu* has to see that it is effectively done, to urge, threaten, and apprehend recalcitrants.

According to the Yakö the name and ceremonial features of *Ebiabu* have been derived from the people of Agwa'aguna to the south, where it is a graded village organization of men, those in the highest grade (*imiedo*) being the political leaders of the village, hearing disputes and making rules concerning farming, trading, and general internal order. The Yakö of Umor say that they established it as a ward organization after visits to Agwa'aguna during which fees were paid for the right to adopt it and for instruction in its insignia and ceremonial procedure. The graded system of Agwa'aguna, if ever introduced in its entirety, had by the thirties been reduced in Umor to a three-grade system of juniors (*Odumugom*—an Agwa'aguna term for a junior on any organization), adults, and seniors (*Abu*). Boys may join the junior branch (*Odumugom*) before they are ten and ceremonies of admission are held following a *Ligwomi* rite; candidates for admission to this junior branch of *Ebiabu* make a payment of four brass rods (2s.), a calabash of wine, and another of *fufu*, and are ceremonially marked

---

[19] According to the sample of the association and other memberships of 111 men of one ward, already referred to.

[20] The insignia of the middle grade in *Ebiabu* were generally similar in each ward and included two staffs (*utubaka*) decorated with dog skulls covered by a ram's skin, the jaw bones of a cow, a short sword (*iwoɲ*), a bifid spear (*ketun*), and raffia bags decorated with bells (*leblabukpa*). Particular songs appear to have been specific to the grades of *Ebiabu* referred to below. Each grade, or a contingent of all grades from a ward, would threaten with physical violence or destruction of livestock any outsider who sang their songs (see Plate XIIa).

with the *Ebiabu* mark in a paste of yellow powder (*kelun*). Admission to the main grade of general adult members who form the rank and file of dancers, participate in feasts, and were formerly called out to quell a disturbance, requires a fee of a goat and 20 rods (10*s*.). For admission to the small group of seniors, most, if not all, of whom are *Yakambən* of the ward, the candidate is expected to provide a cow, which is publicly butchered and stewed in a great iron cauldron, and 140 brass rods (£3 10*s*.). All members may attend the preparations and the feast, of which scraps are given to the juniors, but the brass rods are shared among the senior grade of *Abu* alone.[21]

An assembly of *Ebiabu*, whether for public or convivial purposes, can be called by any member of the senior grade (*Abu*) who has only to shout the *Ebiabu* call, a falsetto go-go-go-go-go, in the ward to summon the Messenger (*Odum*—an Agwa'aguna term), himself one of the *Abu*. If satisfied the Messenger goes first to *Obot Ebiabu*, the Head of the *Abu* grade and of the whole organization, to advise him and get his approval before going round the ward, repeating the cry to summon a meeting of the *Abu*, or, if required, of the rank and file, at the *Ebiabu* meeting-place (*Leblambuma = Ebiabu-lema*), which is the patriclan assembly house of the Head. Meetings for the quelling of minor disturbances or for apprehending a recalcitrant defendant, which have not been superseded by police seconded to the Native Authority Court, are said to have been rare in the past as compared with the convivial and ceremonial gatherings. The latter would be called when some achievement of a member, and especially an *Abu*, afforded occasion.[22] The man so honoured is expected to initiate and make the major contribution to a collection of palm-wine and gin from all members, who then assemble to drink during a public session of songs and dances. If a member stays away from such a feast, a group will go to fetch him and, whether he can come or not, demand a contribution in palm-wine or gin or rods.

On the death of a member, even that of a junior if his father is prominent in *Ebiabu*, the leaders send a shroud cloth for the corpse and proceed to the compound either before or after the burial in the house floor. The heir, or 'maker of the burial', who may not be

---

[21] About a third of the adult members of *Ebiabu* are accepted as *Abu*.
[22] e.g. the gathering of a large yam harvest of 400 sticks or more, or after making or receiving a marriage payment.

a member, if, as should be, he is a matrikinsman, and is from another ward, is responsible for providing a bottle of gin and four pots of palm-wine, while the patrikin have to give 40 brass rods and arrange for the admission of one among them who has not yet joined.

At the dances the insignia of *Ebiabu* are borne by two or three of the leading dancers who are also often decorated with shoulder-pieces or wristlets of ram's fleece[23] and cross-belts of bells (*yati*). The dancers need not be member of the senior grade and are often more vigorous younger men who lead an elaborate ballet of mimic attack and withdrawal supported by the rest of the dancers in close formation carrying belled bags (see Plate XII*a*).

Young men who have not been able to obtain the funds necessary to enter the adult grade, which is alone entitled to dance, sometimes break into the group of dancers who then seize them and force their kinsmen to promise to pay their entrance fees with the threat that they will otherwise 'kill a cow against them'.[24]

It will be apparent that *Ebiabu* serves to enhance the *esprit de corps* of the majority of men in a ward. The members, who include most of the adult men, are accustomed in collective dancing and drinking parties to accept group obligations and also the initiative and prerogatives of the leading seniors—the *Abu*, who, through overlapping membership, can as *Yakambən* rely on their support and action in disturbances involving individuals and small groups even within the *Ebiabu* membership. The Headship of *Ebiabu*, like the role of Messenger, is elective among the *Abu* and passes to one who gets on well with the younger men. It is not held by the *Ogbolia* who, although always an *Abu*, takes only a passive part in the feasts and ceremonies. The role of *Ebiabu* as a men's fraternity and disciplinary force within each ward is ceremonially recognized in a wider framework at the First-Fruits and Harvest rites of the village, when the *Ebiabu* of each ward, with costumed dancers bearing its insignia, comes to receive blessings at the *Odjokobi* shrine in the compound of the Village Head.

[23] Such shoulder-pieces or sleeves (*ŋpabo* = fleeced arms) are common features of the costumes of leading dancers in several organizations, e.g. *Leko, Obam, Ukwa.*
[24] I.e. kill any cow in the village, compensation for which would be due not from the organization but from the outsider who had infringed its rules.

POLITICO-RITUAL CO-ORDINATION OF WARD LEADERSHIP IN THE
VILLAGE *Okeŋka* CULT

The organization of men in the several wards is also integrated
for the village as a whole through the *Okeŋka* organization. *Okeŋka*
is a ritual fraternity embracing the more influential *Yakambǝn* of
the various wards. No one, it is said, who is not an *Okambǝn* would
seek, or be considered for, admission. Entrance fees equivalent to
140 brass rods, paid partly in rods, or now in Nigerian currency,
and partly in livestock are demanded of new members. In Umor
in the thirties there were some 50 members in an adult male population of about 1,750. *Okeŋka* is found in all the Yakö villages and
is regarded by the Yakö as an ancient feature of their organization.
Its prestige and authority derive from its control of a powerful
Leopard Spirit which brings grave misfortune of an unpredictable character on any who offend and fail to appease it. This spirit
resides in a secret contraption (*lekpetu*) which, when manipulated,
gives out a booming noise said to be the Voice of the Leopard
Spirit (*lekpemle*). In Umor it is mostly heard from behind the
closed doors of the *Okeŋka* house in Lebulibulikǝm patriclan in
Idjiman ward and usually at night, when the leading members are
carrying out a rite at the death of a member of the group, or on the
admission of a new member, or are conferring over a dispute that
has been brought to them. But during the First-Fruits and Harvest
rites of the village and when a new Village Head is installed, the
lekpetu is carried into the shrine of the senior matriclan and village
spirit, *Odjokobi*, and the Leopard Voice is heard issuing from it.

There appears to be no fixed limit of membership nor any
strict succession by kinship to membership in *Okeŋka*. New admissions usually follow deaths of members and are incorporated
into the obsequies of the latter, but only men who are senior and
well established among the *Yakambǝn* of their ward are admitted
and acceptability is canvassed in advance before anyone is openly
proposed. In Umor, however, the Head, *Obot Okeŋka*, must be
selected from among members of three patriclans in rotation.
These patriclans,[25] one in each of the three older settled wards of
Umor, are themselves regarded as of early establishment. The
Head of *Okeŋka* is automatically a member of the Priests' Council

---

[25] Lebulibulikǝm in Idjiman (where the *Okeŋka* house is established), Akugum
in Idjum, and Egbisum in Ukpakapi ward.

of the village (the *Yabot*) and election to the leadership of *Okeŋka* is subject to its approval. On appointment a new head provides a cow and a goat for a substantial feast for the members. His office is one of considerable prestige, for his ritual powers are as great as, although different from, those of an *Ina* (matriclan priest). He is often addressed by the Ekoi title: *Ovar Ekpe*, Leopard Head, instead of the Yakö form: *Obot Okeŋka*.

Over the past generation, the influence of *Okeŋka* in social control is said by the Yakö to have waned with the rise of another association *Ikpuŋkara*, and also with the development of the Native Authority Court; but it is held that in earlier times an *Ogbolia* could and would invoke the sanctions of *Okeŋka* if things got out of hand in his ward, while the *Yagbolia* of different wards could and should refer to *Okeŋka* any disputes they could not settle which involved people of their several wards. The knowledge that an issue was being considered by *Okeŋka* was the generally enough to lead the disputants to accept a settlement. If not, *Okeŋka* could place its sign—a small piece of roof-matting—on places or objects involved, and so ritually impound them.

Members of *Okeŋka* and others, who go direct to the Head and make out a good case while offering a calabash of wine, are able ritually to protect their land or trees from suspected or anticipated interference. The *Okeŋka* ritual injunction on interference with protected property is generally the most feared of such taboos in Umor. An offender is not only risking automatic misfortune at the hands of the Leopard Spirit but is apprehended if discovered and threatened with particularly dire consequences that can be averted only by paying a substantial fine to induce *Okeŋka* to remove them.

The men's organizations so far considered—the *Yakambən* in each ward, with *Ogbolia* and *Ogometu* at the head, which unites all boys in the *Ligwomi* ritual; the *Ebiabu* organization, which in part served as the agent of the *Yakambən*; and *Okeŋka*, which supported the authority of the latter and secured settlement of inter-ward issues through village-wide mystical sanctions—can be seen as a co-ordinated series. This implies, not that they were designed as such but, that the gradings and overlappings of membership have favoured an adjustment of activities and authority whereby a considerable measure of cohesion and the reduction of tensions within and between the wards have been secured. But this series of associations by no means exhausts the organization of men in corporate groups within the ward. There are others rising from more specific needs and opportunities which are not explicitly co-ordinated with the organizations described so far.

THE WARRIORS

Within each ward[26] there is an association of the Black Ones (*Eblɔmbe*) whose members were formerly its leading warriors. In those days they blackened their faces with soot when going out to attack; now they do so on ceremonial occasions. The titles of some of the officers are indicative of the former military character. Besides the Head (*Obot Eblɔmbe*) there is a Leader of the Advance Guard (*Okɔlɔbeti: okɔlɔ-be-eti*, going first-them-on the path), a Leader of the Rear Guard (*Okpoibengum: okpoiŋgɔm*, staying back), and a Cook (*Okɔladji*, who tastes first). But today, when local and independent organization for self-defence and attack has ceased, the association continues as a convivial and funerary club confined, it is held, to descendants of the men of the old organization. For membership in *Eblɔmbe* is restricted by succession to close patrikinsmen of former members and the admission of these is both an obligation and a privilege. Some old Yakö say that this was always the rule and that each of the lineages concerned had to provide a successor to be specially trained in fighting. The offices are also restricted to certain patriclans in each ward.[27] A sample count showed that in the thirties there were about 60 members in Ukpakapi and Biko-Biko wards or about 10 per cent. of the adult male population.

The *Eblɔmbe* association will give its members and others, who show good title and pay a fee of a brass rod, protection for their fruit-trees and for raffia and oil-palms being tapped for wine. But the sanction is not, like that of *Okeŋka*, a mystical one. Anyone discovered interfering with property on which the *Eblɔmbe* mark has been set is charged by *Eblɔmbe* itself before the Ward or Village Head and damages are then payable to *Eblɔmbe* for contempt of its authority in addition to the claim for restitution to the owner and the fine for the hearing.

[26] Biko-Biko, a more recently established ward in Umor, has not created its own *Eblɔmbe* lodge but, as for a number of organizations, participates equally in a joint lodge with the adjacent Ukpakapi ward.

[27] e.g. In Ukpakapi and Biko-Biko, the Head must be of Egbisum, Ndai-Lekpaŋkɔm, or of Biko-Biko Lekpaŋkɔm or Lebokɔm; the leader of the Rear Guard should come from Ndai-Lekpankɔm, or Egbisum in Ukpakapi, or Lebokɔm, Ŋpani, or Lekpaŋkɔm in Biko-Biko.

The right of the *Eblɔmbe* organization of each ward to attend in procession to receive blessings from the *Odjokobi* spirit at the First-Fruits and Harvest rites of the village is an index of its recognition in the village. There were formerly war priests (*Yanun Eko*) in each ward, but these offices are obsolete and it is not clear whether there was any special ritual relation between *Eblɔmbe* and these priests. Within the ward, however, *Eblɔmbe* does not appear to have been at the disposal of *Ogbolia* and the *Yakambɔn*.

Meetings today, apart from the annual processions to *Odjokobi* at the First-Fruits and Harvest rites, when the Village Head is expected to provide each ward group with a leg of smoked meat and palm-wine, are confined to the funerals of members, which all should attend, and feasts at new admissions, which are held in the *Eblɔmbe* house. New entrants must bring the equivalent of 200 brass rods, partly in meat, and the rods (or Nigerian currency) are shared, most going to the three leaders.[28] On such occasions leading members carrying weapons perform a ballet of mimic reconnaissance and attack, but there is no drumming or singing.

The insignia of *Eblɔmbe* are the same in all wards: the *abotu*, a pair of skulls each mounted on an oval board with a fishtail projection at the back by which it is held, and the *ebuloti*, a crooked stick to which secret objects are attached by a large ovoid wrapping of bark-cloth near the crook (Plate XII).

Leko Dances

The leaders of *Eblɔmbe*, like the Hunters to be discussed below, call for war-dances which are performed by younger men in the ward who know the songs and steps. These performances are known as *Leko* but there is no formal organization of the dancers themselves. Yakö say that *Leko*, meaning 'the Fighters', refers to the main body of men who would take part in any large conflict, and that in the old days they were under the ritual authority of *Onun Eko*—the war priest of the ward.[29] *Onun Eko* in other words could both encourage and prohibit military action through ritual sanctions. After the fighting, heads of slain enemies were brought

---

[28] The traditionally standard shares are 60 rods to the Head and Advance Guard Leader, 30 rods to the Rear Guard Leader, and the rest equally among the ordinary members.

[29] The wards had their several war priests and in Umor that of Idjiman ward was at the same time a village war priest and a member of the Priests' Council. The *Onun Eko* performed rites at the *Akota* (sing. *Likota*) War Stones (*liko* = war, *leta* = stone).

back and carried round in dances in the ward squares before being thrown in the latrines. Later the teeth were removed to decorate the fibre caps worn in *Leko* dances and only those who had brought back heads could take leading parts in the dances.

Today *Leko* dances are still held during the funerary rites of any important man, including all members of *Ebləmbe*. They are regarded as an adjunct of *Ebləmbe* since it most often sponsors them and rewards the leading dancers. The rank and file wear fibre caps closely sewn with teeth formerly human but now mostly of dog and goat. Their breasts and sometimes their faces are painted with white chalk paste and, like *Ebiabu*, they often wear shoulder-pieces or sleeves made of the long-haired breast fleeces of yellow-white rams. One bears a *Leko* staff (*ekoti: leko, eti*), surmounted by two small opposed carved face-masks separated by a fan of porcu-pine quills and two *ekpense* feathers. Some dancers are masked; one, representing a male, known as *Ekoblami*, is covered from head to foot in a one-piece tight-fitting costume of closely knotted *eteni* fibre, in which there are only small apertures for the eyes. His head is surmounted by a skull; he wears a chest girdle of closely strung fresh palm-leaflets, and carries a bifid sword in his hand. The two ends of a long chain, which passes round his waist, are held by two other dancers who affect to keep *Ekoblami* in leash as he lunges threateningly in all directions. *Ekoblami* may be accompanied by one or more other dancers masked as females and known as *Ukwa*. The carved female heads are worn on top of the dancers' heads, from which voluminous folds of enveloping cloth descend over the body to the ground. Using a reed comb these dancers screech in falsetto while they totter, sway, and turn in the centre of the *Leko* dancers (see Plates XII*b* and XIV*b*).

The masked dancers are not officers of *Leko*—there are none such—but are self-appointed and subject, for continued perfor-mance, to public approbation; they either make, purchase, or borrow their costumes.[30] *Leko* dancing as continued today is an

[30] In the Ukpakapi ward of Umor the only *Ekoblami* costume in the thirties was in the possession of a wealthy member of the *Ikpuŋkara* association who lent it as needed to a dancer of whom he approved, receiving from him a cala-bash of wine. This costume, he said, had been made by Agoi people and any-one who paid for such a costume to be made could have it and keep it. The two female costumes in use in this ward were known as *Ma Oba* and *Ma Eni*. The former, said to be 'for the old men', was kept, and similarly lent out, by a man who had succeeded to its ownership from a dead kinsman; the other had been made only a year or two before by a man of early middle age.

expected and rewarded demonstration by younger men in the ward. The rewards are not only the gifts of palm-wine but the satisfaction of the dancing itself and the approbation of the public, especially of the mourners.

On the death of any member of *Eblɔmbe*, of a prominent *Leko* dancer or of any other man of standing whose fellows can be expected to show their appreciation of a dance by thanks and wine, two dancers from his ward carrying swords (*lewoŋ suwa*) and one a slit drum and the other a skin drum, move stealthily through all wards of the village miming the cautious stalking of a dangerous enemy. This announces the dance which follows a day or two later, beginning in the ward square of the deceased and ending, after visits to all the other wards, in the compound of the dead man, where they are given food and wine and perhaps some rods or money.

THE HUNTERS

Hunters (*yadjɔnen*, sing. *odjɔnen*), for whom also *Leko* dances are commonly performed at death, are organized by wards in the larger Yakö villages although ceremonial expressions of solidarity should be supported by all hunters of the village. In each ward there is a recognized organization known as *Kodjɔ* (Hunting), of which a senior hunter is recognized as leader in the organized hunts from a camp in the forest.[31] Known as *Odjɔnotam* (Old Hunter) or *Obot Kodjɔ* (Head of the Hunters) he should have a younger colleague who leads reconnaissance parties, makes long journeys to and from the bush, and is called *Okop Mpa*, an Efik term signifying a fearless and aggressive fighter. To enter, and be recognized as one of, the ward band of hunters a young man has to have a dane-gun (i.e. the locally available muzzle-loading, flint-lock musket) and must join the band on some occasion when they are going out to their bush camp which occurs once or twice each year before the main harvest. After his first kill he is accepted as a member without fee or formal initiation.

The link between the Hunters and *Leko* is informal but strong. Older men say that only recognized and active hunters should

---

[31] In Umor the camp of Idjum ward is far out in the forest on the Emun path; Idjiman has two established camps, one near the Liplo'opoŋ path and the other far out between the Egoeti and Omini Odji paths; Ukpakapi and Biko-Biko wards, as for the Fighters, share a single leader and camp at the far end of the Ikiki path.

dance *Leko* and that some of the *Leko* dancers today are upstart youngsters. In the old days hunting and fighting went together and no one who had not had experience in the hunting camps would be any good in fighting, nor would he dare to dance *Leko*.[32] Today not only is *Leko* becoming a young men's recreation but some men have dane-guns and go about hunting in ones and twos near their farms without paying attention to the Hunters or going on big hunts at their camps.

At the death of one of the recognized Hunters the Head of the Hunters in his ward goes or sends messages to the Heads in other wards so that the Hunters may be called together to collect wine and carry it to the dead man's compound. The Head of the group in the dead man's ward, which provides the majority of the muster, makes a speech during the drinking and before the burial calling for a successor, that is, for a young kinsman who will have the dead man's gun and join the ward parties in their hunting camp. This successor should be named and should agree to come on the ceremonial hunt that is to follow. The Head is then given gunpowder from the dead man's supply, which is shared round and fired off at any nearby sapling.

At the second mortuary rites some time later, when the dead hunter's grave is 'renewed', i.e. the earth finally stamped down over the grave, the *Kodjə* of his ward decide (in a meeting in the compound of their head to which *Yabot Kodjə* of other wards are invited) on a *kokə* day when they will bring the proceeds of a special hunt for a ceremonial feast in the dead man's compound. A few days before the appointed day a muster of *Kodjə* members from all wards marches out of the village in procession to hunt from the ward camp. When they return to the village they send in a messenger and wait on the outskirts for the *Leko* drums and insignia to be brought out to play them in as they march direct to the compound.[33] If they see any chickens as they march through the village they shoot at them. The dead man's kin produce, besides palm-wine, a goat which is slaughtered in the compound. With the game and the chickens this is immediately prepared for roasting. The killer

[32] In a sample of the Ukpakapi ward of Umor, 31 per cent. of men claimed to be members of *Kodjə* while 56 per cent. said they danced *Leko*. The latter may have included men who had danced in the past but would no longer do so, but the wider participation in the dancing as compared with group hunting was evident.

[33] *Leko* drums should be kept in the house of the *Obot Kodjə* of the ward.

of each animal receives half of his best, as well as a portion of the rest, to carry away after the feast. While the meal is cooking blank guns are fired off and a shooting match is arranged. A live cock is tied to the end of a long raffia rib set up in the compound and those who wish fire at it in turn until the cock is shot to pieces.

Ɔkpe

There is also in each ward in Yakö villages a ritual association which is even more definitely dissociated from that of the Ward Elders, although about a third of the adult men of a ward belong to it. It is called Ɔkpe (the Leopards; sing. ekpe). Although it employs leopard symbolism, like the village cult group of Ward Leaders organized in Okeŋka, it is not associated with Okeŋka; an Ɔkpe member may, however, in virtue of some other status, be invited to join Okeŋka. But no member of the Priests' Council of the village will, after appointment, continue to participate in the activities of Ɔkpe, on the alleged grounds that its supernatural sanctions involve sterility, while the priests' rites are designed to promote fertility.

Each Ɔkpe lodge has a meeting-house in the ward and another in the bush (Kekpetam = ŋkpe ketam). The former, known as Lekpema (ŋkpe lema), consists of a small, open, roofed shelter which is walled in with raffia leaves, cloth, or other light material for rituals. The cult objects are kept in the patriclan house of the head, Ekumbe Ekpe (an Ekoi term). They include a sacred wooden figurine known as Likundu to which requests and offerings are made in secret, and a bellows like that used by Okeŋka which produces the booming leopard voice (lemle), distinct from that of the Okeŋka lekpemle, and is known as Mboko (an Ekoi term) (see Plate XIVa).

Admission to Ɔkpe is obtained on payment of brass rods, or nowadays of Nigerian currency, together with meat to provide a feast for the members. There is a grade of senior members, known as Esuwa, for admission to which further payments are required, and this, under the leadership of the Head, Ekumbe Epke, directs the activities. In the thirties, according to my sample in Ukpakapi ward 40 per cent. of men had joined Ɔkpe.

An Ɔkpe lodge claims to control powerful and mysterious forces which protect its members and punish offences against them especially by women with sickness and sterility. Like many other men's organizations among the Yakö within ward and village, it affixes its sign a plaited loop of raffia palm-fronds (or a fresh branch of a *loseni* tree), to protect trees and other unguarded property of its members and of others who make a small payment.

When a new lodge head is installed the members retreat to their meeting-place in the bush (*Kekpetam*) for six days from one *kokɔ* to the next, taking the cult objects with them. Meat is provided during this period from goats given by the heir of the former head and by the new incumbent, and the 'leopard voice' is heard in the village almost continuously coming from the adjoining bush. They return to the village in procession to dance in the ward, headed by two members wearing carved face-masks known as *Ikoko* (male) and *Nyaŋpe* (female).[34] The masked dancers, also referred to as *Onumian* (water spirits), are accompanied by several drummers. The other members paint the upper halves of their faces with white chalk and two of them carry the *mbŏkŏ* and *likundu* concealed under a chequered cloth. This masked dance is also given in the ward during the funerary rites of any senior member of the *Ŋkpe* lodge.

Their *Ŋkpe* organizations are said by the Yakö to be derived from the Ekoi peoples to the east and it appears that their more recent introduction, and especially their magical threat to fertility, causes them to be looked at askance by the established ritual authorities in the ward and the village. '*Ŋkpe*', I was sometimes told in Umor, 'would not dare to come to *Odjokobi*', that is, the village festivals at the matriclan fertility shrines on the occasion of village First-Fruits and Harvest rituals.

In the small Ekoi communities, *Ekpe* is the dominant men's organization and the senior grade of *Ekpe* is the *de facto* political authority. The validity of the supernatural sanctions of *Ŋkpe* are not doubted. On the contrary, the Ekoi origin of the cult lends great credence to its power, for the Ekoi peoples are credited with remarkable magical powers and the control of most powerful spirits. But both the power of *Ŋkpe* and the organization itself are feared by *Yabot* and also by many *Yakambɔn* in the wards. *Okpebri*, the Village Speaker, and others in Umor said that *Ŋkpe* disturbed the peace among Yakö. It worked, not for the good of all

---

[34] These are Ekoi terms. The dancers wear netted 'one-piece' suits of black *eteni* fibre. The *Ikoko* dancer carries a switch and a length of cloth tightly bound round the waist from which a string of bells hangs down at the back. The *Nyaŋpe* costume consists of a loose covering of strips of cloth extending over the body from the mask to the ground.

the people, but for the power and influence of its leaders. Other
Yakö leaders, on the other hand, told me it was dangerous for a
big man not to belong to *Ɔkpe*. *Ɔkpe* appears to be a cult group
which has appealed especially to those who have not achieved a
recognized position of prestige and authority in the older politico-
religious system. Belief in the effectiveness of the cult of the *Ekpe*
spirit as practised by the Ekoi encouraged its introduction among
the Yakö, but as dangerous and foreign it has stood apart from the
traditional Yakö cults and has tended to attract the dissident and
discontented, while incurring the veiled hostility of those who hold
established politico-religious offices.

Obam

Another independent ward-organized association known as *Obam*
has existed in most, if not all, the villages, but I was unable to
observe its activities while I was among the Yakö in the thirties
and members would give little information. In Umor ceremonies
by *Obam* had been banned by the Ward Heads and the Village
Council on the orders of the Administration following the alleged
ritual murder of a man from a non-Yakö community to the south.
Membership seems to have been considerable formerly, some 60
per cent. of men in Ukpakapi ward having been members. In
Umor *Obam* was said to have been introduced from Ɔkpani, a
village of which little good was spoken since it had been formed
by secession after a protracted quarrel. *Obam* had generally a
reputation for cannibalistic practices and there were suggestions
that in the past it regularly undertook to provide victims for human
sacrifices at the obsequies of members and priests. Its ceremonies
included performances by two dancers wearing masks in which
skulls were incorporated. Membership was apparently not limited
by descent but was open to any who would pay the small fees, and
during a ceremony outsiders could join in the public dance and
the choruses of the *Obam* songs.

Song Clubs

There are also in the several wards of the villages song clubs in
which younger men participate. In Umor one of these, *Nsebe*, has
been adopted from the neighbouring Ekumuru village of Ediba
on the Cross River and some of the songs are sung in their speech
to the accompaniment of skin drums, metal gongs, and cane rattles.
Another such club, *Aiyo*, in which a sun-helmet and dark glasses

XIII. Leaders of *Eblɔmbɔ* dancing during a funeral rite

XIV *a*. Members of *Ɔkpe* carrying the 'Leopard Voice'

XIV *b*. *Leko* dancers with insignia

are *de rigueur* for dancers, specializes in Efik songs learned on visits to Calabar. Many of them allude to adventures in Calabar but others include impromptu mockery of people in the ward who have, in fact or according to gossip, been up to no good. There are no fees for admission to such clubs, and the leadership is informal and changeable. They sing for their own entertainment but they also visit the compounds of leading men who are expected to provide them with palm-wine and small gifts of money.

Ekuruso: WARD ORGANIZATION OF ADULT WOMEN

The solidarity and the interests of the women living in a ward are also organized among the Yakö, and collective action may be taken at times of crisis.[35] Membership of the organization, which is known as *Ekuruso* (*usɔ* = community), is in principle restricted to one junior matrilineal kinswoman of every deceased member, although a married daughter of a senior member is sometimes admitted while the latter is still alive. It is felt that all the matriclans and perhaps all the matrilineages should be represented in *Ekuruso*, but in Umor membership was restricted to a small proportion of the adult women, there being only up to 50 recognized members in each of the wards, while the total number of adult women ranged from 700 to over 1,000, and a tradition of interest and participation seemed to be confined to a few matrilines.

Ward domicile is not as stable for women as for men. Women may leave the ward in which they were born to marry in another, and subsequent divorces with remarriage or return to the paternal compound may involve further changes of ward residence. There appear to be no definite attitudes or rules affecting such transfers. A woman can belong only to the *Ekuruso* of the ward in which she lives, but if she migrates to another ward and is well thought of she will be accepted as a member of the group in that ward.

A new member is called for and admitted to the association during the funerary rites of the late member, whose matrikin are expected to provide a feast of bush-meat and palm-wine for *Ekuruso* when it visits the compound during the mourning and also an admission fee of four rods (2s.) together with a fowl, a goat, and a large bowl of mashed yam (*fufu*) for separate feasts of the group.[36]

---

[35] In Umor the wards of Ukpakapi and Biko-Biko are, as in the case of some men's organizations, a single unit in the *Ekuruso* organization.

[36] A few men join the meetings and feasts of *Ekuruso* and are said to be sons of deceased women members who had no daughters.

Ekuruso meets for discussions and feasts in the compound where its Head lives and the Head keeps in her house a spirit pot (*ekuruso edet*—a clay bowl half filled with Afikpo chalk) from which new members are smeared on their admission. Leadership rests informally with half a dozen of the older women past child-bearing, who select one of themselves to succeed a head who dies.[37] These include the *Omanamana* who carries out the clitorodectomy of nubile girls.

In each ward *Ekuruso* appoints a man associate, known as 'the companion of the women' (*udjegom aneba*), who sounds a metal gong on its behalf to summon an assembly of the members, and sometimes of all women, at the ward meeting-place if trouble in which the women are concerned threatens in the ward. On such occasions *Ekuruso* will go as a body, either alone or supported by a general crowd of women, to the Ward Head, or, especially if several wards are involved, to the Village Head, to demand fair treatment, if they consider that women's interests have been interfered with, or to demand settlement of a protracted dispute which is disturbing the peace of the ward or the village. They will threaten as a last resort to order all women to leave their husbands' compounds in a body and abandon farm work for them. This threat is seriously made and taken, although no occasion on which there was an attempt to put it into effect could be recalled.

Ekuruso will intervene directly in open quarrels among women and girls, as they did in Ukpakapi, when the girls of two adjacent age sets had come to blows in the ward over their ranking *vis-à-vis* the age sets of youths: an issue in which the senior age set disputed the right of their juniors to join courtship parties with youths of an age set they held corresponded to their own. But they have no accepted authority to inflict fines on women or men and can secure suppression of violence or recalcitrance only by enlisting the action of the Ward or Village Heads. The status of *Ekuruso* is, however, formally recognized by the arrival in procession of each ward group to receive the blessings of *Odjokobi* in the compound of the Village Head during the New Yam and the Harvest rites. When *Ekuruso* is in procession in the village, bystanders are expected to stop as it passes by. Any who walk past them or across their path can be summoned to the Ward Head who will order the offender to pay damages of 2–6 rods (1s. to 3s.) to the group.

[37] In the thirties the heads in the wards of Umor were of age-sets VII to IV = 53–64 years in 1935.

A convival dancing club of women, which is also organized in each ward[38] and known as *Oyoŋko*, has no direct connection with *Ekuruso* and its leaders are younger women. It exercises no authority in the ward although it has a spirit pot (*oyoŋko edet*) similar in appearance to that of *Ekuruso* and on which an initiate places her hands to be marked with chalk on admission. It is open to all acceptable women who will pay the fee of food for an admission feast consisting of a goat, four bottles of palm-wine, and a large calabash of mashed yam (*fufu*). The majority of women join *Oyoŋko* soon after marriage, for membership is a sign of good fellowship among women in the ward. Led by its four singers, who teach the songs, which are sung not in Yakö but in Agwa'aguna, and also play the *Oyoŋko* gongs, it organizes public dances in the period between the New Yam and the Harvest rites when women's yams are plentiful, and again after the main harvest; non-members including older unmarried girls may join in the dances. The dancing parties may visit all wards in the village and the compounds of any prominent men whom they will praise in extemporized verses, receiving small gifts of food and money for palm-wine. After the main harvest *Oyoŋko* dancing parties often go on visits of a few days to other Yakö villages in which they can expect a welcome. *Oyoŋko* dances are held at other times to mourn the death of a member or to celebrate a daughter's marriage.

CONCLUSION

Ward organization among the Yakö, as outlined above, shows an interesting adaptation to a considerable aggregation of population in compact settlement. Neither a fully centralized political organization nor a comprehensive segmentary principle of affiliation of clans and lineages has existed in the Yakö village communities. The pattern of village-wide authority under the ritual, moral, and limited juridical authority of the Council of Village Priests, described elsewhere, has been maintained. The ward is clearly a territorial segment in communities grown too large for convenient organization of secular activities on the basis of interpersonal relations, but while the organization of Ward Head and Leaders is ritually and morally linked to the Village Council through the *Okeŋka* society, it is in no sense its agent. Its members are

---

[38] In Umor there is a similarly a single organization for both Ukpakapi and Biko-Biko wards.

recruited within the ward, from the public opinion of which it derives its authority, and its membership predominantly reflects the common interests of the component patriclans and lineages that live as neighbours in the ward. Its rituals promote a sense of solidarity among the people of the ward and through *Ebiabu* and the age-set system it exercises general social control. But the authority, ritual or moral, of the *Yakambɔn* is not exclusive in the ward. Women maintain their own system of social control, while cult groups, such as *Ɔkpe* and others, concerned with public interests such as war and hunting, appear not to be formally linked to the central ward authority. Finally, the sense of neighbourhood developed in the ward channels the development among both men and women of convivial associations such as *Aiyo* and *Oyoŋko*.

VI

VILLAGE GOVERNMENT

(1) INDIGENOUS INSTITUTIONS[1]

IN the study of indigenous African institutions that exercise control while promoting social cohesion and regulating inter-personal and inter-group competition, much attention has been given to the analysis of the governmental functions of kin groups on the one hand and of ritually sanctioned political chiefship on the other. Institutions of these two types, which correspond to the distinction made by Durkheim between segmental and organic solidarity, were the basis of the well-known classification of *African Political Systems* by Fortes and Evans-Pritchard into two contrasted types labelled lineage or segmentary in one case, and centralized or statelike in the other. In their classification these writers were mainly concerned to distinguish politically centralized chiefdoms from those societies in which the exercise of political authority and social control was confined to recurrent but fluctuating combinations of lineages under their ritual leaders. In this they were led to imply, perhaps as a result of the limited range of societies selected for consideration, that apart from small autonomous bands of kindred, the only alternative to an acephalous and segmentary lineage system was a centralized society in which offices and political powers were hierarchically arranged with definite relations of administrative superiority and subordination holding between offices and councils at different levels. 'Administrative machinery' and 'judicial institutions' were treated as concomitants of centralized authority.[2]

This antithesis, while it served to classify broadly the societies actually selected for presentation, took no account of important gaps in its coverage. For it did not consider societies in which neither of these principles of organization and control could be held to be dominant, still less exclusive principles of political

[1] This section was originally published in *Africa*, XXXI, 4, 1961; it was also delivered as a Munro Lecture in the University of Edinburgh in March 1961.
[2] M. Fortes and E. E. Evans-Pritchard in the Introduction to *African Political Systems*, O.U.P., 1940, pp. 5, 6–7, 11–12.

organization. That criteria of social obligation other than lineage membership or chiefly allegiance were prominent in the maintenance of political relations and the exercise of authority in some African societies has, of course, long been obvious. As Paula Brown[3] showed in a comparative analysis of a number of West African societies some years ago, it was necessary not only to distinguish different kinds of authority (moral, ritual, and legal in her terminology), but also to recognize that offices vested in or authoritative over different types of group (kinship, associational, and territorial) might co-exist in varying relations and that there could be different allocations of the various kinds of authority referred to.

But the not uncommon tendency to perpetuate a scheme of apparently clear-cut categories that has served a useful initial purpose would seem to have hindered general recognition that some indigenous forms of government in Africa cannot, even as a first approximation, be fitted into so simple a dichotomy. Among these are societies in which self-perpetuating associations exercise autonomous ritual power and secular authority over part or all of the population with respect to a major sphere of social life. In such societies governmental powers—including both political action and judicial decisions—may be widely distributed among a number of independent and overlapping agencies. Wider political relations then largely resolve themselves into modes of co-operation with and competition between such associations. The coordination of political action in government does not therefore depend directly on the solidarity and co-operation of lineages on the one hand or on the paramount authority of a chief and its delegation to his subordinates on the other. It is achieved to the extent that there is mutual adjustment of their distinct competences by the several associations which may include some form of conciliar organization of their respective leaders. The role of associations among the Yakö, briefly analysed here, affords an instance of political organization of this kind.

The five compact politically independent village communities severally claim exclusive rights over a surrounding tract of terri-

---

[3] Paula Brown, 'Patterns of Authority in West Africa', *Africa*, xxi, 1951. A similar criticism has since been made by Middleton and Tait, in their Introduction to *Tribes without Rulers*, London, 1959. See also A. Southall, *Alur Society*, Cambridge, n.d.

tory which is exploited by its component groups for farming and the collection of forest products. These were, according to their traditions, successively established after an initial migration, perhaps rather more than a hundred years ago, of one or more groups from the Oban forest area to the ·east. These settlements maintained some external trading and other contacts with this eastern area now occupied by Ejagham and other small communities, and appear to have acted as middlemen between it and traders from the Cross River in traffic based on the exchange of camwood, bushmeat, and other forest products for gunpowder and 'trade goods'. At the same time they contributed substantially from at least the beginning of this century to the supply of palm oil and food crops to the Cross River trade. Although they appear to have taken little direct part as traders in the Cross River traffic, the Yakö derived considerable wealth in rods, cloth, and other goods in exchange for their forest and farm products. Their village communities appear to have grown rapidly since at least the beginning of this century. Ranging in population from three to over ten thousand, several of them are as large as were many of the Yoruba or Akan chiefdoms.

Patriclans and Ward Organization

In the nineteen-thirties, the period to which this account relates, Umor, the largest of the Yakö villages with a population of about 11,000, was, as has been described, composed of four wards each occupied by a number of localized patriclans (*yepun,* sing. *kepun*) varying in size from 50 to 200 adult men. These in turn comprised a number of lineages of 15 to 30 adult men, within which patrikinship by birth or through specific adoptions was traced genealogically to a depth of three or four generations and constituted the grounds for heritable rights to house sites and tracts of land. Kinship between lineages, and thus for members of a clan as a whole, was postulated as a norm for further rights and obligations, but it was not generally traced genealogically and often recognized as fictive and derived from the incorporation of incoming lineages and sections of other clans.

Thus little stress was placed on descent within the clan as a whole and there was no ancestral cult. The ritual head of a patriclan (*Obot Kepun*) was the custodian and priest of a spirit shrine. He presided over gatherings of informally recognized elders of the component lineages, arbitrated disputes among them, and formally represented the patriclan in external relations. His ritual capacity to afford the protection of the clan spirit and expiation of offences within the clan gave him moral authority in the interests of clan solidarity and the observance of custom. But the effectiveness and indeed the content of his judgements depended on the strength of his personality and support within the clan.

The unity and distinctness of a ward (*kekpatu*, pl. *yekpatu*) was strictly territorial. Its component patriclans did not claim common descent. It was seen as an aggregation of patriclans formed initially by an early association of a few patriclans among which there had been subsequent fission and to which lineages and sections of patriclans from other wards or villages had attached themselves in the course of the growth of the village.[4] Over the residential areas and lands claimed by its component clans the authorities of a ward had established rights to organize and control certain collective activities, to defend the rights of its clans against other wards and villages, and to arbitrate disputes among them. Within the ward each patriclan controlled and defended occupation of its own dwelling area and the tracts of land in which its members had established and inherited rights to farm plots, clusters of oil palms, and forest resources.

The wards were accordingly compact aggregates of from five to eleven patriclans each, comprising populations of from 300 to 600 men and their households. There was no dogma of common patrilineal descent of the component clans, nor was there any ranking of clans within the ward. Apart from its more general significance as a neighbourhood within a larger community, it was a ritual unit for initiation of boys and other ceremonies, a higher order of grouping for collective protection of rights to land, both residential and productive, and for internal social control. It was also the unit for the organization of age-sets, to the junior of which periodic tasks were assigned. Thus both the wards and the patriclans of Umor were said to have been formed by processes of fission and accretion associated with growth of population, ruptures of relations between lineages within clans, and coalescence of lineages and migrant men in other units. The effects of these processes in the formation, division, and migrations of

[4] Cf. Chapter III above.

patriclans have already been analysed.[5] The tradition with regard to the wards was that two settlement areas, Idjiman and Ŋkpani, were established when Yakö first settled in Umor. Separate wards were subsequently established by groups separating from Idjiman to form Idjum and Ukpakapi, and two generations ago a new ward, Biko-Biko, was established mainly by migrants from Ukpakapi. Meanwhile early in the history of Umor growing friction between Ŋkpani and another ward flared up into serious fighting, which ended by the migration of Ŋkpani to found a separate village of that name.

In each ward there was an association of Leaders (*Yakambɔn* = Men of the Ward), the Head of which (*Ogbolia*)—supported by his deputy (*Ogometu*), the preparer of meat for feasts (*Okaladji*), and Announcer (*Edjukwa*)—claimed a general authority in the name of the association over both ritual and secular affairs. The whole body of members assembled only for periodic rituals and at funerals of their members. The membership of this association of Ward Leaders was said in the thirties to have increased considerably in more recent times, when more than one new candidate had been accepted at the mortuary rites of a member. This was attributed to increased wealth, especially among the younger men, from participation in the oil-palm trade.[6] The heads of the several patriclans expected, and were expected, to be members, but they were a minority within it. The successor to a patriclan headship might already be an *Okambɔn*, if not he became one only when the payments were offered and accepted and the admission feast was held. Any unresolved dispute within the ward affecting the clan or the man concerned had to be settled to the satisfaction of the Leaders before a new clan head would be admitted. Priests of major village cults resident in the ward were normally admitted on succession to their ritual offices in the same way as patriclan heads. Otherwise succession was of one, or sometimes two, close kinsmen of a deceased member at the latter's death. Such memberships were sometimes spoken of as descending within the lineages in which one of their forebears was an original or early member. But provision of a successor to such former members was also an obligation, and a substantial fine, in lieu of admission payments, would be demanded if no suitable candidate were put forward. In proposing and accepting candidates their personal

---

[5] See Chapter III.   [6] See Chapter V, p. 142.

qualities were considered on both sides. Energetic and ambitious younger men could seek entry and in the thirties were often accepted.

There was in any case no fixed numerical or proportionate membership of the Leaders from the several patriclans and this was often very unequal. Nor was membership restricted to patrilineal succession, for successors to matriclan priesthoods joined the Leaders of the ward in which their shrine was situated. Patrikinsmen had only a right and a duty at the death of a member to present and help pay for the admission of a suitable successor from their lineage or clan. The means of a candidate to provide largely from his own resources for these payments in meat and currency was frequently a main consideration in the selection.

Thus the Ward Leaders were not *de jure* an assembly of patriclan heads and elders with an exclusive right to membership representing the clan sections of the ward. On the contrary, the *Yakambən* constituted and were thought of by the Yakö as a self-recruited and self-perpetuating body of notables, including holders of prominent ritual offices. It controlled succession to its own offices (headship, spirit representation in the ward initiation cult, &c.) by selection from its own members, and most of the power of the association was exercised by its Head in consultation with those concerned in any issue that might arise. Rights to succession to the office of *Ogbolia* were claimed by three or four patriclans within each of the wards. These were patriclans which professed to date from the founding of the ward in question and sought to nominate one of their members, normally from among those already Leaders, in rotation.[7] It appeared, however, that neither appointment from a particular clan nor strict rotation had been followed, and much depended on inter-clan relations and the prestige of candidates when succession arose. There appeared to be a general tendency for patriclans and indeed patrilineages within them to claim rights of succession to offices in associations. A similar tendency existed in the matrilineages of matriclans with regard to village priesthoods and both were an expression of the solidarity of kin in relation to

[7] Thus, in Ukpakapi ward the Egbisum, Usadja, and Lekpaŋkem patriclans assumed this right and in Idjiman ward, Lebuli, Kebuŋ, Otalosi, and Ugom made similar claims. In Ukpakapi one territorial subdivision of a large patriclan —the Ndai section of Lekpaŋkem-Ndai—had sought to monopolize the second office (of *Ogometu*) by demanding a right to nominate the successor when an *Ogometu* from the Obeten Ogometu lineage of Ndai had died.

other groupings and the wider society with reference to questions of status and influence.

The office of *Ogbolia* could be held concurrently with other offices in other associations. Thus the *Ogbolia* of Idjum ward in the twenties was said to have been also the Head (*Oboi Yakpan*) of the village association of *Ikpuŋkara*, that of Idjiman was Head (*Obot Obuŋa*) of the village corporation of diviners, and accordingly a member of the council of village priests. The *Ogbolia* of Biko-Biko (Eluŋ Ugopo) in the thirties was also the priest of the village cult of Obasi Oden and a member of the priests council.[8]

The *Ogbolia* in the name of the Ward Leaders had moral authority over other men's associations in the ward, i.e. an association of fighters (*Eblɔmbe*), of hunters (*Kodjo*) and a graded ritual, executive, and recreational association known as *Ebiabu* into which most males were initiated in boyhood. He had to be kept informed of all the important activities and intentions of these organizations. He could demand that they observed customary usages and order them to pay fines to or compensate others for breaches of custom. But these other associations were also self-recruited, with admission dependent on individual capacity and reputation and usually payment of fees. They were autonomous within their own fields of occupational and ritual or recreational activities. Overlapping membership of Ward Leaders in the membership of the Fighters and the senior grade of *Ebiabu* facilitated the co-ordination of their activities. In particular the Ward Head could, through the latter's senior grade *Abu*, request the middle grade of *Ebiabu* to coerce or apprehend recalcitrant offenders to quell intra-ward disturbances.[9]

The Leaders had strong *esprit de corps* with respect to their authority in ward affairs. Their dominance over the component

---

[8] The overlapping memberships in ward and village associations were further shown in the census of one patriclan section referred to above in which eleven of the men who were Leaders in the ward were also members of various senior village associations. Two, both old men of sixty or more, were members of the inner priesthood of *Okeŋka* and one of these was also a priest of *Korta*. Two others were also members of *Korta*. Three were members of *Ikpuŋkara* and three others were members of *Okundom*. There were two other members of *Okundom* who had not joined the Ward Leaders.

[9] The authority and functions of the *Ogbolia* and the *Yakambɔn* as here described were those attributed to them by the Yakö for the period before the Native Court became effective in the twenties. The manner in which the judicial and other secular functions of the *Ogbolia* came to be superseded by those of Court Members ('Warrant Chiefs') selected from the wards will be indicated below, p. 190.

patriclans was also ceremonially and materially emphasized at the death of a member, when they assembled to bid him farewell and dance in his compound. They then demanded from his heirs substantial provisions for holding their own feast in his honour and the nomination of, and admission payments for, a successor.

Within the general body there was also a smaller group consisting of its office holders and a few others who had the privilege of conducting an annual ward rite (*Kɛkpan*) at the time of the clearing of farm land.[10] Apart from the office holders there was again obligatory succession by a kinsman which entailed further payments.

Within each ward there was also, however, an association known as *Ŋkpe* that was not co-ordinated with and did not accept directions concerning its own affairs from the Leaders. Claiming control of a punitive Leopard Spirit derived from the Ejagham (Ekoi) peoples to the east, it offered supernatural protection to its members, and to others for a fee, against theft of crops and stock and also the seduction and insubordination of wives. *Ŋkpe* had no acknowledged right of physical coercion of its members or others. Its secular power consisted in its right to claim damages for the abuse of its protective emblems when these had been placed on the trees or other property of an applicant. *Ŋkpe* also regarded itself as a means of defence against abuse of power both by the Leaders and the village cult groups. These in turn treated it with suspicion and admitted no leading member of *Ŋkpe* to their ranks. It had become a reluctantly tolerated opposition.

Thus within the ward in Umor secular authority, judicial decisions, and the ritual expression of social cohesion and continuity were in the hands of a number of organizations of an associational character. Participation, office, and influence within them depended on acceptance by their own members. Patriclans and lineages could influence their actions and decisions and also derive prestige only through the membership of their own elders and spokesmen within them. Between the associations themselves there was little explicit hierarchy of political authority. The Leaders had recognized authority over the junior age-sets with regard to customary tasks and a *de facto* means of coercing those who flouted a decision that enjoyed general support through overlapping membership in, and a working arrangement with, the

---

[10] See Chapter V, p. 140.

independent association of *Ebiabu*. At the same time the ability of *Ŋkpe* to establish itself as an independent and generally hostile association was a clear indication of the limitations on the authority of the Leaders.

Village Organization

Needless to say, disputes between individuals, lineages, and other groups from different wards could bring the Leaders and other associations within them into conflict. The outbreak of widespread violence arising from inter-ward disputes was recalled as a serious danger in the past. One such occurrence was particularly remembered, since it ended in the extinction of one of the first two wards early in the history of the village. This ward occupied the area south-east of the market in the angle between Idjiman and Ukpakapi wards. Most of its population was said to have left to found, or perhaps to join, the independent Yakö village of Ŋkpani several miles away.

The risk of a resort to force in inter-ward hostilities engendered by such disputes was tempered by the existence of a village cult group to which some Leaders from the several wards belonged. To this ritual fraternity, some fifty strong, known as *Okeŋka*, Ward Heads could and should bring disputes they could not otherwise resolve.[11]

Here again, membership in this village cult association was not a formal right of offices vested in either the patriclans or the wards. But since membership carried prestige and a means of influence both for the member and his patrikin, prosperous, energetic, and reliable men who became Ward Leaders usually sought and were supported for membehip of *Okeŋka*. Only those who were already Leaders in their wards were usually acceptable for membership and each Ward Head (*Ogbolia*) and his deputy (*Ogometu*) was expected to join and be admitted on his appointment if he were not already a member. Membership of *Okeŋka* was not considered to involve obligatory succession. But, on the other hand, the patrikin of a deceased member would usually request that one of them should be admitted. There were also claims that the Headship of *Okeŋka* (*Ovar Ekpe*) should pass in turn to men of one of three patriclans that were reputed to be the oldest in each of the three long-established wards.

[11] This has been more fully described in Chapter V.

Contravention of a judgement of the *Okeŋka* spirit, as made known by the head of the cult group after secret conclave, entailed grave misfortune of an unpredictable character for the offenders and their kin. Ward Heads and Leaders used the sanctions of *Okeŋka* to uphold judgements on intractable disputes both within a ward as well as in the settlement of issues between persons and groups of different wards. Thus common participation of their senior members in the *Okeŋka* cult both provided means for, and accustomed the Ward Leaders to, co-operation and co-ordinated action in maintaining order.

The Head of *Okeŋka* as priest of a village Leopard cult was in turn one of the members of the more restricted body of twenty-four men in which both ritual powers and moral authority in the village as a whole were concentrated. This was a village corporation of priests known simply as the Heads (*Yabot*). Its nucleus consisted of the ten priests of fertility spirits (*ase*) with each of which was associated one or more of the twenty-three dispersed matriclans recognized in the village.

The Council of Village Priests[12]

The sentiments of matrilineal kinship, it will be recalled, are maintained among the Yakö not merely by the customary concern of a man for the well-being of his sisters and their children and by the recurrent transfers of inherited property to matrilineal relatives, but also by belief in the great supernatural power for inducing fertility and well-being in crops, livestock, and women, of supernatural beings known as *ase* (sing. *yose*) to whose beneficence the groups of matrilineal kin severally have access. Each *yose* is believed to be embodied in a shrine set up in a miniature house in the compound of its priest or *Ina* (pl. *Bi'ina*) (Plate XXIII).

There are, as has been shown earlier, 23 matrilineal kin groups or *yajima* in Umor, but several of these have been formed by subdivision of former units. There are only 10 *ase* shrines, each of which is served by an *Ina* who is usually selected from a single *lejima*. The remaining *yajima* are associated with one or other of the *ase* to which their members have access through the priest, who performs rites of supplication and thanksgiving on their behalf.

---

[12] Pp. 174–82 are taken from 'Government in Umor', *Africa*, XII, 2, 1939, pp.129–62. The text has been amended to omit passages on topics more fully dealt with elsewhere and to provide additional material from other references.

Of the 23 groups, 9 have an exclusive right to provide priests, 2 have rights in alternation, while 12 provide no priests. Eight of the existing groups have in the past transferred their allegiance from the *ase* which they formerly recognized, and 5 of these have created new *ase*.

In every *lejima*, as has been seen, there is a small group of elders (*Yajimanotam*, *lejima* old men)—from six to a dozen of the more senior and capable men of the *lejima*, who, although they have no ritual functions and no routine duties to perform, and maintain their numbers by informal co-option from time to time, are able to exert considerable influence on the members of their *lejima* and on village affairs that concern the group. Recompense for offence by one member of the *lejima* towards another can be enforced by requesting the priests of the *yose* to declare the offender excommunicated; and by appeal through him to the village authorities they are able to protect the interests of particular members of the group in the payments and responsibilities involved in the marriages of their matrilineal kin.

On the death of an *Ina* his successor is proposed by the elders of the *lejima* which has the traditional right to nominate to this office. Within a *lejima* there is no restriction of succession to a priesthood, although a close matrilineal relative of a former priest is considered appropriate. The person chosen is not usually one of the elders but a man early in middle life and, although he is selected by the *lejima* elders, he is not appointed or instructed in his ritual duties by them but by the group of *ase* and other associated priests as a whole who thus constitute a sacerdotal village council. These priests are able to veto a nomination of the *lejima* elders by refusing to accept and induct the proposed successor if they consider him unfitted. In practice an appointment is usually discussed by the elders with the priests, and an agreed candidate is selected.

Although each priest carries out private rituals at the shrine for any persons of the *yajima* concerned, the public rites to the *ase* are participated in by all the village priests. Twice a year acting as a corporation they carry out a series of protracted rituals—the New Yam and the Harvest rituals—in which all the *ase* shrines and several other sacred sites in the village are visited.[13]

The pre-eminence of the *ase* fertility spirits as supernatural forces in Umor has thus afforded great prestige and influence to

[13] The New Yam rites are described and discussed in Chapter VIII, below.

their priests, and one of them, the *Ina* of the *yose* Odjokobi, is recognized as the Village Head. Odjokobi, while regarded as the fertility spirit of a set of *yajima* of which one has the recognized right to provide the priest, is also in some sense a fertility spirit for the entire village, and any person, no matter what his affiliation, can make offerings at the public rites, while the leaders of several of the initiation and secret associations are expected to assemble formally and make offerings at the public festivals. The Village Speaker said of Odjokobi, 'He is for all Umor. Yabot *lejima* have him, but he exists for the whole village.' Whether this accounts historically for the recognition of its priest as the Village Head, cannot be known in the absence of records, but the established position is clear. Odjokobi is the fertility spirit of certain matrilineal kin groups, one of which has a particularly close association with it. At the same time it is in a very real sense the fertility spirit of the village as a whole and the most powerful supernatural force in the community. Its priest, although he is selected from a single matrilineal kin group, is as pre-eminent among the priests as is Odjokobi among the other *ase* and is recognized as the religious head of the village. The *Ina* of Odjokobi is regarded and addressed from the time of his installation as '*Obot Lopon*' (Leader of the Village), and the selection of a successor to this office is one in which the other *Bi'ina* priests display correspondingly great concern. At the last appointment in Umor the *Bi'ina* priests refused to accept the first two persons successively proposed by the elders of Yabot *lejima*, insisting that one was too old and the other not a wise and conciliatory man (Plate XV*a*).

The functions of the *ase* priests are not, however, restricted to ritual performances and to securing supernatural benefits. These men are the nucleus and strength of a priestly council which has directed village affairs and attempted to settle major disputes and administer customary law. *Obot Lopon*, the priest of Odjokobi, is the head of this council, which is generally referred to as *Yabot* (The Leaders). His compound, known as Lebokem, is situated on one side of the village assembly square (*Keblapoŋa*) near the centre of the village and not in the territory of any *kepun* or ward. His house, which has the special name *Ebota*, is re-furnished for each new *Obot Lopon* by the men of Yabot *lejima*, and is subsequently repaired and rebuilt from time to time by the co-operative labour of age-sets drawn from all the wards. In his compound all

XV *a*. *Obot Lopon* the Village Head of Umor (1935). His status derives from his priesthood of the paramount fertility spirit, the *Yose Odjokobi*, and he has been recognized as a Warrant Chief of the Native Court in which this photograph was taken

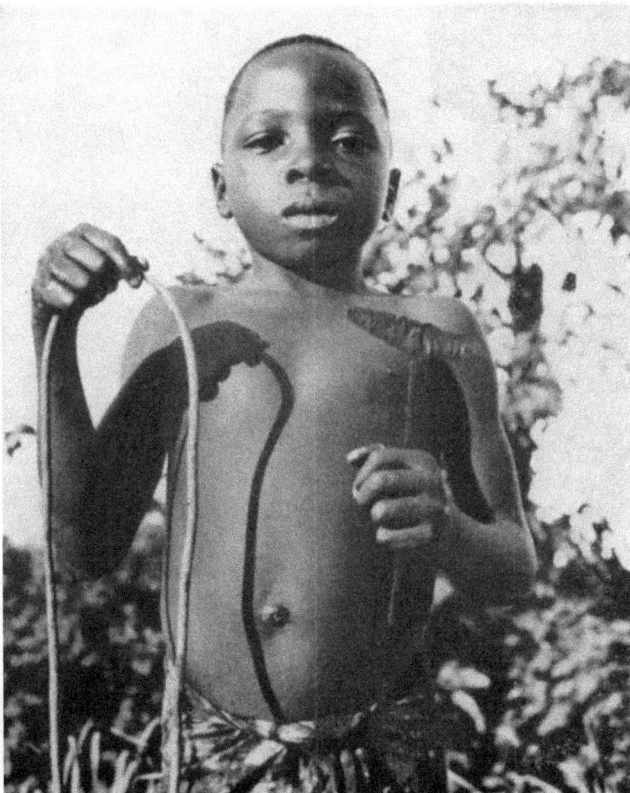

XV *b*. *Ligwomi* initiate. The boy is holding the brass rod and piece of hoe money that is to be paid to the *Yakambən* of his ward

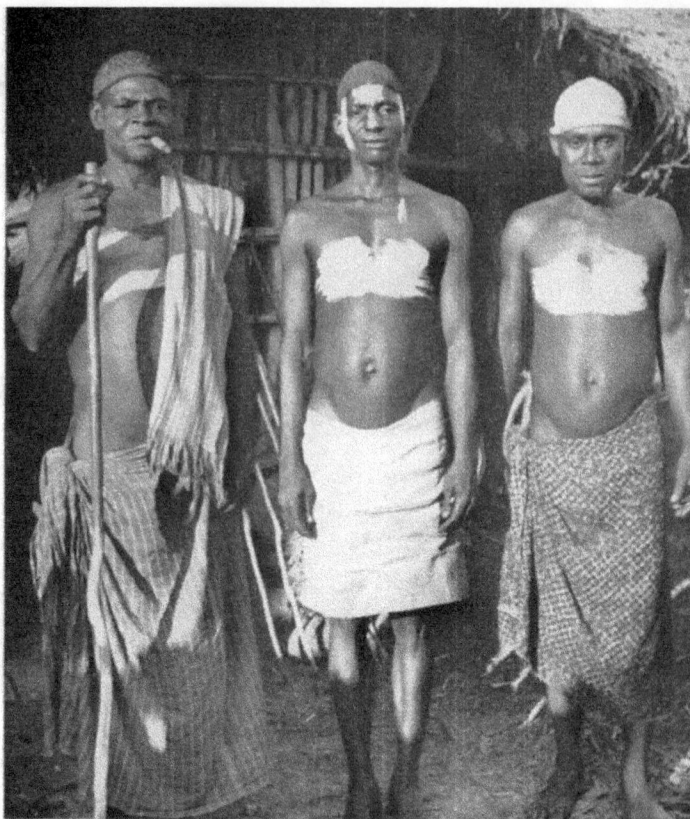

XVI *a. Elamalama.* The *Obot Kepun* of Ugom I, as priest of *Elamalama,* the foundation *epundet* of Umor, is a member of the Village Council, which is mainly composed of priests of the matrilineal kin groups. This status is marked by a teeth-chipping rite, performed by the Village Speaker and a matrilineal priest, seen standing on his right and left at the conclusion of the ceremony

XVI *b.* The leader of one of the younger age-sets with its decorated palm-wine jar. It is prepared for the establishment feast of the set and is kept in the leader's house for use at all later feasts

the public rituals of the village are initiated or reach their climax and in it the council assemble to discuss village affairs and to try cases brought before them.

The village council of *Yabot* does not consist solely of the *ase* priests, but the other members belong to it in virtue of their appointment to ceremonial offices with the consent or at the instance of the priests. They include the heads of the two other ritual organizations, *Korta* and *Okeŋka*, which also perform ceremonies in conjunction with the rites of the *ase* at the annual New Yam Rites; *Obot Yabuŋa*, the head of the corporation of magicians, whose techniques and powers are believed to enable them to satisfy particular human desires, including the diagnosis of diseases, and to combat specific and harmful supernatural agencies, including those evoked by black magic; the priest of one *kepun* shrine in Umor, which is believed to have been established when the Yakö of Umor first occupied the village site; the priest of the village *Obasi* shrine; the priest of a powerful spirit, *Esandet*, whose shrine lies in a tract of uncultivated land remote from the village; and finally a group of persons who have particular ceremonial functions in connection with the *ase* priests but are not associated with a particular spirit or an independent ritual organization. These are *Obot Omeŋka*, who plays a leading part in the initiation of newly appointed priests; *Obot Odere*, the leader of the Trumpeters and Drummers who precede the ceremonial processions of the *Yabot* at the New Yam Feast and other main village rituals; the *Yabot Leko* or *Yanun Eko*, two war leaders who formerly conducted rituals to ensure success in warfare (no appointments to these offices had been made since the last holders died several years ago); and finally the village Speaker, *Okpebri*, who speaks on behalf of *Obot Lopon* and of the *Yabot*, both in rituals and in announcing decisions on disputes and other village affairs.

The *Yabot* thus tend to form a close-knit corporation with community of interests and a strong sense of internal loyalty; for elections to offices in most organizations apart from the wards and patriclans are subject to the approval of the *Yabot*, while appointments to those mentioned above lie with the *Yabot* themselves and men selected come immediately under their instruction and influence. Their prestige in village affairs and their recognition as the paramount body in both legal disputes and public affairs undoubtedly derives from the fact that collectively they perform or direct all the important rituals which control the supernatural forces in whose power for good and evil the great majority of the population profoundly believes.

The Secular Authority of the Yabot.

It would, however, be a mistake to regard the *Yabot* as a ritual-ridden clique indifferent to practical affairs and customary standards of social conduct. They are responsible for announcing the times at which many seasonal activities should begin and they can impose customary penalties for refusal to comply with their regulation of such activities. While the great seasonal rituals are carried through with extreme thoroughness, sincere conviction, and impressive solemnity the *Yabot* do not live withdrawn from the community. They have severally an independent social life in their own *yepun* and *yajima* groups, their households are organized and maintained in the same manner as those of other men, their farms are not usually large, and their harvests are often below the average in size.

All disputes which cannot be satisfactorily settled within *kepun* or *lejima* or by agreement between the elders of the kin groups or the ward of the contestants should be referred to the *Yabot* for their decision. Furthermore, the *Yabot* would intervene on their own initiative, not only if serious disorders threatened, but also in lesser matters involving danger or a breach of custom, particularly if it were believed that supernatural dangers for the village at large have to be averted. Broadly speaking, it may be said that the council of the *Yabot* has functioned both as a civil and a criminal court. In relation to the decisions of the heads and elders of kin groups and wards it has served as a court of appeal, while for serious offences believed to incur the displeasure of supernatural powers it controls it is a tribunal with authority to summon and punish the malefactor on its own initiative.

The *Yabot* have access to powerful sanctions, both physical and supernatural, to enforce their decisions. The supernatural sanctions lie in their own hands. They can refuse an offender all access to the shrine of the *yose* of his *lejima* and can extend this exclusion to his relatives and even to all the members of his *lejima*. They can prevent a man from entering or leaving his dwelling until recompense for an offence has been made, by coming in procession and placing their staffs (which he would not dare to touch) before the entrance to his compound or his house.

If there is a serious disturbance which the *Yabot* are unable to quiet they may request *Okpebri* to bring out the *Edet Lopon* (Village Fetish), a cult object whose safe keeping in the house of *Okpebri* is believed to be necessary if the village is to continue in existence. Bearing it in his arms, *Okpebri* visits the meeting-place in each of the wards, declaring his intention of leaving the village with *Edet Lopon*. He then proceeds to walk out of the village by the path along which it is believed that the ancestors came to Umor. This action is said to have caused great alarm and appears to have effectively distracted attention from the original disturbance and induced a sufficient body of people to restore order, and send messengers to recall *Okpebri* long before he could reach Idomi, the Yakö village a few miles away.

Of the further and larger number of custodians of cults directly associated as *Yabot* with the priests of the fertility shrines, some were priests of particular village spirit shrines. Thus the custodian of the emblems of the Liboku spirit, which was invoked annually in the village First Fruits ritual, was selected and installed by the priests council and incorporated into it. Others were officiants in other organized cult groups. Of these, in addition to *Okeŋka*, which has been referred to in connection with the *de facto* ritual and judicial co-ordination of the Leaders of the several wards, there was, for example, the cult of *Korta*. In the course of a lengthy ritual of renewal of the village held every six years, the spirit of *Korta* sanctioned the initiation of all boys into the male community of the village. Three priestly offices in Korta, that of its head (*Opalapala*), who was custodian of the spirit, his deputy and usual successor (*Ogbodum*) and the chief drummer (*Otomise*), were controlled by, and conferred membership in, the *Yabot*. The headship was expected to pass in turn to men of one of three long-established patriclans, one in each ward. Successions to other positions in the cult, the singer (*Obenebenekpe*) and the drummers (*Yakpapa*), were also claimed by other lineages but these did not confer membership of the *Yabot*.

Further members of the *Yabot* were priests of certain spirits variously associated with the territory or rivers of the village (e.g. *Esandet*) or with its foundation site (*Elamalama*). Two others were responsible for war ritual (*Yanun Eko*), one with sacred

village trumpets (*Odere*) and another with one of the shrines
of the creator god, Obasi Oden. The head of the corporation of
diviners, who was also priest of another diviners' cult of *Obasi*
(*Isɔ Obasi*), and whose office passed from father to son or other
close patrikinsman, was also installed by and became a member
of its council.

But the leading public figure in this priestly council was its
Speaker (*Okpebri*). In his custody were certain village drums and
the emblems of a spirit on whose safe keeping the unity and continuity of the village was held to depend. For public display and
threatened removal of the latter was believed to sanction, under
penalty of general disaster, any prolonged disorder in the village. It
was the Speaker who, during the successive public rituals at their
shrines, actually invoked, on behalf of the village Head and the
priests as a body, the beneficence of the fertility spirits during the
seasonal rites (see Frontispiece and Plate XX*a*).

Although there is no documentation from the past and I obtained only sketchy and sometimes variant traditions to confirm it,
the formation and composition of this council of village priests in
Umor appeared, and was believed by the Yakö, to result from the
combination of these diverse cults. And the original nucleus was
said to have been the association of the priests of the fertility spirits
associated with the various matriclans. However that may be, the
leading priests of these various spirit cults, on which a wide range
of personal and collective benefits were believed to depend or from
which punishment for offences was feared, had come to constitute
a corporation of considerable solidarity.

Moreover, in addition to its powers of ritual interdiction and its
generally effective moral authority in public affairs, the village
priests council had traditionally been a source of judgement with
regard not only to ritual offences, such as incest, abortion, and
homicide, but also to major and refractory disputes between persons and groups. It was still commonly appealed to despite the
establishment of the District Native Court for the area that began
to be effective in the twenties. In an issue of the latter kind one
party to the dispute could request that it be heard by the council.
It was also expected to intervene itself by summoning contestants
to state their cases before it if a dispute was dragging on unsettled
by the Ward Leaders or by the judgements of one of the village
associations. Such judgements were held to have been generally

accepted in the past. Expiatory ritual offerings required were made, compensation awarded to injured parties was paid, and fines demanded of those against whom judgements were given were paid to the priests.

The priests council might also take up on its own initiative important public issues that arose in the village. On internal questions it would summon any Ward Leaders and heads of other associations that might be concerned to give information and to receive its views. On occasions it sent messengers bearing complaints or demands to other villages.

These judicial and deliberative capacities of the priests council were supported only by its combined ritual powers and moral authority. But these were not inconsiderable. The beneficence of matriclan fertility spirits could be withheld from, and the punitive action of other spirits threatened against, those who flouted their judgement. In particular a defiant individual could be ritually sequested in his house and his household and kin excommunicated by the planting of the priests' staves on his veranda. A judgement of the council also afforded moral authority for punitive action by other associations whose intervention could be invoked.

Dependence on Village Cult Associations

For the supernatural powers of the *Yabot* have not been found sufficient to coerce the recalcitrant, and material retribution has also been resorted to. The *Yabot* could not then act themselves. By custom and temperament they should be men of dignity and peace who avoid all brawls and physical violence. But they have found agents for the infliction of material penalties in certain of the village cult associations which acted in both the apprehension and the punishment of recalcitrant offenders at the request of the *Yabot*.

The full coercive powers of these associations have withered in the course of the administrative changes of the past thirty years, and there is some discrepancy between the accounts given of the way in which they operated. The present *Okpebri*, for instance, asserted that the associations could properly take no action without the order of the *Yabot*, but one of the heads of the leading association insisted that certain offences, and in particular theft, could be investigated and punished by them without instructions or inter-

ference from any outside body. One association was outstanding
in the exercise of secular punitive functions in association with the
Yabot. This is *Ikpuŋkara*, which at the time included among its
members only about 40 of the 1,800 adult males of the village.
At the request of the Village Head, announced to the two leaders
(*Yabot Yakpan*) of this society when they had been summoned to
a meeting of the *Yabot*, *Ikpuŋkara* would formerly, according to
Okpebri, have descended on the households of offenders and, if
necessary, their kinsmen, and seized any livestock they might
possess. Such action would be invoked if individuals or a small
group ignored or defied the *Yabot*, not merely with reference to
orders for the settlement of particular disputes but also in connection with bans on particular activities at certain times, such, for
instance, as prohibitions on trading with a neighbouring village
on account of a dispute over lands. But the present leaders also
insisted that formerly it could act independently as a court and
punitive body in certain circumstances. It was claimed that anyone, whether a member of *Ikpuŋkara* or not, could approach its
leaders and, stating a complaint, could ask to have it heard by the
society. Bringing a gift of palm-wine and yams to a meeting
specially called, the complainant could state his case and, if
necessary, the alleged offenders were sent for. Thefts of livestock
and non-payment of marriage money were the offences said to
have been considered by the society in this way. If the accused
were considered guilty and would not offer restitution and a payment to *Ikpuŋkara*, the society would seize sufficient of his livestock or household goods to compensate the claimant and satisfy
itself for its trouble.

As no secular coercive action was directly available to the council
itself, this delegation of its authority directs attention to the fact
that, in addition to the *Okeŋka* cult group already mentioned,
there were in Umor other associations recruited from the village
at large, claiming the custody of other powerful spirits, which did
not participate through their leaders in the village council of
priests, but did claim the right to investigate offences, give judgement, and enforce penalties by direct action.

One such village association, generally referred to as *Okundom*
or 'The Body of Men', was especially concerned with trespass on
farms and the stealing of crops. Against both magical and material
offences of this kind it provided, on receipt or promise of a pay-

ment, the protection of its spirit. When offences were alleged before it, the Heads of *Okundom* undertook detection of the culprits, the presentation or support of an accusation before the Ward Leaders or the village priests council and the enforcement of any compensation by actual or threatened destruction of livestock of the offender or his kin. Where the theft from farm land or trees was explicitly protected by *Okundom*, as marked by the affixing of its sign on the property concerned, the offender was held to have wronged the association and the charge was brought against him specifically on those grounds.

The formation of the *Okundom* association was traditionally ascribed to serious thefts early in the history of the village. This induced the priest of one of the matriclan spirits to sanction its formation and to recognize as its first head a man from the patriclan in the dwelling area in which the spirit shrine was situated. Membership, secured by providing an admission payment and feast, then spread through the village in successive generations. Nomination of a suitable successor to a deceased member became both a right and an obligation of that member's close patrikin. Memorial feasts and admission payments were demanded from them on the occasion of these successions, and the new member shared in the later feasts and the fees provided by those who sought its aid.

Okundom was, however, later overshadowed in prestige by *Ikpuŋkara*, another men's association already referred to, the sphere of activity of which had also extended over the village as a whole. Its forty members, who came from all parts of the village, formed a close-knit group, who were on admission pledged by the supernatural sanctions of their spirit cult, both to divulge within the association and to keep secret from outsiders any information on alleged offences and other issues with which the association concerned itself. *Ikpuŋkara* was said to have been constituted early in the history of the village, but later than *Okundom*, by a group of senior men under the leadership of one of the patriclan heads. Apart from the maintenance of its own prestige, its main concern had been with settling land disputes, which had been numerous in the course of the growth of the community and with detecting and punishing theft of cows which browsed at large in the vicinity of the settlement. As farming and house-building expanded, *Ikpuŋkara* investigated on the ground and gave its judgement on

several acrimonious disputes between men of different clans and
wards over rights to build and to farm certain areas. It had also
gained a general influence in all village affairs including external
relations, concerning which it might declare and enforce a ban on
visits to and trading with neighbouring villages, where bad relations had developed or an unsettled injury had been suffered by
members of the village (Plate XVII*b*).

Ikpuŋkara usually announced its findings and judgements to the
priests council which, in turn on occasion, suggested investigation
by it. It was said to be rare that the council questioned its judgement and the compensation or other action it required. This
liaison was facilitated by overlapping membership, since the Village
Head and several of the other priests of the matriclan fertility
spirits were regularly admitted to *Ikpuŋkara* on succession to their
priesthoods. For the rest, admission to *Ikpuŋkara* was by succession on the death of a close kinsman who had been a member. Most
of these successions were patrilineal, but a few in addition to those
of the matriclan priests were matrilineal. Besides the provision of
supplies for a memorial feast to the late member within *Ikpuŋkara*, the body of kin concerned were required to assist an acceptable successor in making the large admission payments that were
valued in the thirties at some £20.

For its services in investigating offences and settling disputes,
Ikpuŋkara secured payments—fees from those who appealed, and
fines from those it found culpable. Like *Okundom* and the ward
associations, it had an ultimate punitive sanction against those that
would repudiate its authority or flout its judgement. Livestock in
the compounds where the offenders resided were raided and killed
or carried off. The offender was then left to settle as best he could
with his kin and neighbours, who, in fear of a repetition so long as
the matter was unsettled, forced him to accept and act on the
judgement and beg for the return of such stock as had not already
been eaten at a feast.

Both *Ikpuŋkara* and *Okundom* enjoyed ritual recognition and
acceptance by the priests council, for they were among the groups
which included the Ward Leaders, the diviners, and certain
women's associations, that came successively in procession to the
Village Head's compound for the first public rites at the *Odjokobi*
spirit shrine at the seasonal festivals. There, like those of the other
groups, their members received the blessing of the spirit by being

smeared across the breast by the priest with chalk paste prepared at the altar.

On the other hand, neither *Okundom* nor *Ikpuŋkara* regarded themselves as mere agents or subordinates of the village priests council. Indeed, some of their members strongly repudiated such a suggestion. They said that the *Yabot* had their own 'messengers' (i.e. junior kinsmen whom they sent to call people they wished to speak with), and, furthermore, that they had their own spirit, which was independent of the fertility spirits of the matriclans and both justified and protected their own actions.

Ikpuŋkara and *Okundom* resembled the *Yakambən* of the wards in demanding the provision of memorial feasts and fees for the admission of successors from kinsmen at the deaths of members.[14] These were means of increasing the collective prestige of these associations and acceptance of their secular authority. In this they differed from the council of village priests, where membership was directly associated with appointment to ritual office and no question of succession fees or the provision of feasts by the clans arose.

Conclusion

From this outline of the different levels at which various agencies exerted some form of social control in Umor beyond the limits of the local patriclan groups, it will be seen that, with respect to both the ward and to the village as a whole, there were separately developed organizations which claimed independent authority according to the circumstances of the activity or dispute. Supported by the sanction of spirits in their custody, they could require certain actions in the public interest, prohibit other actions, notably violent behaviour, and also demand that alleged offences and disputes within their sphere of authority be brought before them for inquiry and judgement. They claimed, in brief, the right to act as deliberative, executive or judicial authorities; although in many cases their *raison d'être* in the eyes of the Yakö was the performance of rituals which sustained and safeguarded the welfare of part or all of the community. But these bodies did not constitute

---

[14] For an analysis of the relation between these associations and the kin groups of their members in Yakö mortuary ceremonial see: D. Forde, 'Death and Succession: An Analysis of Yakö Mortuary Ceremonial' in *Essays on the Ritual of Social Relations*, ed. Max Gluckman. Manchester University Press, 1962.

a segmentary system of kin groups. Their members did not consist
exclusively or mainly of the heads of clans. Lineage organization
did not extend beyond the patriclan and the matriclan, and
authority derived from it was confined within these comparatively
small unilineal groups.

In the traditionally dominant governing body of the ward—the
Yakambən whom we have called the Leaders—there was succession
to membership from certain lineages and patriclan heads were
admitted. But there was no formal chain of authority or ritual
continuity between the patriclans and the ward. The Ward Leaders
were sustained by their own spirits and were not regarded by the
Yakö as a conclave of clan elders, nor did they function as such.
They viewed their ritual powers, their rights and obligations territorially in terms of the ward and its population. For it they performed an annual rite and a periodic initiation of its boys. They
recognized the formation of new age-sets and through their Announcer (*Edjukwa*) called for the public services of the more junior
ones. The Ward Leaders heard and gave judgement in disputes
within the ward. But they, themselves, had organized no powers of
punishment or coercion with which to enforce their judgements. In
cases of flagrant misbehaviour or defiance of a judgement they
could only rely on their overlapping membership with the senior
grade of an independently organized ward association—the *Ebiabu*
—to secure this. Thus, while they had provided a form of ward
government which, so long as it did not interfere with the established rights of patriclans and of other associations, appeared to
have been respected, they had, in their mode of recruitment and
their stress on spirit powers with respect to initiation and the moral
unity of the ward, also the character of a cult group consisting of a
closed association of notables. It was perhaps their weakness as an
executive body that accounts in part for the rapid decay of their
secular powers in recent times. For when members were called for
from each of the wards to serve on the District Native Court
established in the twenties, only one *Ogbolia* was put forward and
accepted by the Administration as a warrant chief. And within ten
years or so, the Native Court had supplanted the *Yagbolia* and the
Yakambən of the wards as the most general means for securing
redress for private wrongs.

Within the wider framework of the village community, neither
the *Yakambən* as a body nor its priest head *Ogbolia* was directly

responsible to the village council of priests. That the latter had a
different and wider sphere of both ritual and secular authority
which should, in the interest of harmony and prosperity, be
respected, was generally recognized by the Ward Leaders and
Yakö in general. But this implied only a co-operative, albeit in
some contexts a deferential, relation between two organizations
that were autonomous in their respective spheres. Apart from the
Village Head, who had no ward residence, a matriclan priest was at
one and the same time a member of the village priests council and
of the Leaders of the ward in which his spirit shrine was situated.
And other members of the village council were usually also Leaders
in their wards.

When we consider the council of village priests it might be
argued that its ritual head, who was explicitly recognized as Head
of the Village, should be regarded as a chief in the political sense,
as one who, supported by his council, exercised centralized
authority over the village community. If this were acceptable, the
political organization of Umor might still, perhaps without too
much forcing of the evidence, be placed within the category of
'centralized hierarchical, state-like forms of government', which
Fortes and Evans-Pritchard distinguished as the alternative to
acephalous systems of segmentary lineage organization. The
establishment of a separate and central compound, outside the
territory of any of the wards, in which the Village Head resided,
where important village rituals began and where the priests council
assembled to deliberate on village affairs and give judgement on
disputes—all this might give colour to such a view. But it would
not only ignore the crucial lack, and indeed disavowal, of secular
means of enforcing decisions and judgements. In terms of the
combination of features taken as characterizing such a system, we
can recognize the priests council as a 'centralized authority' only
in the moral and ritual spheres. As a judicial institution these were
its only modes of enforcement. Where these were challenged its
sole resort was to approve or accept the coercive action of other
bodies. Furthermore, it lacked 'administrative machinery' for
carrying out any decisions it might reach on public affairs. Here
again it had to depend on the concurrence and action of other
village or ward associations.

Secondly, the status of the priest of the premier fertility spirit
Odjokobi as Head of the Village (*Obot Lopon*) was that of a *primus*

inter pares rather than of a chief enjoying distinctive status who was advised and checked by a body of councillors of lower rank. The priest of Odjokobi was nominated to, and approved and installed by, the council as a whole in the same manner as the other members. The rights of the Village Head with regard to hearing, giving judgement, and in particular collecting fees and fines had been an issue among the Yakö in the past. It was recounted in the thirties that the previous Village Head had sent his messengers on his own account to summon alleged offenders and had heard cases without summoning other members of the *Yabot*. This was held to be against custom and caused discontent and protest. On the other hand it was recognized that, where a minor private wrong was in question, the Village Head, need not summon the whole council, which did not in any case assemble regularly in full session. The practice was for complainants and defendants to inform those *Yabot* with which they were connected by kinship, residential, or ritual ties and for those concerned to meet in the Village Head's compound for the hearing.

It should also be noted that the Village Head did not receive tribute. Small gifts of food were often brought to the priests council during village ceremonials but there was no general obligation to maintain him. His matriclan and the men of the ward from which he came were said to have an obligation to contribute materials and labour for the repair or rebuilding of the house and compound of the Village Head, and he could no doubt get help from both these sources. A compulsory offering that might be regarded as ritual tribute was the bringing of any leopard that had been killed to the compound of the Village Head. But it was *Okpebri*, not the Village Head, who took charge of carcasses and it was the *Okeŋka* cult association which conducted the rituals and admitted the leopard killer to its membership.

The mortuary ritual of the Village Head, while usually more protracted than that of other priests, did not differ essentially in procedure or ideology. Accounts of the burial of human heads and of cannibalism associated with it, which were discreetly placed in the past, were probably not distinctive, for the 'head hunting' associations that were formerly active were said to have obtained victims for the mortuary rituals of other priests.

We must conclude, therefore, that despite their considerable moral as well as ritual authority and the very general acceptance of their judgements on public issues and private disputes, the council of village priests in Umor and, so far as they are known, those of the other Yakö communities, cannot be regarded as the apex of a pyramidal form of centrally administered government. Individually the powers and the authority of the priests of the Yakö fertility and other spirits find closer analogues in those of the custodians of Earth shrines among the Southern Ibo, or again among the Lowiili, Tallensi, and other peoples of Northern Ghana.

The tradition of compact settlement and the double system of descent among the Yakö has resulted in a pattern of large communities composed of closely neighbouring territorial patriclans and of dispersed matriclans in each of which membership is scattered over the whole community. With a considerable growth of population these conditions appear to have fostered a closer association of the matriclan priests who embodied positive values of peaceful co-operation. Their formal organization for the conduct of public rituals on behalf of the community would have further enhanced their moral authority. The priests of other cults were incorporated into this body, which accordingly acquired an essentially associated character as a self-regulating corporation that co-ordinated both the complex series of ritual activities significant for the village as a whole and the exercise of ritual sanctions by the priests of these various cults.

In the large and dense aggregation of population, a number of other punitive spirit cults were adopted and linked in some cases to material coercion for the protection and regulation of individual and kin-group rights within the framework of both major territorial divisions or wards and of the settlement as a whole. The absence of secular powers of enforcement in the case of both the Ward Leaders and the village priests facilitated the emergence and exercise of such powers through independent associations, notably *Ebiabu* within the wards and *Okundom* and *Ikpuŋkara* in the village at large.

Thus indigenous government in Umor was effected through the loosely co-ordinated deliberations, judicial decisions, and executive acts of self-perpetuating spirit cult associations, the ritual powers and moral authority of which were in some cases buttressed by physical coercion of recalcitrants. These associations were operative at two general levels of organization—the ward and the village. But neither within nor between these two levels was there an explicit hierarchy of authority. Respect for generally acknowledged rules of public conduct, the maintenance of order, the settlement of disputes, and the compensation of wrongs ultimately depended on the measure of authority, common understanding, and coincident interests among the associations. And this was in part at least fostered by the considerable overlapping of their memberships both within and between these two levels of organization.

(2) Changes Under British Administration[15]

The 'Native Court' of Warrant Chiefs

To the indigenous organization for the regulation of village affairs and the punishment of wrongdoers new elements were introduced with the establishment of British administration in the Cross River area. In the nineties of the last century, after two expeditions had been sent to quell disturbances in the riverside villages, a Cross River Division was set up, with headquarters in the village of Ediba, and a Native Court, the first which affected the Yakö people, was established there in 1899. Ediba is one of the villages of a distinct linguistic group, Ekumuru, whose settlements extend along a riverine stretch of about fifteen miles lying between the territory of Umor and the Cross River. The court at Ediba at first dealt with cases among the Ekumuru, Yakö, and two other smaller linguistic groups to the north, all of whom sent recognized representatives to the court. But in 1920 a separate court for the Yakö was established in Umor as a branch of the Ediba court, and a few years later, on account of jealousy and hostility between Umor and its large Yakö neighbour, Ekuri, a separate branch court for Ekuri was set up.

These courts were given powers to award damages and impose penalties of fine or imprisonment within certain limits for all cases save those which were reserved for the jurisdiction of Magistrates or the High Court. Civil actions, such as claims up to a certain limit of value for the settlement of debts, jurisdiction over claims concerning land rights, inheritance and marriage, criminal charges, including assault, and also breaches of native custom formerly

---

[15] Reprinted from 'Government in Umor', pp. 142–61.

punished by the native elders or councils, were all actionable before these courts.[16]

As in the past, the Resident and the District Officer had access to the Court and its records and had power on application by any person, or on their own initiative, to review any of the proceedings. They could order any case to be retried before the same or another competent Native Court or to be transferred to a Magistrate's Court or to the High Court. The District Officer might sit as an adviser in the Court at all times, as President when any suit relating to the ownership or occupation of land was being heard, and was

---

[16] The status and powers of the courts were codified and revised by the 'Courts and Native Authority Legislation for Nigeria' which came into force in 1934 (*Courts and Native Authority Legislation in Force on 1st September 1934*, Government Printer, Lagos, 1934; to be cited below as C. & N. A. L., 1934). In the schedule of 'An Ordinance to prescribe the powers and duties of Native Authorities' (No. 43 of 1933) the Native Courts of the Ediba- Ugep (= Umor) —Ekuri—Abini—Akuna-kuna Native Court area are recognized as Native Authorities pending the reorganization of administration among these peoples. The former powers of the several courts, of which that at Umor was one, were substantially maintained by recognizing them as of Grade D. The powers of a Grade D court were laid down in the schedule of Ordinance 44 of 1933 as having jurisdiction over:

> 'Civil actions in which the debt, demand or damages do not exceed twenty-five pounds.
> 'In the Southern Provinces such jurisdiction concerning land, or in which the title to land or any interest therein comes in question as may be stated in the warrant or annexure thereto.
> 'Full jurisdiction in causes relating to inheritance, testamentary dispositions, the administration of estates and in causes in which no claim is made for, and which do not relate to money or other property, and full jurisdiction in all matrimonial causes other than those arising from or connected with a Christian marriage. . .
> 'Criminal causes which can be adequately punished by imprisonment for three months, or in the case of theft of farm produce or live stock by imprisonment for six months, twelve strokes, or a fine of five pounds, or the equivalent by native law or custom'.

The Court was also empowered to administer: '(a) the native law and custom prevailing in the area of the jurisdiction of the court, so far as it is not repugnant to natural justice or morality, or inconsistent with any provisions of any other Ordinance; (b) the provisions of any Ordinance which the court may be authorized to enforce by an Order . . .; (c) the provisions of all rules or orders made under the Native Authority Ordinance, 1933, or under the repealed Native Authority Ordinance, and in force in the area of the jurisdiction of the Court.' Unless the warrant for a summons were issued at the direction of the Court petitioners must pay a fee of 5s. for the issue of a summons against the accused, or 10s. where the claim in a civil action exceeded £10, and a fee of 1s. for the issue of a summons for a witness or for the adjournment of the hearing of a case. Any person who was aggrieved by an order or decision of the Court could appeal within 30 days to such higher court or to the District Officer as might be set out in the warrant. From the Court at Umor appeals might be made to the Magistrate's Court at Obubra or, if the District Officer had sat as President or Adviser, to the High Court.

required to do so when the parties to a suit were not members of a single village group.[17]

There were no available records of the manner in which appointees to the bench at the first Ediba court were selected, but by 1910 there appear to have been representatives of all the villages in the court area and these 'Native Court Members' came to be referred to as 'Warrant Chiefs' on account of the warrant of appointment handed to each. It appears that throughout the period one member had been appointed from each ward of Umor, and in 1927 the Village Head (*Obot Lopon*) was also appointed. There is no precise information as to the way in which representatives were actually selected from each of the wards of Umor. As has been seen, organizations based on the wards have but restricted functions and have not formed part of the central authority of the village. In any case the Warrant Chiefs of the various wards in Umor have not been appointed in virtue of any official position in the native ward organization. Neither the present nor most past Warrant Chiefs from Umor, concerning whom information could be obtained, had for instance been *Yagbolia* in their wards. The persons appointed seem to have been senior men who were supported by a strong following in their ward. I was told that prosperous and generous men who were good speakers and had a reputation in their ward for shrewdness and courage (and likely to deal effectively with the Administration) were proper persons to put forward. The actual selection for some of the later appointments seems to have taken place at public assemblies of the adult men of the ward concerned. Here in the presence of the District Officer various men have been nominated by different groups in the ward and the one receiving the greatest acclamation has, if he appeared worthy and capable, been recommended for appointment by the District Officer. Needless to say, this procedure, however effective it may have been in

[17] No. 44 of 1933, paras. 23, 25; C. & N. A. L., 1934, pp. 133–4 and Text of Grade D Court Warrant, Lagos 1053/35.

Being of Grade D the court at Umor had, however, no jurisdiction over reserved classes of cases which had to be tried before a Magistrate's Court, in this case the District Officer sitting as Magistrate at Divisional Headquarters at Obubra, or before the High Court.

The reserved classes as enumerated in the Warrant of Grade D Native Courts, Lagos, 1053/35, were homicide, treason, sedition, counterfeiting, trial by ordeal, practice of witchcraft, slave dealing and child stealing, defilement of girls, procuration, rape, documentary defamation, false pretences, forgery, corrupt practices, official secrets, perjury (if the Native Court considered a penalty more severe than it could impose were required), offences against Public Revenue, Posts and Telegraphs or Railway, official corruption.

XVII *a. Obot Obuŋa*, Head of the Diviners outside the shrine of Obasi

XVII *b. Ikpuŋkara* initiate

XVIII *a*. Scene during a ritual dance of *Ikpuŋkara*

XVIII *b*. The Bench of the Native Court at a sitting in Umor

practice, is very different from the customary Yakö method of deliberation by an appointing body.

By 1935, at the time of my first residence there, the Native Court in Umor was a firmly established institution. On its bench sat Warrant Chiefs not from Umor alone, but also from the other Yakö villages of Idomi, Nko, and Ɖkpani, and from the smaller settlements of Agoi Ibami to the west of Yakö territory which were included in the court area; cases from all these settlements were regularly heard before it. The Court sat monthly, the bench at each session being occupied by certain of the Chiefs who were selected in rotation from the full list of Chiefs (Plate XVIII*b*).

But the four wards of Umor had not been represented with equal effectiveness. The Chief of Idjiman, a man of late middle age who had been severely crippled since his appointment in 1924, played no prominent part in the life of his ward and was a very passive member of the bench, speaking publicly at no session that I attended. There had been considerable agitation for his replacement among the younger men of Idjiman. Biko-Biko ward had in recent years had no member on the bench, for the last Warrant Chief of this ward died in 1931 and, in anticipation of the proposed reorganization of Native Administration among the Yakö, no successor had been called for by the Government. The Warrant Chief of Ukpakapi ward was the outstanding member of the Court. This man, Arikpo Egede, secured appointment in 1928 after serving an unofficial apprenticeship to his predecessor, Okoi Mpangi, who had held a warrant from 1909 to 1927. During his later years of office Okoi Mpangi had been an invalid. Arikpo provided for his household and took over his unofficial duties such as the informal hearing of allegations and complaints which might later be tried in the court, and the provision of food and sleeping quarters for messengers and police who came to his ward from Divisional headquarters. According to accounts I obtained from him and others, he acted for Okoi in most matters during this period, and apart from Court sessions appears to have been regarded as a virtual Warrant Chief in his ward. Okoi indeed asked the District Officer to allow Arikpo to replace him during his lifetime, but the request was refused. When, after Okoi died, a successor was to be appointed the District Officer visited Umor and asked a meeting of the people of Ukpakapi to nominate a successor. There were rivals to Arikpo, but at the meeting the majority supported him and he was appointed by warrant in 1928.

Arikpo Egede had no office in the traditional ward organization, nor was he a *kepun* head or a *yose* priest; his only title to prominent status in the native organization was his position as one of the two 'speakers' of the *Ikpuŋkara* association. But as a result of his confident bearing and effective counsel in the Native Court he had won great prestige in the village and he regarded himself as the administrative head of Ukpakapi ward.

The Village Head (*Obot Lopon*), who had been appointed a Warrant Chief in 1927, exercised no right of precedence or seniority on the bench on which the heads of the other Yakö villages also sat when summoned and, although he commanded respect in virtue of his status in the village, he took a less commanding part in the proceedings than Arikpo Egede, the Warrant Chief of Ukpakapi ward. The Village Head was the only member of the *Yabot* who was also a Warrant Chief. I was told both by some *ase* priests and others that it was not really appropriate that a *yose* priest should concern himself with the Court.

It must be clearly realized, nevertheless, that in Umor, and perhaps more in Umor than in the other Yakö villages because the court sat there, the Native Court was regarded as an established institution. Although it had by no means entirely superseded arbitration by *kepun* heads or the authority and decisions of the *Yabot*, everyone was prepared to take his case to the Court if he considered that his grievance or claim had not otherwise been met. Although some persons might seek its judgement in preference to traditional means of securing justice, and might even make claims in the Court against the desire and advice of their kinsmen who would wish the dispute to be settled by arrangement between elders, there was no widespread or strongly expressed dislike of the Court as an institution superseding older methods of administering justice. The indigenous organizations had themselves taken advantage of the Court in order to compel breaches of custom against recalcitrant individuals and even to enforce successors to take up office and make the appropriate offerings or payments. Criticism of the personnel of the bench, of which I heard much, was indeed a measure of the recognition that had been accorded to the Court in village opinion.

At some time since the appointment of ward representatives as

Warrant Chiefs for Umor a new term, *Obot Kekpatu* (the head of the Ward), had come into use to describe them. The use of this term implied more than a desire to employ a native term: it indicated not merely the recognition of the authorized powers of the Warrant Chiefs but also an unofficial extension of their authority. All Warrant Chiefs in Umor, save *Obot Lopon*, were so styled and participated in the implied authority, but it was to be seen best developed in Ukpakapi ward where Arikpo Egede, the most active and intelligent of the Warrant Chiefs, was indeed a *de facto* ward head. Many disputes arising in his ward, and others which might also concern people of other wards, were first ventilated and often settled in an unofficial hearing in his compound. The heads of *yepun* would come there with disputants, and their attitudes in the few instances I saw or had described in some detail showed an unmistakable deference to the judgement and authority of the Warrant Chief.

When the last *Edjukwa* of the *Yakambən* died in Ukpakapi, Arikpo Egede took over his drum. He did not call himself *Edjukwa*, but regarded his position as *Obot Kekpatu* as superseding that of an *Edjukwa* in sounding the drum to summon age-sets to a ward meeting. He had also assumed direction of the age-set organization in his ward. He took the initiative among the men of the senior age-sets in proposing the execution of public tasks, and his personal messengers went to the heads of the several classes to announce arrangements.

The two Warrant Chiefs of other wards in Umor were men of less force of character, but they were also looked to for advice on public affairs in their wards, and disputes were often brought to them in an attempt to settle matters out of Court. Indeed, it was the importance attached to the unofficial functions of a Warrant Chief that accounted in great measure for the dissatisfaction of men in Biko-Biko and Idjiman referred to above. The former practice of referring disputes involving men of one or more *yepun* in a ward to the *Ogbolia* had apparently been superseded by resort to the Warrant Chief, for the *Obgolia* exercised no judicial authority.

The Warrant Chiefs apart from *Obot Lopon* had, however, no standing among the *Yabot* and they were not regarded by the *Yabot* as having any right to participate in their deliberations or judgements. On the other hand, in a legal dispute as distinct from a matter of ritual or customary village organization, the advocacy of a Warrant Chief might be obtained by men of his ward or his opinion sought by the *Yabot* themselves during the public hearing. There is little doubt that the Warrant Chiefs had in their unofficial as well as their official capacities encroached on the former powers of the *Yabot*. Disputes over farming rights, debt, and marriage which would formerly have been taken to the *Yabot* were sometimes settled in the wards by the Warrant Chiefs. But there was no open hostility between the two groups and the *Yabot* accepted the Warrant Chief's Court as a valuable means of bringing wrong-doers to book.

Taxation

In 1928 taxation was first levied on the Yakö, and from that time each able-bodied adult male had been required to pay an annual tax of five shillings. As was the general practice in the Obubra division, the tax was collected by issuing receipt disks in proportion to the number of men listed in the official Nominal Roll. For Umor these disks were issued in groups allotted to each *kepun*, the head of which was to be made responsible for the distribution of disks as receipts and for handing in the amount of tax corresponding to the number of disks issued. Actually only 4 of the 23 *Yabot Yepun* assumed this responsibility, ostensibly because they did not wish to leave the village to journey to the Government Station, and other men, usually younger than the *Obot Kepun*, were thought more suitable to undertake this Government imposed task. In four cases the *kepun* tax-collectors were the assistants of the *Obot Kepun*, while the two active Warrant Chiefs acted as collectors in the *yepun* to which they belonged. As a result the '*kepun* heads' listed in the Nominal Roll for tax purposes were nearly all of them men other than the actual *Yabot Yepun* recognized as priests, arbitrators, and leaders of the *yepun* themselves. There was also some discrepancy between the official list of groups and the native reckoning of kinship grouping, for some subdivisions were recognized as separate groups while others were not.

Bendom—'The Young Men'

More recent than the establishment of a Native Court and the emergence of the Warrant Chiefs as persons of influence in the community was the development of another breach with tradition in Umor. Although very much less effective and far-reaching it merited serious consideration because it reflected changes in the wider social and economic environment of the community. It was a movement among younger adult men, particularly those who had travelled for trading purposes to large centres such as Calabar and Port Harcourt, whose interests were directed to external economic opportunities and in a vague way to development in the village itself. This self-appointed group of men called itself 'Bendom'—the ordinary Yakö word for 'the young men'. The implication of this title, namely opposition to the old men, the conservative heads and elders of kin groups and the Yabot, was further and paradoxically indicated by their adoption of the English term 'Elders' to which they had no right by age or status.

In 1935 there were about 24 active members of Bendom, most of them in their thirties or forties. They claimed that their group had been formed about ten years previously. They usually met only at irregular intervals whenever one or more of their number called the group together to discuss an issue of importance; but during the last year or two prior to 1935 they had instituted regular monthly meetings—a practice apparently imitated from the monthly sessions of the Court and based on the European not the native calendar. At each meeting every member was required to contribute sixpence to a fund intended to finance mutual aid in case of trouble, including the costs of summonses in the Native Court.

But the activities of Bendom were not directed against the Warrant Chiefs' Court to which they tended to look for support for their claims. It was with the actions and decisions of the Yabot affecting village affairs that they were mainly concerned. When issues of general importance or interest, whether legal cases or questions of an administrative order, arose, it was the customary obligation of the Yabot to hold a public meeting at which anyone might speak. The Bendom group endeavoured to act as a unit on such occasions and succeeded after much dispute and recrimination in obtaining de facto recognition of its group existence by the Yabot. A spokesman of Bendom claimed a right to speak on their behalf at all public meetings called by the Yabot. It appears that they protested publicly at such meetings if they disliked the decision of the *Yabot*, and were able in this way to compel reconsideration of some decisions which have on occasion been modified. The opposition between the *Yabot* and the *Bendom* group centred on the person of *Okpebri*, the Speaker of *Yabot*, who had attempted to deny any special status to the men of *Bendom* and to discredit their claims and views. *Okpebri*, a massive slow-moving man of deliberate speech, had a deep knowledge of native custom and a real belief in the need for its preservation. He played a prominent part in all the great public ceremonies in Umor, and, while not narrowly self-seeking, claimed the respect which he believed to be due to his position, and quietly resisted encroachment on the authority of the *Yabot* as far as he was able. In Idjiman ward where he lived his position was anomalous. He collected the tax in his *kepun*, and as *Okpebri* he assumed that he should be consulted on any issue arising in the ward. But some of the younger men, led by a member of *Bendom* who was assistant and unofficial deputy of Ofem Ntum, the paralysed Warrant Chief from Idjiman, denied him any right to authority in ward affairs. In fact many minor disputes were settled in his compound, and with a large number of the people in Idjiman his advice and judgement carried great weight. *Okpebri* and the invalid Warrant Chief backed by men of *Bendom* in fact divided, in uneasy partnership, the direction of affairs in Idjiman.

The opposition of *Bendom* to the *Yabot* was to some extent reinforced by the objection of the small Christian Mission element in the village that priests of the 'jujus' should not govern the village. *Bendom* was not, however, a Christian group. Its procedure and views had no religious qualities and many of its members were not Christians. Nor was it hostile to all the *ase* priests and other members of *Yabot* individually. Its members did not boycott the public rituals, associations or other native institutions of the village, nor did they refuse office in them. Indeed one of their members had become a *yose* priest, and although some of the members of *Bendom* claimed that he should leave them he had refused to do so and insisted on regarding himself as still a member of the group. When at the end of 1934 the question of the reorganization of native administration among the Yakö was first introduced by the District Officer in public meetings in the villages, the *Bendom* group in Umor, understanding that the establishment of a Village Council recognized by Government was in question, became the spokesmen of extreme claims for the supersession of the *Yabot*.[18]

(3) THE PROBLEM OF REORGANIZATION

The Implications of Indirect Rule

The Yakö did not have sufficient knowledge of the facts and and problems of Nigerian Government administration to envisage the question of reorganization in terms of particular developments in the future and with regard to new powers that the Council might assume. The *Yabot* and the Warrant Chiefs evinced less interest in the matter than *Bendom* and rarely talked of it. In the case of the *Yabot* this was, I believe, largely because they could not see what it was all about. They knew their own customary powers and duties; they accepted existing institutions, and thought of *Bendom* as a group of gadflies who made an irritating stir from time to time. The Warrant Chiefs for their part appeared not to grasp the fact that reorganization was likely to involve changes in the method of appointment to the bench of the Native Court.

The Native Court was an institution to which all the people were accustomed and they tended to consider the question of future changes in terms of the Court alone. When reorganization was first discussed with them their own suggestions almost all concerned modifications in the Court. The views which I heard expressed made it clear that the functions and personnel of the Court were the subject of lively and intelligent concern, but that few could envisage a new Council which whould exercise administrative functions in the village. Many, even of the younger men, felt that the general control of village affairs should be left with the various persons and bodies that now controlled them, *kepun* affairs with the *yepun* priests and elders, *lejima* affairs with the *yajimonotam* and the *Bi'ina*, the activities and duties of age-sets to the men of senior sets in each ward, and the maintenance of general law and order and respect for customary behaviour with the *Yabot*, who also had responsibility for the rituals that safeguarded the well-being of Umor. In fact, however untidy and amorphous it might appear

---

[18] An attempt had been made in 1923 by a District Officer to establish a new Village Council in Umor, but the body then called into being is said to have been unsuccessful. It was abolished two or three years later and no particulars of the composition or its failure were available. I failed to discover whether any of the members of *Bendom* were appointed to it.

to an outsider, there was, as would be expected, no general desire to revolutionize the habitual conduct of affairs.

On the other hand, acceptance of the going concern was, as has been indicated, not accompanied by a sufficient realization of the opportunities for development implied by the general principles which lay behind the Government's initiative in proposing reorganization.[19] The opportunities for establishing a Native Treasury in the village into which the share of the tax payment allotted to local administration would be paid, of drafting a budget for the spending of this revenue, and of establishing thereby public services for which a Council would be financially responsible, all implied serious consideration of the fitness of any existing or proposed body to perform such functions. The native system in Umor could be said to maximize the decentralization of authority; the *Yabot* took cognizance only of major issues which threatened disturbance in the village or were believed to be offences against custom and belief which would incur supernatural penalties on the community as a whole. Neither the *Yabot*, the Ward Leaders, nor the councils of elders of the patrilineal and matrilineal kin groups were bodies which customarily initiated new activities whether social or economic, and in the more recent period the changes consequent on the establishment of Nigerian administration and the growth of external trading had been effected either by outside bodies or through individual initiative. The palm-oil and kernel trading of Umor was in the hands of a few enterprising persons; most of them were men who had little prominence in the affairs of the kin groups and none of them were members of the *Yabot*. A mission church and school had been established by the Mission of the United Free Church of Scotland and two small congregations of African-organized Christians groups had been formed. The Native Court, as has been seen, was a creation of the Nigerian administration.

All this might suggest that in the development of a responsible and progressive local administration native institutions could play little part. But an essential point, frequently emphasized in connection with the policy of 'Indirect Rule', was the need for avoiding a break in the continuity of the social life of the community and for minimizing any sense that new developments were foreign things

[19] As expounded in Sir Donald Cameron's memorandum on *The Principles of Indirect Rule*, Lagos, 1935.

for which the people themselves had little responsibility. To this one might add the need for great care to avert the growth of hostile factions representing dispossessed traditional authorities. These dangers were clearly real in Umor and a sufficient reason for preserving all that could usefully function in the native organization.

Another serious danger was that of weakening the corporate spirit of the kin groups which still, as in the past, formed effective co-operative groups safeguarding the rights of their members and restraining them from misconduct. The strength of the kinship organization had already been weakened to some extent, for the development of external trading had provided opportunities for enterprising and self-reliant but selfish persons to evade obligations to their kinsmen. Men who devoted much of their time to trading, were tending in fact to become socially as well as economically divorced from the community and to acquire an independent and commercial outlook. Among such men one heard too the view that a person's wealth was no concern of his *lejima* and they might attempt to evade the Yakö rules of matrilineal inheritance. Serious weakening of the kinship structure would undoubtedly increase this tendency towards economic individualism.

The Native Court, although it had in general upheld local custom, including both ceremonial obligations and rights of succession, had also to some extent weakened the bonds of kinship, in that men with a grievance could and often did take action in the Native Court instead of seeking the arbitration of the heads and elders of the kin group concerned. Save in disputes over marriage payments this practice had not yet become general, and the fact that the fixed fees payable for summonses to the Native Court were more considerable than the gifts made by complainants to the elders served to encourage traditional methods of seeking justice in the first instance.

Before attempting to assess the possible modifications that might be introduced in reorganizing the local administration of Umor in consonance with the aims of Government policy it would also be necessary to estimate the social and economic trends. Assuming that there would be no organized effort to transform the economic life of the people during the next decade or two, and that the existing social and economic forces would continue to operate, a useful estimate of conditions in the near future could be made.

In the first place the indigenous system of land holding was in full vigour. The practice of acquiring farm plots for household cultivation within the framework of the patrilineal clan organization was not threatened by external economic forces, and as has been shown elsewhere the minority of the population that gained its basic livelihood by other means was still very small.[20] Furthermore there was room within the recognized territory of the village for a considerable expansion of the area of cultivated land with the existing methods of farming. An increase and improvement in the palm oil produced by Umor and the other Yakö villages could be provided by encouraging the extension to oil palms of the native custom of permanent private ownership of planted trees, without interfering with the native system of land tenure.

On the other hand, the current forms of external trading were certainly likely to continue and might be expected to develop. This implied that there would be more persons who, although still a small minority, would devote most or all of their energies and interests to the collection and transport of palm products to the riverside trading-posts and to the port of Calabar. These and others would also continue to act as village merchants for European trade goods. This element in the population would not, however, grow to large dimensions and need not, if the strength of the kinship organizations were maintained, become sharply set off from the rest of the community. But it would be in touch with the external commercial world, might have less interest in the traditional culture of the village, press for innovations, and be over-ready to break with the past. The same could apply to the small number of youths who had gone away to residential schools and, perhaps, in a lesser degree, to those who attended the Mission School in Umor itself.[21] But the way in which returned scholars of an earlier generation had settled down to take up a full and normal part in the activities of the village suggested that this was not likely. A man who could read and write English was respected for his skill in Umor, but he was accorded no particular prestige by his fellows in village affairs. It was more probable that those who had been to school would either obtain clerical or other work outside the community

---

[20] See Chapter I.

[21] There were said to be about 130 children attending the Mission School in 1935, a very small proportion of the total number of minors (under 18) in the village, which I estimated at nearly six thousand.

and cease to be active members of it, or would return to find that the vigour of the native culture was too great for them to force the pace of social change.

The Christian element in the population might increase, but the United Free Church Mission suffered competition from the small 'African Episcopal' and 'Apostolic' sects, the adherents of which appeared to combine membership with respect for, and underlying belief in, the spirits of the clan and other shrines. The Mission Christian element was hostile to the authority of the Village Priests mainly, it would seem, because it had learned to doubt the benefic-ence of the public seasonal rituals at the *ase* shrines and to regard as sinful certain indigenous practices, such as the exposure of twins, which had been upheld by them. But, unless there were a very great increase in missionary activity, it would be many years before this would seriously affect the importance of the native shrines and rituals in the eyes of the mass of the people.

Unless their prestige were undermined by external forces the Council of Village Priests would continue to command the respect of the majority as spiritual leaders of the community, as those who had access to the supernatural forces which affected the daily lives of the people and who knew the time-honoured rules of proper conduct and the recompense that must be made if one who had offended the spirits were to avert personal and even public disaster. Resort to the 'Native Court' as a means of recovering a debt or accusing another of theft or assault by no means excluded profound belief in the *Yabot* as the possessors of knowledge and wisdom.

On the other hand, although the process was likely to be slower than might at first be imagined, belief in the aboriginal super-natural powers, and with it the sense of the importance of the native rituals and the prestige of the *Yabot* were likely to decline during the next few generations; for Umor, whatever happened, would no longer be a closed society.

The Possibilities for Reorganization

What, then, could, at that time, be reasonably proposed as a basis for the reorganization of local government in this African village? With religious beliefs and organization there might appear to be no direct concern. But in the native view supernatural sanc-tions lay behind the authority of the leaders of indigenous social groups. On the other hand, Christians who in varying degrees repudiated the aboriginal religious beliefs could not be excluded from participation in local government. The institutions had therefor to be secular in formal character, but to allow for the actual beliefs of the people. It would be well to re-state first the particular difficulties in Umor.

First, there was the existence of a dual system of unilineal kinship grouping as a result of which there was a double system of authority backed by supernatural forces, and the safeguarding of the civil rights of the individual was partitioned among these two authorities. Rights of residence and of land use were the concern of the elders and the priest-leaders of the *yepun*; rights of inheritance of stock, goods, and currency were protected by the elders of the *yajima* and the *ase* priests.

Second, there was a territorial division of this large community into four wards, and the wards had provided the basis for an indigenous authority overriding that of the leaders of the kin groups. But in the native system only a few specialized administrative and ceremonial functions were organized on the territorial basis of the wards.[22]

Third, the paramount native authority in the village had rested in a corporation dominated by the priest-leaders of the matrilineal kin groups. This body, the *Yabot*, was one which had no concern, until a major dispute arose, with the organization of affairs in the territorially compact patrilineal kin groups and wards. Its prestige was, moreover, closely bound up with native beliefs in supernatural fertility spirits which were not likely to be maintained indefinitely in their original vigour. At the same time the *Yabot* were individually and collectively the guardians of the rights of matrilineal inheritance which were firmly established in Yakö society.

Finally, for at least a generation a Court of Warrant Chiefs had offered a means of securing justice and punishing offenders which had rivalled the authority of the *Yabot* and had enjoyed the prestige of recognition and the enforcement of its judgements by the Nigerian Government. The mode of selection of judges in this court had not been based on the native social structure and it had

---

[22] This paper was written after the first period of field-work and before the former authority of the *Yakambən* was appreciated. This passage has been revised, but their possible role in future organization has not been considered.

given an anomalous authority in his ward to the Warrant Chief appointed from it.

With these facts in mind we could consider possible forms of reorganization, assuming in the first place that there were to be recognized in Umor both a Council to administer village affairs, probably with some financial control of the funds derived from taxation, and a Court with powers generally similar to the present Native Court.

It will have been realized that there were objections to the recognition of the corporation of the *Yabot* alone and as then constituted as the Council of Umor. Real and paramount as its powers had been in the past, the changes during the last generation and the probable future trends of social development in Umor rendered it inadequate as the sole representative and executive body for the community. The well-defined, stable, and autochthonous authority of the heads of the patrilineal kin groups (the *Yabot Yepun*) might, on the other hand, have suggested that these leaders should collectively constitute the Council. But it had to be realized that such an arrangement would be a complete innovation. No council of *kepun* heads had existed up to then and the authority of a *kepun* head had always been confined to his own patrilineal kin group. Moreover, the prestige and authority of the priests of the matrilineal kin groups had been and still was much greater than that of the priest-leaders of the patrilineal clans, while the Village Head, who had been recognized by the Government and had for nearly ten years served as a Warrant Chief, was not a *kepun* head but the priest of a matrilineal kin group and the leader of the *Yabot*. A council of *kepun* heads was what the vocal members of the *Bendom* group had asked for, but if the Council were constituted in this manner and the *Yabot* were ignored, an entirely new corporate authority would have been created, while the traditional central authority of the village would have been deposed. But the *Yabot* as a social force would not quickly disappear for, however adverse the social conditions, their prestige both individual and collective would continue for considerable period. The result would thus be to perpetuate in a new and more aggravated form the uneasy relation of overlapping *de facto* authority between an official body recognized by and responsible to the Government and an indigenous institution. This situation had existed in recent times between the Warrant Chiefs and the *Yabot*. During the past few years there had been little apparent friction, but that was in large measure due to the fact that the Warrant Chief's Court had in fact recognized the authority of the *Yabot* in matters concerning native custom and had acted in conformity with their declarations and demands in such matters. The Court had on its own initiative sent complainants to the *Yabot* or to similar authorities in other Yakö villages for the decision of disputes involving matters of customary law. So amicable a relationship could not be counted on in future between the *Yabot* and an independent and powerful Village Council.

Since the matrilineal as well as the patrilineal organizations and rights of succession might be expected to continue in Umor for a considerable period, it would appear to be desirable to recognize the traditional leaders of both sets of kinship groups. This would imply the appointment to the Council of both the *kepun* heads referred to above and those members of *Yabot* who were *ase* priests and leaders of matrilineal groups. There were actually fewer *Bi'ina* than there were matrilineal clans since several groups of these combined in recognizing a single shrine. But, in view of the potential importance of the territorial patrilineal organization in the administration of village affairs and in economic development, it would probably be wiser to give the *kepun* heads, who would start with less prestige, this numerical preponderance over the leaders of the matrilineal groups. If recognition as council members was accorded only to the *Bi'ina* and not to other members of *Yabot*, who had no direct connection with the matrilineal organization, there would be ten of these as compared with the twenty-two *Yabot Yepun*.[23]

But to these should be added, in order to avoid a breach with native custom, the *Okpebri* who speaks officially on behalf of the *Yabot* both on ceremonial and public occasions. It would have been possible on the demise of the then *Okpebri* to have allowed the office to lapse or to fill it from among the members of the Council. It might also have been desirable to appoint to the Council one or two members nominated by the members of the Mission Church. The appointment both of the *Bi'ina* and of Christian representatives might have proved valuable for reasons quite other than the need for maintaining continuity and representing particular interests.

---

[23] It would probably be desirable to encourage the appointment of heads of the three anomalous territorial groups which had been derived by fission from one or more of the other *yepun*. See Chapter III above.

For those members would not be representatives of territorially compact groups like the *kepun* heads and might help to smooth out difficulties arising from rivalries and disagreements between different *yepun* in administrative matters.[24]

The then Village Head, whom even the *Bendom* group agreed— somewhat illogically since his office depended on his priesthood of the premier *yose*—in recognizing as the proper head of any village council, was the most appropriate person to function as President or Head of the Council. The presence of the *Bi'ina* and the presidency of the *Obot Lopon*, all of whom had experience of orderly consideration of village affairs, might be expected to impart a sense of accustomed order and coherence into what would otherwise in its early stages be a very amorphous body. It was not, however, necessary to assume that the procedure in appointing the Head of the Council in future should be that whereby the *Obot Lopon*, the *Ina* of Odjokobi, and the Head of the *Yabot* had been appointed in the past. It could be left for the Council to devise a procedure satisfactory to itself and to the Government for future appointments to the office.

Since the age-sets which performed useful public services capable of being further extended were organized on a ward basis in Umor, it was desirable to encourage the *kepun* heads from each ward to act as a sub-council, each if necessary appointing its own leader, which would be responsible for purely ward affairs and could direct and develop the public functions of the age-sets.

The social functions of both *kepun* heads (*Yabot Yepun*) and *yajima* heads (*Bi'ina*) were still intimately bound up with the performance of rituals which expressed and maintained the solidarity of these groups. It would have been a profound mistake to attempt to divorce these men as members of the Council from their traditional ceremonial duties, above all for the reason that at that time the rituals commanded great respect among the majority of the members of the kin groups. In time the ritual functions might become less important in the eyes of the people, but their continuance need be no bar to efficient local administration. An *Obot Kepun* was chosen with reference not merely to religiosity of temperament but to personal qualities of impartial judgement, gener-

---

[24] Such, for example, as the siting of latrines or the opening of new bush paths, both of which are instances of questions over which adjacent *yepun* could not agree on mutually satisfactory arrangements during my stay in Umor.

osity, and dignity. The same applied to the priests of the matrilineal kin groups in whom qualities of leadership and respect for
native custom were sought. It had also to be borne in mind that as
new fields of activity developed the qualities sought in men to be
appointed to the Council as representatives of the groups would
themselves tend to change in consonance with the new conditions.

The question of the appointments to the bench of the Native
Court depended in certain measure on its area of jurisdiction. At
that time the court at Umor served all the Yakö villages, save
Ekuri, and also the smaller Agoi settlements to the west. Although
a continuance of this system might be necessary for reasons of
economy and administrative convenience, it seemed desirable that
a community as large as Umor should constitute a distinct court
area, and that the possibility of inter-village friction, which is said
to have arisen in the past from dissatisfaction with non-local courts,
should be avoided if possible. If the court at Umor were restricted
in its jurisdiction to Umor itself the bench could be quite small.
As the notion of ward representation had been firmly implanted by
the practice of appointing Warrant Chiefs on this basis for the
past thirty years or more, a procedure likely to be satisfactory both
to the people and to a council constituted in the manner described
above would be nomination by the members of the Council resident in each ward of one or more or their number to serve as court
members. These might serve regularly or in rotation as was thought
fit. The Village Head as president of the Council could also be
chairman of the bench of the Court. A Court whose bench was
constituted on these lines would accord with native ideas in which
no separation is made between administrative and judicial functions. In order to avoid the possible development of disgruntled
factions the then Warrant Chiefs might reasonably be allowed to
continue in office as court members with the understanding that
new appointments would be made through the Village Council.

I have endeavoured here to indicate by an analysis of the social
structure of one village community the nature of the problems
that arise when an attempt is made to develop local government
on the basis of native institutions under conditions of social change
and after the indigenous system has itself been modified by a
prior period of external control. In Umor there had been no serious
difficulty in discovering and defining the traditional native authorities. But some thirty years of direct administration, with the aid of a

XIX *a.* *Opalapala*

XIX *b.* *Odjokobi*

XX *a*. Invocation by the Village Speaker before the altar of *Odjokobi*

XX *b*. The *Ekui* dance before the *Yabot* on *Ledemboku*

Court of Warrant Chiefs which originally had no status in the native society, had, together with other external influences, to some extent outmoded those authorities and created a new situation. The modifications in social structure had been sufficiently extensive to have created difficult problems in the application of the principles of indirect rule, both for the people themselves and for the administration. In such circumstances detailed analyses of social organization, of the sentiments and beliefs which supported the various institutions, of the external forces affecting the community, and of probable future trends are essential prerequisites for adequate judgement on the organs of local government that are most likely to offer possibilities of smooth transition and useful development in the future.

VII

SPIRITS, WITCHES, AND
SORCERERS[1]

UMOR, the largest of the five Yakö[2] villages, was in the thirties already a very largely closely settled community which exploited the surrounding forest area by agriculture, collecting, and, formerly, substantial hunting. It lay within the economic hinterland of the lower Cross River, which had long afforded its eleven thousand people economic relations as producers rather than traders with many peoples along and beyond the river. Thus, from the later part of the nineteenth century at least, Umor had enjoyed considerable security and prosperity based on adequate local resources and increasing quantities of imported goods from other parts of Nigeria and from overseas in return for exports of yams, palm products, and camwood. The Yakö shared many cultural features with surrounding peoples. Some of these were conspicuous in the field of ceremonial and supernatural belief, such as the seclusion of girls before marriage, mortuary practices, and cosmological beliefs concerning the creator Obasi. In particular, several spirit forces invoked by Yakö associations were claimed by their custodians to have been derived from one or another neighbouring people.

A salient feature of Yakö ritual was the juxtaposition without conceptual integration of distinct rites and of the mystical forces that were posited in different contexts. Thus, firstly, in the context of the village as a whole, seasonal rites were centred on the invocation of the tutelary *ase* spirits of the dispersed matriclans. These avowedly sought to protect and foster the unity and well-being of the community as such and implied a collective capacity of the *ase* spirits to do so. But when defiance of village authority or in-

[1] The substance of this Chapter was presented at the Spring meeting, 1958, of the Association of Social Anthropologists and it was originally published in *J.R.A.I.*, vol. 88, 1958.
[2] While for convenience I refer to the people as Yakö, the studies in 1935 and 1939 on which this account is based, were, apart from some comparisons of ritual objects and procedures, virtually confined to the village of Umor.

ternal disruption was feared, other spirit agencies were brought into play—*Edet Lopon, Okeŋka* and (in one aspect) *Korta*—of an especially punitive character.

Secondly, component sections of the community, both territorial units such as wards and localized patrilineal kin groups and associations, looked to further and separate spirit agencies to sanction their internal coherence and harmony, sometimes to protect their members collectively or individually against outsiders.

Thirdly, when an individual, a household, or small *ad hoc* body of kin, was faced with hazard or misfortune, the beliefs in the protective role of spirits associated with the village or more restricted groups, although not explicitly rejected as inapplicable, did not always suffice, for there was resort to the aid of spirits that were not tutelary to any groups, but linked to shrines, the cults of which were in the personal custody of individuals who had acquired or inherited them.[3]

This suggests that the beliefs and rites connected with collective protection of the community and its segments, while sustaining and sustained by a generalized sense of security that they normally induce in the members of relevant groups, are not accepted as adequate by component sub-groups or by individuals in the face of actual or feared misfortune. In such circumstances, particularistic beliefs concerning the capacities of specific punitive spirits, which constitute a distinct category known as *ndet*, are most commonly brought into play to threaten, punish or alleviate. In more limited contexts witchcraft and sorcery are suspected and corresponding protective measures are taken.

Sociologically all this reflects a salient characteristic of Yakö village society, where the field of interaction of the individual is both wide and heterogeneous as a result of the large concentration of population and the organization of activities and interests in series of distinct, non-congruent units. Thus, for example, while the twenty or more men of a patrilineage occupying adjacent compounds have farming interests in common, they may associate in this with lineages of clans other than their own, while their wives who live and farm with them are likely to have come from many other parts of the village. These patrikinsmen will, moreover,

---

[3] The conceptual framework within which these spirits are differentiated and invoked is analysed in Chapter IX.

belong to a number of different matrilineages which severally make claims and confer benefits on them. The men of a given lineage are also separated by their differing seniority and capacity with regard to their status and activities as members of different age-sets and associations in the affairs of the ward. Individual memberships in recreational clubs and, especially for the older men and women, in associations for mutual protection and influence in village affairs, and also the holding by a few of politico-ritual offices of the ward or village (offices that are not formally or necessarily vested in or representative of patrilineage or patriclan), all further differentiate both the various fields of activities of individuals and their social differentiation within the localized patrilineage and patriclan.

Ritual actions involving diagnosis and sacrifice, invocation, or control of spiritual beings, went on unceasingly in Umor. Such rites varied widely from actions on individual initiative, as for instance an unostentatious daily, offering made by a household head to the creator, Obasi; a consultation with a diviner to discover the supernatural risks or source of a misfortune; a sacrifice to a spirit on behalf of a barrren woman or an ailing person, or the burning of owl feathers under the eaves to keep away witches; to the annual cycle of public village ceremonies at the seasons of first fruits and harvest extending over many days. The names, attributes and particular range of effect variously ascribed to the beings involved suggest a discordant and fluctuating congeries of beliefs from among which a process of *ad hoc* selection was continuously taking place to meet the exigencies of human aspirations and fears.

Indeed it can be shown on analysis that Yakö beliefs concerning the supernatural beings and entities which influence their lives, fall into several distinct categories that are conceptually independent and operationally unintegrated. These can be indicated in a preliminary way as, first, an omniscient creator, Obasi; secondly, protective tutelary spirits that can be invoked on behalf of the matriclans and the community at large; thirdly, an indefinite number of spirits capable of inflicting sickness, sterility, and death, some, but by no means all, of which operate on behalf of the community or established kin groups and associations; fourthly, witchcraft power; and finally, the ghosts of the recently dead.

It also becomes apparent that the allocation of this conceptually discrete but limited range of supernatural means over the unlimited field of human concern is informed by notions of economy through which it is sought to maximize, in terms of the character and limitations of the supernatural resources available, the satisfactions of reassurance and of rewards, or at least to secure the restoration or termination of loss, with respect to both personal and collective ends.

If only because the Yakö, as they have grown into a series of large compact village communities, have long been in continuous contact through the Cross River traffic with many peoples, it would be pointless to regard their specific beliefs and procedures concerning supernatural action as being indigenous developments in response to their local situation. In fact, the names of many spirits and the stories connected with the introduction of particular cults point to the derivation of particular beliefs and ritual procedures from Efik, Ejagham (Ekoi), Mbembe, Ibo, and other peoples. Moreover, some more general notions concerning, for instance, the creator, the nature of witchcraft, or the qualities of leopard spirits are part of a common heritage of the peoples of eastern Nigeria and further afield. We are concerned here not with the derivation of specific beliefs, but with the extent to which their fields of relevance have been selected and distinguished.

It will be suggested that both in the formulation and the selection of ritual action, the Yakö of Umor appear to be guided less by a sense of the logical implication of particular dogmas or of need to establish intellectually coherent relations among them, and more by the opportunities that they severally afford to allocate among specific supernatural agencies means for the achievement of particular ends of groups and persons. In other words: the various supernatural entities which have come to be established as objects of Yakö thought and ritual action are handled as a series of alternative and complementary, but at the same time largely dissociable, means for attaining material and social benefits and for averting threats to these. Thus ritual activities seen as a whole take on something of the character of an economic system in which needs, opportunities, and risks are assessed, and the most appropriate and advantageous among the available means are sought. The efficacy of the latter in a particular situation is judged by results. Their inadequacy in the event in a particular instance or context is normally taken to imply faulty estimations of that situation and does not discredit acceptance of the capacity of a super-natural entity in principle. The *ceteris paribus* principle is an under-lying reservation of Yakö thought when considering any question of explanation or action on the supernatural plane and this is applied *ex post facto*. If a rite on a given occasion does not prove effective in terms of the desired end, some element in the super-natural context of the misfortune or the aspiration has not been allowed for and remains to be diagnosed and coped with.

A review of Yakö beliefs forces one to the conclusion that there are marked fluctuations in the selection for expression of a particular belief. In part, these appear to depend on differences of mood which in turn reflect different and often subconscious appreciations that people make of their material and social situations.

This may be conveniently illustrated by reference to two dissoci-ated sets of belief and ritual concerning the fertility of women. Married women who have experienced reproductive misfortunes, miscarriages, illness during pregnancy, failure to conceive or neo-natal deaths of their children, commonly resort to the custodians of *ndet* (sing. *edet*) in, or in the vicinity of, their husband's com-pounds. They seek through requests and offerings to have their fertility restored by the *edet* in question. These *ndet* are believed to be able both to cause and to remove such disabilities. But they are not in such cases specifically alleged to have caused them. They are merely requested to 'give' or 'allow' the bearing of a healthy child. *Ndet* of this kind, to which control over other maladies of men as well as women are often ascribed, are not explicitly associated with any fixed social group. The custodian has an individual capacity and a right to invoke it, that has been secured by ritual transfer associated with purchase, inheritance, or occasionally personal innovation. The clientele of such an *edet* is indefinite and may be small or large, and the custodianship is valued accordingly.[4]

When I asked the custodians why women came to them to secure children, since these were ensured to them by the *ase* (fer-tility spirits) of their matriclans, replies were to the effect that the *ase* were 'far away', that it was a long time since the First Fruits or

[4] The social context of, and the qualities ascribed to, these *ndet* are more fully discussed in Chapter IX.

the Harvest rites, or more elliptically, that a woman was now living
with her husband's people. When one then inquired not only of the
matriclan spirit priests, but of custodians of *ndet*, whether the *ase*
really did give women the power to bear children, this was readily
confirmed, but referred to as a capacity which could be interfered
with. Although I did not talk directly with women on these topics,
cases discussed by husbands suggested that in the situation of
anxiety concerning childbirth, a wife tended to be much affected
by local opinions in and around her compound. Thus she gave
credence to beliefs and claims concerning a particular and usually
local *edet* that had assisted others among her neighbours—beliefs
often reinforced by the husband or other affines—and lost sight as
it were of publicly declared and matrilineally sustained belief in
the beneficent and protective power of the *ase*. This is not to say,
of course, that there was any conscious sense of conversion from
one belief to another. Indeed, it appeared that both beliefs might
be entertained in successive conscious reflections and be likewise
acted upon. Appeal to an *edet* did not imply repudiation of the
yose. Nor did Yakö generally appear to consider that the *ase* con-
demned or would punish resort to *ndet* for a proper purpose,
including conception and the safe delivery of a child.

But at the time of the First Fruits and Harvest ceremonies in
Umor, when offerings and invocations were made successively to
the *ase* and their priests participated collectively in other rites,
women came in large numbers to the shrines associated with their
matriclans to secure the blessing of the *ase* and in particular sought
'many children who would live long'. Furthermore, if after her first
marriage a young wife did not soon conceive or if she feared miscarriage, it was expected that her mother would bring her with an
offering before the shrine of the *yose* of their matriclan. At such a
time, it should be noted, a young wife would often still be living
with her mother. In collecting a series of marital histories, I also
noted cases where older women had on their own initiative and
apart from village festivals gone, usually with a senior matrikins-
woman, to the *ase* to ask for conception. All in all, however, I gained
the strong impression that faith in the fertility conferring power of
the *ase* was of a generalized character, regarded as part of their
general and protective beneficence which expressed and sustained
by its publicity a confidence that fertility was normally assured.
When for a particular woman this inital confidence was not borne

out, beliefs in other supernatural agencies usually became dominant, inducing action to secure other aid.

This apparent discrepancy between the basic dogma expressed
in the public invocation of the *ase* of the several matriclans at the
village First Fruits and Harvest rites, namely, that each *yose* confers fertility on the women of 'its' matriclan in response to the
periodic invocation and offerings of its priest, and the fact that
married women fearing sterility, miscarriage, or the loss of infants,
for the most part resort, not to the *ase*, but to *ndet* in their immediate neighbourhood to secure alleviation, finds explanation in the
multiple roles of women as daughters and mothers on the one hand,
and as wives on the other. All Yakö are agreed in principle that a
woman derives the capacity for childbearing from the *yose* of her
matriclan, whose priest, so long as certain ritual and moral norms
are observed, is able in association with the other *ase* priests, to
ensure this by their periodic invocations and offerings. As a daughter of the matriclan this blessing is, as it were, automatically conferred on a woman and it can be confirmed, or even restored, for
the individual by special offerings and expiatory rites. But in this
context, the woman as herself the child of a matriclan is important
as the bearer of children that will also become members of it and
of the village community as a whole. These children will not only
ensure the continuity of clan and community but will participate
in the inheritance of such rights and goods as pass matrilineally
from men to their sisters' sons and from mothers to their daughters. The fertility of women as sisters and daughters is therefore
of concern to their brothers and mothers' brothers as members of
a matriclan and more especially of one of its component matrilineages.

But once married and gone to live with her husband, the daily
life of a woman, her productive activities and household supplies,
her most frequent informal contacts and the occasions for companionship, competition and hostility, are provided within the
cluster of adjacent compounds that are occupied by her husband,
his patrikinsmen and other neighbours and their households. In
this neighbourhood group which is, according to circumstances,
focused on one or more patrilineages, it is as a wife and as the
mother of her husband's children who will belong to the next
generation of his patrilineage and patriclan, that the prestige and
security of a woman is determined. Here she finds herself admired

or criticized as a wife and neighbour by her husband and his patrikin, and by other wives who are co-resident as a result of marriage
but with no necessary kin ties among them. The immediately adverse effects of sterility, miscarriage or loss of children on a
married woman's position are, therefore, greater among the neighbourhood group centred on the patrilineage and its wives, than
they are among the dispersed members of her matrilineage. It is
only later in life that a woman without sons and daughters may
suffer as a widow from the lack of these close matrilineal kin who
will succour and protect her. Meanwhile, any sense of failure or
anxiety in connection with childbirth and consequent need to
restore her position as a wife and mother in her husband's patrilineage and local group is more immediate. So, correspondingly,
are her responses to remedies which are available and approved
within this neighbourhood. Her husband's confidence in the
efficacy of an *edet* in the custody of one of his patrikinsmen, and
the success that other wives of his kin are believed to have had in
securing benefits from it, loom larger than the doctrine of matrilineally conferred fertility. But the same man who, as husband,
counsels or approves his wife's resort to a neighbourhood *edet*, may
as an elder of a matrilineage urge that one of his matriclan sisters
or their daughters should seek an invocation of their matriclan
spirit for a similar disability.

Further striking instances of the limitation of effective belief and
of the selection of ritual action in relation to the total field of
needs were afforded by Yakö attitudes to witchcraft and sorcery.
Human agents of injurious supernatural action might be suspected
or divined in the absence of any specific evidence of hostility.
The subject of the divination and those acting for him, or more
occasionally the diviner himself, might suggest that an ailment
was due to witchcraft or to sorcery.

Yakö concepts of witchcraft conformed in general to patterns that
occur widely in Africa. Since the contexts in which they were believed to operate correspond closely to those which have been so
well elucidated in a number of detailed studies among African and
other peoples, they need only be referred to briefly here. For the
Yakö witches (*yatana*, sing. *otana*) were the possessors of a mys-

terious capacity for disembodiment whereby their souls could leave their sleeping bodies to alight on other sleepers whom they invisibly attacked. The severity and persistence of their attacks were believed to vary greatly and range from mere nuisance of disturbed sleep and waking in a breathless or choking condition, to endangering or even occasionally taking the life of their victims. Witches were thought to take a victim's breath with effects ranging from a sense of mild suffocation after sleep to a debilitation that could develop into severe weakness and bodily wasting. Witches were also believed to be able to take blood from their victims, and an ulcer that would not heal, especially one that grew larger or went gangrenous despite treatment, was likely to be regarded as visible evidence of continued blood-sucking by a witch. People affected by one or other of these symptoms, which in various degrees were, of course, far from uncommon, might justifiably suspect the action of witchcraft. As a first protection they could employ one or other of the magical means, such as the burning of owl feathers, that were believed to repel witches. If the ailment was severe, they might consult a diviner in an attempt to identify the witch or learn of an *edet* which by punitive action might afford a more drastic protection.

In Umor, however, witchcraft was not commonly associated with more serious, still less sudden, afflictions. Moreover, while it was held that witches were in one sense malevolent in that they lived and flourished on the breath and blood of others, gaining strength at the expense of their victims whom they thereby debilitated, it was also accepted that witches could be unconscious of, or might only dimly recognize, the practices in which they were believed to engage. This was indeed a generally expressed assumption when, as only occasionally happened, a particular person was openly and directly accused of witchcraft against another. Individuals thus accused were not declared to have acted with deliberate malice, but they were expected tacitly to admit the possibility of witchcraft action on their part by participating in a ritual to end it and to remove its supposed effects. The allegation was of an activity of which the person charged might not have been aware and the demand was that she or he should by spraying water on the hands and feet of the supposed victim before his or her husband's patriclan spirit shrine (*epundet*) 'cool' and remove sickness and her or his own witchcraft, if such it were. This ritual action also supposedly exposed the suspected witch to punitive action by the *epundet* if the attacks did not cease.

The social contexts of witchcraft fears, rumours, and accusations in Umor also conformed to patterns which have been well analysed for a number of other societies.[5] For they were linked to resentments and jealousies among persons who were associated in small groups but also had competitive or conflicting interests which engendered fears of surreptitious hostile intent. Allegations of witchcraft result in such situations from a linking of increasing malaise to the fear of hidden malice. Allegations whether private or open serve to relieve anxiety at least temporarily on both these counts, for counter measures can be taken, which it is expected will protect or eliminate the malice and thus alleviate the sickness.

Nearly all suspicions and accusations in Umor were said to concern neighbours occupying the same or adjacent compounds, or living within the wider patriclan area. They were, however, dogmatically excluded between the men of a lineage and more generally of a patriclan who shared a patrimony of house sites and land, even though there was frequently intense rivalry and there could be much envy among the men of a lineage or clan with regard to their prosperity and prestige and competition for offices in ward and village associations. In this situation, a distinct supernatural resource was brought into play not, as in the case of failure in child-bearing, to remove a supposed specific obstacle to a capacity provided by other supernatural means, but on the contrary, to suppress belief and action in respect of the acknowledged mystical power of witchcraft in a particular context. For witchcraft was held to be prevented between patrikin by the intervention of the patriclan spirit (*epundet*) which would punish with sickness and the loss of vitality any one who attempted to bewitch a clansman. In other words, the supernatural protection of the solidarity of clansmen was accepted as a more powerful axiom than fear of witchcraft.

While both men and women were believed capable of witchcraft, one effect of this allocation of supernatural resources was to direct most suspicions and allegations of witchcraft on to women, who as wives had come to live in a patrilineage or patriclan area. And it was moreover these wives, not excluding co-wives of the

[5] E.g. Max Marwick, 'The Social Context of Cewa Witch Beliefs', *Africa*, xxii, 1952, pp. 215–33.

same husband, who commonly suspected one another of witchcraft against themselves, their husbands, or their children. Since the patriclans were exogamous, and there was otherwise a wide choice in marriage, the wives in the households of such an area came from various other parts of the village and a few even from other villages. Thus, few of the women in a neighbourhood formed around the men of a lineage or clan were close kinsfolk, sharing a loyalty developed from a common home and upbringing. Nor were they severally supported in their daily activities and contacts by the presence of their own kin. Nor again did they develop close ties of common interest. Each was concerned for the most part with her own household and children and however close her attachment to her own husband and his interests, there was little motive or pressure to extend this to other men of the clan or their wives. Thus they could and often did remain without close ties of mutual obligation to one another, severally maintaining their separate attachments to their kinsfolk or age mates living elsewhere. On the other hand, open quarrels among them or offensive behaviour on their part towards men of the lineage or clan were not tolerated, and if persisted in might incur the physical sanctions of a beating. That this situation of close proximity and emotional ambivalence tended to evoke suspicions of witchcraft directed against one or other of the women either by another wife or her husband, when they or their children were ailing, was borne out by the accounts of particular cases. In these a reciprocal series of old grudges over slights or supposed unfriendliness and suspicious actions among the women, were recalled as supporting evidence of an accusation.

Since it was from women that witchcraft was mostly feared, and it was also axiomatic that attacks would not come from people of one's own patrilineage or clan,[6] any transmission of the power of witchcraft from generation to generation was attributed to maternal descent. The daughters of a woman reputed to be an active witch were eyed askance and young men warned against, or even prevented by their parents from seeking to marry them for fear of bringing witchcraft into the compound. A retrospective line of

[6] Yakö also said, however, that there was a witchcraft risk involved in the adoption of persons into a patrilineage and clan. Such adoptions were frequent through the initiative of men who bring sisters' sons to live with them or marry and adopt the children of widows. Men joining a lineage in this way, and even their children, might find this circumstance the basis of a later witchcraft charge within the patriclan, if there had been hostility between them and some other clansmen.

witchcraft also tended to be built up to account for a current suspicion. Past sicknesses, deaths and other misfortunes of people
among whom lived the mother or other matrilineal kin of the newly
suspected witch would be retrospectively ascribed to the former's
witchcraft and be used to buttress the suspicions of her daughter.
Through this reminiscent linkage of present and past instances,
supposed chains of witchcraft incidents could be built up whereby
a matrilineage as such might get the unsavoury reputation of
witchcraft power and any member of it would be among the first
to be suspected in connection with a relevant sickness. Such a suspicion would, in turn, reinforce the evil reputation of the matrilineage as a whole. This appeared to account for the fact that the
various indications I was given concerning particular lineages
reputed to carry witchcraft showed not only sporadic but far from
consistent distribution. Different neighbourhoods in the village
from which they originated appeared to have built up their separate speculations from local incidents.

But this *de facto* association of witchcraft with matrilineal descent was not in my experience reconciled or brought into an explicit relation by the Yakö with their doctrine that health, fertility,
and prosperity and, indeed, general beneficence, were conferred
and protected by the matriclan spirits of the *ase*. Apart from a
general and moralizing view that witches like sorcerers would be
punished for their actions by loss of the vitality conferred by the
ase, the two notions were simply kept apart. The latter was significant in an internal and the former in an external context from the
point of view of any person and his or her matriclan. Indeed the
implicit but unrecognized contradiction afforded a striking instance of the different context of belief with reference to a single
class of social group. Although members of a matrilineage would
be aware that allegations were made by others and that one of their
members had perhaps recently 'cooled' her supposed witchcraft,
it would not be accepted by them that they did indeed carry a
strain of witchcraft. For them, such a charge was a slanderous suggestion by others to excuse their own neglects or involve others in
their misfortunes. In other words, belief in the matrilineal transmission of witchcraft was evoked and expressed only in regard to
other matrilineal groups and repudiated with reference to one's
own. The elders and the *yose* priest of one's own matrilineage
and clan sought harmony, peaceful co-operation, and prosperity

for its people and for all Yakö. They sought to harm none. The *yose* itself was invoked *inter alia* in the village rites to extirpate witches. How then could witchcraft develop and persist among them? On the other hand, how could one be sure that other matrilineages were respecting their *ase* and deserving of their protection? Thus the incompatible beliefs in the corporate generation of good and evil in the matriclans were kept in separate social contexts related to a distinct personnel for each believer and were acted on with respect to mutually exclusive ends.

A further point that should be stressed concerns the effect of the localized sphere of application of witchcraft beliefs on the manner and intensity of its expression. Yakö were generally agreed that witchcraft suspicions did not frequently emerge as open accusations. A man who came to believe that he or others close to him were being persistently attacked by a particular person, would first speak of it privately to his kinsmen. Should the ills continue, he might declare his fears to his patriclan head and request his aid. If the morale of the victim and his local relatives was high with reference to the suspected witch in their midst and any people who might retaliate on her or his behalf, one of the senior men (or the husband if his wife were the victim) would go to the supposed witch, announce their suspicions and request him or her to 'cool' the witchcraft. This, as has been seen, could be done without verbally admitting responsibility. Such open demand and compliance was said to be conducted usually with great deliberation avoiding abuse or overt expression of anger on either side.

The circumspect manner with which witchcraft gossip and direct challenges were conducted is likely to be due to the severely disruptive local effects of the open breach which would follow from an acrimonious levelling and repudiation of such charges. For the context was characteristically that of a compact, although not sharply defined, residential group, sometimes that of a single house cluster or even occasionally, where between co-wives, of a single compound family. Within that group, which had a common round of daily tasks and a corresponding sense of the need for give and take, at least among the men, there would be some whose interests were strongly tied by kinship, marriage and the needs of their own households to the supposed victim and others similarly linked to the alleged witch. As Yakö themselves pointed out, if the charges and their repudiation became matters of open and noisy conflict, estrangement between men and their households on either side would follow and more and more people would be forced to take sides if it persisted, the outcome being the breaking away of part or perhaps an entire lineage which would go elsewhere to live. There was, therefore, a strong general interest within a lineage or patriclan, in which relations had hitherto been fairly harmonious, to prevent such an outcome. Influential persons who were not directly involved sought, while not being categorical in their judgements, to suggest that either the cause of the ill or the identity of the witch were not certain, or that while the accused person might be genuine in any repudiation, he or she might have manifested witchcraft power of which they were quite unaware and which it was in their own interest to 'cool'.

In instances where witchcraft accusations had in fact been associated with the occasional secessions of households or lineages from their patriclan areas, there had been a history of disputes over other and practical problems, concerning succession to farm plots and house sites, material support for association membership, and the development of factions on this account.

The factors that damped down witchcraft accusations, confining them largely to semi-secret gossip, and sustained an attitude of doubt on the part of those not directly concerned, with regard to the identity of any witch that might be responsible in a particular case, were reflected in the handling of witchcraft fears and allegations by diviners. While a divination might well suggest that witchcraft lay at the root of a lingering malady or of female sterility, and that protective measures should be taken, I heard of no instance where a diviner explicitly identified the witch. Even the witchcraft itself was, it seemed, left as a more open possibility than were divinations of ritual and moral transgressions. Such divinations would usually be confined to suggestions that charms should be used to prevent witches entering the house or for temporary change of residence to make sure that any local witch would not continue the attack. While these hesitancies were consistent with the risk of legal penalty under Nigerian ordinances for open accusation of witchcraft, such risk of action before the Native Court of the area was not stressed by Yakö themselves as a reason for caution.

Thus, while divination might in some cases generate or reinforce beliefs that ailments or disabilities were due to witchcraft, it did not discover particular witches and so precipitate open conflicts in a neighbourhood or bring a decisive judgement to bear on them. Furthermore, the supposed identification of a witch by the victim in a dream which was considered fairly common was not relied on by others since it was held that witches were able to shield themselves behind the appearance of another person who alone was seen and wrongfully suspected.

Uncertainty as to the identity of particular witches, which was thus much greater than doubt concerning the occurrence of witchcraft, was increased by the coexistence of divergent beliefs as to acquisition of witchcraft powers. For, while it was generally accepted that these were likely to be inherited from other witches, especially by daughters, it was also believed that they could be acquired by an aspirant who secretly received from a witch leaf medicines that were kept in a hidden camwood-smeared pot (*yitanasowa*). It was also told that medicines given to barren women by the custodian of an *edet* might miscarry and, while failing to restore her fertility, unwittingly give her witchcraft power instead.

Finally the responsibility, and hence the culpability, of a supposed witch could be mitigated by the view not only that this injurious power had usually been acquired unawares, but that a witch might also have been a victim of coercion of other witches who formed a secret corporation within the village. Thus, the sterility of a woman, if her matrilineage were suspect, could be regarded as a penalty inflicted by the corporation for her failure to exercise her power to associate with them in their invisible gatherings. A similar explanation might be offered for a man whose harvests despite sound husbandry were continually poor. And in such cases a change of fortune was likely to be regarded as a reward that had been accorded for responding to this coercion.

The Yakö response to the doctrine of witchcraft power thus appeared to be mainly one of averting or neutralizing the supposed effects rather than of the exposure and destruction of particular witches. And an alleged witch could, where the attribution of grave sickness or death was not directly in question, be spoken of in pity for the disabilities that possession of this involuntary anti-social power entailed.

Since the dwelling areas of patriclans were adjacent to one another, forming a continuous built-up area which brought members of several clans into frequent contact, and there were sources of friction and suspicion between lineages of different clans, especially concerning ground for house building in the village and conveniently situated farming and oil palm collecting areas outside, one might have expected to find frequent inter-patriclan fears and accusations of witchcraft. But this was not regarded as a serious or likely danger in Umor. Its rarity was accounted for on various grounds. Some said that the patriclan spirit protected its household against attack from outside witches by inflicting sickness on such disembodied intruders. But another reassurance against both fear of external witchcraft and of accusations from persons outside the patriclan area was afforded by the politico-ritual authority of the Ward Leaders, the *Yakamban*, who were drawn from all the patriclans.

The Leaders of a ward under their Head the *Ogbolia*, and backed by the *Ebiabu* association of the younger men of a ward, could also be appealed to in such matters, both by accusers and those who sought to repudiate such accusations. The *Yakamban* were responsible for the periodic *Ligwomi* initiations of boys in each ward which ritually expressed the value of ward solidarity and their dominant attitude and findings with regard to intra-ward disputes were conciliatory. They accordingly served to damp down and even discredit accusations and consequently the intensification of fears concerning witchcraft between different clan areas in the ward.

By the thirties the political authority of an *Ogbolia* had already been diminished after the introduction by the Nigerian Administration of a system of Warrant Chiefs. One of these had been appointed from each ward in Umor to serve on the Native Court of the area, before which, as already noted, charges of open allegation of witchcraft could be brought under Nigerian ordinances. But a Warrant Chief had no interest in letting a charge of witchcraft accusation from his ward come before the area Court. His involvement in a possible external sanction was, by promoting faction, likely to prejudice the authority and prestige to which the more capable of them had attained in internal affairs.

The virtual absence of witchcraft accusations before the *Yabot*, the village council of matriclan and other priests, could be accounted for by similar factors. The ordinances which rendered witchcraft accusations punishable by the Native Court of the area may again have played their part. But only cases involving persons from different wards which could not, therefore, be dealt with in the patriclan or ward, would be likely to be brought before the *Yabot*. And such would be rare since suspicion of distant persons was not part of the ideology of witchcraft. Finally, the *Yabot* would on principle seek to allay suspicions and remove fears in such a case by requesting the 'cooling' of possible witchcraft before the patriclan or sometimes, it was said, the matriclan shrine of the victim without definitely declaring its occurence.

Thus the Yakö of Umor knew and in principle accepted a pattern of beliefs concerning the nature, processes, and symptoms of witchcraft common to many African peoples, including such widespread special features as the manifestation as witches in owls, and flitting lights at night. But, unlike many other peoples, including some of their neighbours whose reputation for intense and destructive witchcraft was well-known to them, they relegated witchcraft to a minor role as a supernatural souce of injury.

Correspondingly, although they knew of the *essere* bean ordeal whereby both an accusation and a repudiation of witchcraft could be simultaneously tested and sanctioned to the destruction of the guilty, they had not adopted it. To the Yakö, the appropriateness and efficacy of this practice for the Mbembe and the Efik seemed not so much a matter for questioning as something irrelevant to their own situation. Having in their patriclan, ward and village groupings, cults which provided strong politico-ritual sanctions against such covert inter-personal hostility, the fears these would engender were correspondingly reduced. Their own witches were accordingly different. They allocated the main responsibility for both causing and alleviating misfortune to the extra-human *ndet* whose supernatural actions were open to the alternative interpretations of caprice on their own part or an offence, witting or unwitting on the part of the sufferer or, exceptionally, as will be seen, of a sorcerer. Thus Yakö were, by other elements of dogma and their patterns of social relations, inhibited from exploiting the aggressive possibilities of witchcraft belief and accusation.

Yakö attitudes were in some respects similar to sorcery, a supernatural process which was formulated with equal definiteness and recognized as a danger but was in practice circumscribed as an explanation of disasters. And the effect was again, largely to exclude the building up of extreme hostility between persons and groups.

While witchcraft could be suspected where there was loss of

vitality and ill-defined malaise, any sudden and severe illness and especially death without premonitory symptoms was often attributed to sorcery (*nkɔbi*, lit. 'destruction', from *okɔbi*, to spoil). Severe losses or destruction of crops or goods could also be similarly ascribed. Sorcery was regarded, implicitly, and in contrast with witchcraft, as a practice for which the propensity lay with men and not with women. It was believed to be achieved by abusing the power of punitive spirits, *ndet*. Materials taken from the shrine of one of these were surreptitiously obtained and introduced into the food or drink of the intended victim or placed in a position that he frequented; or again, something intimately associated with the victim (a scrap of soiled clothing, hair, excreta, or matting from his house floor or roof) was surreptitiously placed and left in contact with an *edet*.

The custodians of *ndet* were themselves dogmatically excluded from the practice of sorcery and those joining an association or cult group protected by an *edet* commonly took an oath, sanctioned by death at the hands of the *edet*, that they would not practise sorcery. But the practice of sorcery seeking the death of the victim was also believed to be further and more generally restricted by attributing to it a suicidal character, for the sorcerer who employed means to encompass the death of his victim, died himself and triumphed only as a ghost. When speaking of sorcery in this context the Yakö attributed it to the consuming envy of the unsuccessful who accepted their own destruction as the cost of destroying those whose good fortune and prosperity pointed their own failure. They would say in stressing deterrents that, while the Creator, Obasi, did not prevent men from playing this dangerous game, he had decreed that as a condition of success they should also die by the action of the *edet* they abused. But it was believed that lack of success in life materially and in gaining the admiration of others could so embitter men that they welcomed this desperate means of displaying their power to ruin others at the cost of their own lives, which no longer had any satisfaction for them.

In sudden and severe illness, the sufferer might become aware of the identity of the sorcerer as a ghost from among the recently dead, who, appearing in sleep or while the victim was awake but solitary, struck him to hasten the departure of his soul to the underworld. A sudden fainting fit and especially prolonged unconsciousness was also thought likely to be an attack of a recently deceased sorcerer and those who found anyone in that condition had to shout his name loudly and repeatedly to recall his soul before it had reached the underworld.

Thus the theory of sorcery was linked in Umor to more general beliefs concerning the capacity of the remembered dead to appear as ghosts, mostly in dreams, to coerce the living. On the one hand this placed the death-dealing sorcerer beyond the reach of further human intervention to secure his punishment and so eliminated violence in quest of revenge. On the other it postulated a prior and extreme supernatural sanction since the sorcerer himself was already excluded from further material and social benefits by his death and was also destined to fade into a speedy and impotent oblivion. For the soul of anyone strongly suspected of sorcery could never be reincarnated in a later generation as most souls were believed to be. This was not only dogmatically given, for the stigma of suspected sorcery would prevent either a mother or a diviner discovering the reincarnation of such a soul in a later-born child.

The dogma concerning the self-destructive character of death-dealing sorcery was also applied in mitigated form to lesser misfortunes whereby anyone who sought through abuse of an *edet* to destroy another's harvest or stock or house, would himself suffer corresponding, but not necessarily similar, loss. Yakö asserted, and appeared reassured by the assertion, that on this account only the desperate or the deranged among them would resort to sorcery save in a minor degree. Fears were, however, expressed concerning Ibo and other strangers, visiting Umor to trade or to work there temporarily, whose sorcery might be immune from these automatic sanctions. The destruction of such foreign sorcerers was explicitly sought from the normally beneficent *ase* spirits in the seasonal village rituals. Besides subjecting strangers to an exceptional supernatural sanction, this had a significance for the Yakö themselves that was analogous with the dogma of the self-destructiveness of homicidal sorcery in applying it to those outside the living community. Beliefs concerning sorcery could not therefore be harnessed to exacerbate conflicts and intensify factions within the wards or the village as a whole. Diviners, ward leaders, and village priests concurred in repudiating the belief, and would reject an accusation that a healthy and flourishing person within the community could have destroyed another by sorcery.

When discussing transgressions or ritual neglect that could forfeit the beneficence of the *ase* spirits or incur the harmful effects of *ndet*, and when characterizing witchcraft and sorcery, the Yakö never claimed to have definite criteria for differentiating in advance between their effects. The sequence of events in particular illnesses, misfortunes, and deaths, whereby various divinations, allegations, and offerings were made at different stages, showed that the initial attitude towards suspected supernatural action was one of uncertainty and of implicit questioning in an endeavour to discover and influence the supposed cause. Any apparent certainty expressed with regard to supernatural action was retrospective and particular. A favourable outcome in a particular case was held to have demonstrated, for example, the capacity and the responsiveness of the spirit appealed to on that occasion and an expectation that it could operate similarly in the future. But the complexity of the material and social background of any particular need or failure, and the existence of a multiplicity of possible supernatural entities and actions was recognized as excluding certainty concerning the cause of misfortune or the best means of ensuring success.

It is in this context that the role of the diviner is to be assessed. For his essential service in the Yakö view was to narrow down the initial field of uncertainty and choice for those seeking supernatural aid. This sense of uncertainty and need for selection was expressed in Umor in terms of an omniscience that was otherwise confined to the creator Obasi. The diviner was believed, through a supposed gift of Obasi, to be able to transmit that knowledge. Furthermore, since supernatural actions by spirits, witches, or ghosts were all conceived as conditional, and capable of being reversed or deflected by offerings or supernatural protections, the diviner indicated in many situations not only the probable mystical cause of a misfortune, but the means of alleviating it.

But diviners were not assumed to be infallible. Not only would unfavourable comments be made on the capacity of a particular diviner, but some accounts of particular divinations and their outcome concluded with the statement that the diviner had not been able to 'see clearly' or 'see enough'. Even with the services of a diviner, both uncertainty and the possibility of further alternative or supplementary action remained.

In contexts of frustration, the Creator, Obasi, was commonly portrayed fatalistically as a predetermining agent of destiny, as distributing talents and opportunities, health, and wealth unevenly and inscrutably, if not capriciously, among men. All these attitudes, however, assumed the omniscience of Obasi, who thus became the ultimate source of supernatural knowledge and power. And it was through a power conferred by Obasi during initiation and training that the diviner was able to discover the hidden causes of misfortunes and thereby the supernatural means by which they may be averted.

Divining was practised by both men and women. While both, were known as *Yabuŋa* (sing. *Obuŋa*), Ibo terms which are distinct for men and for women, viz.: *Obla* and *Idja*, respectively, were commonly used in addressing or naming a particular diviner. But only those who had shown convincing signs of a 'call' from Obasi—in recurrent and vivid dreams and/or by a temporary but not disabling attack of madness (*keto*)—would be accepted for initiation. In Umor, with a population of over 10,000, there were in the thirties only twenty-five recognized diviners. While two of these said they had become initiated on account of persistent dreams in which Obasi had appeared to order them to do so and one of them described how ghosts had flogged him in dreams when he delayed, several practitioners were found to have succeeded a kinsmen whom they had served as an assistant and replaced on death or incapacity. It appeared that diviners looked for temperamentally suitable persons among their kin to serve them as their assistants, but this did not, in the view of the diviners or others, provide the essential power which was conveyed by Obasi himself in a ritual initiation performed only when the candidate had been accepted as suitable by the other diviners in the village.

For the diviners constituted a corporation of which one was installed as the ritual head, was custodian of the main shrine, and was associated with the *ase* priests as a member of the village cult group and council, the *Yabot*. The shrine of the head, *Obot Yabuŋa*, was considered to be a manifestation of Obasi himself, under the name of *Isɔ Obasi*, the Ekoi term for the masculine aspect of Obasi which the Yakö in other contexts referred to as *Obasi Woden* (see Chapter VIII and Plate XXVI).

From accounts of a considerable number of seances, obtained from persons who had consulted diviners, it became clear that while all were concerned with the discovery of particular hidden causes of events, the consultations related to a very wide range of situations. Some of them concerned routine or recurrent situations of low emotional intensity, such as the customary divination of the identity of the 'soul' that had been reincarnated in a child.[7] Others sought guidance as to means of averting a possible misfortune, such as the risks associated with the clitoridectomy carried out on nubile girls and with childbirth, especially on the part of a woman who was bearing her first child or had lost children previously. But a large number concerned sterility, sickness, death, or other misfortunes that had already taken place and here the purpose of the divination varied according to the circumstances. As already mentioned, diviners were frequently consulted by wives when they had failed to achieve pregnancy or suffered several miscarriages. Their aid was also sought for both men and women in cases of sudden and severe illness, serious accidental injuries, and exceptional losses (such as the rotting of a large part of a harvest or the destruction of goods by termites). Finally, divination was resorted to when a man or woman died suddenly.

In some instances of all these kinds, the divination accounted for the misfortune in terms of ritual neglect or moral fault on the part of the victim, spouse, or kin. In other words, the responsibility was placed on persons closely concerned whose imprudence in neglecting to make appropriate offerings or failure to meet social obligations had led supernatural powers associated with patriclan or matriclan or *ndet* to withhold benefit or protection. For lapses in ritual observance, as in those mentioned earlier, or where protection was sought against anticipated risks, the diviner commonly prescribed only ritual means of alleviation or preventing a recurrence of misfortune. Thus, according to the situation, he would provide a concoction of leaves to be applied or drunk and require an undertaking to make a further offering to Obasi

[7] There is a season each year at which recently born children are brought to the diviners by their mothers and other female kin and are identified, after questionings about the life history of the parents and their relatives, as reincarnations of recently deceased kin or prominent persons with whom these had been associated.

when a favourable outcome had materialized or he would indicate
the shrines at which offerings should be made, and those who
should participate in them.

But where, as quite frequently, the questioning had elicited
specific acts of hostility, obstruction, or other failures affecting
rights and duties between the patient and a spouse, relative, or
neighbour, the loss of supernatural protection would be implicitly
attributed to this and the prescriptions then included an explicit
moralizing element. In such cases a 'cooling' rite was also enjoined
at one or more shrines in which the offending party, whether the
patient or another, should make offerings and also promise such
material or behavioural amends as were appropriate.

By such procedures, since his seances were not private and his
prescriptions were in any case quickly made known to those
concerned, a diviner could, and sometimes undoubtedly did,
establish a quasi-official and public demand, through moral
declarations in a ritual context, for the restoration of harmony
and material adjustment in conformity with norms applicable to
the situation. In this way considerable and often effective social
pressure for right conduct between spouses, siblings, co-wives,
affines, and others could be exerted through the procedure of
divination. Those who were tempted to flout a diviner's findings
in such a case were reminded not only that they ran the supernatural risk of injury through the spirit concerned, but were
admitting an ill-will which could lead to graver charges.

But from a cosmological, as distinct from a moral point of view,
the diviner was seen as an adviser on the interplay of supernatural
agencies. Apart from sudden deaths in which sorcery might be
suspected, there appeared from the cases studied no close or
asserted correlation between the nature of the misfortune or fear
in question, or the character of the moral failure, if any, that might
be brought to light, and the specific spirit agency which was
suggested as instrumental. Punitive *ndet*, whether tutelaries of
groups or not, matriclan spirits, witchcraft and minor sorcery,
and even Obasi, were severally suggested as the supernatural
sources in various cases of very similar kinds of malady or misfortune. The diviner, guided no doubt by the particular configura-
tion of personal relations and the possible repercussions of his
diagnosis and the sacrifices or other ritual that he might recom-
mend, acted in one sense as a kind of broker with regard to a

supernatural investment. He did not guarantee an immediate or sure return. His implicit claim was to understand the workings of the supernatural economy and to discover the factors involved in it that were most likely to underlie a particular risk or dislocation and should be manipulated to safeguard or restore the situation. That the Yakö recognized and valued this service as such is suggested when, as they commonly did outside the ritual situation, they spoke of their initial and fulfilment offerings to the spirits of the divination shrines as payments to the diviners themselves for the exercise of their powers.

VIII
FIRST FRUITS RITUALS *

Introduction

LIKE so many peoples who depend directly on the cultivation of the soil for the maintenance of both the individual and the community, the Yakö mark the main phases of the agricultural cycle by collective ceremonies. These seasonal rites are undoubtedly an expression of the values attached to the thorough and punctual performance of successive tasks in cultivation and of the appreciation of the rewards that flow from these farming activities. But a close study of the ritual forms, of the social groups and persons prominently associated with them, of the social relations posited among these persons and groups, and finally of the values directly expressed in prayers, gifts, and magical acts, reveals an integrative function with respect to the community which far transcends the maintenance of effective patterns of agriculture. These rites are an occasion for the re-affirmation and the inculcation of the total values of the traditional way of life among the Yakö; of the rights and duties of villagers among themselves as individuals and as members of different organizations, of the attitudes to be expected from and adopted towards strangers; in fact, of the proper relations between the components of the social system both within the village community and its external relations.

I will attempt here to demonstrate the validity of this view by a brief analysis of the First Fruits Ceremonies which I witnessed and discussed among the Yakö of Umor in 1939. These rites, known, for reasons which will appear later, as *Liboku*, take place every year in early July. They have been preceded six moons before, at the beginning of the rains, by the *Lisetomi* rite, Offering to the Soil, and are followed towards the end of the rains by the Harvest rites, *Ase*, in mid-November.

Organizations Concerned in the Rites

It will be recalled that the Yakö villages were formerly politically as well as ritually autonomous. In each a dual series of corporate

* Reprinted from *J.R.A.I.* Vol. 59, 1949 (1951)

groups, matrilineal and patrilineal, established on the basis of unilineal descent, provide the foundation of the social system. But there is also a territorial organization which in the larger villages is based on the wards and also an elaborate development of restricted associations and of cult groups for men and for women. Office and influence in these ward and other organizations overlap to a considerable extent with the authority of the Village Council of Priests of which the leaders are the priests of the matriclans. Their prestige and authority vary according to social context. There are particular fields of competence with reference to specific ritual and juridical actions and there are accepted lines of successive intervention and appeal, but there is no rigid hierarchy of offices and authority. An organization of Ward Leaders, with which the age-set system is associated; the Council of Village Priests, known as the *Yabot*; the Corporation of Diviners, the *Yabuŋa*, and the more powerful men's associations such as the *Ikpuŋkọra* society, exist in their own right and for the most part operate their own sanctions. Twice a year, however, in the First Fruits rites, and in the Harvest rites at the end of the agricultural year, the relative status of these organizations is symbolically expressed in an elaborate series of ceremonials. This expression of the mutual relations of the various groups and cults is not the overt intent of the rites. The explicit purpose is to secure with spirit aid, prosperity, fertility, security, and harmony in the village. But the roles of various group leaders and spirit priests, their mutual relations and their position in the community as expressed in the rituals, serve to integrate and adjust them one to another on occasions when the value of harmony and solidarity within the village is emotionally inculcated.

Before giving some account of the rites of the First Fruits ceremonies themselves and of their significance from this point of view, it will be necessary to recall briefly the character of the organizations concerned in them. In each of their five compact villages which range from over 1,000 to nearly 11,000 in population, there is an organization which controls through rituals at the shrines of matriclan spirits and elsewhere both sources of fertility, health, and general well-being for man and crops and beasts, and sanctions against grave offences whether ritual or moral. These priest leaders, known collectively as *Yabot*, the Leaders, thus constitute a sacerdotal village council, the juridical aspects of whose authority have been described elsewhere.[1] The composition of this sacerdotal council in Umor, where it has twenty-three members, may be summarized as follows:

Its nucleus consists of the ten priests (*Bi'ina,* sing. *Ina*) of matriclan shrines of whom one, the priest of *Odjokobi* of the *Yabot I* matriclan is leader of the Council and priest-head of the village.

To these are joined the holders of other ritual offices, appointments to which are made or approved by the Council. Of these the most prominent is the Village Speaker (*Okpebri*), who, on both ritual and secular occasions, is the usual spokesman of the *Yabot,* and is the custodian of the Village Drum and Spirit which ritually ensure and enforce peace in the village.

The remainder, while recognized as members of the Council and participating in both rites and deliberations, have a secondary place in discussions and in ritual activities, save on the occasion of rites which are their special concern. They include:

The chief priest (*Opalapala*), the deputy priest (*Ogbodum Ogu*) and the chief drummer (*Otomise*) of *Korta,* a village organization into which all males are initiated in boyhood, which performs seasonal and sexennial rites.

The chief priest of *Okeŋka* (*Ovar Ekpe*), a village cult to be described later, which also arbitrates secular disputes between the wards of the village.[2]

The priest of *Liboku,* the spirit especially invoked in the First Fruit ceremonies to be discussed here.

The head of the Corporation of Diviners (*Obot Yabuŋa*).

The priests of two shrines connected with the foundation of the village (*Elamalama* and *Esandet*).

The War Priest of *Idjiman,* the oldest ward and the site of first settlement in Umor (*Onun Eko*).

The Tooth Chipper (*Omeŋka*), who has the duty of ritually chipping and blackening the teeth of all *Yabot* when they are installed in office.

The custodian of a set of Village Drums and Trumpets (*Obot Odere*).

It will be seen that the *Yabot* include, beside several officials such as *Okpebri* and *Omeŋka,* who act on its behalf, the heads of a number of cults distinct from those of the matriclan spirits. It is necessary to look a little more closely at some of the latter since they are prominent in the First Fruits ceremonies.

[1] See Chapter VI.　　　　　　　[2] See also Chapter V.

Korta is a ritual organization of all the men of the village into which boys are initiated in childhood following their initiation into the ritual organization (*Ligwomi*) of the ward to which they belong. Its major ritual takes place at six-year intervals when its priest leader (*Opalapala*) performs a masked dance on successive nights at a series of sacred sites in the village while the five *Korta* slit-gongs are beaten. The *Korta* house in the compound of *Opalapala* is then renewed. The power of *Korta* is believed to be derived from a ritual object *Ekpe Edet* (Leopard Spirit) contained in a sealed box to which initiates are introduced. It is reputed to include a skull wrapped in a leopard skin and is kept in the *Korta* house with the slit-gongs, which are beaten only in the six-yearly rites. The punitive power of *Ekpe Edet*, which is thought to be able to inflict severe illness and swift death, is held in considerable awe and the person of *Opalapala* is sacred. His office should rotate among certain patriclans. He is assisted in rituals by an assistant priest (*Ogbodum Odu*) and by a Singer (*Otomise*), the chief of five *Korta* Drummers. These may, on behalf of *Korta*, taboo objects and places by affixing its sign and levy fines for infringements and for attempts to witness its secret rites. All three are, as has been seen, members of the Village Council of Priests (Plate XIX).

There is also a ritual organization of women known as *Ekao*, parallel to *Korta*, the leaders (*Yadjeika*) of which, while not members of the Village Priests Council, participate in the First Fruits rites. All girls are initiated by presentation to the cult object embodying its powerful spirit, which is at other times kept in the house of the senior priestess (*Odjeika*). This spirit is believed to cause and cure sickness, particularly a crippling stiffness of the joints. The sacred site of *Ekao* lies outside the village under a rock ledge by a stream, supposedly known only to senior members (*Yakaledji*), who have been taken to make offerings to the slit-gongs kept there to cure ailments or secure a child. Membership of the officiating group is obligatory on those obtaining cures or children in this way. Every six years, in the year following the major *Korta* rite, the *Ekao* drums are set up in the Village Square inside a raphia-palm leaf screen and beaten at intervals over a period of days. At such times any woman who is sick may seek a cure from the drums without special fee or obligation. The *Yadjeika* have a general moral authority over women and are believed able to invoke the ritual sanctions of *Ekao* against those who misbehave.

Okeŋka, the head of which is also a member of the Council of Village Priests, is an association recruited from the Leaders (*Yakambǝn*) of all the wards of the village. The Leaders of each ward constitute a politico-ritual authority with regard to the initiation of boys, the recognition and control of age-sets, the settlement of internal disputes and representation of ward interests in the village. *Okeŋka* unites the several ward organizations since only Ward Leaders are admitted and then at a considerable fee. Serious disputes and offences involving two or more wards may be taken to *Okeŋka* for judgement. The Head (*Ogbolia*) of any ward could appeal to it to intervene. It will also protect the property of members and others for a fee by affixing its sign. Its supernatural sanctions, which are greatly feared, are founded on belief in the powers of another Leopard Spirit which brings misfortune and even death on those who flout its commands as announced by *Okeŋka*. Its head is also known as *Ovar Ekpe*, Leopard Chief, and it speaks with a leopard's roar by sounding its *lekpetu* (a booming instrument) kept in the *Okeŋka* house. Thus, *Okeŋka* consists in practice of a body of men who have secured leading positions in their several ward organizations, gaining thereby the support and the means to make the payments and receive admission, and to participate in the ritual control it exercises. It will be seen that the members of *Okeŋka* accompany the *Liboku* priest in his nocturnal circuit of the wards of Umor, sounding two bull-roarers (*Ewoŋwo*), while all others must remain concealed in their houses. The bull-roarers of *Okeŋka* are also sounded in the bush at a place called *Kewoŋwoŋtom* on the day for announcing the time of First Fruits ceremonies and nightly after the day of the main rite, when bull-roarers may be sounded in the village by any young man.

The Diviners (*Yabuŋa*), whose head is again a member of the Village Council of *Yabot*, are a corporation of diviners and healers who practise under the auspices of the Sky Spirit, Obasi. A manifestation of Obasi known as *Isǝ Obasi* inheres in a figurine in the shrine of which the Leader of the *Yabuŋa* is custodian and priest. To this sacrifices and prayers are made at the initiation of every new *Obuŋa*. The *Yabuŋa* are recruited by dream visitations of a deceased *Obuŋa* to one who is called to succeed him. Initiation involves a secret ritual which includes prolonged sun staring, the payment of fees to the corporation, and a period of instruction in divination and in herbal and ritual treatment. Each *Obuŋa* is instructed in the means of preparing a sacred and purifying water and in the making of a figurine (*Opata*), which is consulted in divining the sources of ills and the reincarnation of the dead in children. Each *Obuŋa* practises independently but he or she relies on the support of the whole corporation, which, through its leader *Obot Obuŋa*, can invoke the sanctions of the Village Council against one who refuses to make promised sacrifices and payments for services. At the First Fruits and Harvest rituals of the village, as will be seen, the *Yabuŋa* act collectively to secure the blessing of *Isɔ Obasi* and to purify the community as a whole. On both these occasions the *Yabot* ritually visit the shrine of *Isɔ Obasi* and receive its blessing.

Certain female ritual officiants, *Yamanamana* and *Idjadja*, who are not members of the *Yabot* but carry out the clitoridectomy of nubile girls and the chipping of their teeth after marriage, participate in the public ceremonies of the First Fruits, receiving blessings like other priests.

A number of restricted associations, especially of men, receive public recognition in the rites. These associations, admission to which is variously dependent on fee-paying, succession and special aptitudes, have no authority or active role in the rituals, but they attend as groups seeking blessings from the premier matriclan spirit at the public rites. Their acceptance appears to be critical for public approval of the moral worth of these associations.

Before considering the sequence and actual organization of the First Fruits rituals, it should be first explained that *Liboku*, the term by which the rites are known, is also the name given to a powerful spirit or medicine which inheres in a bundle enclosed in four flat pieces of wood bound with cord. This ritual bundle is kept in the shrine of the matriclan Spirit *Obolene*, but a special priest, *Obot Liboku*, is appointed to carry out the rituals connected with it. He is assisted in the secret rituals by the following priests: *Okpebri*, the Village Speaker; the Head of *Okeŋka*; *Obuŋa Omenka*, the ritual officiant at village-priest installations; the Head of Diviners; *Opalapala* and *Ogbodun Ogu*, the head and deputy head of *Korta*; and four priests of matriclan spirits, including *Obolene*, in whose shrine the *Liboku* cult objects are kept, the others being *Okarefoŋ*, *Esukpa*, and *Atewa*.

THE RITES

The rites extend over a period of thirty-two days and begin with a ceremonial announcement. On the day before this announcement, *Obot Liboku* collects obligatory contributions of palm wine from all returning to the village with wine, and places the large jars of wine in the Village Head's compound. The next morning he visits and summons successively each of the other ten *Liboku* priests indicated above, beginning with the Village Speaker. They go in procession to the compound of the Village Head, who receives them in silence, and gives them food and the large jar of wine collected on the previous day. They proceed again in procession with the pot of wine to the compound of the priest of the matri-clan spirit *Obolene*, in whose shrine *Liboku* is kept. *Obot Obolene* announces to his spirit that the rites are to be performed and asks its blessing. The Speaker then declares before it that the *Liboku* rite proper, the Night of *Liboku*, will be held in twenty days' time and the wine is drunk. Throughout these procedures all other villagers must keep out of sight. Any seen by the priests are later required to pay a fine of four rods (two shillings), which is enforced, if necessary, by the Village Council of Priests after the rites.

Eleven days later, in the early morning, the *Liboku* Priest collects firewood from any convenient heap of 'marriage firewood', that is, a large and special accumulation provided for a girl who is in seclusion prior to her marriage. He chops it up for the later Night of *Liboku*. Anyone infringing the secrecy of this rite is fined one rod.

Three days later the Village Head takes from the inner shrine and places on the outside altar some of the ritual objects and materials of the premier matriclan spirit, *Odjokobi*, of which he is priest. *Obot Liboku*, waiting at the compound entrance until the Village Head retires, then takes these to the *Korta* house, where *Opalapala*, the priest of *Korta*, awaits him. The sacred *Liboku* bundle is brought to the *Korta* house from the shrine of the matri-clan spirit of *Obolene* and into it are put some of the ritual materials from the *Odjokobi* shrine. Others are set aside for use during the rites. *Opalapala* eats and drinks wine with *Obot Liboku*, who then returns the ritual objects to the *Odjokobi* shrine. *Odjokobi*, the premier fertility spirit of the village, thus validates and 'strengthens' *Liboku* in a rite at the place sacred to the village initiation of men.

XXI *a*. *Lite* dancers

XXI *b*. Diviners collecting leaves and roots

XXII *a*. Cooling the village

XXII *b*. The *Odere* dancers

On the same day, having been requested in advance by *Obot Liboku*, prominent members of *Ekao*, the village cult for women, go in procession about forty strong and led by the senior *Odjeika* to its secret forest shrine, perform rites, and return smeared with camwood in late afternoon to feast in the compound of its leader. Thus the separate cult organizations for men and for women are associated in the 'strengthening' of *Liboku*.

The Night of *Liboku*, the major secret rite of the First Fruits, takes place after nightfall two days later. It is preceded during the day by other rites. In the early afternoon the Village Head summons all the Village Priests (*Yabot*) to the *Odjokobi* shrine, where they receive the blessing of the spirit and their breasts are smeared with sacred chalk. The members of *Okeŋka* follow with their Leopard Voice and are blessed at the outer altar. They are also given meat and wine, which they take back to their meeting-place and prepare for the rites that night.

Later in the afternoon the priest (*Ina*) of the matriclan spirit *Atewa* conducts the *Lekpeduŋa* rite, in which the *Liboku* priests participate. Any newly appointed member of the *Liboku* group offers a goat on this occasion. Assembling in *Ina Atewa's* compound wine is drunk and meat put on to cook. *Ina Atewa*, who has his own Leopard Voice (*Lekpetu*), takes this and leads the group to the *Lekpeduŋa* site on the edge of the village containing a boulder, also called *Atewa*. Chalk is sprinkled on the stone and on the Leopard Voices of *Atewa* and *Okeŋka*. A piece of hoe money (*ekase*) is provided successively by *Atewa*, *Okeŋka* and any newly appointed *Liboku* priest, scraped over the bellies of all present and buried by the boulder. The *Atewa* priest then slices pieces of new yam as an offering to *Atewa* with this prayer:

> Today we will eat new yams
> When a man lies with a woman let her conceive and bear a live child.
> *Atewa* take this offering of yam.
> We will eat new yams.
> The man who carries witchcraft let him die.

Slices of yam are then offered to the booming instruments (Leopard Voices) without speech. Yellow powder is rubbed on the boulder and the instruments. Each priest then chalks his hand as it rests successively on these objects. The *Atewa* priest then takes a new yam, which has been roasting on a fire made when they first arrived, and gives a slice to each priest, who puts it to his tongue and drops it by the stone. The instruments are next taken into the adjacent bush and are played by the priests of *Atewa* and *Okeŋka*. The meat is then eaten and the wine drunk.

In the evening, when all who are not officiating must remain indoors and out of sight, *Obot Liboku* goes with the ritual firewood collected earlier to the compound of the Village Head, who has again set out materials on the *Odjokobi* altar (hoe money, chalk, yellow powder, smoked meat, and palm wine). *Obot Liboku* calls the Village Head, who remains in his shelter and does not answer. *Obot Liboku* leaves some of the firewood and takes the ritual materials from the altar to the adjacent Village Square and lays a fire there. He returns to the Village Head's shade and calls him four times in the name of his matriclan spirit. The latter answers, uttering only huh! huh!; the fourth time, and with his eyes shut, he hands *Obot Liboku* burning brands kindled from the wood he left. With these *Obot Liboku* lights the fire he has laid in the Village Square. He then goes round the village to summon all the other *Liboku* priests, except *Ina Atewa*, calling each four times, and takes the *Liboku* itself from the *Obolene* shrine to the Village Square. The Village Head now emerges and brings an offering of meat and wine for the *Liboku*, which is ritually consumed at the fire, which is then put out.

The *Liboku* priests next proceed in file to the compound of *Ina Atewa*, who has lit a similar ritual fire. Ritual objects and materials from the *Atewa* shrine have been put out on the altar and the *Liboku* is blessed (with smeared chalk) by *Ina Atewa*, who says 'Let us all live but the witch should die.' Two tusk trumpets are sounded, meat and wine provided by the priest of *Atewa* are consumed. The blessing by the Spirit *Atewa* (the only matriclan spirit visited besides *Odjokobi*) arises, according to the Yakö, from the special position of the *Atewa* cult, believed to have been brought by immigrants from Ekumuru neighbours whose premier fertility spirit it is.

The priests now file out into the village. The *Liboku* is first replaced in the *Obolene* shrine and they proceed successively to each of the four ward squares, where the local ward members of *Okeŋka* have assembled and are sounding the *Okeŋka* Leopard's Voice, which is carried on ahead to each ward in turn. A tusk trumpet, three bull-roarers, and mouth whistles are also sounded, while the priests are given meat and wine and accompanied to the sacred War Stones (*Likota*) in that ward. The priests then go to the Village Head's compound, where the *Okeŋka* Leopard's Voice is placed in the *Odjokobi* shrine. Throughout this rite all but the priests and members of *Okeŋka* must remain indoors on pain of fines and/or compulsory fees for membership of *Okeŋka*.

Earlier in this day the chief village drum (*Ekui*), kept in the Village Speaker's shelter, is ceremoniously re-covered with a new skin at a sacred place near the Village Square by the *Korta* Drummer (*Otomise*) and his assistants, while all outsiders are warned off by shrill cries.

The main public celebrations occur on the following day, known as Liboku for the People (*Yanen Liboku*). Most, but not all, of the *Yabot*, assemble at the Village Head's compound in the morning, where invocations are made before *Odjokobi* in its shrine house and their chests are smeared with sacred chalk. The ritual objects of the spirit *Odjokobi* are then brought out from the shrine house and set out on the public altar by the Village Head, while the *Okeŋka* instrument remains in the shrine house, where any Village Priest who belongs also to *Okeŋka* can play it during the day.

In the afternoon the Village Head summons the Village Priests, the leaders of *Okeŋka*, the Chief Drummer (*Otomise*), and other drummers of *Korta* by a trumpeting messenger. The Village Priests assemble on their stools round the *Odjokobi* altar with the others nearby and the laity crowded in the background (Plate XXa).

The Village Speaker speaks before the shrine of *Odjokobi*:

> Ah! Ah! Ah! Ah!
> All Yakö stand still (and listen) [repeated four times.]
> All *Yabot* (Village Priests) stand still!
> [All members of the *Yabot* present are then called upon by the names of their office or spirit.]
> All women priests stand still.
> [These are similarly named by their offices.]
> Village Head I show my hands (I beg leave to speak).
> It was time to clear farms.
> We started clearing farms, we took farms, we burnt them.
> We got ready the hoes. We gave them to women. We told them to dig yam hills.
> We cut the yams. We put them in the hills.

When we had put yams (in the hills) we dried some.
We put them on the ritual stones of *Yakö*.
We made supports (for the yam vines). We weeded.
We have cut new yams of the ritual farm.[3]
We have put *Odjokobi* outside.
We say we will eat new yams.
We say no one's belly should ache.
Let the whole village be well.
Do not let fire destroy our village.
A man lying with a woman copulating
Let her conceive and bear a child that will live long.
Let those of Umor wishing good things bring them in Umor.
Let harm befall the stranger who comes to Umor and tears off a
    roof mat to do magic against Umor.
[The *Yabot* respond in chorus: 'Let it be so!   Let it be so!']
Let the right hand be lifted against the stranger who comes to
    Umor and lies against a man of Umor.
[The *Yabot* respond in chorus: 'Let it be so!   Let it be so!']
But the stranger to the Umor people who comes to live in peace
    with the Umor people let his body be cool (he should be allowed
    to live in health and peace).

The priest of *Okarefoy*, a matriclan spirit, who officiates at the
altar, now slices a new yam in offering to *Odjokobi*, saying:

We shall eat new yams; our heads should not pain us.
Let us be well and children be born alive.

He then takes a piece of hoe money, scrapes it across his belly and
passes it round so that each may scrape it over his belly in turn.
He prepares a chalk paste on the stone before the altar, smears his
own chest, then that of the Village Head and of all the other
priests, of the *Korta* drummers and of the priestesses.

Food, prepared in considerable quantities by women of the
matriclan of the Village Head, is now brought out. Mashed new
yam is set out in large bowls. Meat is cut up by *Obot Liboku* and
distributed by him with kola nuts to the circle of priests. The
Odjokobi trumpet is then blown by a messenger of the Village
Head while *Ekui*, a ritual dancer, described below, dances with the
spears of *Odjokobi*.

A series of groups now approach the altar ceremoniously to be

---

[3] This refers to the digging of new yams, for use in this ceremony, from the
ritual plot earlier prepared and planted by the Village Priests in the Earth
Offering which marked the opening of the agricultural year.

blessed and receive gifts of food. These include the *Ikpuŋkara* society, an association of leading men in the village, some forty strong; the Leaders (*Yakambən*) of each ward; the members of *Okeŋka*; and the members of several other organizations of different wards, including the 'Fighters' (*Ebləmbe*) and recreational Dance Clubs (*Nsebe* and *Aiyo*) (see Chapter V). Members of the general public and especially members of the Village Head's matri-clan, then come up in ones and twos to receive blessings.

During the night which follows, the village drums, of which the chief, also known as *Ekui*, is kept in the compound of the Village Speaker (*Okpebri*), are brought to a site, *Lekuibla* (*Ekui* screen) by the grove adjacent to the Village Head's compound and, as soon as the palm frond screens are erected, are beaten during the night and the following day, known as *Ledemboku* or *Ekui*. On *Ledemboku* two distinct rites are held in the Village Head's compound close to the *Ekui* drums:—

(1) A mid-day feast known as *Ekui Kaŋa* (Green leaves of *Ekui*) shared by the Village Priests (*Yabot*), including the *Korta* Drummer and his assistants, and other leaders of *Korta* and of *Okeŋka*. The leaves are placed on slices of roasted yam and distributed by *Obot Liboku* to all present. This is followed by a further beating of the *Ekui* drums.

(2) A rite known as *Ekui Kemle* (*Ekui* enters), for which the *Yabot* reassemble and *Obot Liboku*, *Opalapala* of *Korta*, *Obot Okeŋka* and *Obot Omeŋka* attend in ritual costume and a bowl of sacred water is brought from the *Korta* House. Each of the *Yabot* is accompanied by a hunter. These, in succession, fire their Dane guns into the trees overhanging the *Ekui* drums. Others with guns then join in while *Obot Liboku* walks round asperging those present with water from the *Korta* water pot. Finally, the *Ekui* dancer appears with ram fleece shoulder pieces, wicker shield and sword and dances to a crescendo of drumming and firing guns (Plate XX*b*).

On the following day the Village Priests (*Yabot*) assemble with *Obot Liboku* at the *Korta* House for the *Ntoŋe* (Okra) rite, a ritual feast including a dish of new season's okra provided by the Head of *Korta* and served by *Obot Liboku*. In the evening and continued on the next day there is mass dancing known as *Lite* by all the unmarried girls of each ward, who are marshalled by the young married men and move round the village from ward square to ward square (Plate XXI*a*).

The night and day following the *Lite* dances are occupied by rituals performed by the *Yabuŋa* (Diviners). They assemble at their Head's compound in the evening for *Yekpi* (Tortoiseshell), in which they make ritual visits throughout the night and next morning to the assembly house of every patriclan in the village (over twenty in all), accompanied by kinsmen who play tortoiseshell rattles. At each patriclan house they are given food and wine including uncooked green leaves and *Obot Yabuŋa* sprinkles yellow powder on cult objects. Finally, they go to the *Korta* House, where the *Korta* priest, *Opalapala*, and the *Obolene* priest meet them and all proceed to the compound of the Village Head for the *Keboŋatam* rite. Already assembled there are the Village Head and Speaker with the several women who perform rituals, viz: the *Yamanamana* (who perform the clitoridectomy at marriage for girls), the heads of the women's ritual group *Ekao* (*Yadjeika*) and the leader of the Women Clowns (*Kekoŋ*). The Head of the Diviners (*Yabuŋa*) leads them in procession to a place in the adjacent grove known as *Keboŋatam* (Stones of the *Yabuŋa*). Here the Village Speaker addresses the group and the shrine while holding a series of ritual objects, described below, which are provided by the Village Head:

> Ah! Ah! Ah! Ah!
>
> All *Yakö* stand still (and listen)! [repeated four times.]
>
> All *Yabot* stand still (and listen)!
>
> [All members of the *Yabot* present are then called by the names of their offices or of the spirits of their cults.]
>
> All women priests stand still (and listen)!
>
> [These are similarly named by their offices.]
>
> Village Head I show my hands (I beg leave to speak) [repeated four times.]
>
> The Village Head says every *Okö* feels hunger.
>
> He says he shall eat the new yams. If he eats new yams let him not be ill.
>
> The Village Head speaks. He says people should be born in plenty and live long.
>
> He says his village should be good.
>
> If a stranger to *Yakö* says he wishes to bring harm to the people of Umor, let the right hand of the people of Umor go up and let his go to the ground.
>
> We say the *Yakö* are all one people.

The Speaker then gives the ritual objects to the Head of the

Diviners, who scrapes a piece of hoe money on his belly and passes it to others to do likewise, and, on receiving it back, twists it up and drops it among the stones. Next he prepares a chalk paste which he smears across his own chest and that of others present. He pours palm wine into a buffalo horn goblet which he drinks from and passes to others. The tortoiseshell rattles are played and the whole group files out in procession across the village to the compound of the Head of the Diviners. Here the latter pours water from a calabash on to the roof of his shrine house, saluting *Obasi Oden* by name. The whole group then files past and each places first the right hand and then the left foot in the pool of water that has trickled off the roof of the shrine, saluting *Obasi Oden* as they do so. All except the Diviners then leave and all villagers save for the Village Head are now free to eat new yams.

The Diviners, who remain behind, are feasted by their leader. A considerable number of young men, patrikin of Diviners, have meanwhile been out in the bush to drag up saplings by the roots and bring them to the compound. During this, silence is enjoined on them despite customary provoking jeers from parties of children. Early in the morning on the next day, known as *Yeboŋeti*, the Diviners prepare materials from the saplings for ritually cooling water. The Village Priests (*Yabot*) together with the women priests assemble in the compound of the Head of the Diviners early in the morning and are given food, including new yams, while the Head of the Diviners himself remains concealed in the Diviners' meeting-house and the saplings are being piled high, lying all one way with their roots together, by the other Diviners, who strip off the leaves and chop up the roots. Each Diviner makes his own pile of leaves and roots, which he later takes away for the preparation of a finely chopped mixture which is placed in the bowl of magically 'cooled' (healing) water with which clients are asperged. The matriclan priests then leave and the Head of the Diviners emerges to provide a feast for the Diviners and the other priests who have remained, during which the tortoiseshell rattles are played (Plate XXI*b*).

Later that night the Head of the Diviners himself prepares chopped leaves and roots to provide a large supply of the sacred water kept in the *Isɔ Obasi* shrine for the rite on the next day, 'the Cooling of the Village' (*Lopon Fawa*). This begins early in the day with the arrival at the compound of the Head of the Diviners of the two priestesses (*Yamanamana*) who perform clitoridectomy. They are given a large calabash of the sacred fluid consisting of chopped leaves and roots in a mixture of water and palm wine. They also carry a large empty calabash and a meat dish for food offerings. Accompanied by the Head of the Diviners, they go first to the *Korta* House, where they are received by *Opalapala* and *Obot Liboku*. Some leaves from their calabash are placed in the *Korta* bowl of sacred water and *vice versa*. The magical powers derived from *Isɔ Obasi* and from *Korta* are thus combined in both. Food (yams, meat, and palm wine) is offered, some is consumed and the rest placed in the offering bowl, save for the wine, which is added to the calabash, and a yam, which is given to the Priest of *Liboku*. With a fibre brush they then asperge all those present, including many women and children in the compound, and give them some of the sacred fluid to drink. They then proceed on a lengthy circuit of the village, visiting every matriclan shrine and every patriclan assembly house, where a similar procedure is observed. Men, women, and children in the vicinity of each assemble, make gifts of food and are asperged, the priestess saying, as she does so, 'Liboku ends today'. The circuit continues after nightfall with the aid of a torch carried by the Head of the Diviners and at intervals, whenever the offering calabash is full, they go to the Village Head's compound, where half the offerings are given to the Village Head and the rest left for safe keeping. Finally they return to the Chief Diviner's compound, where he puts the leaves and roots left in the calabash into the bowl of sacred water in the *Isɔ Obasi* shrine and makes an offering to it (Plate XXIIa).

During this same day an independent celebration is carried out by the *Odere* dancers (trumpeters, drummers, and a warrior dancer), who visit every patriclan assembly house and matriclan shrine compound and receive small gifts of wine, kola, and meat. Their songs vaunt the powers of Yakö men both in fighting and in their superiority over women. Thus they sing: 'Girls are very many, boys are few. But if there is fighting they (the boys) will win'. The food and wine they collect is taken to the compound of the head of *Odere* and prepared for a feast on the next day (Plate XXIIb).

Various men's clubs also make preparation for a feast on the following day, posting some of their members at the entrances to the village to take a toll of palm wine from men returning. On this day of separate feasts among men grouped in their various associations, the First Fruits rites end with the ceremonial eating of his first new yams by the Village Head. For this the senior *Omanamana* representing women who have planted and cultivated the yams,[4] takes a new yam to the compound of the Head of the Diviners and puts it to roast on a fire she kindles *inside* the *Isɔ Obasi* shrine. She then collects edible leaves sacred to *Isɔ Obasi* from the bush nearby and, with some of the meat given her the previous day, makes a stew. When the food is ready the Village Head is summoned and he, the Head of the Diviners, and the two priestesses, eat it quietly and depart separately.

INTEGRATIVE FUNCTIONS

As indicated at the outset, I am concerned here only to analyse briefly the integrative character of these rites in relation to basic values and social solidarity among the Yakö. The first and most obvious point is that they are rites of the village and not of the Yakö people as a whole. Although general Yakö solidarity may be implied in some of the invocations which call for blessing or virtues for the Yakö people as a whole, the term *mömö*, people of Umor, is used almost as frequently in these perorations. Furthermore, the personnel of the rites is drawn from the single village alone and there are few unofficial and no official participants from other villages. The other Yakö villages have analogous rites in their own communities. The *Liboku* or First Fruits rites, then, and to a greater degree than the Harvest rites later in the year, stress the moral and social autonomy of the village unit in opposition to the outside world from which dangers threaten. These human dangers of physical violence, of deceit and misrepresentation, and of sorcery are recalled in the prayers.

Within the village, as suggested at the outset, the rites give public approval and assign varying moral status and social authority to a series of organizations and cults, and, at the same time, express their relations to one another. It is seen in the first place that the central cult of the *Liboku* spirit itself is intimately linked with that of the matriclan spirits and with the ritual authority of the Village Head and his council of priests. The Village Head is *not* a member of the *Liboku* cult group and his separation from it is ritually stressed on a number of occasions. On the

---

[4] The early variety of yam which is alone available at this season and known as *lidjofi* is normally planted only by women (see chap. I).

other hand, the *Liboku* spirit is ritually approved and 'strength-ened' by the tutelary spirit of the Village Head's matriclan when at the outset *Obot Liboku* receives some of the *Odjokobi* cult objects and materials for insertion in the *Liboku* bundle, when again on the Night of *Liboku* the Village Head provides the burning brands for the *Liboku* fire and a food offering for *Liboku* and its priests. Finally, the public rites are held at the shrine of *Odjokobi* in the compound of the Village Head. A special feature of this integration of the *Liboku* rites with the cult of the matriclan spirits is to be observed in the rites linking it with the *Atewa* spirit. For the *Atewa* spirit is held to be that of an incorporated group from the neigh-bouring Ekumuru and here, again, the recognition and ritual strengthening of *Liboku* through the integration of the *Atewa* cult and people with the rest of the village is stressed.

It is next to be observed that the *Korta* organization, and the cult of its Leopard spirit to which all males are initiated in child-hood, with its sanctions of severe illness and death for ritual offences, is presented in these rites in its more beneficent aspects and as the 'host', as it were, of *Liboku*, the ritual value of which is enhanced thereby. *Korta*, in turn, in the public rites is accepted by the Village Head and the matriclan spirits as an approved mech-anism of social control.

The *Okeŋka* organization, which unites the ward leaders, is also associated in these rites directly with *Liboku*, on the one hand, as when the *Liboku* priest attends an *Okeŋka* ritual in each of the wards and in the joint rite of *Lekpeduŋa*, and also with *Korta* and the Village Priests council in the public rites at the *Odjokobi* shrine. When it is recalled that the personnel of the *Okeŋka* group expressly consists of the leaders of the *Ligwomi* rituals in each ward, who in turn control public affairs and disputes in the ward and give ritual expression to ward solidarity, it will be recognized that a further system of social control in the village, that based on the major territorial components in which the age-sets are organized, is also ritually integrated in the total system on this occasion.

A further and prominent theme concerns the role of the village Corporation of Diviners and the spirit *Isɔ Obasi* from which their powers of divination and healing are believed to come. The Head of the Diviners (*Obot Obuŋa*) is himself a member of the Council of Village Priests, but on this occasion he is given a position of great ritual prominence as the priest of *Isɔ Obasi*. The Council of Village

Priests, including the Village Head and the *Liboku* priest, together with the Diviners and Priestesses of women's cults, attend a rite in which the Head of the Diviners invokes health and peace for the village, and they then proceed to the *Isɔ Obasi* shrine and receive blessings there. Before this, the Diviners have collectively visited every patriclan house in the village, receiving gifts of food and blessing cult objects. Later the Diviners prepare a new supply of the chopped leaves and roots which are essential ritual ingredients in the cooling and healing water that they use. The Head of the Diviners then provides a supply of this sacred water, with which is mixed sacred water of *Korta,* and with this the whole village is ritually cooled, after the other ceremonies, in rites of asperging at every patriclan house and at every matriclan shrine. Finally, on the last day of the whole series of rites, a ritual meal, including a new yam and leaves sacred to the Diviners, is prepared at the *Isɔ Obasi* shrine for the Village Head. The power of healing and cooling bestowed by Obasi is in these final rites represented as effective and necessary for all the other cults. The final rites connected with Obasi not only, as is expressly stated, 'cool the village', that is, remove the implicit danger from the ritual power of the other cults that have been activated; they also place the patriclans, the matriclans, the Council of Village Priests, the *Korta* and *Okeŋka* cults, and the women's cults, under the ultimate ritual power of Obasi, the Supreme Being, and support the role of the Diviners as the source of ultimate knowledge of the causes of sickness and of the origins of the human souls that are reincarnated in every generation.

Finally, some important features of the two days of public rites at the *Odjokobi* shrine in the Village Head's compound must be noted. One element, expressed in the setting up and prolonged beating of the Village Drums and the dance of *Ekui,* who appears to symbolize the village, has already been noted in other contexts The emphasis is on the unity and solidarity of the village. The other is implicit in the successive visits of a number of organizations to the *Odjokobi* shrine for blessings while the priests are assembled there. These include, on the one hand, certain restricted village associations of men and women, outstanding among which is *Ikpuŋkara,* an association of eminent men which arbitrates land disputes and acts as an executive agent of the Council of Village Priests. Others are the Warriors, the Hunters, and a number of recreational groups in the wards. In addition to these, the *Yakam-bən*, or ritual and executive Leaders of each ward, attend as corporate groups. To all in turn the blessings of *Odjokobi* are administered by a priest on behalf of the Village Head. This expresses, on the one hand, the status of these several groups as ritually dependent on, and as practically subordinate to, the *Odjokobi* spirit, the Village Head and the Council of Priests. At the same time, it gives them recognition as approved and valued organizations in the life of the village. In this connection it is particularly to be noted that certain other associations, notably *Ɔkpe* and *Obam*, which, while admitted to control powerful spirit forces, are regarded as dubious in character and potentially anti-social, are excluded from this rite. '*Ɔkpe* would not dare to come to *Odjokobi*,' I was told, 'and the *Yabot* would not permit them.' Much could be said on this last point, for among the Yakö, as among neighbouring Cross River peoples, there appears to have occurred over several generations a considerable proliferation of secondary associations and of particular cult groups. Spirits, the cult objects which embody them, and particular ritual techniques, have been carried from locality to locality, being modified in the process and adjusted to the particular conditions. Among the Yakö there is a welter of *ndet*, spirit beings or forces in the control of individuals and small groups. Similarly, new associations combining in varying degrees the pursuit of the pecuniary and social advantages of their members, the diagnosis of causes of disease and the performance of public and secret rites have been introduced. Possibly, if the history were known, some of the cults such as *Okeŋka*, which are fully accepted and have great prestige, and some of the leading associations such as *Ikpuŋkara*, grew up in this way.

But, in relation to particularist groups and cults the First Fruits rituals in Umor reaffirm the ritual and moral authority of the older and more basic organization. Yakö social structure is not, as will have been seen, hierarchical. It consists of a series of largely independent organizations of patriclans, matriclans, wards, and associations with special functions. Cults are similarly specialized and restricted in social context. The First Fruits ceremonies serve in this situation to integrate the major elements in this complex structure of overlapping groups in a series of rituals which subordinate special village cults and organizations to the Council of Priests and the Village Head. The thirty days of *Liboku* in Umor are a period in which everyone is made aware both of the status and powers of the various spirits and groups, and at the same time feels them to be part of the ritual life and social foundations. In this respect they have a profound effect in integrating a very large and complexly organized community.

IX

THE CONTEXT OF BELIEF[1]

SIR JAMES FRAZER devoted a long life of unremitting industry to the assembling of a vast corpus of material on supernatural beliefs and associated customs in the ancient and in the savage worlds. In the successive and ever-expanding editions of the *Golden Bough* and other writings, he succeeded in conveying his sense of the mysteries which he found equally challenging in the texts of classical authors and in contemporary accounts of aboriginal Australians, American Indians or Polynesian Islanders. His leisurely and ornate prose succeeded in evoking for countless readers a wonderland of strange belief and mysterious enactment.

But alongside his obvious delight in weaving his elaborate tapestry of myth and rite, Frazer also sought both to emphasize and explain the mental gulf that he believed existed between the primitive and the modern world and accordingly to trace the sources of the egregious errors in which, as it appeared to him, primitive mankind had been so prone to fall. In his interpretations Frazer closely followed Tylor—his great predecessor in the study of primitive belief—to whom on more than one occasion he expressed his debt as one who had 'opened up a mental vista undreamed of by me before'. This vista was that of a comparatively simple and comprehensive formulation and classification of the beliefs of mankind under differing conditions of intellectual advancement. Tylor, writing in the sixties and seventies of last century under the influence of contemporary conceptualist and associationist psychology, accounted for supernatural ideas among primitive peoples in ancient civilizations and their modern survival in terms of two basic principles.

One concerned the foundations of magical belief. Tylor perceived and demonstrated a common cognitive element in the most diverse magical beliefs, namely, a tendency to transform a conceptual association between two entities or situations into a causal relation whereby it could be supposed that action with regard to

[1] First published as the Frazer Lecture for 1958 by the Liverpool University Press.

one would correspondingly affect the other. This he ascribed to an erroneous inversion of the normal human capacity to reach correct inferences by associating ideas whereby it was imagined that, as he put it, association in thought must involve similar connection in reality—thus mistaking an ideal for a real connection. Frazer elaborated this in an analysis and classification of magic which has proved of great value for the purposes of formal classification of types of belief and ritual action.

Tylor's other thesis, exemplified even more fully, was his theory of animism. Considering the notion of human souls, in the sense of separable immaterial entities surviving death, as an expectable conception generalized from commonly occurring dream and hallucinatory experiences of apparitions of absent or deceased persons, he argued that belief in the existence of other non-human spirits could be satisfactorily accounted for by other hallucinations and, as we might put it, a universal tendency to objectify conceptual entities and by analogy to endow them with personality. Tylor's often quoted minimum definition of religion—the belief in spiritual beings—depended on and implied this conceptual distinction between a palpable material world and an immaterial essence of being and power, a distinction between body and soul. For Tylor, as for Frazer after him, the concept of animism and the nature of animistic beliefs involved not merely a vague recognition of a distinction between the quick and the dead, but a belief to account for this.[2]

But little consideration was given by Tylor or Frazer to the contexts in which such beliefs found expression, nor, in particular, why they were significant for those who held them, and afforded a basis for action. This can be ascribed to the fact that with rare exceptions, the accounts of primitive beliefs, on the basis of which Frazer and, still more, Tylor, made their interpretations, came from observers who, however reliable and objective by contemporary Western standards, were not mainly concerned to evaluate

[2] Frazer, regarding this conceptual discrimination which had played so great a part in the early history of Western philosophy and religious doctrine, as a great intellectual achievement which marked off religious from magical beliefs, assigned it to a crucial stage in the development of human thought and sought to explain it in terms of a rejection of magical beliefs, assuming that by a slow erratic process of ratiocination 'mankind came to realise that all his efforts to work by means of these imaginary causes had been in vain' and that 'if the great world went on its way—it must surely be because there were other beings like himself but far stronger who unseen themselves directed its course . . .' and thus attained to a religious conception of the existence of supernatural beings.

such beliefs in terms of the material, cultural, and social conditions in which they had meaning for the people themselves. It was such an external and abstracted relation to the data which, for example, had led Tylor to make a sweeping condemnation of all magical belief as a pernicious delusion.[3]

The defects of the interpretations which Frazer adopted from Tylor lay not, as has been sometimes suggested, in the fallacious character of the particular psychological principles that they invoked. Indeed, we can hardly claim that the propensity to derive erroneous causal relations from associated events or the argument from dream and hallucination to the supernatural mobility and survival of human souls and the existence of other immaterial spirits has now been extinguished. Both the capacity of dream and hallucination to convince their subjects of the reality and supranormal character of such appearances, and the suggestibility which leads others to accept the validity of such accounts and interpretations, have been confirmed and documented both by the ethnographer and the psychologist.

The inadequacy of these views lay rather in a failure to consider the importance of the context in which such phenomena and their interpretation were given meaning and made to serve other and often subconscious ends. Thus what was lacking in the first place was consideration of the powerful drives of desire and anxiety to which such beliefs were everywhere harnessed, and the recognition that they were not detached explanations, not only the objects of dispassionate thought. It was not appreciated that, in circumstances of recognized hazard and very limited knowledge of natural processes, such beliefs, on the one hand suggested means of action urgently sought to secure individual and common ends, and, on the other, generated fears concerning the harm that such supernatural entities might work. In the other words, nineteenth-century anthropology of belief tended to neglect consideration of the emotional context in which manifestations of supposedly supranormal phenomena were interpreted, of the further beliefs they

[3] One could as well condemn all belief that could be classified under the rubric of a divine creator of the universe on the grounds of frequent and often cruel mistreatment of heretics and non-believers in the history of Christendom. Both the intellectual criticism and the ethical condemnation of the character and supposed consequences of primitive beliefs which Frazer inherited from the 19th century would seem to derive from this failure to penetrate beyond the conceptual status of the beliefs to the human aspirations and fears, the material conditions and the social relations with which they were associated.

XXIII *a.* *Yose* shrine house and cult objects

XXIII *b.* *Kupatu* shrine interior

XXIV *a*. Invocation to *Yose Otabalusaŋa*, Ina Ibiaŋ

XXIV *b*. One of the *Akota*, the foundation war stones

generated, and also of the uses to which these were put in seeking to further or protect human ends. This, as has already been pointed out, was due in considerable measure to what we may call the disembodied character of most of the data on which they were based, as well as to the remoteness and detachment of these writers from the situations in which the beliefs with which they were concerned had found expression.

In a series of essays written at the beginning of this century, and later republished in his *Threshold of Religion*, Marett recognized and sought to remedy this defect. Relying very largely for documentation on the evidence that Frazer was himself so carefully assembling, he sought to show not only that the concepts implied in primitive supernatural beliefs were often vague and fluctuating so that, for example, it was sometimes impossible to apply the Frazerian distinction between magical spell and religious prayer; but more importantly that declarations of belief and the performance of rites were only secondarily concerned with problems of evidential truth and logical validity, since they were basically verbal and motor reactions to emotional needs. To confine analysis and interpretation to questions of conceptual content was, therefore, inadequate, since the essential aspects of hope, and fear, desire and will which occasioned them, were left out of account.[4]

In Marett's writings, however, the character and context of the

[4] It may be well to recall Marett's own summary of his basic contention, namely, that generally among mankind 'in response to, or at any rate in connection with, the emotions of awe, wonder and the like, wherein feeling would seem for the time being to have outstripped the power of "natural", that is, reasonable, explanation, there arises . . . a powerful impulse to objectify and even personify the mysterious or "supernatural" something felt, and in the region of will a corresponding impulse to render it innocuous or better still, propitious, by force of constraint, communion or conciliation'. It was therefore in terms of equally generalized and universal emotions and will that Marett sought to define the sphere of 'supernaturalism'. On these grounds he held that both magical and religious beliefs (in Frazer's sense) were to be regarded as 'differentiated out from a common plasm of crude beliefs about the awful and occult' (Ch. ix.), and that 'impersonal magical' forces and qualities may and do possess, not secondarily and by derivation, but primarily and in their own right, religious value . . . and even tend to possess such value in a predominant degree'.

It has to be borne in mind that Marett was particularly concerned to question what he and others after him called the 'intellectualist' criteria for the definition and explanation of magical and religious beliefs and for the distinctions between them, that Frazer had inherited from Tylor. He had no difficulty in showing that magical assumptions of potent association between phenomena on the basis of their similarity or their continuity in space or time were not dependent for their special character on any particular 'process of reasoning', or 'laws of thought', but depended on some 'continuity of interest'.

hopes and fears themselves still remained vague.[5] The value of his critique consisted rather in his demonstration that the meaning and value of supernatural beliefs lay, for those who accepted them, not in their capacity to solve intellectual problems concerning ultimate causes, but to channel emotions and provide a pattern of action in the face of powerful impulses. Marett wrote, however, as if these emotional reactions to the ostensible objects of cult were directly generated by their intrinsically impressive qualities as natural phenomena or extraordinary artifacts. Overlooking the fact that the material objects associated with awe and reverence were often in themselves unremarkable—a heap of stones or an inconspicuous plant—he did not appreciate that their evocative power depended on their symbolic character, and was not led to explore the cultural and social contexts of the intangible entities which could be so often shown to be the more ultimate referents of belief.

One aspect of this symbolic function of the objects of supernatural belief was, however, being given the greatest stress at this time by Durkheim and his colleagues in France. For them, too, the interest and significance of dogmatic belief and ritual enactment lay not in any manifestation or limitation of conceptual capacity, nor any tendency to fantasy to which the human mind might be prone. Durkheim claimed to eschew psychological inquiry and explanation as irrelevant to his chosen problem. Supernatural entities and qualities whether expressed in prayer or spell, in myth or ritual, were, he held, to be interpreted as symbolic expressions of the common sentiments that sustained the collective life of a society. The awe which they evoked derived neither of necessity nor frequently from any intrinsic qualities of the symbols, but was a sacredness inherent in a primitive and otherwise unformulated human apprehension of the mysterious omnipotence of society and its indispensibility as the framework of the life of the individual. The names, objects, actions, and incorporeal entities to which this sacredness was attached, while they might be drawn from some manifestation in the world of nature or elaborated in terms of human personality, derived their impressiveness from the sentiments they enshrined and the awe they evoked as creations of

[5] In characterizing the life of savage peoples as insecure, at the mercy of both natural catastrophes and human enemies, and therefore likely to evoke frequent and intense emotions of apprehension and a generalized attitude of awe towards unusual occurrences, Marett did little more than make explicit the underlying assumptions of Frazer and others.

society. They were, therefore, as expressions of these sentiments, essential clues to their existence and character, and a means for tracing the constraint exercised by society on its members.

The particular form and experiential derivation of a belief or ritual action became in this context of little consequence. For the meaning to be sought depended not on the particularity of the ideas, nor on a closer understanding of psychological process. It resided in the manifestation of sentiments of social obligation, through which the individual was both incorporated into society and provided with a sense of purpose in his social life.

It is not difficult to point to the exaggeration and one-sidedness of some of Durkheim's more categorical formulations—formulations which suggested that all knowledge is derived from a religious apprehension that is, in its turn, a mystical and symbolically expressed recognition of society as an all-powerful and external entity compelling the sentiments and beliefs of the individual.

* * *

These psychological and the sociological approaches to the study of the beliefs of primitive peoples that were developed at the beginning of this century have, however, in the hypotheses they offered and the further problems they raised, deeply influenced the outlook of those who undertook and guided the large body of more sustained intensive field studies carried out over the last forty years. This phase may be said to have begun with the now classic studies of Radcliffe-Brown among the Andamanese and of Malinowski in the Trobriand Islands, whose first monographs were both published in 1922. Radcliffe-Brown had gone in 1906 to study the life of the hunting and fishing camps of the Andaman Islanders in terms of problems very different in kind from those which Frazer posed to his far-flung correspondents. His concern was only initially with what the Andamanese might do or say that they believed. Stimulated mainly by the hypotheses of Durkheim and his colleagues concerning the maintenance of social relations and pressures through ceremonial behaviour and collective belief, the basic problem for Radcliffe-Brown lay in discovering how such social sentiments were built up, symbolically expressed and thereby maintained in an orderly on-going pattern of co-ordinated activity. The social processes involved in a given pattern of human relations needed to be explored in detail, if the meaning of belief and ritual were to be discovered. In his interpretation of such Andamanese beliefs and practices as those attaching to the cyclic changes of the seasons and restrictions on the use of and distribution of foods, he applied Durkheim's hypotheses concerning the continuous renewal of the social framework through a symbolization of what was proper in human action and relations. A myth had validity and a rite its rationale in the consequent regulation of the sentiments and activities of persons as members of a social body. Invested with emotional inertia through the effect of beliefs in external and transcendental forces, routines of both practical and symbolic actions were thus established which sustained a viable pattern of social interaction and exploitation of material resources for the self-maintenance of the community in the given material circumstances.[6]

Malinowski, who first went to Melanesia in 1913, also adopted in his early essays a sociological interpretation of belief and ritual as evoked by and directed towards socially sanctioned objectives. In his detailed studies of the Trobrianders he described the social contexts in which myths came to be told and sometimes pitted one against another, and portrayed the complex social interplay in which, for example, mortuary rites and garden magic were carried out. These beliefs, he suggested, served to safeguard and establish morality, to justify existing differences in rank and power or to substantiate new claims to precedence where changes in social influence were taking place.

But he also recognized and repeatedly stressed the psychological mainsprings of belief and ritual, dealing hardly with Durkheim for failing to appreciate the part played by common but individual human desires and fears in generating and sustaining them. Through his close and prolonged study in the field he was also able to carry this psychological analysis much further than Marett. While the latter had appreciated that the interpretations of primitive supernatural beliefs required consideration of their emotional as much as of their cognitive aspects, he had been content to as-

---

[6] While Radcliffe-Brown did not specifically embrace, and may well have had reservations concerning some of Durkheim's more comprehensive claims, such that 'in the Divine I can only see society transfigured and thought of symbolically' (Durkheim, E., *Sociology and Philosophy*, London 1953, p. 75), or his attribution to a reified Society 'its own passions, habits and needs which are not those of individuals', he adopted an essentially Durkheimian approach in this and later studies in religious belief, presenting the entities and associations found in mythology and ceremony and taboo as symbols of powerful sentiments that sustained a pattern of recurrent activities and a system of social relations.

cribe the formulation of such ideas to some direct apprehension of mystery derived from the intrinsic impressiveness of phenomena external to man. Malinowski, however, had had borne in on him in the field that individual emotional reactions of fear and aspiration, in recurrent but specific situations and the consequent tendencies to generalize and objectify means for assuaging them, were the essential basis on which magico-religious conceptions were developed. In particular he portrayed and placed the greatest emphasis on the concern of the individual with reference to hazardous enterprises and the fear of death in the evocation and persistence of beliefs in supernatural sources both of danger and of aid.

More recently, however, interest has tended to focus intensively again on the sociological aspects of belief. As part of the great advances that have been made over the last twenty years in the detailed analysis of primitive social systems, transcendental beliefs and ritual observances have been closely analysed both as indices and sanctions of social obligation and the cohesion of social groups.

But in exploring so effectively the significance of supernatural beliefs as symbolic expressions of social relations there has been some tendency to lose sight of the fact that supernatural beliefs and the rites with which they are associated are by no means always evoked by concern for a particular social pattern, but may be stimulated by other conditions of the human environment through the values and hazards attached to material resources and techniques, the incidence of disease and other risks to health and life. These equally with social groupings and conflicts are reified or personified in supernatural entities and lead to the performance of ritual acts. Here the social framework of belief is secondary and may sometimes even be limited to that of a conveniently available field of communication within which individuals draw guidance for interpretation and action with respect to their common but discrete concerns. While beliefs and cults focused on material needs and physical well-being may be associated with or lead to the further development of patterns of social organization, such as priesthoods or institutions deriving from the prestige of a sacred chiefship, it is important to recognize that it is the ecological factors, stemming from biological and physical conditions and the character of particular techniques, that have called them into being and sustain their significance. The significance of the inevitable human concern for control of the non-human environment figured prominently in some earlier studies of primitive religion and did not escape Frazer's attention in his accounts of cults of vegetation. This underlying biological and ecological context of primitive belief has as important a claim on anthropological attention as those of individual psychology and social structure. It is, moreover, one which the facilities for intensive and technically developed field research have made it possible to explore more systematically.

The history of anthropological thought on mystical belief has tended to be one of controversy and even of division into schools, largely, it would seem, because the complex character of the context of belief, while not repudiated in principle, has received too little explicit recognition. Interpretations have too often tended to concentrate on particular factors or aspects of that context. But patterns of belief are likely to reflect, both in their content and in their fields of relevance, not one, but many elements of human interest and response. In seeking to reach any adequate degree of understanding of the supernatural beliefs accepted and acted upon by a given people, it would seem necessary, therefore, to consider not merely one or other of their aspects but to explore empirically the actual contexts in which they are manifested, so that the interplay of psychological and ecological factors can be determined. The extent to which the various conceptions and beliefs evoked in particular contexts are integrated in any wider system of ideas and are related to more general conditions, then becomes a matter for scientific research rather than a methodological assumption.

*   *   *

It will, I hope, be useful in this connection to illustrate the diversity of the factors involved in the evocation of a single type of magico-religious concept that is manifested in widely differing contexts. I will consider the part played by a type of belief that has been called fetishism in the older literature as it occurs among the Yakö. A fetish consists of one or more objects to which a supernatural personality and power are attributed. The spirit thus associated with a fetish is not a distant god, nor a still sentient human ancestor, but a vaguely personalized indwelling power believed to intervene in human affairs and subject to influence by appropriate offerings. Belief in the existence and power of fetishes is not the whole of Yakö religion, but it is a predominant conceptual element in that recourse to supernatural explanation and aid, whether protective, punitive, or restorative, is most frequently through invocation of one or more of them.

We may begin by distinguishing the main classes of fetish object recognized by the Yakö and then consider both the beliefs associated with each and the range of contexts in which these are expressed and acted upon. The Yakö used two general terms in this connection: *yose* (pl. *ase*) and *edet* (pl. *ndet*).

In village ceremonies and affairs, the *ase* were the more prominent category. Each consisted of a varied collection of objects: clay mounds sometimes sculpted and painted to represent a human head, bronze manillas and helices, pottery flasks and bowls, and a flat slab on which a white chalk paste was prepared for smearing on the face or breast of the participants in a rite to convey the blessing of the fetish. These objects were normally arranged on a low platform within a miniature house situated in the compound of its custodian-priest known as an *Ina* (pl. *Bi'ina*). But adjacent to the house was a crescent of boulders on or within which the objects were displayed for public ceremonies. There were ten *ase* in all and each was said by the Yakö to 'belong' to one or more of the matriclans whose members were dispersed through the village (see Chapter IV). The custody of each *yose* normally passed to men within one of these groups. But the installation, and therefore the public recognition, of an *Ina* depended on acceptance by the other *Bi'ina* and other priests associated with them in public ceremonies who were known collectively as *Yabot* (The Heads). One of the *ase* was given ceremonial precedence and its custodian was styled *Obot Lopon* (Head of the Village). At ceremonies held in connection with each of the main phases of the farming year—before the clearing of farm plots, when the early yams first became available, at the main harvest—and also at the beginning of the river fishing season, rituals were carried out successively by the *Yabot* collectively at the several *ase*.

The essential Yakö beliefs concerning the *ase* can be explicitly stated, since formal declarations and requests were made on these and other occasions. From these it is clear that in the context of invocation the *ase* were regarded as sentient and sympathetic beings, capable of conferring benefits not only on the members of the associated matriclans, but on the people of the village as a whole and associated within it. The nature of these benefits was also explicit, namely, material well-being through the fertility of crops, protection against outbreaks of fire, the continuity and growth of the people through the birth of children, internal social harmony by disposing people to peaceful conduct, the destruction of anti-social persons especially those practising witchcraft or sorcery, and particularly the frustration of such attempts by visiting strangers.

Thus the blessings sought from the *ase* were comprehensive and diverse. They included, on the one hand, the beneficent working of what we should regard as the forces of nature to maintain and protect the population. Others were social—peaceful and benevolent conduct on the part of the individuals and groups and the punishment of those infringing this whether physically or supernaturally. In public ceremonies certain associations and special cults in the village were blessed on the implied condition that they would act for its welfare.

Confidence in the capacity and disposition of the *ase* to ensure all this, and in the consequent benefit derived from the ceremonies, was apparent in many discussions. These beliefs expressed the ambivalent attitude of recognition of benefits already derived from orderly and productive conditions together with concern for their continuance. Thus a synthetic conception of a favourable total environment, both material and social, emerged, the source of which in the context of an anxious sense of its complexity and precariousness was personalized in the invocation of the *ase*. When such matters as the security of the yam harvest, the fertility of woman and the survival of children, the risk of disastrous fires, and of serious dissensions leading to protracted brawls, were discussed and investigated in a non-ritual context, it became clear not only that these anxieties were strong and widespread, but also that they had very solid foundations in experience. In the physical sphere severe crop losses from pests and floodings, high infant and maternal mortality, and devastating fires were recounted from the past. The other concern for what may be summarized as the social stability of the village had an equally objective foundation in the history of many past disputes which from small beginnings in offences, jealousies, and fears, among a few had ramified through the cross-cutting groups of patrilineal and matrilineal clans, wards,

age-sets, and associations to generate complex and extensive align-
ments of hostility and occasionally widespread disorders. The
general hope and approval for the orderly settlement of disputes
arising from conflicting claims to land, forest resources, succession
to offices, and the meeting of obligations connected with marriage,
were by no means matched by a conviction that this could be easily
achieved. When I asked Yakö how *ase* were able to effect such
things, I usually received a standardized reply that they cooled men's
hearts. This notion that egoistic passions destructive of the interests
of others could be 'cooled' by the supernatural means was expressed
in many other contexts, notably in *ad hoc* rites of reconciliation
between disputants within a patrilineal or a matrilineal kin group.
And one assurance of penitence and desire for reconciliation between men of different matriclans was the provision of materials for
a sacrifice at the offender's *yose*, by which its continued beneficence
for him was felt more assured. In this context, the effect of belief
in the power of the *ase* was thus both to indoctrinate, and to give
confidence in, respect for moral rules. The attitude was similar
with regard to fears of witchcraft and sorcery. The witch and the
sorcerer were not only declared to be public enemies, they were
held vulnerable to loss of the vitality conferred by the *ase*. When
comparing their relative immunity with the more devastating witchcraft and sorcery believed to be practised among some of their
neighbours, Yakö were apt to attribute it to the beneficent power
of their *ase* by whom such persons were sooner or later destroyed.
But, if, as beliefs expressed at the public seasonal rites indicated,
there was indeed a clearly expressed conception of collective village
welfare, we have to recognize and account for the fact that beliefs
concerning its source and maintenance were not expressed in the
cult of a single village deity, but in that of a series of discrete
spirits whose efficacy was, in other contexts, partitioned among the
population. This appears to have resulted from the prior patterning
of the beliefs themselves, whereby the hopes for material well-
being and social harmony had clustered round a central concern
for the fertility of women. This fertility was conceived as passing
from mother to daughter, and matrilineal descent groups provided
the social framework for supernatural beliefs and ritual concerning
its maintenance. With the growth of the Yakö communities into
large compact settlements, the cults of several matrilineal spirits
had been integrated into a village priesthood performing rites for

the whole community. But the importance of particularistic dogmas concerning the maintenance of human fertility within the matriclans had precluded the dominance of a separate supernatural symbol of village unity and prosperity which might have been expected on purely sociological grounds. The social unity of the village was symbolized by the collective actions of the *ase* priests, whose functions as village priests derived conceptually and probably historically from their prior capacity for their several matriclans. Symbols of other supernatural spirits that were believed to protect resources and sanction conduct in the village as a whole were operative only within the framework of the village priesthood and were ritually subordinate to the *ase*.[7]

Thus, while the Yakö did, as Durkheim would have had us recognize, conceptualize social solidarity in their religious beliefs, this was not totally expressed through a single direct symbolic expression of the social aggregate, but by associating and integrating symbols of special capacities, namely human fertility and prosperity, initially sought within smaller collectivities. In their common desire for collective well-being, the Yakö believed that the *ase* in severally aiding and protecting the people of the various matriclans, did not interfere the one with the other. The obligation of certain *ase* and other cult priests, the heads of wards, and some village associations to serve and respect the interests of the village as a whole, was supernaturally sanctioned at their installation through observances conducted by the Village Speaker at a series of fixed sacred sites associated with the foundation of the village, marked only by stones known as *akota* (sing. *likota*; lit. war stones) which at the same time protected the health and life of these office holders. While offerings, blessings, and invocations at the *akota* resembled those at the *ase* as sources of beneficence and harmony, the *akota* were not addressed as personalized entities, and the declarations were oaths of office rather than prayers. As a conceptual category, therefore, the *akota* were distinct. The context of the observances and beliefs was also specific in that they both constrained and protected persons entitled to invoke spirits that affected the public good. Furthermore, the apprehension of the village as a total social entity was not symbolically distinguished

---

[7] This is the case with reference to the village fetish *Edet Lopon* and the village drums *Ekui* (see p. 268 below and Chapter VI).

from the non-human resources and biological processes affecting human well-being.

The powers attributed to the *ase* were also invoked for the benefit of individuals through their membership of one or other of the matriclans. The fertility and safe delivery of women, for which there was much concern, was thought to depend in the first instance on the beneficence of the *yose* of a woman's matriclan. In the course of her marriage ceremonies and again, if pregnancy was not achieved or unsuccessful childbirth was feared, a woman went with close matrikin to the shrine, making a small offering of yams, palm wine, and meat, at which the *Ina* invoked the aid of the *yose*. The *yose* was also invoked in the expiation of offences, notably on behalf of one who had committed homicide.

Although it was believed that for some unexpiated offences, a *yose* might withhold fertility from a person, or generally in the matrilineal kin group concerned, punitive sanctions were not primarily stressed with reference to the *ase*, in which, as it were, generalized productive and protective capacities had been mystically segregated. On the other hand, it was commonly accepted that to ignore the *ase* by failure of due observance at the seasonal rites, or to flout them by conduct which endangered the material and social benefits they conferred, was to risk the loss of those benefits for the persons or group concerned.

But associated with the *ase* priests in the seasonal collective rites, there were officiants of other cults believed to involve negative sanctions for any in the community at large who threatened the social order, whether by physical or supernatural means. These cults centred round fetishes that the Yakö assigned to the class of *ndet*.

Two of them were manifestations of Leopard Spirits, each in the custody of priests regarded as acting for and responsible to the village. The priests of *Korta* who controlled the cult of *Ekpe Edet* (Leopard Spirit), performed a highly secret ritual on successive nights every six years. During these the leader, *Opalapala*, danced in a mask at the series of sacred sites associated with the foundation of the village. At this time adolescent boys were ceremonially presented to the *Korta* gongs and the wooden box that contained *Ekpe Edet*, reputed to include a human skull wrapped in a leopard skin. The role of *Ekpe Edet* was as negative as those of *ase* were positive, for its powers were held to be essentially punitive, inflicting severe and painful illness or sudden death, according to the flagrancy of the offence, for infractions of declared prohibitions. These included any action which the village priesthood declared that *Ekpe Edet* should sanction, and had mainly concerned settlements appertaining to hotly disputed claims to land and inheritance of goods, as well as restrictions on external trading and other movement following inter-village quarrels. The mystery and impressiveness of the six-yearly rites and the initiation of adolescent boys, together with the seclusion in which *Opalapala* the chief priest lived, surrounded *Korta* and its fetish with a particular awe.[8]

A further and separate Leopard Spirit cult, *Okeŋka*, was maintained by an association whose members were drawn from the leaders of all the wards. Its Head was also installed by and became a member of the village priesthood. Disputes and offences involving people from different wards were formally brought before the *Okeŋka* association for settlement, under the sanction of the Leopard Spirit (*Lekpetu*) that it was believed to control. The cult objects included a bellows, the sound of which manifested the existence of the spirit to all in the village. The rights of property of members and others were protected by such judgements.[9]

The perpetuation of the village was also given symbolic expression at Umor, by a further cult object called *Edet Lopon* (Spirit of the Village). This was in the custody of *Okpebri*, the Speaker of the *Yabot*, who made the formal declarations and prayers on their behalf at the *ase* and elsewhere. It was generally believed that to remove it would cause the village to disintegrate and this had been

---

[8] A cult of *Ekao*, believed to sanction the conduct of women by sterility, sickness, and death, was in charge of a priestess, *Odjeika*, who performed similar rites in the village in the year following the *Korta* rites, and into it all girls were initiated.

[9] The symbolic association of the leopard with swift supernatural punitive sanctions in these and other cults is not far to seek. Belief in the supernaturally destructive power of Leopard Spirits, common to many peoples in S.E. Nigeria and beyond, is modelled on the swiftness and ferocity of unsuspected attack of actual leopards not only on game but on unwary travellers in the forest. The Yakö regarded the leopard as the one really dangerous beast in the forest, difficult to kill, hunters said, even with Dane guns, and likely not only to attack when wounded, but to spring from hiding in the deep forest. When a leopard was killed in Umor, an elaborate ceremonial was carried out by certain of the *Yabot* including the head of *Okeŋka*. The leopard was presented to all the foundation stones, *akota*, in different parts of the village and was 'cooled' at the *Yose* of the killer by its priest. The killer became a member of the *Okeŋka*, without paying fees.

acted upon in cases of uproar in the village when the Speaker threatened or actually proceeded to leave the village with it. The *Okpebri* I knew told me of two occasions when the village was in an uproar and he had acted on this belief as a sanction to restore order. Carrying *Edet Lopon* he went first to the compound of the Village Head and then to the assembly place of each ward, solemnly declaring at each in the name of *Edet Lopon*: 'The peace I need in this village I cannot get from the people of Umor. I am going away.' He then walked out of the village along the *Elomite* path by which the first settlers were believed to have arrived. He turned back only after the crowd which assembled and followed him begged that he should turn back with *Edet Lopon*, with promises that they would see order restored and force the brawlers to accept the judgement of the *Yabot*. Here again, and unlike the *ase*, the notion was one of latent punitive capacity which became operative after offence. *Edet Lopon* was invoked in crises to restore social co-operation under threat, not recurrently to symbolize its maintenance and normality.

Cults were also associated with the territorial segments of which the Yakö villages were composed, the wards (*yekpatu*) and the localized patriclan groups (*yepun*) within these. Each of the wards at Umor had a sacred grove where small boys were periodically initiated in a rite conducted by the ward Leaders (*Yakambɔn*) every few years. In this initiation, known as *Ligwomi*, masked figures impersonated spirits specifically attached to the ward. These were conceived not as ancestors, but as *genii loci*. While believed to bring misfortune to anyone living in the ward who refused to accept the authority of its elders, they were not stressed as important sources of collective prosperity, like the *ase* on the one hand, nor as punitive agents for specific offences on the other. In other words, the antithetical beliefs concerning supernatural public agents of welfare and of punishment were not emphasized at this level of social organization in the village.

But for each of the patriclans (*yepun*) in Umor, the men of which lived together in a distinct dwelling area of fifty or more households, there was a clan spirit or *epundet* (*kepun edet*—spirit of the clan). The beliefs concerning this spirit were consistent with the name of *edet*, for the rites conducted before it by the head of the patriclan sought to remove or avert misfortune connected with internal offences or the exposure of members to external danger, and not, like the *ase*, positively to promote the collective prosperity of the group. Most rites concerned expiations for offences and reconciliation after quarrels within the patriclan area and were precipitated by sickness or sterility in a clansman's household alleged to result from some failure to fulfil clan or household obligations. When daughters of a patriclan left on marriage to join their husbands in other patriclans, they were given the protection of their natal *epundet* in a rite associated with the delivery of their first child.

* * *

But Yakö beliefs concerning supernatural agencies of misfortune and punishment were not confined to *ndet* that were specifically linked to, and acted on behalf of, definite social aggregates such as *Ekpe Edet* and *Edet Lopon* in relation to the village or the *epundet* for each patriclan. More frequent everyday verbal expressions of belief and ritual actions were concerned with *ndet* of which the cults were in the custody of individuals, and had no specific clientele. For the Yakö there was an indefinite number of these discrete vaguely personalized, ethically neutral supernatural powers which were thought able to cause and remove sickness, sterility and other misfortunes, and might be induced on a *do ut det* principle to give effect to the desires of an individual supplicant.

Each of these *ndet* had a name and was physically manifest in a collection of objects, again mostly pottery vessels, but sometimes including curiously shaped stones or carved wooden figures (*yapata*, sing. *okpata*), often placed in a miniature house. The custodian, nearly always a man, could be regarded as its agent rather than its priest, since his attitude to it was emotionally neutral. He had, as it were, a property right in the administration of offerings to it that could be acquired by inheritance or purchase. After he had invoked it and divined its capacity or willingness to meet a request, he received offerings on its behalf. Custody usually passed from a man to one of his sons or other patrikinsmen, who had served as his assistant in its invocation, but not by any explicit transmissions of mystical power. The paraphernalia and capacities of a particular *edet* could be multiplied and segmented if its consent were obtained on divination, one portion being transferred to another custodian on payment of a fee. Many known to me in Umor were obtained in this way, several of them from other villages and from other neighbouring peoples.

Despite the variety in their material character and some special-ization in their supposed capacities, the routine of request was highly standardized. When a person had told the custodian what aid was sought, the latter reminded the client what offerings must be brought in making the request, and also what further offerings should be promised when the request was granted. The offerings, in contrast to those to the *ase*, normally included a fowl and other animals for a blood sacrifice. Typical first offerings consisted of a live chicken, cooked yam and sauce, a piece of bushmeat, a cala-bash of palm wine, a four-sectioned kola nut, a stick of chalk (made into a paste for smearing the body in blessing) and a piece of cam-wood (used for grinding into a powder for body decoration). The offerings of reward were similar but usually more substantial and often included a dog or a goat, of which the custodian took posses-sion. The offerings were placed before the *edet* which the custodian addressed by name in a rite of supplication (*kupawa*), thus: '*Ekpin* I speak, I ask do you agree that this woman here shall conceive?' I have heard a custodian repeat part of the request as expressed by the client, e.g. '*Odjilebo!* she says; she begs a child to be born. Let me see its face alive and let it grow. I will give a chicken and a dog and cooked yam with sauce and a back leg of *ituna* (duiker) and a back leg of *kemen* (small duiker), a piece of yellow dyewood, a chicken's egg, four calabashes of wine, and a pod of guinea grains.' He then 'threw' a pair of *kepeseni* leaves four times before it to divine the will of the *edet*. If all 'throws' gave a refusal after the request had been put in both a positive and a negative form, the client would be sent away with the offerings. But if at least one was favourable, the request was taken to be accepted. The offering chicken was beheaded over the objects, to be later cooked and eaten by all participating, together with the other food, and the power of the *edet* was transferred by smearing chalk paste and breathing on the supplicant. The custodian held the chicken over the *edet* while his assistant ('he who pours wine') chopped off its head so that the blood spurted over the objects. Then, using some of the supplicant's wine and chalk, he made a chalk paste on a stone slab, set at the front. He smeared this on the various objects; on his breast, on his assistant's, and on the suppli-cant's. They then ate the cooked yam together and waited while the chicken was cooked by the assistant, to be eaten in turn, portions being given to any who had accompanied the client. The kola nut was divided and eaten, the wine drunk and the client finally extended his or her hands placed together with palms upturned on which the priest and his assistant breathed loudly several times. The custodian sometimes, especially in the case of sickness, provided a 'medicine' which was to be rubbed on the body, hung in the house or placed in a bowl of water. Such medicines were not regarded as herbal remedies, but as containing power from the *edet* itself.

If later the request was thought to be granted, the further promised offerings had to be brought for a rite of thanks (*kutukpi*) in which a similar procedure was followed. The custodian would remind anyone failing to make these further offerings and warn them that the *edet* could and would punish them, by, for example, causing the death of the child that had been born or a more severe recurrence of the sickness from which relief was sought.

In Umor these *ndet* were not distributed entirely at random in the community. From sampling in two wards it appeared that there were several in all the larger patriclan areas and one in many of the component patrilineages containing from a dozen to two dozen households each. It was only in an informal sense that such an *edet* belonged to the patrilineage or patriclan in question. It was used by those men and their wives more than by others and they knew and had confidence in its powers. Accounts that custodians gave of the number and provenance of their clients showed that the great majority of appeals to most of these *ndet* were from persons living in the patriclan and quite often from within the patrilineage. Custodians and clients both accounted for this in terms of the members of the patriclan and their wives 'knowing' the power of the *edet*, having confidence in it, but not, as was the case with *ase*, there being any restricted affinity between the group and the *edet*. Its custody was expected to remain in the group. Thus it could be regarded as in some sense belonging to the group but it did not in any way symbolize it. Its services were open to all and where it had a reputation for a particular capacity it would be appealed to by persons outside. Such an example was an *edet* believed capable of curing smallpox, situated in the Idjiman ward of Umor which had gained a great reputation during an epidemic in the twenties, and to which all Umor were wont to resort. Other instances related to the protection of children whose cranial sutures did not close, and specific ailments such as chronic diarrhoea. Furthermore, requests

XXV *a*. *Kepun* funeral insignia. During the rites held for elders of the *kepun* the *yekpanun* (smoke-blackened staves to which hare skulls are bound with decorative lashing) are displayed and the *leniga* (elephant tusk horn) is blown. At other times these are stored under the roof of the *kepun* house.

XXV *b*. *Edet*, Odjilebo in Idjiman

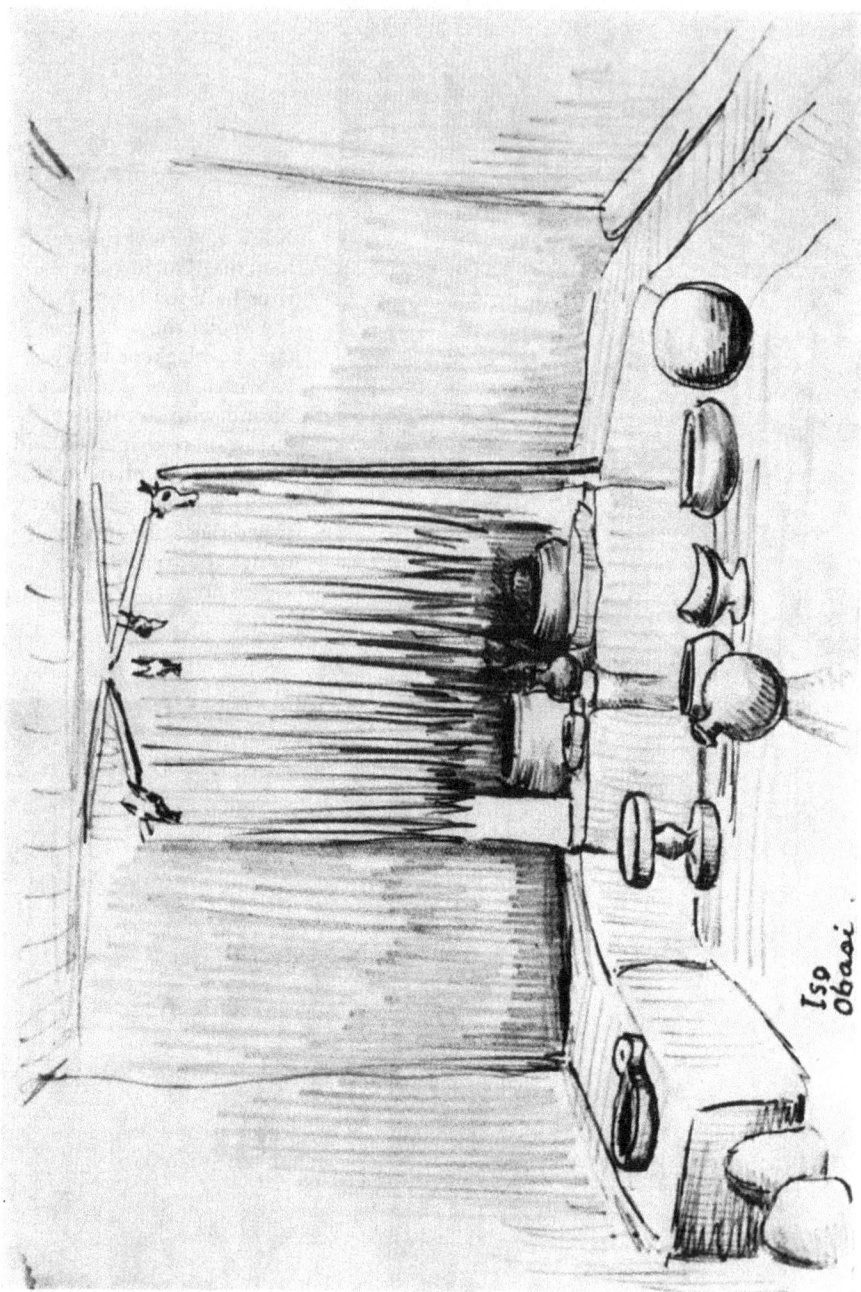

XXVI. The shrine of *Iso Obasi*, spirit of the diviners

to a particular *edet* would often be made on the advice of a diviner who might specify one situated outside the patriclan or even the ward of his client.

Moreover, people who were refused or, in the event, not helped by one *edet* would try another, often after consulting a diviner. Thus, the association between an *edet* and a neighbourhood group was felt to be one of familiarity and confidence, not one of mystical identity. *Ndet* also differed among themselves according to whether they were 'new' or 'old', well known or used by a few persons. Of the 'newer' ones, the custodian would describe how he had himself 'bought' it from another custodian, either in Umor or elsewhere, who had taught him how to speak to it. The reasons for acquiring it always related to some personal misfortune generally in his own household or lineage, such as a run of sickness, sterility or crop failure which had not been alleviated by other *ndet* that had been appealed to, and the installation of the 'new' *edet*, after payment and instructions, usually followed a successful appeal for aid to its 'original'.

From these accounts it became clear that a proliferation of *ndet* had occurred in Umor in response to a continuous quest for means of alleviation of sickness or the satisfaction of other individual needs. Whether a particular *edet* achieved a considerable reputation and clientele appeared to depend on the degree of coincidence between its adoption and the occurrence of relevant needs, together with improvement of conditions among those who gave it a trial. Thus an obvious problem arising from this multiplication of *ndet*, many of which were believed to perform similar services, concerned the motives for seeking their aid, and the basis of continued belief in their efficacy.

While custodians were often reticent or had no established claim concerning the range of powers of their *ndet*, the accounts of their 'cases' showed that by far the most frequent appeals, especially to the less widely known *ndet*, were by or on behalf of women seeking pregnancy or, when pregnant, the safe delivery of a child, usually after a history of previous miscarriages. Ambiguous and contradictory beliefs were expressed by Yakö concerning the supposed actions of *ndet* in relation to failure to conceive and to miscarriage. For the most part stress was laid on the capacity of an *edet* to counteract these misfortunes. But occasionally, and most frequently in connection with *ndet* to which wider powers were

ascribed and where the approach had been made on the instructions of a diviner, it was stated or implied that the *edet* was the
cause of the misfortune. This was not, however, necessarily associated with any explicit ritual or moral fault in the victim, or a
diagnosis of sorcery. Thus the *ndet* were generally regarded as
ethically neutral agencies. This was consistent with the type of
story given concerning their associations with a local group, namely
that someone in the lineage or patriclan had learned of an *edet* in
use elsewhere that was powerful in securing the fertility of women
and had 'bought' it, i.e. made payment for the objects and the
routine required in order to establish it himself.

Finally, it should be noted that there existed an objective correspondence between the great frequency with which *ndet* were
resorted to by the Yakö in connection with human fertility and
both the desire for and the hazards of bearing children. A sample
study of the marital histories of women in Umor confirmed the
high incidence of sterility, miscarriage, and neo-natal death. At the
same time, the respect accorded to a woman both as a wife and as
a member of her matrilineage, and the prestige of a man within his
patrilineage and clan, depended so greatly on their having children,
that deep and frequent anxiety concerning the hazards of pregnancy
and childbirth existed among the Yakö.

There were, however, other *ndet* which were not appealed to
only or mainly with these ends in view, but were associated with
distinct and more specialized afflictions and hazards such as male
impotence, madness, and dysentry. Thus I learned in Umor of
three or four *ndet* all known as *Kebo* which were believed to control
the sexual potency of men. Impotence, while held to be less common than barrenness in women, was just as damaging to the prestige
and status of the individual and the lineage. The routine of appeals
and offerings was similar to that already described and a medicine
was provided, a supernaturally potent concoction of herbs to be
placed in water and drunk, to assist the cure.

The belief that an *edet* could cause as well as remove incapacity
and sickness, found expression in its invocation for protection
against offences by others, and in particular, against theft of crops
in the farms, stores of goods and wandering livestock. Anyone
suffering or fearing such losses could make an offering to the *edet*,
invoking the infliction of a disease it controlled on anyone stealing
his goods. The conventional sign of the *edet* was often provided by

its custodian to affix to these, and served in its turn as a warning of protection. Thus men commonly used the fear of impotence by making offerings to the *Kebo edet* to secure protection for their groves of oil palms in the bush. The special bunch of leaves provided for tying on the palms warned that impotence would befall any man who stole fruit or wine from them or who magically poisoned the palm wine.

The supposed destructive powers of some *ndet* were also invoked collectively for the protection of crops. The bulky yam harvests were stored not in the villages but on tall scaffoldings erected in the open a mile or more out on each of the main paths leading through the farm lands. These yam stacks greatly economized labour since a considerable proportion of the harvest had to be replanted and the supply of yams for domestic use could be brought in from day to day when returning from work in the farm lands. The households farming tracts that were reached from one of the main paths erected their stacks together in a cleared area running back on either side of the path.[10] Most of the households using one such yam stack area were often those of one or a few patriclans within a single ward but the exigencies of shifting cultivation and population growth had led to considerable clan and even some ward heterogeneity. The harvests of individuals were thus exposed to the risk of theft not only from strangers, whose presence might be suspect, but from other users. Although a yam thief ran considerable risk of detection, since on most days there were usually people about who might well notice any trespassers, theft of yams, even between co-wives within a stack, was quite often alleged. Individuals often sought to protect their harvests by making an offering to an *edet* and obtaining its sign to affix on their own stack. Members of the *Ŋkpe* association commonly obtained its protection in this way. Collective attempts were also made to prevent theft by establishing an *edet* with great destructive powers at the yam stack area to which seasonal offerings were made at the opening of each phase of the farming year. Usually derived from a reputedly powerful *edet* in the village, such *ndet* were not in the custody and control of a ward or clan head, but had been set up on the initiative of users of the stacks, often leading women, who demanded general contributions to the offerings. At the time of my first stay at Umor an *edet*, *Ekurikpana*, said to have been derived

[10] See Chapter I.

from the Mbembe people of Adun, was installed at all the stacks
on the paths leading from two of the wards. The custodian of its
original manifestation in Umor, which was set up in his compound,
had in each case provided the component objects and performed
a ritual of establishment for which offerings of food and money
were required from all households using the stack. At each stack
two women had been selected as the local custodians to make seasonal offerings to the *edet* at the stack with materials provided by a
levy on all who used it. Some of the offerings were carried back to the
custodian of the original *edet* in the village for further offerings there.

The ritual objectives and procedures were not, however, uniform throughout Umor. At another yam stack men took a positive
part in the main rite each year before the farms were cleared,
engaging in a hunt over the surrounding bush and bringing in such
game as were caught for a feast after the offerings to the *edet* concerned, the name of which (*yedjodet*) suggested that it was conceived as being specifically a yam spirit. The invocation; 'Let the
yams be good, let children be born, let food give life, let the thinker
of witchcraft against another die' also reflected a wider concern for
the food supply, the birth of children, and protection against the
evil-doer more characteristic of the seasonal rites of the *ase*. The
undertaking of the ritual custody of an *edet* by women was accounted for by the fact that it was the women who spent most of their
time in and around the stacks and carried yams from them into the
village and the plots. It would seem that since it was the women
who not only had most opportunity to steal but were responsible
for the regular provision of supplies in the village, the periodic
reinforcement and reminders of the power of the *edet* was felt to
be appropriately placed in their hands. The *edet* was regarded
especially as a supernatural sanction for good behaviour and mutual
respect for each other's property among the wives of the households. For it was believed to punish by sickness and even death not
only theft but also violent altercations (again especially among
women) at the yam stack. A woman accused of theft, trespass, or
brawling would be told to make an offering to the *edet* swearing
her innocence to it if she refused to admit the offence. Women
could be made to pay fines by the patriclan elders if caught
stealing or judged guilty in a quarrel, but they made an offering
to the *edet* as well. The stretch of path alongside the *edet* was said
to be the favourite, because the safest place, to leave unattended a

headload of yams and other produce—for no one, it was said, would dare to risk its punishment by stealing so close to it. Thus these collective *ndet* at the yam stack area served in the eyes of the Yakö to keep an admitted nuisance within bounds and the periodic requests that anyone who offended the *edet* by stealing should die was certainly not without a deterrent effect.

Ndet were also collectively held and invoked by voluntary associations and again primarily for protection of their members or to sanction their claims. One such association, mainly of younger men in Umor, had as its *raison d'être* the protection of its members' goods and their interests, especially against insubordination and witchcraft by women. It was known by the name of its *edet*, *Ɔkpe*, a further Leopard Spirit, believed to be manifested in a bellows-like contraption that was manipulated to produce a leopard-like roar. This, it was said, had been originally obtained from the Ekoi on account of its reputation for great potency among them. Members and others for a fee could obtain its protection for their goods and also its sanction for claims in disputes over debts and, in particular, marital rights over women. Control of women and especially profligate or runaway wives by threat of sterility or death in pregnancy from *Ɔkpe* was often given as a reason for the large membership of the *Ɔkpe* association among younger men. It was also said by some elders to be misused against them by ambitious and envious young men. Its supposed activities were frowned on for their unregulated and destructive character by the village priests and ward Leaders, who said that no man prominent in *Ɔkpe* would be accepted for office among them. The cult of *Ɔkpe* was not recognized in the village festivals and one factor in the development of the association appeared to have lain in opposition to alleged past injustices by the village priesthood and by ward Leaders.[11]

But the Yakö also believed that the power of *ndet* could be harnessed to injure others where no offence was involved. This was the supposed procedure of sorcerers motivated by unprovoked malice. Beliefs concerning sorcery among the Yakö are significant here as further illustrating the ethically indifferent character that can be ascribed to *ndet*. Sorcerers were believed to encompass sudden and severe illness or death in their victims by bringing objects associated with them into unsuspected contact with an *edet*. They might secretly place near the *edet* some object intimately associated with

[11] See Chapter V, pp. 158.

the victim, or they might secretly take small objects from the *edet* to put in the victim's food or his sleeping place. In either case, such action would be entirely unauthorized by the custodians of the *edet*. Indeed the custodians of the *ndet* of the village and of associations had to swear at their installation under penalty of their own destruction that they would not themselves abuse the power of these *ndet* for sorcery. Death-dealing sorcery was believed by the Yakö to be a very dangerous and even suicidal enterprise practised only by the recklessly embittered.[12] Where a death was ascribed to sorcery, the identity of the sorcerer himself was sought among the recently dead. For to have evoked so destructive an *edet* the sorcerer had exposed himself to its action. Here again, as in the protective use of *ndet* against offenders, the moral relation lay between men. The *edet* itself was an indifferent agent.

This sketch of Yakö beliefs concerning *ndet* shows that they are conceived as discrete, autonomous personalized entities that, according to the particular powers ascribed, can produce and avert sterility, sickness, and death. Many persistent maladies and any death were likely to be regarded by the victims or those close to them, as due to the action of some *edet*. *Ndet* were not thought of as primarily beneficent, for any benefit individually obtained from an *edet* was usually that of withdrawal of the disability it was believed to control. To this extent, *ndet* were conceptually antithetical to the *ase*, which were believed positively to confer health, fertility, prosperity, and peace. Beliefs concerning the existence and actions of *ndet* were characteristically evoked in a context of actual or anticipated misfortune. While those concerning the *ase* were manifested in connection with a desire for the continuance or renewal of benefits already known and enjoyed. The cult of *ndet* appeared not to be completely or expressly dissociated from that of the matrilineal fertility cults of the *ase*, however, for I learnt of a supposedly very powerful *edet*, *Edet Eteto*, which was said to belong to the *Yabot* matriclan to which the premier *Yose Odjokobi* was also attached. Two women of the matriclan in different wards were custodians of separate manifestations of this *edet*, offerings to which could not only restore fertility but afforded protection against sorcery by the secret misuse of other *ndet*. Its status appeared to be exceptional, and perhaps anomalous, not only in that its clientele was drawn from members of the matriclan and their children as well as people

[12] See Chapter VII pp. 227–8.

from the two patriclan areas where its cult was situated, but that its aid and protection was sought in a general manner by these through making a small offering; and those girls and boys who did so for the first time carried out a collective rite at a secret place in the bush where they passed a night before returning in procession to the compound of the village head, where all who had been thus initiated assembled and drums kept in the *Odjokobi yose* house were brought out to which they danced.

In another context, however, it was accepted that *ndet* could be employed to protect against offences by other persons by invoking their capacity to injure against such offenders. Thus the protection of the village at large was sought through Leopard Spirits in the custody of *Korta* and *Okeŋka* which were not only linguistically classified as *ndet*, but were conceived as supernatural punitive agencies against transgressors. An *epundet* sanctioned offences among and against the members and dependents of a patriclan. *Ŋkpe* protected the interests and property of those associating themselves with it. The *ndet* established at yam stacks had similarly for those installing them, the function of protecting their goods and the security of their rights. Thus, while most spirits categorized as *ndet* were in the custody of individuals and had an indefinite clientele among persons seeking relief from actual misfortune, some were controlled by custodians accepted as acting on behalf of the village community, of its clan segments or of formal and informal associations and were believed to sanction offences by or against the members of such groups.

The conceptual link between the personal and the collective resort to *ndet*, and the explanation of the fact that the same term could be used for spirits receiving ritual offerings to restore health or fertility and for others held to injure offenders, would appear to lie in an underlying belief in the indifferent character of supernatural agencies of disability, disease, and death which could be activated by offerings to serve human ends. On the one hand, an *edet* might be invoked and rewarded by, or on behalf of, an individual to secure relief from suffering. On the other, the same could be done by individuals or groups to bring suffering on those who infringed their rights and claims. Sorcery, in this conceptual context, consisted in the extreme case of action by an embittered person whose envy transformed the success of others into a wrong against himself and sought to punish this through the action of an *edet*.

While the custodian of an *edet* might advise or require restitution for some offence disclosed by or alleged of those invoking restorative aid, the *ndet* were not themselves addressed or described as judges of morals. The moral relations were always between men, who, it was believed, were able to use, and even misuse, the powers of *ndet* for human ends.

Invocation of an *edet* on behalf of an individual afforded him and those close to him, some relief of anxiety, and some restoration of confidence. For the community or any section of it, such offerings operated in a psychologically parallel manner with reference to collective concern over actual or feared infringements of property and other rights and the disruption of orderly life.

Collective offerings in protection of rights had the secondary psychological effect of inducing in individuals, whether members of the collectivity or not, a fear of committing any act which the *edet* had been invoked to punish. Thus belief also served as a negative sanction against infringement of the rights of others which the ordinary person was loth to incur. It is possible, but more difficult to ascertain, that individual offerings to *ndet* for the removal of suffering and disability also inculcated a heightened sense of the risk of incurring further attacks by *ndet* through subsequent offence or improper conduct.

With the rapid growth of their villages, greater social differentiation and increasing external contacts, the tendency among the Yakö to discover and placate or invoke a particular supernatural agency with respect to individual misfortune, together with the continuation of the misfortunes themselves, had led to an indefinite multiplication of *ndet*. In these circumstances, Yakö resorted to further supernatural means to obtain guidance in the discovery of the *edet*, or other supernatural entity, from which relief should be sought especially in serious and prolonged illness. This guidance was provided by the diviners.

Faith in the powers of diviners to discover the mystical cause of a particular misfortune was set in a wider framework of belief concerning the ultimate ordering and control of the universe and hence of the personal fortune of individuals. For the capacity to discover hidden supernatural action was believed to be bestowed by a supernatural being Obasi, who had created the universe. To Obasi the Yakö attributed the ultimate power and responsibility for organizing and controlling the world as they knew it. While in some contexts Obasi was regarded and addressed with gratitude as conferring order on the world and benefits on mankind, he was not generally believed to intervene directly or with particular intent. On the other hand, as creator and maintainer of the universe he was aware of all the hidden causes of events.

The diviner, endowed by Obasi with a capacity believed to be first manifest spontaneously in his temperament and strengthened by an initiation, was believed to communicate such of this knowledge as was relevant to particular circumstances. In Umor the diviners (*yabunga*, sing. *obunga*) constituted a small corporation whose head participated with the *ase* priests in the village priesthood. They trained and initiated approved new members in the methods of divination and the conducting of seances. Yakö differed among themselves concerning the nature and extent of a diviner's knowledge. Uncertainty was not mitigated by the indirect character of the questioning and suggestions regarding the context of a request, and the laconic instructions concerning reconciliations, sacrifices, and other rites to be performed. But their most important capacity was seen to consist in the discovery whether fetishes or other supernatural agents might be responsible for sickness, untimely death or other grave misfortunes. This usually led to suggestions that one or other of the *ndet*, for reasons which might or might not be specified, was immediately responsible and should be invoked to secure relief. Consistently, however, with the role ascribed to Obasi, the diviner did not claim to secure any other supernatural benefits for his clients. He was a diagnostician of supernatural action. His prescriptions were confined to the suggestion of further actions, both ritual and moral, that might favourably alter these.

* * *

This brief sketch of the contexts of fetishism among the Yakö will, I hope, have confirmed the significance of the several general processes psychological, sociological, and ecological, on which stress has been placed in the history of anthropological thought concerning the development and acceptance of supernatural beliefs. Equally, however, it has sought to show that any one of them has but limited explanatory value, so that such restriction of attention conceals the complexity of the factors and the range of contexts in which such beliefs take form and acquire significance.

It has exemplified the conceptual tendency to objectify, as supernatural beings or spirits with various attributes of human personality, the hidden causes of human prosperity and misfortune. It
has also, I hope, shown how strong and recurrent are the emotional
drives under which this search for causes proceeds in the endeavour to safeguard or restore both individual and collective needs.
Marett, while recognizing their importance, often wrote as if these
emotions were directly generated by external phenomena that were
intrinsically mysterious. Yakö fetishism confirms Malinowski's
insistence on the middle term of concern and uncertainty in relation to human needs and aspirations. In the objects visibly associated with Yakö fetishism there is no intrinsic mystery. Indeed,
the fetish objects are treated as mysterious and regarded with awe
only when the belief in the doctrines is being acted on during an
actual rite which seeks to influence the spirits. It would be more
true to say that the mystery and awe derive from the doctrines
concerning spirit powers. And the doctrines become significant
and the belief important only in the context of concern for the
continuance or restoration of benefits.

Explicit among those benefits for the Yakö are the harmony and
perpetuation of the village community, its component groupings
and approved leaders. Similarly explicit are the hazards of social
discord and individual offence. The *ase* and some *ndet* are invoked
to maintain and protect the welfare of the village and smaller
groups. The social context of the concern and the beliefs is clear,
but the spirits do not thereby become mere symbols of society.
They are associated with particular collective ends. Moreover,
need and concern are not confined to the desire for social harmony
and means of overcoming attacks upon it. Individual life and prosperity and its protection against hazards of all kinds, especially
those connected with farming, health, and child-bearing, are equally
stressed. That one important context of these beliefs consists of
public and collective rites does not make the benefits sought less
individual or their fulfilment conceptually dependent on society.

The cults of the lesser *ndet* are sustained even more explicitly
by individual fears and uncertainties directly related to personal
interests. Here both the occasion and the substance of invocation
are often derived from the material and biological conditions of
life. Here too it is necessary to distinguish the immediate context
of belief, the experience or the fear of misfortune which induces

the invocation of spirits, and the secondary social effects whereby people may be deterred from theft or sorcery or brought to admit and expiate offences to which conscience or suspicion may attribute the injurious intervention of an *edet*. Such effects are undoubtedly of significance for social control and the reaffirmation of moral values. But they are conceptually and logically secondary to concern for the hazards of life and livelihood.

Among the Yakö the belief that health, fertility, and long life are conferred by the *ase* spirits of the matriclans on all who respect them finds its complement in the face of particular fears and misfortunes in belief that these can be caused and removed by *ndet*. Conceived as morally indifferent sources of sickness, sterility, and death, they are believed to respond to those who make appropriate offerings. And this aid can be sought both to relieve individual suffering and also to protect individual and collective interests.

INDEX

Adoption, 71–81, 89, 104, 131
Adultery, 90, 92, 126–7
Age-set, 20, 67, 72, 87, 92, 122, 127, 142–8, 162, 164, 168, 172, 176, 186, 195, 199, 207, 212, 220, 235, 238, 250, 265; ill., p. 177
Akota, see War Stones
Ancestors, 3
Ase, see Ritual, Harvest
Atewa, vii, 239, 241–2, 250
Authority, vi, 124–5, 131, 142–4, 147–54, 159–60, 162–4, 165–8, 171–4, 178–9, 181, 185–6, 189–90, 195, 198, 200–1, 203–5, 225, 235, 237–8

Bananas, 9
Basket, 41
Beans, 8, 23–24, 42
Bendom, 196–9, 205, 207
Betrothal, 122
Biko-Biko, 56, 58–59, 101–2, 135, 153, 193
British Administration, 190, 192
Brother, 90, 92, 96, 107–8, 130, 216

Carbohydrate, 43
Cassava, 8, 23–24
Cattle, 27, 31
Census, 4, 13, 63, 171
Chalk, 41, 44, 68, 137, 144, 155, 159, 162–3, 185, 241–4, 247, 271
Chicken, 28, 43, 271
Childbearing, 215, 217, 231, 264, 267, 274, 282
Children, 26, 45, 49, 53, 71–82, 86–88, 92–93, 98, 102–3, 108, 111–12, 124, 126, 131, 133–4, 137, 214, 216–17, 220, 231, 237, 239, 248, 264, 274, 276; table p. 80
Christianity, 198, 200, 202–4, 206
Clearing, 7, 11, 17–24, 30, 68, 92, 96, 109, 127–8, 140–1, 146, 172
Climate, 6–7
Cloth, 13, 27–28, 38–40, 43, 45, 48
Coconuts, 9
Coco yams, 8, 23, 40, 42, 45
Colocasia, 8
Compensation, 92, 110–13, 124, 126–7, 162, 171, 175, 178, 180, 182–4, 190
Compound, 55, 92–93, 115, 125–6, 128, 130, 132, 135, 149, 161, 176, 178, 187, 211, 214–16, 222; ill., p. 16; fig., p. 94
Consumption, 31–48
Cosmetics, 38, 44–45
Cow, 140, 149–50, 152, 184
Crops, 8–9, 23–24, 49, 87–88, 131, 134, 167, 174, 227, 235, 264, 273–4
Cultivation, 3, 5, 7–13, 29
Currency, 13, 96, 107–8, 123, 132–3, 142, 148–51, 154, 158, 170
Cutlery, 27, 45

Dance, 136, 138–42, 145, 149–50, 154–6, 159–60, 163, 172; ill., pp. 129, 160, 161, 193, 209, 240, 241
Daughter, 71–84, 89–90, 95, 107–8, 116, 122, 124, 216, 220, 224
Death, 72, 74–75, 80–82, 107–8, 110–11, 125–6, 139, 141–2, 146, 149, 151, 156–7, 163, 169–70, 172, 175, 212, 221, 224, 227, 229–32, 237–8, 250, 261, 268, 272, 276–9, 281, 283
Debt, 107, 111–12
Descent, 49, 69, 71, 74, 83, 85–134, 103, 135–6, 160, 167–8, 189
Distribution, viii, 9 ff.
District Officer, 191–3, 198–9
Diviner, 171, 181, 184, 212, 217–18, 223, 228–33, 235, 238–9, 246–7, 249–51, 273, 280–1; ill., pp. 192, 240; ill., spirit of, p. 273
Divorce, 72, 75, 80, 81, 89–90, 92, 95, 126–7, 161
Dream, 224, 227–8, 238
Duck, 28
Duiker, 27, 41, 271
Dwelling area, 49–61, 72, 98, 122, 135, 168, 183, 224

Ebiabu, 147–50, 152, 155, 164, 171–2, 186, 189, 225; ill., p. 144
Eblɔmbe, 153–5, 171, 245; ill., p. 160
Edet, 211, 214–18, 224, 226–9, 231–2, 252, 263, 267, 269–83; ill., p. 272; *Edet Lopon*, 179, 211, 268, 269–70; *Ekpe Edet*, 237, 267–8, 270
Ekao, vii, 237, 241, 246, 268
Ekui, 243–4, 251; ill., p. 209
Ekuri, 3, 63, 96, 135, 190, 208
Ekuruso, 161–3
Elamalama, 61, 181, 236; ill., p. 177
Eponama, 53, 93, 146
Epundet, 50–51, 58, 60–61, 70–71, 74, 95, 113, 218–19, 269–70, 279; ill., p. 112
European goods, 27, 36, 38
Exchange, ix, 31–48
Exogamy, 52, 56, 58–60, 62, 95, 105, 123, 220

Farming, viii, 5, 7–13, 28, 51, 53, 63, 86, 132, 167, 184, 210, 234, 243, 282; fig., pp. 8, 12, 15; farming paths, 5, 16–20, 24, 148, 207, 275–6; farming path elders, 17, 20–21, 53, 56, 72, 76, 132; farming plots, 10–13, 16, 18–19, 21, 30, 93, 108, 202, 223; farming produce, 37, 40; farming land, 16–20, 49, 62, 72, 76, 79, 93, 116, 135, 143, 224; farming rights, 17, 29, 87, 125, 168, 196
Fat, 43
Father, 18, 85, 90, 92–93, 96, 106, 116, 123–5, 130, 134
Father-in-law, 18, 122, 128–9

Fertility, 7, 113, 115–16, 121, 131, 136, 158–9, 174, 176, 182, 204, 214–15, 217, 221, 224, 235, 240, 242, 264–7, 273–4, 278–9, 283; fertility shrine, vii, 159, 180–1

Fetishism, 262–81

Fine, 115–16, 147, 153, 240, 243

Fish, 28, 38, 40, 42–43

Food, 7–8, 19–21, 23–24, 27–28, 30–32, 34, 36, 40, 43, 48, 55, 86–87, 93, 227, 240, 246–8, 250–1, 260, 276, 278

Forest, 5–7, 210, 265; forest produce, 3, 32, 53, 167–8

Foster-father, 71–74, 76–78, 81–82, 92, 113, 123

Funeral, 29, 54–55, 72, 77, 107, 109, 112, 116, 126–7, 140, 154–5, 159, 161, 169; ill., pp. 128, 160, 272

Geological conditions, 6–7

Goat, 27, 43, 140, 149, 152, 155, 157, 161, 163, 241, 271

Ground nuts, 8, 23–24, 42, 140

Gun, 111, 156–7, 268; gunpowder, 38, 40, 157, 167

Hardware, 38–39, 43

Hausa, 24

High Court, 190–1

Hoe blade, 41

Hoeing, 11, 146, 243

House, 86, 90, 146, 228; ill., pp. 81, 97; house-building, 24, 44–45, 93, 116, 122, 128, 176, 184, 188; ill., p. 81; house plan, fig., p. 91; house sites, 3, 49, 51, 53, 62, 72, 79, 93, 121, 135, 167, 223, 225; table, p. 54

Household, viii, 9, 11, 13, 18–19, 25–26, 30–32, 41–42, 47, 54, 63, 77, 79, 80–82, 86–93, 97, 107, 121, 132, 216, 223; fig., p. 10; household consumption, 41–45; household expenditure, 43, 46–47; table, p. 45; household income, 26, 31, 33–35, 41–48; table, p. 46

Humidity, 7

Hunting, 27–28, 164, 210; hunters, 156–8, 251; ill., p. 96

Husband, 18–20, 23, 32–33, 46–47, 80, 86–88, 95–96, 108, 121–2, 124–9, 214–17, 220, 222; ill., p. 97

Ibo, 22, 27, 31, 39, 60, 89, 213, 228, 230

Idomi, 3, 135, 143, 193

Ikpuŋkara, 179–80, 183–5, 189, 194, 235, 245, 251–2; ill., pp. 192, 193

Illness, 212, 214, 218–21, 223, 225, 227, 229–31, 237, 250, 252, 261, 268–9, 272–3, 276–81, 283

Ina, 174–6, 236, 241–2, 263, 267

Inheritance, 29–30, 49, 63, 75, 83, 85–86, 96, 106–8, 111, 113, 190, 201, 204, 211, 268

Isɔ Obasi, 247–51; ill., p. 273

Kebo, 274–5

Keboŋatam, 246

Kɛkpan, 140–3, 172

Kɛkpatu, 55, 135–64, 195, 269

Kepun, 11, 16–17, 21–22, 25, 30, 49–54, 56–60, 62–63, 66, 68, 70–82, 93, 96, 99, 110–13, 128, 135–6, 176–8, 196, 198–9, 204–6, 269; ill., pp. 113, 272; kepun head, 21, 68, 70, 78, 194–6, 207

Kinship, viii, 4, 11, 16–17, 24, 29–30, 48, 56, 71–73, 76, 89, 117–22, 130, 132, 165–6, 178, 201–2, 204, 220, 230–1; Yakö terms for, fig., p. 118; table, p. 54

Kodjɔ, 156–7, 171

Kola nuts, 9, 248, 271

Korta, 177, 180, 211, 236–7, 239–40, 243–6, 248, 250–1, 267–8, 279

Kupatu shrine, ill., p. 256

Labour, ix, 1–30, 49

Land, ix, 1–30; land resources, vi; land rights, viii, 10, 28–29, 190, 202, 268; land use, viii

Ledemboku, 245; and see also Ekui; ill., p. 209

Lejima, 96, 98, 100, 102–6, 111, 114, 116, 136, 174–6, 178, 199, 201, 204, 207; table, p. 105

Leko, 150, 154–7; ill., pp. 129, 161

Lekuma, 49, 56, 73

Leopard cult, 139, 151, 158–9, 188, 213, 237–8, 241–3, 250, 267–8, 277, 279; ill., p. 161

Liboku, 8, 29, 180, 234, 236, 238–40, 242, 248–52

Ligwomi, 137–43, 148, 152, 225, 236, 250, 269; ill., p. 176

Lineage, 17, 23, 30, 53–55, 57, 59–63, 66–69, 72, 75, 82, 106, 119, 221, 223; fig., pp. 60, 94; table, p. 54, 64–65, 70; lineage head, 69–71, 74

Lisetomi, 234

Lite, 245–6; ill., p. 240

Livestock, 27–28, 31, 49, 96, 107, 126, 131, 141, 151, 174, 180, 183–4, 228, 235, 274

Lopon Fawa, 247

Magistrate, 190–1

Maize, 8, 23, 42

Manihot, 8

Marriage, ix, 18, 20, 52–53, 72–73, 77, 79–80, 82, 88–89, 95, 105–7, 121–9, 144–6, 161, 163, 175, 190, 196, 210, 215, 217, 222, 239–40, 265, 267, 269; marriage payments, 47, 72, 80, 82, 92–93, 96, 104, 113, 121–9, 135, 149, 201

Matriclan, 96–102, 104, 106, 109–10, 112–15, 117, 119, 121, 123, 129, 133, 136, 142, 161, 170, 174, 181–2, 184, 188–9, 206, 212, 214–17, 221–2, 231–2, 235, 239, 244, 248–52, 263–7, 278, 283; fig., p. 104; table, p. 105

Matrikin, 96, 107–8, 113, 116–18, 120–4, 126, 131, 161, 217, 220, 267

Matrilineal kin-group, 28–29, 46, 75–77, 80–84, 97, 99–103, 105, 115, 123, 130–1, 134, 161, 174, 176, 200, 204–6, 208, 212, 217, 221, 264–5, 267, 274; table, p. 101

Meat, 27–28, 40–43, 45, 140–1, 154, 158, 161, 167, 170, 241–4, 248–9, 267, 271
Medicine, 38
Meeting house, 51, 53, 56, 61–62, 110, 137, 139, 141, 149, 158, 248
Men, 8, 21–22, 24–25, 29, 49, 51, 77, 81–82, 85–86, 88, 102–3, 116, 219, 227, 230–1, 235, 239, 248, 274, 276; men's associations, 182–5, 248; man's house, 90, 92; ill., p. 91
Miscarriage, 216–17, 273–4
Mother, 71–85, 90, 92–93, 98, 116, 131, 134, 216–17, 228, 231
Mother-in-law, 128–9

Native court, vii, 46, 96, 107, 115, 133–4, 147, 149, 152, 171, 182, 186, 190–1, 193–4, 196–7, 199–201, 203, 205, 208, 223, 225; ill., p. 193
Ndai, 4, 11, 19, 21–25, 27–28, 52, 54, 57, 61–63, 66–68, 70–71, 74, 76, 77–78, 80–81; ill., p. 16; fig., p. 15; table, pp. 54, 64–65, 70, 80
Nigerian Administration, vi, 1, 107, 199–200, 204, 225; Forestry Department, 7, 29
Ŋko, 3, 135, 193
Ŋkpani, 3, 135, 160, 173, 193
Ŋkpe, 158–60, 164, 172, 252, 275, 277, 279; ill., p. 161

Obam, 160, 252
Obasi, 210, 212, 227, 229–32, 238–9, 247, 251, 280–1
Obolene, 240, 242, 246
Obot kepun, 68, 167, 196, 207, and see also Kepun head
Obot Liboku, 239–42, 244–5, 248, 250
Obot Lopon, 99, 104, 114, 176–7, 188, 192, 194–5, 207, 263; ill., p. 176
Obuŋa, 230, 235, 238–9, 281; Obot Yabuŋa, 171, 177, 230, 236, 239, 250; ill., p. 192
Odere, 248; ill., p. 241
Odjokobi, 115, 150–1, 154, 159, 162, 175, 185, 188, 207, 236, 240–4, 250–2, 278–9; ill., pp. 208, 209
Ogbolia, 137–43, 147, 150, 152, 154, 169–71, 173, 186–7, 192, 195, 225, 238
Ogometu, 137, 139, 141–3, 152, 169, 173
Okambən, 137–40, 142–4, 147–52, 154
Okarefoŋ, 244
Okeŋka, 151–3, 158, 163, 171, 173–4, 177, 180, 182, 188, 211, 236, 238–9, 241–3, 245, 250–2, 268, 279
Okpan, 116–17, 120
Okpebri, vii, 115, 159, 177, 179–81, 188, 198, 206, 236, 239, 245, 268–9; ill., frontispiece
Okra, 8, 23, 42, 140, 245
Okundom, 182–5, 189
Opalapala, 180, 236–7, 239–40, 245–6, 248, 267–8; ill., p. 208
Oponotameta, 17, 53
Ornaments, 44–45
rthography, v
tomise, 180, 237, 243

Pachylobis edulis, 9, 43
Palms, 9, 24–27, 47, 51, 88, 108–9, 153; ill., p. 33; palm collector, ill., p. 96; palm fronds, 24; palm fruit, 24–25, 32, 34; palm kernels, 9, 25–26, 31–41, 46, 88, 127, 132, 200; palm oil, 9, 25–26, 28, 32–38, 43, 46, 78, 88, 127, 132, 200, 202; ill., pp. 33, 80; palm wine, 9, 17, 21–22, 24–25, 29, 32, 34–35, 43, 45–46, 68, 71, 109, 122, 129, 136–7, 139–41, 144, 148–50, 152, 154–7, 161, 163, 167–8, 180, 240–3, 246–8, 267, 271–2
Patriclan, ix, 49–84, 92–96, 106, 108–10, 112–14, 117, 119, 121–3, 131–2, 134–5, 140, 142–3, 146, 151, 153, 164, 167–73, 180, 183, 185–6, 189, 202, 211, 216, 219–20, 222–6, 231, 237, 246, 248, 251–2, 270, 272–3, 275–6, 279; ill., p. 112; fig., p. 60; table, pp. 57–58; map, p. 50
Patrikin, 96, 110, 116–17, 119–22, 125, 130, 133, 140–1, 150, 173, 183, 211, 216–17, 219, 247, 270; table, p. 54; patrikin group solidarity, ix, 3
Patrilineal kin group, 11, 16, 24, 28–29, 51, 54, 58–59, 62–63, 77, 79–80, 82–84, 88–89, 92–95, 97, 103, 105, 109, 130, 132, 200, 204–6, 211–12, 220, 264–5, 272, 274
Patrilineal kinship, ix, 72, 125
Pawpaws, 9, 42
Payment, 22, 36, 39, 44–45, 47, 77–78, 107, 110–12, 137, 139–42, 144, 148–51, 153–4, 156, 158, 160–3, 169–72, 183–5, 196–7, 201, 233, 237–40, 243
Pears, 9, 42–43
Peppers, 8, 23, 40, 42
Pigs, 28
Plantains, 9, 42
Planting, 8, 11, 18–19, 23, 47, 88
Political organization, 1, 3–4, 165–7, 187, 234–5
Polygyny, 80, 86, 88–89, 127–8
Population, 3–4, 10, 30, 55–56, 67, 78, 84, 135, 167–8, 189, 211, 235
Pots, 41, 43, 60, 68
Price, 31–33, 36–37, 43
Priest, 13, 55–56, 58, 61–62, 68, 70–71, 73–74, 89, 97–100, 102–4, 111, 113–16, 131, 133, 136, 142, 144, 151, 154, 158, 160, 167, 169–71, 174–8, 181, 183–4, 187–8, 198, 203–5, 208, 215–16, 221, 225, 228, 235, 239, 241–4, 246–52, 261, 263, 265–8, 277, and see also Yabot
Production, viii, 9 ff., 31–36, 134, 210
Property, 10, 17, 29–30, 46, 49, 75, 86, 96, 100, 107–8, 112, 125–6, 174, 227
Protein, 43
Pumpkins, 8, 23

Rain, 6, 7, 234; drought, 7; monsoon, 7
Resident Officer, 191
Ritual, 1, 21, 28–29, 51, 53, 56, 58, 68, 71–72, 95–99, 104, 106, 110–16, 127, 131, 133–6, 140–5, 147, 151–3, 158–60, 166, 169, 175, 186–7, 203, 207, 210,

213–14, 217, 228, 230–2, 258–61, 263, 265, 267, 270, 276, 279, 281–2; ill., p. 193; burial, ill., pp. 128, 160; fertility, 112–13; first fruits, vi, 8, 29, 68, 122, 128, 145, 150–4, 159, 162–3, 175, 177, 180, 212, 214–16, 234–53; first planting, 29; harvest, vi, vii, 29, 150–1, 154, 159, 162–3, 175, 212, 215–16, 234–5, 239; initiation, 137–40, 168, 237, 238; ill., pp. 176, 192; pregnancy, 51, 62, 113, 123; war, 181
Rope, 32, 34, 35, 41, 46

Salt, 38
Schooling, 133–4
Seasons, 6, 19–20, 147, 234, 260; dry, 6–7; wet, 6
Sheep, 28
Shrine, 104, 114, 136, 151, 206, 211, 215, 226–7, 230, 232–3, 235–6; ill., 256, 273; map, p. 50; fertility shrine, vii; *kepun* shrine, 28, 51, 53, 56–62, 68–69, 73, 97
Sister, 90, 96, 108, 122, 129
Soap, 38, 43
Soil, 7
Son, 71–84, 90, 92–93, 96, 106–7, 116, 124–6, 130, 133–4
Song, 148–9, 154, 160, 163; song clubs, 160–1
Sorcery, 217, 221, 226–9, 232, 249, 264–5, 274, 277–9, 282
Spirits, 210–33, 235–6, 238–9, 255–6, 262
Sterility, vii, 212, 216–17, 223–4, 231, 268, 270, 273–4, 277–8, 283
Succession, 49, 69, 71, 74, 83–86, 96, 109, 113–14, 125, 130, 133, 143, 151, 153, 162, 169–70, 172–3, 175, 183–6, 201, 206, 223, 230, 238–9, 270
Sugar, 23–24, 38
Swamp land, 5, 29, 109

Taxation, 4, 26, 45, 63, 196, 198, 200
Temperature, 6
Territory, 4–6, 49, 168; map, p. 2
Tobacco, 41, 45
Trading, 20, 25–28, 31, 36–41, 47, 88, 132, 167, 169, 180, 184, 197, 200–2, 210, 268; table, p. 35

Ugep, *see* Umor
Umor, vi, 1, 3–4, 6–7, 16, 22, 24, 26–7, 29–31, 33, 35–39, 46–47, 49, 53, 55–56, 59, 61–63, 71, 75–78, 83–85, 92–93, 95–97, 99–100, 102–4, 115, 135, 137, 142, 144, 148, 151, 155–6, 159, 167, 169, 172, 174–7, 181–2, 185, 189–203, 205–8, 210, 212–13, 218–19, 225–6, 228–30, 234, 236, 238, 244, 246, 249, 252, 268–9, 270, 272–7, 281; ill., frontispiece and pp. 128, 176, 193; map, pp. 5, 50; fig., p. 104; table, pp. 57–58, 105
Uwo womon, 69, 93

Vegetation, 7
Village, 3, 16, 49, 75–76, 163, 226, 234, 249, 251, 263, 266, 268, 282; village

associations, 30, 107, 109, 116, 148, 171, 179–82, 185, 187, 219, 235, 245, 252, 266; village council, 104, 107, 133, 143, 160, 163, 175, 198–9, 205–8, 225, 230, 235–40, 250–2; village head, 92, 100, 110–11, 136, 147, 150–1, 153–4, 162, 176, 179, 181, 184–5, 187–8, 194, 205, 207–8, 240–4, 246–52, 269; ill., p. 176; village government, 28, 115, 164–209; village markets, 38–39, 41; village speaker, vii, 110, 115–16, 176, 236, 239, 243, 246, 266; ill., frontispiece and p. 209; village territory, 4–6, 16, 27, 29–30, 53, 109, 143, 166–7, 202, 235

Ward, 28, 55–56, 135–64, 167, 178, 185, 187–8, 192, 204, 207–8, 211, 219, 226, 235, 250, 252, 269, 272–3; ward head, 20, 46, 48, 115, 137, 139, 141–2, 144–5, 147–8, 153, 160, 162–3, 169, 171, 173–4, 195, 266; ward leaders, 136–7, 139, 141–4, 147–8, 158, 163, 169–74, 180, 182–4, 186–7, 189, 200, 225, 228, 235, 238, 242–3, 245, 250, 252, 264, 268–9, 277; ill., p. 128
Warrant Chiefs, 190–7, 199, 204–6, 208–9, 225
Warrior, 153–4, 251
War Stone, 154, 243, 266, 268; ill., p. 257
Wealth, 10, 29–30, 43, 49, 74, 77–78, 96, 106, 112, 132–4, 167, 169, 201, 230
Weeding, 8, 23, 88, 145, 244
Wife, 13, 18–20, 23, 25–26, 32–33, 35, 41, 44, 46–49, 76–77, 80, 86–90, 93, 95, 107–8, 121–2, 125–9, 131, 172, 211, 214–17, 219–20, 222, 231, 274–7; ill., p. 97
Witchcraft, 212–14, 217–26, 229, 232, 241–2, 264–5, 276–7
Women, 8, 18, 20, 22–23, 26, 29, 31, 33, 36–37, 40, 51–52, 75–77, 85–86, 88–89, 95–96, 102–3, 108, 116, 131, 161–3, 214–16, 219, 227, 230, 231, 235, 237, 243, 248, 274–5, 278; women's associations, 185, 237, 251; woman's house, 92; ill., p. 91

Xanthifolia, 8

Yabot, 111, 115–16, 126, 152, 159, 174, 176–80, 182–6, 188–9, 194–200, 203–7, 225–6, 230, 235–6, 238, 241, 243–7, 252, 263, 268–9, 278; ill., p. 209
Yakö, v, vi, 1, 17, 20–22, 26, 28, 33, 40–41, 43, 47, 49, 53, 59, 63, 69, 71, 74–75, 83, 86–87, 89, 92–93, 95–96, 100, 107, 109, 113, 117, 122, 124, 127–35, 137, 142–3, 147–8, 151, 153–4, 156, 159–61, 163, 167, 170, 173, 177, 185–90, 192–4, 196–9, 201–2, 204, 206, 208, 210–17, 220–4, 226, 228–9, 233–4, 242–4, 246, 248–9, 252, 262–3, 265–6, 268–70, 274, 277–8, 280–3; map, p. 2; fig., p. 118
Yams, 6–7, 12, 18–20, 31, 34–35, 40–41, 45–47, 68, 87–88, 97, 107–8, 129, 137,

141, 161, 163, 180, 210, 241–7, 249, 251, 264, 267, 271, 276; ill., pp. 17, 80, 96; yam consumption, 41–42; yam harvest, 8–9, 13–14, 19, 23–24, 29, 31, 41, 47, 87, 107–8, 122, 126, 149, 275; fig., p. 15; yam hills, 7, 11, 19, 22–23, 41, 243, 244; ill., pp. 16–17; fig., pp. 12, 15; yam stacks, 8–9, 13–14, 87, 275–7, 279; ill., p. 32; map, p. 5; seed yams, 18

Yose, 100, 102–4, 106, 113–14, 116, 174–7, 194, 198, 203–4, 206–7, 210, 214–16, 221, 222, 228–9, 230, 263–9, 271–2, 276, 278, 281–3; ill., p. 257; yose shrine, 111–12, 174–5, 178; ill., p. 256

For Product Safety Concerns and Information please contact our EU
representative GPSR@taylorandfrancis.com
Taylor & Francis Verlag GmbH, Kaufingerstraße 24, 80331 München, Germany

www.ingramcontent.com/pod-product-compliance
Lightning Source LLC
Chambersburg PA
CBHW070716280326
41926CB00087B/2307